RESTRUCTURING LARGE HOUSING ESTATES IN EUROPE

Edited by Ronald van Kempen, Karien Dekker, Stephen Hall and Iván Tosics

First published in Great Britain in November 2005 by

The Policy Press
University of Bristol
Fourth Floor
Beacon House
Queen's Road
Bristol BS8 1QU
UK

Tel +44 (0)117 331 4054
Fax +44 (0)117 331 4093
e-mail tpp-info@bristol.ac.uk
www.policypress.org.uk

British Library Cataloguing in Publication Data
A catalogue record for this book is available from the British Library.

Library of Congress Cataloging-in-Publication Data
A catalog record for this book has been requested.

ISBN 1 86134 775 8 paperback

A hardcover version of this book is also available.

Cover design by Qube Design Associates, Bristol.
Front cover: photograph kindly supplied by Iván Tosics
Printed and bound in Great Britain by Hobbs the Printers, Southampton.

Contents

List of tables, figures and boxes

Tables

Figures

Boxes

Preface

In the three or four decades following the Second World War, most European cities were extended by large housing estates, many of which were built on the cities' outskirts. These estates were built in order to resolve the housing shortages resulting from wartime devastation and the increasing number of households in the first couple of decades after the war. At that time, the estates were considered attractive, not only because they provided a home for the many people waiting for one, but also because the estates were clearly different from the pre-war urban areas. The open housing blocks, the extent of green space, the separation of traffic from other functions, and dwellings of good quality seemed to mark a stark contrast with the situation before the war. A new kind of living environment seemed to have emerged: one based on the ideas of such architects as Le Corbusier.

This book is about these large post-Second World War housing estates; on most of them, the once ideal situation has developed into a complex and problematic one that deserves the attention of both policy makers and researchers. With the help of a European Union (EU) subsidy within the 5th Framework Programme, we have been able to carry out a research project in which the current and future situations of these estates have been brought to the fore. This research project (RESTATE: Restructuring Large-scale Housing Estates in European Cities: Good Practices and New Visions for Sustainable Neighbourhoods and Cities) commenced in November 2002 and ran until October 2005. RESTATE has described and compared the history and current situation of the large housing estates in ten European countries, the policies aimed at these estates, the effects of these policies, and the expectations of the policy community and the inhabitants for the future of these estates. This book offers an overview of a multitude of aspects concerning these estates.

We selected the authors on the basis of their interest in, and knowledge of, the specific topics addressed in their chapters. Preliminary versions of the chapters were discussed with the authors, and the consequent revised versions of each chapter were sent to a team of external reviewers. We extend our thanks to these external reviewers for their willingness to read the draft chapters and their very helpful and fruitful comments. All the chapters have improved significantly following the comments made by Judith Allen, Justin Beaumont, Gideon Bolt, Danny Burns, Frans Dieleman(†), Mats

Franzén, Patsy Healey, Peter Marcuse, Clara Mulder, Jacob Norvig Larsen, Peter Somerville, Richard Turkington, and Frank Wassenberg. We, as editors, have had detailed conversations and correspondence with each of the contributors about their chapters, so that this book has become more than a collection of disparate papers, but has addressed common questions in a cohesive way. We would like to thank Wanda Verweij and Alexandra de Jong for the technical changes they made to the text and Anne Hawkins for correction of the English. We thank Adèle Lydon, Bo Larsson, and Eric Ponthieu of the European Commission for their confidence in our efforts to carry out the RESTATE [www.restate.geog.uu.nl/] project and serve as the editors for this book.

Ronald van Kempen
Karien Dekker
Stephen Hall
Iván Tosics

June 2005

Notes on contributors

Manuel Aalbers is a junior researcher at the Amsterdam Institute for Metropolitan and International Development Studies, Department of Geography, Planning and International Development Studies, University of Amsterdam, the Netherlands.

Roger Andersson is a Professor of Social and Economic Geography at the Institute for Housing and Urban Research, Uppsala University, Gävle, Sweden.

Fatiha Belmessous is a researcher at the Institute for Urban Research, RIVES (UMR 5600-CNRS), ENTPE, Vaulx-en-Velin, France.

Agnieszka Bielewska is a PhD student at the Institute of Philosophy and Sociology, Warsaw University, and worked as a junior researcher in the Department of Urban and Population Studies, Institute of Geography and Spatial Organization, Polish Academy of Sciences, Warsaw, Poland.

Åsa Bråmå is a junior researcher at the Institute for Housing and Urban Research, Uppsala University, Gävle, Sweden.

Barbara Černič Mali is an economist and researcher at the Urban Planning Institute of the Republic of Slovenia, Ljubljana, Slovenia.

Franck Chignier-Riboulon is a senior lecturer in social and urban geography at the Blaise Pascal University, Clermont-Ferrand, France, a researcher at the Céramac (Clermont-Ferrand) and associate researcher at the UMR5600-CNRS, Lyon, France.

Nicole Commerçon is Director of Research CNRS at the UMR 5600-CNRS, Institute of Human Sciences, Lyon, France.

Karien Dekker is a researcher in urban geography at the Urban and Regional research centre Utrecht, Faculty of Geosciences, Utrecht University, the Netherlands.

Christiane Droste is a researcher in urban studies at the Institute for Regional Development and Structural Planning, Erkner, Germany.

Lídia Garcia Ferrando is a junior researcher at the Department of Economics, University of Barcelona, Spain.

Anna Guszcza is a junior researcher at the Department of Urban and Population Studies, Institute of Geography and Spatial Organization, Polish Academy of Sciences, Warsaw, Poland.

Stephen Hall is a lecturer in urban and regional economic development at the Centre for Urban and Regional Studies, School of Public Policy, University of Birmingham, UK.

Thomas Knorr-Siedow is a senior researcher in housing, urban and regional development at the Institute for Regional Development and Structural Planning, Erkner, Germany.

Irene Molina is an Associate Professor of Human Geography at the Department of Social and Economic Geography, Uppsala University, Sweden.

Silvia Mugnano is a researcher at the Faculty of Sociology, Department of Social Research, University of Milan–Bicocca, Italy.

Alan Murie is Professor of Urban and Regional Studies at the Centre for Urban and Regional Studies, and the Head of the School of Public Policy, University of Birmingham, UK.

Sako Musterd is a Professor of Social Geography at the Amsterdam Institute for Metropolitan and International Development Studies, Department of Geography, Planning and International Development Studies, University of Amsterdam, the Netherlands.

Eva Öresjö is a Professor at the Department of Spatial Planning, Blekinge Institute of Technology, Karlskrona, Sweden.

Wim Ostendorf is an Associate Professor at the Amsterdam Institute for Metropolitan and International Development Studies, Department of Geography, Planning and International Development Studies, University of Amsterdam, the Netherlands.

Montserrat Pareja-Eastaway is an Associate Professor at the Department of Economics, University of Barcelona, Spain.

Lars Pettersson is a researcher at the Jönköping International Business School, Jönköping, Sweden.

Rob Rowlands is a researcher at the Centre for Urban and Regional Studies, School of Public Policy, University of Birmingham, UK.

Richard Sendi is a researcher at the Urban Planning Institute of the Republic of Slovenia, Ljubljana, Slovenia.

Teresa Tapada-Berteli is an Associate Professor at the Cultural and Social Anthropology Department, Autonomous University of Barcelona, Spain.

Iván Tosics is a sociologist and researcher. He is one of the principals of the Metropolitan Research Institute, Budapest, Hungary.

Ellen van Beckhoven is a junior researcher in urban geography at the Urban and Regional research centre Utrecht, Faculty of Geosciences, Utrecht University, the Netherlands.

Brechtje van Boxmeer is a junior researcher at the Department of Economics, University of Barcelona, Spain.

Ronald van Kempen is a Professor of Urban Geography at the Urban and Regional research centre Utrecht, Faculty of Geosciences, Utrecht University, the Netherlands.

Francesca Zajczyk is a Professor of Urban Sociology at the Faculty of Sociology, Department of Social Research, University of Milan-Bicocca, Italy.

Marcus Zepf is an architect and contractual researcher at the UMR 5600-CNRS, Institute of Human Sciences, Lyon, France.

ONE

Restructuring large housing estates in European cities: an introduction

Karien Dekker, Stephen Hall, Ronald van Kempen and Iván Tosics

We really believed, in a quasi-religious sense, in the perfectibility of human nature, in the role of architecture as a weapon of social reform ... the coming Utopia when everyone would live in cheap prefabricated flat-roofed multiple dwellings – heaven on earth (Philip Johnson, US architect, quoted in Coleman, 1985, p 3).

... during the evening and night ... a violent disturbance took place at the Broadwater Farm Estate, Tottenham. A police officer ... was killed. Several buildings were set on fire, as well as many motor vehicles ... the disturbances were the most ferocious, the most vicious riots ever seen on the mainland (Broadwater Farm Inquiry, 1986, p 3).

The first quotation refers to the 1930s-1960s, the second to the 1980s. What happened in between? Why did so many large housing estates change from celebrated urban innovations into problem areas no longer liked by their residents? Are the origins of the problems of housing estates internal to the estates themselves or are they simply spatial concentrations of more general problems of society? How widespread are the problems of large housing estates? What are the chances that large estates, developed in haste and proliferating across Europe, will disappear with the same speed?

Large housing estates in European cities: an historical note

All over Europe huge numbers of people live in large housing estates built after the Second World War. The philosophy according to which these estates were built was socially progressive and common to the different European countries involved. The origin of the estates can be traced back to the poor housing situation of the majority of the working classes at the turn of the 20th century. The principal period of construction for the large housing estates, however, came after the devastation of the Second World War, when massive building programmes were needed to replace the dwellings that had been destroyed or damaged in the war, to make up for the lack of housing production during the war, and to house the millions of people searching for a home. Demand for housing was high and further inflated by an unprecedented natural growth of the population in the early post-war years. Hundreds of tower blocks were constructed in the UK, in the *Banlieue* projects of France, and in the 'One Million Programme' in Sweden, and the Netherlands saw new housing estates built in almost every city (Murie et al, 2003).

The early cases were followed by the construction, from the 1960s to the late 1970s, of even more ambitious housing estates, containing large high-rise blocks. Many of these new urban areas were built on the fringes of the cities. Later, large building projects were also completed in Eastern Europe. In addition to dominating the large Eastern European cities, *socialist new towns* were built, often deliberately sited far away from the existing urban areas, but close to the places where the major new socialist industries (such as steelworks) were located. The estates built in these countries were much larger than those in the West, and the period of construction prevailed much longer, practically until the collapse of socialism in the late 1980s.

Today, about 40% of the population of cities in post-socialist countries lives on large housing estates. In Western European cities this percentage is typically below 10%. The difference between these proportions exemplifies an important fact: large housing estates are far more important relatively in the urban housing markets of the post-socialist cities than in Western Europe.

Initially, many large housing estates in European countries appear to have conformed to similar design principles (see also Turkington et al, 2004): medium- to high-rise apartment blocks, sometimes (but not always) interspersed with single-family dwellings. The architecture is simple, and the layout of the estates was, at least at the time the estates were built, quite revolutionary. A generation of pre-war modernists (such as Le Corbusier in France, Walter Gropius and Max Taut in Germany, and Oskar Hansen in Poland) put their stamp on the new estates. The result was large blocks, large open spaces between the blocks, and a separation of functions. Carefully designed urban landscapes emerged; they were praised by many urban designers of that period. Positive opinions on, and evaluations of, the large housing estates were very common at the time. In most cases, at the time of construction, the dwellings were considered to be spacious and affordable and many of the estates were characterised by extensive green areas, which were safe and traffic-free. At the same time, many of the estates were socially cohesive communities in which a considerable number of residents were involved in neighbourhood activities.

A closer look at the estates reveals, however, that there were many differences between countries, within countries, and even within cities, even from the initial date of construction. When the appropriate statistics are consulted, an enormous diversity in structures, populations, and problems is revealed. Even greater diversity would have been discovered had the people living in these estates been asked to give their opinions about them as places in which to live.

In many cases the estates were not built for the poorest of the poor. The quality of the housing on the estates was often high, at least compared with the older segments of the city, and this quality was reflected in price terms. In some countries, such as the Netherlands, the dwellings in these areas were not initially affordable for the poorest households, and the tenants who were attracted to the new flats had reasonable incomes. In the socialist countries the allocation mechanisms, rather than property prices, were decisive. In the early years the high-prestige flats were mostly allocated to what were considered the 'deserving' strata of society (Konrád and Szelényi, 1969). As time passed and ever-larger new estates were built in ever-more peripheral locations, the relative position of these newer estates within the local housing market hierarchies fell. In many countries this decline led to cases of large housing estates that were problematic from the beginning, and the poorer and less influential strata of society were deliberately allocated to them.

Large housing estates in Europe: the contemporary challenges

There have been radical changes in the course of the last 20 to 30 years. Many of the assumptions that informed the development of the large estates have been undermined by the dramatic economic, social, and political changes that occurred across Europe during the late 20th century. In particular, the end of the post-war prosperity underwritten by the Keynesian welfare state in Western Europe, and the failure of statist central planning in Central and Eastern Europe have resulted in new forms of social and spatial polarisation. Increasingly, regions, cities and neighbourhoods (not least the large estates) are differentiated according to their position within a new economic and social hierarchy.

The impact of these changes on the large housing estates has been uneven. Many of them continue to function well, economically and socially, and resident satisfaction remains high. Not all large estates are, therefore, problematic. However, an increasing number of large housing estates in European cities are no longer popular. In many areas – especially in cities where the initial housing shortages have been eliminated and the large housing estates have consequently been relegated to the bottom of the housing hierarchy – the estates evolved from problem-free and attractive residential neighbourhoods into areas that are very problematic in many respects. Many of these estates now share a long list of common problems although, of course, the combination of problems experienced locally varies considerably (Power and Tunstall, 1995; Wacquant, 1996; Hall, 1997; Power, 1997; Evans, 1998; Social Exclusion Unit, 1998; Taylor, 1998; Burrows and Rhodes, 1999; Musterd et al, 1999; Cars, 2000; Costa Pinho, 2000; Kearns et al, 2000; Andersen, 2001; Murie et al, 2003):

- physical decay because of shoddy construction work, rapid attrition and dereliction, and increasing amounts of litter and rubbish in open spaces;
- concentration of households with low incomes;
- low demand and abandonment of dwellings in areas where new and more attractive developments are being built nearby;
- increasing unemployment, because of declining job opportunities in the urban area as a whole, and because of a process of increasing spatial concentration of the unemployed on the large housing estates;
- visible anti-social behaviour: crime, disorderly behaviour, vandalism, drugs, alcoholism, young people loitering;
- social and racial tensions and conflicts among residents;

- high turnover leading to partial breakdown of social cohesion and reduced resident activity;
- deterioration of the housing and management services;
- deterioration of local private (and sometimes also public) services;
- educational problems because of a high concentration of children from poor families or minority ethnic groups in local schools.

The uncritical recital of such a list is dangerous, however. The impression might be conveyed that these problems have taken root and nothing can be done about them. Much of the existing literature tends to view the destiny of housing estates as an inevitable negative trajectory with increasing physical decay, and more and more social and economic problems. This literature seems to deny the significance of social and physical action or policy action in influencing what happens on these estates (see also Power and Tunstall, 1995; Hall, 1997; Taylor, 1998; Vestergård, 1998; Andersen, 1999; Gibb et al, 1999; Morrison, 1999). At the same time, the literature is very much centred on Western Europe and, within Western Europe, very much on the UK. This bias means that we should be very careful in generalising all these problems to estates in other parts of Europe.

In this book we definitely do not accept the proposition that the large housing estates in European cities have reached the limits of their useful existence and that nothing can be done to 'save them' for the future. In fact, in the last decade of the 20th century, housing, spatial, and urban policies were increasingly directed towards large post-war estates: a clear sign of the desire of policy makers and other stakeholders to work towards securing a better future for these areas. Moreover, we would argue that large estates have an important part to play in promoting sustainable urban development more broadly, given their compact morphology, abundant open space, and their potential to benefit from public transport links and the development of green heating and energy systems. In the recent past, other parts of the urban fabric have been the subject of state-led (slum clearance) or market-led (gentrification) restructuring processes, often (but not always) with positive results. It is now the turn of the large estates.

In most cases, however, a better future will not arrive automatically. As we have already observed, the large housing estates do not usually occupy favourable market positions. They are not, for example, attractive places for the processes of spontaneous gentrification. In many cases the estates are places for low- and middle-income households and will probably remain unattractive to higher-income households and other potential investors such as private sector service providers (shops, financial services, for example). In some cases, because of deficient demand or technical failures, radical solutions such as demolition will be necessary to reanimate the appeal of the estates for present and future residents and investors and thereby avoid a future permanently supported by overstretched public service.

Since the late 1990s (and before then in some cases), 'urban restructuring' and 'urban renewal' of large housing estates have become frequently heard catchphrases in many European countries. After the, often radical, renewal of older areas, some built before the Second World War, the post-war large housing estates have increasingly become the areas where new policies are needed. Renewal and restructuring policies aim for radical change in post-war neighbourhoods. In some countries this restructuring is clearly directed towards the rectification of physical decline; in other countries social decline has been the main concern. Elsewhere, the desire to make the areas more mixed in terms of housing tenure and the population profile became central to the policy agenda. There has been a clear recognition that improvements can be achieved in every case; although many large housing estates of the second half of the 20th century have become problematic living areas, most of them still have a future. This future is not assured automatically, however; collaborative efforts to improve their situation are necessary. Many studies have revealed that restructuring and renewal processes are increasingly the result of partnerships between a whole host of actors, including at least some of the following: central government; the relevant ministries; regional government; local government; housing associations; private companies; residents' organisations; and individual residents.

Place making, large housing estates, and looking ahead

The state intervenes in many aspects of people's lives on a daily basis. This intervention is felt most keenly in the context of the large estates, in which the public sector is often responsible for meeting the most basic needs of many of the residents (housing, benefits and income, for example). In many European countries, public policy has become preoccupied with the short-term minutiae of managing cities and neighbourhoods, such as the bureaucratic regulation of land use and routine service delivery, much of which takes place in an un-coordinated manner. However, public policy is not usually well adapted to meet:

(1) *the importance of place*: people who have the resources can choose where to live, work, and invest, while people who do not have these resources are confined to less desirable places; and

(2) *the importance of diversity*: every place has a multitude of problems (economic, social, environmental, political) and a multitude of stakeholders (central, regional, and local government, business, local residents).

Patsy Healey (1997, 1998a, 1998b) argues for a more proactive approach in which a variety of stakeholders may be mobilised in support of a holistic, long-term vision for an area. Healey argues for the consideration of means to initiate proactive development strategies based on agreements around what places might look like and the opportunities and limitations of transforming them, a process she refers to as 'place making'. A more sophisticated attempt is required than previous physical, economic, or socially deterministic approaches to address the problems of territory – in the context of this book, the large estates. In our opinion, place making (see Chapter 3) can be seen as an essential feature for the large housing estates in Europe, since place making might help in many cases to find ways to improve the situation in these problematic areas. Collaborative planning and place making are therefore two central concepts in this book.

This choice is not based on a belief that the specific problems of places (on large estates, for example) are generated exclusively locally and, by implication, may be resolved by local intervention (a belief that has handicapped the area-based approach that has traditionally characterised estate regeneration in Europe). Rather, the notion of place making – the pursuit of positive social, economic, and environmental outcomes in a given place – acknowledges the impact of a variety of causal process operating at different spatial levels and the need for multi-level intervention by a variety of stakeholders.

The concept of place making does not imply that all problems are local and have local origins and can be resolved locally. We wish to point out from the outset that care should be taken to avoid over-enthusiastic concentration on the local arena. The following notions should, as a minimum, be taken into account when looking at the problems and possible solutions with respect to large housing estates:

• The problems of large housing estates are, to a significant extent, the expressions of more general economic, demographic, and sociocultural developments (see also Murie et al, 2003, for example). The post-industrial transformation of the economy in the late 20th century decimated employment opportunities in almost all European cities. The unemployed are likely to find themselves in a position of declining income and declining choice in the housing market, and thereby relegated to the cheapest housing alternatives and the most unattractive neighbourhoods. Increasing immigration may increase the number of people looking for a home and the competition for dwellings. In neighbourhoods where demand exceeds supply for some dwelling types, some people might find themselves in situations they find undesirable and inappropriate. Conversely, some households may face increasing choice as a result of a combination of rising incomes and newly built alternatives elsewhere. Those people who can afford to do so will vacate the problematic areas, to be replaced by others who move more through compulsion than choice.

- The quantitative and qualitative supply of housing in a housing market can affect the position of large housing estates. In the case of a tight housing market, there is a significant chance that some areas that are not very attractive may remain relatively popular because of the lack of alternatives. When supply exceeds demand, the chances of vacancies in the most unattractive areas of the city are much greater.

- A crucial factor affecting housing estates is the process of housing allocation. In the case of public rental housing, local housing officers act as keepers (Pahl, 1975), often discriminating against certain housing estates through the allocation of dwellings to problem families.

- In Western European welfare states, decisions made by central government can have an effect on the characteristics of large housing estates and their position in the housing market. For example, a decision to demolish certain large housing estates will have an impact on not only these estates, but also estates not directly affected by the demolition policy.

- Decisions made by local government authorities can also affect large housing estates. For example, decisions to invest scarce capital resources might affect some areas positively and other areas negatively.

- The role of various non-public institutions, such as housing associations and private developers, can be crucial. The red-lining practices of banks and the prejudice of employers towards residents of certain areas can be very influential.

- The attitudes of all kinds of people not living on the estates can be important. First, all professional organisations are staffed and managed by people. The crucial role of these managers has been stressed by authors such as Pahl (1975, 1977), Lipsky (1980), and Tomlins (1997). Staff may find themselves torn between pressures that originate from the management board, the housing consumers, colleagues, and, of course, their own preferences (Karn, 1983; Murie et al, 2003).

- Changes in some areas invariably effect changes in other areas. Spill-over effects (see also Chapter 8) always occur. The dispersal of some groups from one area will almost inevitably lead to new concentrations in other areas.

The context of this book

The research material for this book has been drawn substantially from the EU Fifth Framework research project RESTATE, an acronym for: 'Restructuring Large-scale Housing Estates in European Cities: Good Practices and New Visions for Sustainable Neighbourhoods and Cities'. This cross-national research project took place in ten countries (France, Germany, Hungary, Italy, the Netherlands, Poland, Slovenia, Spain, Sweden, and the UK), in 16 cities, and in 29 estates in the time period November 2002 to October 2005.

The principal aim of this research was to find out how large housing estates built in the first three or four decades after the Second World War have developed in physical, social, and economic terms. In the project, we have paid explicit attention to the role of policies and other actions aimed at improving the quality of life on these estates. Following Anne Power (1997), we have defined post-Second World War 'large housing estates' as "areas built in the second half of the 20th century as groups of at least 2,000 housing units that are recognised as distinct and geographical areas, planned by the state or with state support". Some more detailed information on RESTATE, and the research methods used in this project, can be found in the Appendix.

From the beginning we decided to include ten European countries in the project. The basic idea behind this selection was that we should have a representation of all geographical parts of the European Union (EU) (north, east, south and west), in order to have countries with different historical and political backgrounds. We considered it especially important to have a number of Central European countries in the project, first, because these countries have witnessed radical political reforms in the past 15 years and, second, because large housing estates are a very prominent phenomenon of the urban housing markets in most of these countries. Also we wanted to include both larger countries, such as France and Germany, and smaller countries, such as Slovenia and the Netherlands.

Large post-war estates are now prominent on the policy agendas of all Western European countries. *France* developed a high-profile policy agenda following disturbances on some estates. In France the Habitations à loyers modérés [low-rent dwellings], which tend to be the major societies of housing suppliers in these areas, are relatively independent of local government, and the areas concerned are often located on the periphery of cities. In *the UK*, local government is often the owner of property as well as the provider of services. Many of the estates built in the post-Second World War period were built in different parts of cities and associated with slum clearance. In *the Netherlands* concern about segregation and deprivation on large estates has generated action. The Netherlands has financially independent housing associations but at the same time a strong interventionist tradition of government. In *Sweden* the organisation of housing is different again and the role of social partners is more specifically built into policy making.

In Southern Europe the situation of large housing estates is rapidly changing. In *Italy* these estates were built to house rural–urban migrants and also those moving from South to North. In *Spain* these areas were built at a different stage in economic development associated with rural-urban migration and under the previous political regime. Owner-occupation is much more prominent in these countries compared to those of Western Europe.

There are several examples of estates operating in transitional economies. In *Germany* distinctive features can be identified but in this project we mainly refer to estates in East Germany, built under a different political system. In addition to the German examples of estates operating in transitional economies we have included two large (*Hungary, Poland*) and one smaller (*Slovenia*) Eastern European transitional economy. This enables us to reflect upon the different contexts and resources that affect policy initiatives both now and in the future. Especially in the Central European countries privatisation is a crucial process affecting the lives of individuals in the large housing estates, as will become clear later in this book.

With respect to the *cities* under review we focus on a wide variety. Capitals (such as Amsterdam, Budapest and London) as well as former industrial cities (such as Birmingham and Milan) have been included. Large cities (Lyon, Berlin) as well as smaller ones (Koper in Slovenia, and Utrecht in the Netherlands) have formed part of the research. In the selected cities at least one but in most cases two or more large post-war estates have been identified as research locations.

Can the results of this study be generalised? This is a question that can only be answered very cautiously. Within this book we will make clear in many places that when interpreting the results with respect to the different estates in this project, the national and local context should never be overlooked. This means that local circumstances and developments are always at least partly shaped by developments on different spatial levels. In other words, developments within an estate should always be interpreted with various elements of the local and national context in mind. The same holds for policies. Policies might look more or less the same in different estates. However, it may well be that these policies find their origins in very different ideas, that the organisation of these policies is rooted in very different traditions and that the outcomes of policies and other actions depend much more on other factors than the policies themselves. Again, different contexts may be decisive.

Believing in the contextuality of developments must mean that generalisation is at least difficult, if not impossible. However, we do believe that some generalisations are possible, as long as the contextual developments are kept in mind. Throughout the book some generalisation may be found, and especially in the last chapter. But again and again we want to stress that developments within one estate, city or country cannot automatically be generalised to other estates, cities and countries.

The structure of this book

The specific contribution of this book compared with other publications on large housing estates is that it has grown out of a comparative exercise in which the housing estates of ten countries were analysed against a common framework (see previous section). The chapters in this book have been written by multi-national teams, drawing on original research into the economic, social, and cultural experiences of a number of estates.

The book concentrates on a number of topics that we consider essential for the present and future position of the large housing estates in their respective cities and housing markets. The chapters are grouped into three main parts.

In the first part of the book we present the basic information that is needed to understand the more detailed topics which follow. For this first part we have formulated the following research question:

> What factors and developments are crucial for the development and present state and position of large housing estates in European cities?

In Chapter Two Dekker and van Kempen provide a quantitative overview of the present state of the large housing estates that stand central in this book (see Table 2.1). This chapter makes it clear that although there are broad similarities between estates in European cities, they are most definitely not all the same. Their diversity is crucial when implementing policies. Chapter Three, written by Hall and Rowlands, is a more theoretical chapter, in which the concept of place making is elaborated and where the notion of collaborative planning is introduced. This chapter provides a theoretical framework for the book. In Chapter Four, Hall, Murie, and Knorr-Siedow describe the (historical) developments that have been crucial in influencing the evolution of large housing estates in European cities. This chapter provides a general historical background to the estates. In Chapter Five, the crucial process of the privatisation of housing is discussed by Murie, Tosics, Aalbers, Sendi, and Černič Mali. Privatisation is a crucial process, not only in the post-socialist countries, but also in Western European countries, where it appears in different forms with differential effects for the estates.

In the second part of the book, the focus is on the ideas that lie behind the policies that are implemented on large housing estates. In this part it is not the policies themselves, but the ideas and philosophies behind these policies that are central. The following research question is addressed in this part of the book:

> What ideas and philosophies inform potential policy interventions in European large housing estates? What are the advantages and disadvantages of these approaches?

In Chapter Six, the concept of *social cohesion* is addressed. This concept has become crucial in the academic literature and in political practice, not least in EU research programmes. In terms of urban policies, particularly those concerning the future of large housing estates, the idea of social cohesion can be seen as a crucial notion. In this chapter, Dekker and Rowlands investigate the problematic issues and the opportunities for creating social cohesion in large housing estates with mixed population compositions.

Another crucial concept in present-day urban restructuring policies is the idea of social mix. In general, social mix in housing estates is seen in a positive light: a socially mixed neighbourhood would create better opportunities for the people living there. In Chapter Seven, Andersson and Musterd consider the validity of this idea.

In Chapter Eight, Musterd and Ostendorf take up an idea that many studies have often neglected: that of displacement effects. The idea is that when policy interventions are applied in one area, that area may experience some positive effects (and these positive effects are often mentioned in evaluation studies), but the problems may be exported to other areas where they might become just as severe as they were in the original areas. It will be evident that the supposed effectiveness of policies might be reduced when one looks across the borders of a narrowly defined target area.

When areas are restructured, the most important effect is that some people can stay in the area where they used to live, while others have to move. When inexpensive housing stock is demolished, or upgraded, and replaced by more expensive stock, the new dwellings will not be affordable for low-income households. In some cases, this is the precise reason underlying the demolition and rebuilding. Bråmå and Andersson address the question 'who stays and who moves?' in Chapter Nine, drawing on the Swedish estates as an example.

The third part of this book concentrates on policy intervention and the organisation of the policies. The contents of the policies, as well as the way they are organised, are central here:

> Which policy interventions are important in large housing estates in European cities? How are they organised? How effective are they?

These questions have been addressed from a number of perspectives and are discussed in several chapters. When discussing the restructuring and renewal of housing estates, it is clear that demolition can be seen as one of the most radical interventions. Demolition can be used as an intervention for various reasons. Rebuilding an area can be carried out in different ways, with different aims in mind. In Chapter Ten the reasons for demolition and the aims of rebuilding are assessed critically by a French team of researchers (Belmessous, Chignier-Riboulon, Commerçon, and Zepf).

Chapter Eleven concerns the partners in the restructuring process and the ways in which they work together. In their case study of Italian and Spanish estates, Mugnano, Pareja-Eastaway, and Tapada-Berteli argue that different kinds of partnership are feasible and that each kind has its own advantages and liabilities. In Chapter Twelve, participation within neighbourhoods is discussed. On the basis of a comparison of local participation in neighbourhoods in Dutch and Spanish cities, van Beckhoven, van Boxmeer, and Garcia Ferrando conclude that the level of participation is explained more by neighbourhood characteristics than by national (policy) differences.

Chapter Thirteen, by Pettersson and Öresjö, focuses on local practices to fight unemployment in Swedish large housing estates. Chapter Fourteen is about an increasing problem in large housing estates: inhabitants' feelings of insecurity as a consequence of the criminal behaviour of young people in the area. This chapter also considers the measures taken to curb young criminals. The conclusion drawn by the authors of this chapter (Aalbers, Bielewska, Chignier-Riboulon, and Guszcza) is that different kinds of strategy should be employed to combat criminal behaviour and decrease feelings of insecurity. Chapter Fifteen starts from the question of whether gender mainstreaming is important in restructuring large housing estates. Droste, Molina, and Zajczyk describe the practices in Sweden, Germany, and Italy. These authors conclude that gender sensitivity is of great importance in urban development processes, but that there are still many constraints, especially in the interactions between top-down incentives and bottom-up initiatives.

Chapter Sixteen, by Knorr-Siedow and Tosics, gives an account of the role of knowledge. This chapter is not about a policy concept, but is organised around the question of how to use (scientific) knowledge in different practical situations.

Chapter Seventeen, the concluding chapter, summarises what feasible future there might be for the large housing estates in European estates.

Most chapters in this book do not feature all the 29 estates that are incorporated in the RESTATE project. We have deliberately chosen to publish an edited volume in which certain topics that are, in our opinion, essential with respect to large housing estates are central in the chapters. After selecting these topics, we selected the estates, cities, and countries in which each topic could best be described and explained. This gave us the opportunity to deal with the central topics in more depth than would have been the case had we been obliged to cover all 29 estates.

References

Andersen, H.S. (1999) *Byudvalgets indsats 1993-1998. Sammenfattende evaluering*, Copenhagen: Danish Building Research Institute.

Andersen, H.S. (2001) 'Excluded places: on the interaction between segregation, urban decay and deprived neighbourhoods', paper presented to the International Sociological Association, Research Committee RC21 conference, Amsterdam, the Netherlands, 14-16 June.

Broadwater Farm Inquiry (1986) *Report of the independent inquiry into disturbances of October 1985 at the Broadwater Farm Estate, Tottenham, chaired by Lord Gifford*, London: Karia Press.

Burrows, R. and Rhodes, D. (1999) *Unpopular places? Area disadvantage and the geography of misery in England*, Bristol: The Policy Press.

Cars, G. (2000) *Social exclusion in European neighbourhoods – processes, experiences and responses*, Brussels: European Commission.

Coleman, A. (1985) *Utopia on trial: vision and reality in planned housing*, London: Shipman.

Costa Pinho, T. (2000) 'Residential contexts of social exclusion: images and identities', Paper presented to the European Network for Housing Research conference, Gävle, Sweden, 26-30 June.

Evans, R. (1998) 'Tackling deprivation on social housing estates in England: an assessment of the housing plus approach', *Housing Studies*, vol 13, no 5, pp 713-26.

Gibb, K., Kearns, A. and Kintrea, K. (1999) 'Low demand, housing preferences and neighbourhood choices', Paper presented to the European Network for Housing Research conference, Balatonfüred, Hungary, 25-29 August.

Hall, P. (1997) 'Regeneration policies for peripheral housing estates: inward- and outward-looking approaches', *Urban Studies*, vol 34, no 5, pp 873-90.

Healey, P. (1997) *Collaborative planning – shaping places in fragmented societies*, Basingstoke: MacMillan.

Healey, P. (1998a) 'Collaborative planning in a stakeholder society', *Town Planning Review*, vol 69, no 1, pp 1-21.

Healey, P. (1998b) 'Building institutional capacity through collaborative approaches to planning', *Environment and Planning A*, vol 30, no 11, pp 1531-46.

Karn, V. (1983) 'Race and housing in Britain: the role of the major institutions', in N. Glazer and K. Young (eds) *Ethnic pluralism and public policy: Achieving equality in the US and Britain*, Lexington: Heath, pp 162-83.

Kearns, A., Atkinson, R. and Parker, A. (2000) 'A geography of misery or an epidemic of contentment? Understanding neighbourhood (dis)-satisfaction in Britain', Paper presented to the European Network for Housing Research conference, Gävle, Sweden, 26-30 June.

Konrád, G. and Szelényi, I. (1969) *Az új lakótelepek szociológiai problémái*, Budapest: Akadémiai Kiadó.

Lipsky, M. (1980) *Street-level bureaucracy: Dilemmas of the individual in public services*, New York, NY: Russell Sage.

Morrison, N. (1999) 'Addressing the difficulties in letting social housing across the UK', Paper presented to the European Network for Housing Research conference, Balatonfüred, Hungary, 25-29 August.

Murie, A., Knorr–Siedow, T. and van Kempen, R. (2003) *Large housing estates in Europe: General developments and theoretical backgrounds*, Utrecht: Urban and Regional research centre Utrecht, Faculty of Geosciences, Utrecht University.

Musterd, S., Priemus, H. and van Kempen, R. (1999) 'Towards undivided cities: the potential of economic revitalisation and housing redifferentiation', *Housing Studies*, vol 14, no 5, pp 573-84.

Pahl, R.E. (1975) *Whose city?*, Harmondsworth: Penguin.

Pahl, R.E. (1977) 'Managers, technical experts and the state: forms of mediation, manipulation and dominance in urban and regional development', in M. Harloe (ed) *Captive cities: studies in the political economy of cities and regions*, London/New York, NY: Wiley, pp 49-60.

Power, A. (1997) *Estates on the edge: The social consequences of mass housing in Northern Europe*, Basingstoke: MacMillan.

Power, A. and Tunstall, R. (1995) *Swimming against the tide. Polarisation or progress on 20 unpopular council estates, 1980-1995*, London: Joseph Rowntree Foundation.

Social Exclusion Unit (1998) *Neighbourhood renewal*, London: Cabinet Office.

Taylor, M. (1998) 'Combating the social exclusion of housing estates', *Housing Studies*, vol 13, no 6, pp 819-32.

Tomlins, R. (1997) 'Officer discretion and minority ethnic housing provision', *Journal of Housing and the Built Environment*, vol 12, pp 179-97.

Turkington, R., Wassenberg, F. and van Kempen, R. (eds) (2004) *The future of high-rise housing estates in Europe*, Delft: Delft University Press.

Vestergård, H. (1998) 'Troubled housing estates in Denmark', in A. Madanipour, G. Cars and J. Allen (eds) *Social exclusion in European cities*, London: Jessica Kingsley Publishers, pp 115-29.

Wacquant, L.J.D. (1996) 'The rise of advanced marginality: notes on its nature and implications', *Acta Sociologica*, vol 39, no 2, pp 121-39.

TWO

Large housing estates in Europe: a contemporary overview

Karien Dekker and Ronald van Kempen

Introduction

In this chapter, we consider the present situation of large housing estates. The chapter is based on data obtained from detailed studies of estates in the RESTATE project (see Chapter One), and the aim is to provide a clear overview of their characteristics. We therefore provide some basic data and present a systematic inventory of the current situation on these estates.

We show that, although in many respects the estates are very similar, there are some issues that are typical of only some estates in some cities and countries. It is not our intention to explain all these differences and similarities. We do believe, however, that the overview in this chapter may be helpful as a backdrop for understanding the more empirical chapters in this book, where some aspects of the estates have been investigated in more depth. At the same time, the overview gives an up-to-date account of the present situation in large housing estates throughout a large part of Europe.

In this chapter we have drawn on ten reports in the RESTATE series (Aalbers et al, 2003; Andersson et al, 2003; Černič Mali et al, 2003; Chignier-Riboulon et al, 2003; Erdösi et al, 2003; Hall et al, 2003; Knorr-Siedow and Droste, 2003; Mezzetti et al, 2003; Murie et al, 2003; Pareja Eastaway et al, 2003; Węcławowicz et al, 2003). Here we refer to the estates without too many references to avoid repetition. It should be clear, however, that most of the data in this chapter are taken from these reports. An overview of the estates in the RESTATE project can be found in the Appendix.

It is important to appreciate that the large housing estates in the RESTATE project (and in this chapter) may not be typical of all large housing estates in their respective countries. The presence of urban or housing policies was a prerequisite for the selection of the estates. This means that, in general, it was not the most thriving estates that were included in the project. The somewhat negative picture that emerges from this chapter is therefore no coincidence. Evidently, in most countries there are also more positive examples of large housing estates.

A final introductory note: in this chapter we refer to the estates as if they can be seen as homogeneous areas. This is not always the case, because in some estates there are clear internal differences with respect to housing quality, the socioeconomic status of the population, and the quality of life in general. However, it is not the purpose of this chapter to consider these internal differences.

Large housing estates in Europe

The large housing estates were originally built according to the ideas of CIAM *(Congrès Internationaux d'Architecture Moderne)* [International Conference on Modern Architecture] and Le Courbusier, with the idea of creating pleasant, spacious, green, and light places in which to live. Of course, some of these positive notions are still true today, but many problems have also emerged. A number of authors have already discussed these problems (Power, 1997; Murie et al, 2003; Turkington et al, 2004; PRC Bouwcentrum International, 2005). We summarise here the current developments in these kinds of estates on the basis of the reports published in the RESTATE series. We concentrate on five sets of issues:

- physical developments;
- economic developments;
- demographic and sociocultural developments;
- liveability;
- safety.

The subsections within these basic sets feature such issues as regeneration, the housing market, unemployment, and social cohesion. Although this division is somewhat arbitrary and issues sometimes overlap, it enables us to give a systematic account of the current problems.

Physical developments

Building period and size

The estates in our study were all built after the Second World War to house large numbers of people. Some early estates were built and finished in the 1950s and 1960s, while others are of more recent date (see Table 2.1). The plans for the construction of the large housing estates were in accordance with the ideas current at that time about the ideal housing environment: spacious apartments in multi-family blocks with large green areas between them. Often, services such as shops, schools, and meeting places were clustered in service centres, although in many cases they were constructed later than the housing units. Urban planners also had definite ideas about managing traffic; in some areas, such as the Dutch Bijlmer or the Hungarian Jósaváros, pedestrians were separated from car traffic and through traffic was led around the estate.

The estates in our study are of very different sizes (Table 2.1). In all the estates, the units are situated in 3- to 12-storey flatted accommodation, sometimes mixed with single-family homes nearby. In many cases the initial composition of the area was based on a repetition of a certain composition of high-rise housing blocks: London's Poplar HARCA (87% high-rise), or Hungary's Jósaváros, where the centre of the estate is formed by 11-storey high-rise blocks, surrounded by a ring of 5-storey buildings are examples.

Location

The location of the estates is usually outside the urban city centre. These peripheral locations can cause accessibility problems, but at the same time nature is close by. Rillieux-la-Pape (Lyon) is beautifully situated on a plateau and overlooking a valley. The Swedish Tensta in Stockholm is surrounded by beautiful (protected) natural areas that are used for leisure activities.

Some more negative points must be mentioned, however. Post-Second World War large housing estates are in some cases situated in a very peripheral situation, even separated from the city by green areas or wasteland. Problems of accessibility can lead to feelings of isolation. The presence of large motorways, canals and rivers can also cut off a relatively new housing estate from the rest of the city. Lyon's Rillieux-la-Pape is separated from the main city by a canal, a river, and a ring road. Koper's Žusterna-Semedela is also bound by several large roads.

Table 2.1: Physical characteristics of the RESTATE research areas[a]

	Housing units (number)	Building period	Social sector[b] (%)	Owner-occupied (%)	Average housing size (square metres)	Average housing size (number of rooms)
France, Lyon						
Rillieux-la-Pape	7,422	1960-1976	92	Na	Na	3.6
Les Minguettes	7,751	1965-1974	97	3.2	Na	Na
Germany, Berlin						
Marzahn NorthWest	23,784	1977-1992	0	14/86[c]	62	3
Märkisches Viertel	16,000	1963-1975	0	10/90[d]	65	2 or 3
Hungary, Budapest						
Havanna	6,200	1977-1983	16	65/19[e]	47	Na
Hungary, Nyíregyháza						
Jósaváros	3,600	1970s	11	64/25[f]	51	Na
Italy, Milan						
Sant'Ambrogio	2,268	1960s	96	4	Na	Na
San Siro	12,564	<1945-1971	38	62	Na	Na
Comasina	2,404	1946-1960	23	77	Na	Na
the Netherlands, Amsterdam						
Bijlmer Centre	9,440	1980s	97	3	80+	1-4
Bijlmer East	12,072	1970s	85	13	80+	1-4
Kolenkit	2,634	1946-1960	94	2	50-60	3
the Netherlands, Utrecht						
Nieuw Hoograven	2,595	1956-1965	85	6	50-60	3
Kanaleneiland	2,676	1956-1965	78	13	50-60	3

Table 2.1: contd.../

	Housing units (number)	Building period	Social sector[b] (%)	Owner-occupied (%)	Average housing size (square metres)	Average housing size (number of rooms)
Poland, Warsaw						
Ursynów	13,143	1976-1981	1	99[g]	61	3.8
Wrzeciono	13,122	1960-1970	26	74[h]	39	2.6
Slovenia, Ljubljan						
Nove Fužine	4,322	1977-1988	6	92	65	2.36
Slovenia, Koper						
Žusterna-Semedela	2,040	1973-1989	5	94	65	2.44
Spain, Barcelona						
Trinitat Nova	3,215	1950s	–	71	71	Na
Sant Roc	3,395	1960s	–	70	70	Na
Spain, Madrid						
Simancas	9,035	1950s-1980s	0	70	50	4
Orcasitas	6,375	1970s & 1980s	0	91	90	6
Sweden, Jönköping						
Råslätt	2,216	1968-1975	99[i]	1[i]	66	2.5
Öxnehaga	2,041	1970-1975	68	32	78	3
Sweden, Stockholm						
Tensta	5,931	1968-1972	54	28	Approx. 65	3
Husby	4,725	1970-1975	53	24	Approx. 60	3

Table 2.1: contd.../

	Housing units (number)	Building period	Social sector[b] (%)	Owner-occupied (%)	Average housing size (square metres)	Average housing size (number of rooms)
UK, London						
Bow HAT	2,295	1968-1977	26.0	21.0	80	3.94
Poplar HARCA	6,304	1930s-1960s	29.0	16.0	Na	4
UK, Birmingham						
Central Estates	3,305	1960-1970	46.0	18.0	Na	4.15
Hodge Hill	3,937	1930-1950	4	51.0	83	4.8

Notes:
[a] all data are from years 2001, 2002, or 2003 unless otherwise stated. All French data are from 1999.
[b] social sector and owner-occupied sector is not necessarily 100%, since on some estates there is also a considerable share of private-rented dwellings.
[c] 14% private, 86% public shared ownership
[d] 10% private, 90% public shared ownership
[e] 65% private, 19% cooperative housing
[f] 64% private, 25% cooperative housing
[g] this is 62.4% owner occupied and 37.2% cooperative housing
[h] this is 60.9% owner occupied and 12.9% cooperative housing
[i] municipal housing association
[j] including cooperative housing
Source: RESTATE reports

Although this estate is beautifully situated near the coast, busy traffic makes it very difficult for the residents to reach the beach. Some of the Birmingham central estates are located at the crossroads of major routes into and around the city centre and these estates have become a focus for drug dealing and hijacking cars.

In other cases the estates are not peripherally located at all. Hoograven and Kanaleneiland in Utrecht are almost within walking distance of the centre of the city (no more than ten minutes away by bicycle). Some central Birmingham estates adjoin the city centre, although the authors of the UK report state that the residents do not seem to derive many benefits from this location.

Public transport is a service that determines to a large extent how connected people feel with the rest of the city. The residents on some estates, Utrecht's Hoograven for example, evaluate public transport positively. On other estates, Barcelona's Trinitat Nova for example, public transport has improved significantly, turning a highly isolated estate into a well-connected one, leading to increased housing prices but also more job opportunities for the residents.

Sometimes public transport is not available, while in other cases services do not run to the most important places. What has been reported are long walking distances to the nearest stops sometimes necessitated by detours to avoid nearby crime hotspots (such as in London's Bow Housing Action Trust [HAT]). In Milan's Sant'Ambrogio there is only one small supermarket and one bar for more than 6,000 people. Here, the only bus stop is a 15-minute walk from the estate, creating huge problems for people relying on public transport for daily shopping and other needs.

Maintenance

The dwellings are often light and offer a relatively large space for low prices. But dwellings built some decades ago now show signs of decay, especially in buildings where poor quality building materials were used. The list of physical housing problems can be extensive, as in the case of Sant'Ambrogio (infiltration of water in the dwellings, unsafe balconies, poor functioning of lighting systems, defects in the heating systems), and the more recently built Ljubljana's Fužine (leaking roofs, defects in water and sewage systems, crumbling plasterwork, problems with heat insulation). London's Bow HAT shows a similar list of housing problems; it has sometimes been described, as have other estates, as a vast area of grey concrete.

Housing market

The ownership structure varies markedly from country to country (Table 2.1). In the Southern European countries most of the housing units are owner-occupied. Examples are Comasina (77%) and Orcasitas, where 91% of the residents own their houses, while in both Germany and Sweden most units are owned by the government. Home ownership is also common in the Eastern European countries, although this is a more recent development since the apartments were sold to the tenants after the change to the political system (see also Murie et al on privatisation in Chapter Five). In Western Europe the majority of the houses on the estates are in the social-rented sector, with the highest proportions in Amsterdam: Bijlmer Centre has 97% and Kolenkit 94% of dwellings in the social-rented sector. More recently, restructuring policies in the UK, the Netherlands, and France have started to replace social-rented multi-family apartment blocks with new owner-occupied single-family houses.

Different forms of tenure in an area can create different feelings of involvement. In Jönköping's Råslätt, for example, the initially strong social bond between the residents was broken by the demolition of the government-owned houses and replacement by cooperatives, thereby replacing a uniform social-economic group with a more heterogeneous one with fewer opportunities for identification.

The prices of the housing units are mostly in the cheap or affordable range, although the differences between countries, and sometimes even within the same estates, can be huge. In Fužine (Slovenia) one can rent a social-sector house for as little as €52 a month, while the private-sector rent is €320 for a similar flat. A flat in Hoograven costs between €250 and €400 a month in the social sector, while private rents start from €700. Also in Spain, Trinitat Nova is cheaper than the city average: €1.960 per m² for a flat in Trinitat Nova compared to the average for Barcelona of €2.690 per m². Les Minguettes is the cheapest estate in Lyon, although in spite of the low prices a large share of the housing stock is empty.

All the estates are relatively cheap places in which to live, but not necessarily the cheapest in the city. With a rent of nearly €500 a month the Bijlmer, for example, is not much cheaper than the rest of Amsterdam.

Most of the estates in our study are at the bottom of the housing market, but not all. To buy a house in Ursynów (Poland) would cost between €700 and €900 per m², which is slightly above the city average. Also the turnover rate on this estate is very low. The estate is a place where people want to live. It cannot be characterised as a neighbourhood at the bottom of the housing market.

Unattractive dwellings in an unattractive location are likely to stand empty when there are other alternatives on the local housing market. As soon as other opportunities open up, the risk of vacancies immediately arises. In Rillieux-la-Pape (Lyon) in 2000, about 6.5% of the dwelling stock was empty and much of the evident vandalism and anti-social behaviour can be attributed to the relatively large number of vacancies. In Les Minguettes (Lyon) vacancies amounted to 14% in 2001. The number of vacancies can increase when an area is on the brink of a renovation process.

On most estates the size of the dwellings is small by modern standards or when compared with more recently built houses. At the time the estates were built, 60 m² for a family was regarded as spacious. Having three bedrooms was seen as a luxury. As can be seen in Table 2.1, most families have 65 m², with some smaller average housing units (Wrzeciono: 39 m²) and some larger (Bijlmer: >80 m²; Orcasitas: 90 m²). At present, housing size is one of the problems on the estates, especially when related to the influx of large migrant families. The limited floor space combined with a relatively large number of rooms leads inevitably to small rooms. There is an example in Hoograven where the famous architect Rietveld designed four-storey apartment blocks. He was very concerned about the well-being of working-class families with their limited budgets, so he thought the interior design through thoroughly. Every room was exactly large enough for its purpose, while at the same time the floor plan was very inflexible for other uses or other standards; today's 2-metre-long beds would not fit into the children's rooms.

Economic developments

Employment

The housing estates were built in a period when industrialisation was booming and low-skilled workers were needed in large numbers. Mass employment led to housing that was built especially for these employees and their families (see also the historical and theoretical chapters in this volume). Initially, low-skilled industrial workers inhabited many of the estates; even today, the educational level is below average on all estates (Table 2.2). On some estates the situation is very worrisome, for example in the Barcelona cases, where nearly three quarters of the population has only completed primary education. Also in the Dutch

Table 2.2: Economic characteristics of the RESTATE research areas[a]

	Unemployment (%)	Gross participation (%)	Receiving social assistance (%)	Maximum primary education (%)
France, Lyon				
Rillieux-la-Pape	19	Na	59	36
Les Minguettes	29	Na	72	38
Germany, Berlin				
Marzahn NorthWest	18	50	11	Na
Märkisches Viertel	16	45	8	Na
Hungary, Budapest				
Havanna	4	48	21	35
Hungary, Nyíregyháza				
Jósaváros	7	39	28	30
Italy, Milan				
Sant'Ambrogio	15	Na	Na	41
San Siro	13	Na	Na	37
Comasina	15	Na	Na	45
the Netherlands, Amsterdam				
Bijlmer Centre	19	69	12	Na
Bijlmer East	18	69	12	Na
Kolenkit	4	69	10	Na
the Netherlands, Utrecht				
Nieuw Hoograven	4	55	10	45[b]
Kanaleneiland	5	54	10	53
Poland, Warsaw				
Ursynów	3	41	6	11
Wrzeciono	16	30	12	34
Slovenia, Ljubljana				
Nove Fužine	Na	Na	Na	Na
Slovenia, Koper				
Žusterna-Semedela	Na	Na	Na	Na
Spain, Madrid				
Simancas	28	46	Na	15/79[c]
Orcasitas	31	49	Na	25/72[c]
Spain, Barcelona				
Trinitat Nova	22	49	Na	70
Sant Roc	31	50	Na	72
Sweden, Jönköping				
Råslätt	6.5	47 (men) 35 (women)	31	Na
Öxnehaga	5.5	70 (men) 60 (women)	6	Na
Sweden, Stockholm				
Tensta	5	51	25	31
Husby	5	56	17	25

Table 2.2: contd.../

	Unemploy-ment (%)	Gross participa-tion (%)	Receiving social assistance (%)	Maximum primary education (%)
UK, London				
Bow HAT	Na	Na	Na	Na
Poplar HARCA	Na	Na	Na	Na
UK, Birmingham				
Central Estates	Na	Na	Na	Na
Hodge Hill	Na	Na	Na	Na

Notes:

[a] all data are from years 2001, 2002 or 2003 unless otherwise stated. All French data are from 1999.

[b] lower educated people, not clearly defined

[c] % with maximum primary education/with maximum secondary education

Source: RESTATE reports

cases of Nieuw-Hoograven and Kanaleneiland, about half the population has a poor educational level, an even worse situation when the generally high educational level of the rest of the city's population is taken into consideration. Some estates were even especially built for poorly educated manual workers: Les Minguettes was built for employees of the Renault industry. Another estate, Trinitat Nova, was built to house low-skilled immigrants from the rural areas in Spain who were looking for a job in Barcelona.

In every country the change from an industrial to a service economy led to increased unemployment among the low-skilled manual workers. As a consequence, nearly all estates have unemployment rates that are above the city as a whole, although the real concentration of the unemployed is often still to be found in the old city centres. The post-Second World War housing estates have had relatively high unemployment rates, but certainly not the highest of the city. In Sant'Ambrogio (Milan), unemployment is 7.4%, which is slightly higher than in the rest of Milan (4.8%), but certainly not bad. A positive exception is Warsaw's Ursynów where unemployment is lower (2%) than in the city as a whole (6%) and much lower than the national average (18%).

Some caution is needed when comparing the data in Table 2.2 on employment, participation, and dependency. Since the definition and therefore the registration of unemployment differ in each country, a strict comparison is not always possible. In addition, social assistance is granted to different groups in each country. However, gross participation (the share of the total population that has a job) does give a comparable indication of participation. On many estates gross participation is declining. Many reports explain this decline by reference to the changing population structure of the estates and a changing demand for employees.

Another reason for the decrease of participation is the increased proportion of pensioners among the residents; people who started their professional and housing careers in the 1960s have now retired.

Furthermore, as shown below, there has been an influx of migrant families on many estates. Unemployment among migrant groups is higher in all countries. In Les Minguettes, for example, unemployment among migrants is 10-15% higher than for French-born people. On top of that, in many cities employment opportunities for young people are limited. Again in Les Minguettes, 42% of young people are unemployed. Therefore, on nearly all the estates, the most vulnerable groups on the job market are young migrants with a poor educational level.

Income

A general low participation in the labour market leads to low average incomes. On nearly all the estates, the average disposable income is below the average disposable income in the city and the country as a whole, and reliance on social welfare is greater. On many estates, but especially in Southern and Eastern Europe, the black economy is of great importance for many families as a way of supplementing their limited income. Although less frequent in Western and Northern Europe, the provision by the poorly educated of such services in the black economy as cleaning and hairdressing represents an important source of income for many. In Eastern Europe many small businesses (construction, transport) can be found on the estates. This kind of business is relatively easy to start since no special education, floor space, or capital is required.

Opportunities within the estates

Many estates lack employment opportunities on the estate itself. In a highly mobile society it might be questioned whether the presence of employment in the near vicinity of the home is very important. People can commute to work by car or by public transport. In some countries a person can easily travel by bicycle or moped to a job situated more than ten kilometres from home. Lack of local employment is therefore not always a problem.

The increased spread of employment from the inner cities towards locations near motorways or public transport facilities offers opportunities on some estates. In the Bijlmer (Amsterdam), for example, the metro station that was built to connect the housing estate to the city centre is now a major point of attraction for high-profile businesses.

In some places and for some groups, the presence of local employment opportunities can be crucial, particularly for physically isolated estates, from which it is not at all easy to reach employment opportunities elsewhere, and possibly also for poor people who do not have the financial resources to buy a car or even to use public transport and for single mothers who want to be at home when their children arrive from school (sometimes twice a day). The lack of jobs in the near vicinity of the home can then become an impediment to employment. From Lyon's Rillieux-la-Pape to the city centre of Lyon takes about half an hour by car or public transport; many inhabitants are consequently prevented from having a job in the city of Lyon.

Lack of employment in an area can also lead to its mono-functionality. This is what was planned for the estates: a quiet, healthy and green living environment for the residents. This scene still holds true in many cases, but some areas are virtually empty during daytime, leading to uneasy feelings with regard to safety for those (like the elderly) who stay behind, or resulting in dormitory settlements.

In short, while the position of the residents of large housing estates on the job market is not as bad as in other parts of the city, it is also not the best. The estates are characterised by a separation of functions that concentrates on housing rather than employment. Usually there is little employment on the estates, and the traditional industries are closing down, creating unemployment among low-skilled workers. New businesses are spreading from the city centres, creating new employment in the service sector. Since the most vulnerable groups on the job market – youngsters and migrants – are often overrepresented on the large housing estates, their share of the unemployed is also higher than in most other parts of the city.

Demographic and sociocultural developments

Population structure

The large post-Second World War housing estates were planned with a certain population structure in mind. In many cases the estates were initially built for traditional family households. Since the areas were built up 30 to 40 years ago, the original population is now ageing, leading to an overrepresentation of the elderly (Table 2.3). This is especially the case in Southern Europe, where the elderly stay in their homes but their children leave as they cannot find suitable housing on the estate. The supply of services has not always been well adapted to this changing population structure. A lack of services for older people has been reported on several estates, such as Sant'Ambrogio in Milan. In some cases, such as San Siro in Milan, the apartment blocks have no lifts, so the elderly have problems reaching their dwellings.

In Eastern Europe there is an overrepresentation of the 19-65 age cohort on the estates, which is related to the estates' position on the housing market. Warsaw's Ursynów, for example, was very popular among well-educated families, communist officials, and artists and has therefore been able to maintain its attraction for the working-age cohort. In Budapest's Havanna, families with many children have moved out over the past ten years and have been replaced by young childless couples. On the Eastern European estates, immigration from abroad is not an issue.

In Western and Northern Europe the position of the estates on the housing market is less favourable, leading to an influx of migrant families. These families often have more children than the original population, leading to an overrepresentation of young people. The original population started leaving the estates in the 1970s, moving to neighbourhoods with single-family homes and making room for less prosperous households, often migrants. There are some exceptions, however: white working-class residents predominate in London's Bow HAT, for example.

In short, we can identify three broad groups of estates related to population structure: first, the Southern European estates, with an ageing population; second, the Eastern European estates, with a relative overrepresentation of people of working age (19-65 years old); and finally, the majority of the Northern and Western European estates, which are often characterised by an influx of immigrants.

Table 2.3: Demographic and sociocultural characteristics of the RESTATE research areas[a]

	Inhabitants (number)	Age < 18 (%)	Age > 65 (%)	Non-native people (%)	Main immigrant groups	Average household size (%)	Single parent households (%)
France, Lyon							
Rillieux-la-Pape	18,302	33	21	13	North Africans	2.7	Na
Les Minguettes	21,312	Na	34	Na	North Africans	3.0	13
Germany, Berlin							
Marzahn NorthWest	42,835	25	12	7	Vietnamese	2.0	29
Märkisches Viertel	38,000	17	18	13	Turkish	1.9	Na
Hungary, Budapest							
Havanna	16,990	20	9	Na	Immigration is not important	2.6	21
Hungary, Nyíregyháza							
Jósaváros	8,494	21	12	Na		2.4	16
Italy, Milan							
Sant'Ambrogio	6,259	11[b]	34	1	None	2.8	Na
San Siro	25,182	11	38	12		2.2	Na
Comasina	5,432	9	39	3	None	2.4	Na
the Netherlands, Amsterdam							
Bijlmer Centre	21,350	30	5	84	Surinamese	2.3	18
Bijlmer East	27,605	30	8	76	Surinamese	2.3	17
Kolenkit	6,799	36	8	84	Moroccans/Turks	2.6	13

Table 2.3: contd.../

	Inhabitants (number)	Age < 18 (%)	Age > 65 (%)	Non-native people (%)	Main immigrant groups	Average household size (%)	Single parent households (%)
the Netherlands, Utrecht							
Nieuw Hoograven	5,903	25	32[c]	45	Moroccans	2.3	5.7
Kanaleneiland	7,819	33	16	74	Moroccans	2.9	4.0
Poland, Warsaw							
Ursynów	33,600	20	7	0.5	None	2.6	Na
Wrzeciono	31,379[d]	16	25	0	None	2.4	0.1
Spain, Madrid							
Simancas	20,916	11[e]	29	13	None	2.7	18
Orcasitas	18,716	11	24	3	None	3.2	14
Spain, Barcelona							
Trinitat Nova	7,686	11	30	2	None	2.4	Na
Sant Roc	12,476	17	17	4	None	3.7	Na
Slovenia, Ljubljana							
Nove Fužine	12,086	14[f]	4	Na	Former Yugoslavia	3.0	Na
Slovenia, Koper							
Žusterna-Semedela	5,397	12	11	Na	Former Yugoslavia	2.9	Na
Sweden, Jönköping							
Råslätt	4,242	29	15	47		Na	Na
Öxnehaga	5,197	33	10	27		Na	Na

Table 2.3: contd.../

	Inhabitants (number)	Age < 18 (%)	Age > 65 (%)	Non-native people (%)	Main immigrant groups	Average household size (%)	Single parent households (%)
Sweden, Stockholm							
Tensta	17,763	34	8	58	Iraq, Somalia	12	31
Husby	11,874	29	8	56	Iran, Iraq	13	25
UK, London							
Bow HAT	4,869	24	17	32	Bangladeshi	2.1	10
Poplar HARCA	17,741	37	12	58	Bangladeshi	2.82	11
UK, Birmingham							
Central Estates	6,582	25	16	39	Black Caribbean	1.77	11
Hodge Hill	9,015	31	19	13	Black Caribbean	2.27	13

Notes:

[a] all data are from years 2001, 2002, or 2003 unless otherwise stated. All French data are from 1999.

[b] includes only the social housing sector, not the owner-occupied sector

[c] older than 55

[d] 1988, estimates for 2003 are 34,000

[e] younger than 14

[f] younger than 14

Source: RESTATE reports

Ethnic diversity

In France, the Netherlands, Sweden, and the UK the influx of migrants from abroad is a major issue on the estates. Often more than half of the population originates from another country. A relative homogeneity of the population is replaced by a large share of a variety of ethnic groups. In Amsterdam's Bijlmer Centre (Surinamese) and Kolenkit (Moroccans and Turks) the proportion of migrants is 84%. The increased ethnic variety can lead to a vibrant civic culture, with a lively public social life and a concomitant variety in services. Unfortunately, however, in most cases the differences in culture, language, and religion are perceived negatively, in particular by the older native Dutch population. An exception is the Bijlmer in Amsterdam, which has gone past the stage where multi-ethnicity is a problem; some authors now consider the prospects for the Bijlmer to be good (Helleman and Wassenberg, 2004).

In London's Poplar HARCA it is reported that the influx of large families of black and minority ethnic groups in relatively small dwellings is leading to overcrowded housing situations. When too many people live in a dwelling, various problems are bound to arise. The situation may be uncomfortable for the people involved, but the main problem is for the neighbours who have to cope with the noise and other nuisances. When there are too many of these over-occupied dwellings, there may be significant pressures on the area and on its public spaces. The definition of overcrowding depends on the local context. In some cases, as in Fužine (Ljubljana), it is not uncommon for a poor family of five to live in a 20 m^2 flat, while the average housing size is 65 m^2. A situation like this would seldom occur in a country such as the Netherlands, where a two-bedroom apartment of 65 m^2 housing a family of four is considered to be overcrowded.

A heterogeneous population structure does not always have to generate problems. The ethnically diverse population of the Birmingham central estates seems to exist without major tensions or problems. But problems are reported in many cases. The original inhabitants of Milan's Sant'Ambrogio, for example, find it difficult to accept the newcomers, however low their numbers, meeting them with reticence and resistance.

Stigmatisation

Many estates have social problems related to a lack of meeting places, drug abuse and drug dealing, and other criminal activity, which may lead to the stigmatisation of the area. A neighbourhood more easily gains a stigma than loses it; repetition by the media often bears some responsibility here. A stigma can become attached to an area that becomes known for its problems with crime or with a large proportion of minority ethnic groups. Some estates were stigmatised from the beginning, such as Råslätt (Jönköping). In the early years the estate was perceived as something different and not as a 'regular' or 'average' housing estate. However, the characteristics that constitute 'difference' are changing over the course of time. This change has an influence on the everyday life in the area as well as the identity of the residents and their image of Swedish society. In the course of time, Råslätt has taken on an ethnic character. The Amsterdam Bijlmermeer is another example of a highly stigmatised neighbourhood. Despite many physical and social changes in recent years, the area is still known to many people from both within Amsterdam and outside it as one of the worst places in the city in which to live.

Social cohesion

Originally, the community feeling on many estates was strong. The population consisted mainly of young working- or middle-class families. Nowadays a new feeling of local solidarity has emerged in many cases, sometimes as a result of living together in harsh situations. There is evidence in Lyon's Rillieux-la-Pape of a high degree of local solidarity. The residents help each other, mainly through the women on the estate; and they have developed local community and voluntary activities. In Comasina (Milan) there is a strong sense of social cohesion, resulting in activities such as the joint cleaning and redecoration of the common areas in apartment blocks and maintaining the green areas of the estate. These self-organised groups are all homeowners. In Warsaw's Ursynów there are also clear signs of mutual support, especially among those who have lived there for a long time. London's Bow HAT is said to have a well-developed community and voluntary sector infrastructure, particularly in relation to the relief of poverty and to housing.

Local solidarity or social cohesion can also be enhanced as a consequence of the (perceived) peripheral location of the estate. This seems to be the case in Birmingham's central estates, where the sense of isolation and neglect felt by the residents has led to a significant bond between them. This bond has been used and turned into positive action, resulting in the implementation of a regeneration programme. In some cases, social cohesion can be found among a limited number of groups. In Fužine in Ljubljana, social cohesion seems particularly strong among Serbians and Bosnians, as can be seen from their joint celebration of national holidays and joining in folk music together.

Liveability

Public space

Large post-Second World War housing estates and high-rise housing blocks are by no means invariably the worst places in the city in which to live. Older neighbourhoods often have lower-quality dwellings; in many cases there are more negative neighbourhood characteristics in the older areas than on the more modern estates, for example, higher population densities, traffic problems, a lack of playing facilities for children, and a general lack of green areas. It is clear that many people like living on some of the post-Second World War estates. Warsaw's Ursynów is a case in point, as is London's Bow HAT. In the latter area a survey revealed that 81% of the respondents thought the area was a good place in which to live and the residents of this area are said to leave only when they die or are evicted.

A separation of functions can be seen as a typical characteristic of the estates that were built according to the principles of CIAM and Le Courbusier. The large green public areas between the housing blocks and the separation of functions are nowadays often evaluated as an asset. The estates were often designed by famous architects with clear ideas about urban design, creating a feeling of spatial grandeur. As a result the estates are spacious and provide ample opportunities for leisure activities such as jogging and fishing; pedestrians are not bothered by traffic; and disturbances by public functions are minimised when they are not located close to dwellings. In Ljubljana's Fužine, for example, the design is described as 'excellent' and said to contain some beautiful places.

In some cases, however, such as Milan's Sant'Ambrogio and Utrecht's Kanaleneiland, the green areas and other public spaces are very poorly maintained. In former state-socialist countries, unclear ownership structures generate problematic issues with respect to public spaces and lead to poor maintenance. Consequently, sometimes these spaces cannot be used, or they are vandalised. Areas where cars are not allowed also minimise the opportunities for police patrol, and all kinds of criminal behaviour may be attracted, as in Amsterdam's Bijlmer. In a part of Milan's San Siro a central courtyard is used as the central meeting point for drug dealers and drug addicts, so that other people no longer dare to use this space. On many estates the quality of the playgrounds leaves much to be desired.

When the post-Second World War large housing estates were built, nobody suspected that the number of cars in the city and the neighbourhood would increase to the extent it has done in the last 20 years or so. This increase means that within these estates – as in other city neighbourhoods – there are traffic problems of all kinds. Small streets generate traffic jams (as in Ljubljana's Fužine neighbourhood), as do situations where only one or two roads give access to an estate. Parking problems are a direct consequence of the growth of car ownership in combination with too few parking spaces, although the large green public spaces provide a solution that cannot be found in inner city areas. In Fužine the original plan for the estate envisaged underground parking, but this was never realised because of a shortage of resources. During the winter piles of snow reduce the limited parking opportunities even further and parking becomes particularly chaotic.

A high population density leads to problems with the liveability of an estate. The number of people living in a designated area does not matter as much as the number of people who feel uneasy about this density. The high population density in Lyon's Les Minguettes, where the presence of many dwellings was accompanied by a lack of public space, has been reported to have led to many problems. In the meantime some of the high-rise blocks have been demolished in order to create more open space in the area. According to a spokesperson, this intervention has resulted in a reduction of vandalism in the vicinity.

Services

One or two shopping centres were planned on most of the estates. The needs of the residents have changed in the course of time, so the kinds of services provided have often been updated and adapted. On estates where many migrants have moved in, the number of foreign shops has burgeoned. On other estates the perceived lack of 'normal' shops has led to an increasing number of small informal shops, especially in Eastern Europe after 1990. This is also where the number of services on the estates is currently no problem and large shopping malls with big French and English supermarkets are sprouting up in the direct vicinity of the estates.

In some cases the number of shops is limited, satisfying only the most basic of shopping needs (as in London's Bow HAT); in other cases the shops are too expensive. The closing down of smaller shopping centres on some estates causes problems for the elderly, who now have to walk longer distances to the supermarkets for their daily supplies.

All the reports note a lack of health services and community centres. Barcelona's Trinitat Nova is worth mentioning here, since this shared problem has led to a cohesive community. No facilities were available on this estate, so the residents organised their own community centre. This has now become the neighbourhood's focal point, leading to the empowerment of the residents and increased influence on policy-making processes. On other estates, in Jósavarós in Hungary, for example, the limited facilities are used very efficiently, in that they are used extensively by a wide range of groups. In Žusterna-Semedela in Slovenia the lack of community centres is compensated by a large number of extra-curricular activities in schools not only for the students, but also for other groups in the community such as the elderly and the unemployed. A lack of community facilities has particularly been mentioned in the UK cases, for example on one London estate (Poplar HARCA), where local healthcare provision is very poor.

Safety

The literature on post-Second World War large housing estates in general, and high-rise housing complexes from the same period in particular, makes it abundantly clear that dwellings in these areas and complexes hardly belong at the top of the housing hierarchy. A multitude of safety and social problems can arise in neighbourhoods at the bottom of the housing market. Many people live there because they have no other choice; vacancy rates are often high. Empty dwellings can lead to anti-social behaviour, vandalism, feelings of insecurity, and, of course, lower incomes for the landlords, who may decrease their investments in the housing stock. A spiral of decline then emerges (see also Prak and Priemus, 1985). Vacant dwellings can also attract squatters. In Milan's San Siro an estimated 9% of the total number of dwellings are illegally occupied.

Another safety problem is related to a lack of meeting places. When people cannot meet outside the home in pubs, youth centres, community buildings or similar venues, they start looking for alternatives. Hanging around in common parts of buildings, shopping centres, and other external spaces seems to be typical, particularly for the young people in Rillieux-la-Pape in Lyon and the Wrzeciono estate in Warsaw. In France's Les Minguettes the population of Arab children and teenagers dominate the public space. Their prevalence enhances feelings of insecurity among the other local inhabitants and can even mar social life in general in the area.

Feelings of insecurity among the residents of the neighbourhood are often fed by the anti-social behaviour of some groups in the area. In the case of Rillieux-la-Pape (Lyon) the anti-social behaviour of youngsters inside and outside the buildings is seen as one of the most pressing problems. Communal spaces are vandalised and public spaces destroyed by some of these youngsters.

It has been noted earlier in this chapter that drug dealing and drug abuse may be related in part to the physical structure of an area. Drug problems are mentioned on many of the estates in our research project. That is not to say, however, that these areas are invariably the most prominent sites in the city involved in drug dealing and drug abuse. It should also be noted that drug abuse probably relates to some extent to the age structure of the area's inhabitants. When an estate accommodates many people in the 15- to 25-year age range, the chance of drug abuse is higher than when there are greater numbers of younger or older people living on the estate.

From the Wrzeciono estate in Warsaw it is reported that the number of alcohol and drug addicts has risen by 50% in the last two years. Related to this situation are problems such as theft, assault, and burglaries. Drug-related crime is also a big issue in London's Bow HAT. Residents may suffer from drug-related problems, however large- or small-scale they may be.

Crime is not always related to drugs. The perception of crime in the area can easily lead to a negative evaluation of an estate. This holds for the Polish Wrzeciono estate. The Polish researchers noted that the general opinion in Poland is that city streets are dangerous places. In some cases there is clearly a relatively high incidence of criminal activities. In London's Bow HAT area, for example, robbery is a significant problem, and figures are much higher there than in the rest of the country. The same holds for burglary figures in London's Poplar HARCA. Gang culture and related crimes add to the criminality figures and feelings of insecurity in, for example, Bow HAT.

Conclusions

In conclusion, in spite of all the differences, some generalisations can be made about the estates. The physical layout is mostly the same: low- or high-rise multi-family dwellings with large green public spaces seem to predominate. At the same time, there are not many large housing estates that consist of just one housing type (such as high-rise blocks). In most cases the areas include a mix of housing types, leading to a variation in physical quality, surface, tenure, and kinds of resident. In Southern and Eastern Europe most houses are owned by the residents, while in Northern and Western Europe the housing associations are the predominant landlords.

In many of these areas several positive points can be identified. Many people value the design of the estates with their large green public spaces. The separation of functions is sometimes an asset, since it provides safe traffic handling and no industrial pollution. The estates also provide relatively large, bright and sunny dwellings at a good price. The estates clearly serve an important function for the people at the bottom of the housing market. Some of the estates offer many opportunities because of their location close to the city centre or near natural areas. Others have become new business centres as a result of their easy accessibility and available building space.

Unfortunately, many negative points can also be found. In most cases, dwellings show clear signs of physical decay and sometimes long lists of physical housing problems can be produced. Estates are often sited in a peripheral location, which diminishes accessibility to the city centre and other business locations. Furthermore, the estates are often below the average level on the housing market, although this is less true in Eastern Europe. Relatively cheap housing attracts those households who cannot afford to live elsewhere, leading to a concentration of low-income households.

Nearly all the estates have higher unemployment rates than the cities to which they belong, especially among young people and immigrants. The educational level is generally below the city average. Often there are few employment possibilities on the estates. Increasingly, they are inhabited by elderly people, especially in Southern Europe, as a consequence of the ageing process taking place there. On most Western estates the elderly population is increasingly accompanied by households from minority ethnic groups. In Eastern Europe the estates are still predominantly inhabited by people in the economically active 19- to 65-year age group, owing to their position on the housing market. The combined effect of unemployment, large numbers of children, and many retired people is that a relatively large proportion of the population is inactive and incomes are generally low. Not surprisingly, in Southern and Eastern Europe, where there are no extended social security systems as in Northern and Western Europe, the black economy is an important source of additional income.

The estates also experience problems with liveability: the separation of functions that is so typical of most of these estates leads to unsafe spots and conflicts about the maintenance of public spaces. The increasing numbers of cars (especially in Eastern Europe) in the last two decades cause traffic jams and parking problems. The pollution of the large public spaces is a problem on many estates; a lack of maintenance of the public spaces is also frequently mentioned in Southern and Eastern Europe. Shopping centres are sometimes closed down and they then degenerate into crime spots, while other shopping areas do not seem to meet the needs of the local population. In addition to this, a lack of health services and community centres seems to be typical of most of the estates.

Safety problems on the estates are related to vacant dwellings, drug abuse, the lack of meeting places for youngsters, and the anti-social behaviour of some groups in the area. Problems of these kinds occur everywhere in Europe. The criminal behaviour of just a small group of people can make all the difference between living comfortably and quietly and being engulfed by feelings of unease and fear. The stigmatisation of an estate can be the consequence of processes of decline in the area, especially when the processes of decay are given broad coverage in the media. Eradicating these negative images is often very difficult.

When listing all these problems, it should of course be acknowledged that they never appear alone. In fact, many problems are the consequence of other problems, which in their turn may create new problems. Spirals of decline have often been described in the literature (see Prak and Priemus, 1985, for example) as typical of post-Second World War large housing estates in Europe.

However, we also see in several chapters in this book all kinds of policies, actions, and efforts being undertaken to reverse such spirals. That is the most important message for this chapter: although problems may seem to predominate, most of these areas are still important housing areas for a large number of people and there are many opportunities to remedy the situation. Trying to find solutions to the problems is a necessity and a challenge.

References

Aalbers, M., van Beckhoven, E., van Kempen, R., Musterd, S. and Ostendorf, W. (2003) *Large housing estates in the Netherlands: Overview of developments and problems in Amsterdam and Utrecht*, Utrecht: Urban and Regional research centre Utrecht, Faculty of Geosciences, Utrecht University.

Andersson, R., Molina, I., Öresjö, E., Pettersson, L. and Siwertsson, C. (2003) *Large housing estates in Sweden: Overview of developments and problems in Jönköping and Stockholm*, Utrecht: Urban and Regional research centre Utrecht, Faculty of Geosciences, Utrecht University.

Černič Mali, B., Sendi, R., Boškič, R., Filipovič, M., Goršič, N. and Zaviršek Hudnik, D. (2003) *Large housing estates in Slovenia: Overview of developments and problems in Ljubljana and Koper*, Utrecht: Urban and Regional research centre Utrecht, Faculty of Geosciences, Utrecht University.

Chignier-Riboulon, F., Commerçon, N., Trigueiro, M. and Zepf, M. (2003) *Large housing estates in France: Overview of developments and problems in Lyon*, Utrecht: Urban and Regional research centre Utrecht, Faculty of Geosciences, Utrecht University.

Erdösi, S., Geröházi, É., Teller, N. and Tosics, I. (2003) *Large housing estates in Hungary: Overview of developments and problems in Budapest and Nyíregyháza*, Utrecht: Urban and Regional research centre Utrecht, Faculty of Geosciences, Utrecht University.

Hall, S., Lee, P., Murie, A., Rowlands, R. and Sankey, S. (2003) *Large housing estates in United Kingdom: Overview of developments and problems in London and Birmingham*, Utrecht: Urban and Regional research centre Utrecht, Faculty of Geosciences, Utrecht University.

Helleman, G. and Wassenberg, F. (2004) 'The renewal of what was tomorrow's idealistic city. Amsterdam's Bijlmermeer high-rise', *Cities*, vol 21, no 1, pp 3-17.

Knorr-Siedow, T. and Droste, C. (2003) *Large housing estates in Germany: Overview of developments and problems in Berlin*, Utrecht: Urban and Regional research centre Utrecht, Faculty of Geosciences, Utrecht University.

Mezzetti, P., Mugnana, S. and Zajczyk, F. (2003) *Large housing estates in Italy: Overview of developments and problems in Milan,* Utrecht: Urban and Regional research centre Utrecht, Faculty of Geosciences, Utrecht University.

Murie, A., Knorr-Siedow, T. and van Kempen, R. (2003) *Large housing estates in Europe: General developments and theoretical backgrounds*, Utrecht: Urban and Regional research centre Utrecht, Faculty of Geosciences, Utrecht University.

Pareja-Eastaway, M., Tapada-Berteli, T., van Boxmeer, B. and Garcia Ferrando, L. (2003) *Large housing estates in Spain: Overview of developments and problems in Madrid and Barcelona*, Utrecht: Urban and Regional research centre Utrecht, Faculty of Geosciences, Utrecht University.

Power, A. (1997) *Estates on the edge: The social consequences of mass housing in Northern Europe*, London: Macmillan.

Prak, N.L. and Priemus, H. (1985) 'A model for the analysis of the decline of post-war housing', *The International Journal of Urban and Regional Research*, vol 10, no 1, pp 1-7.

PRC Bouwcentrum International (2005) *Sustainable refurbishment of high-rise residential buildings and restructuring of surrounding areas in Europe*, Den Haag: Ministry of Housing, Spatial Planning and the Environment.

Turkington, R., Wassenberg, F. and van Kempen, R. (eds) (2004) *The future of high-rise housing estates in Europe*, Delft: Delft University Press.

Węcławowicz, G., Kosłowski, S. and Bajek, R. (2003) *Large housing estates in Poland: Overview of developments and problems in Warsaw*, Utrecht: Urban and Regional research centre Utrecht, Faculty of Geosciences, Utrecht University.

THREE

Place making and large estates: theory and practice

Stephen Hall and Rob Rowlands

Introduction

This chapter provides a theoretical overview that can be seen as the basic framework for this book. The framework starts from a premise that the large estates were planned, developed, and allocated during a socioeconomic paradigm that characterised the four decades following the Second World War, the basic tenets of which (social and economic stability created by the Fordist industrial process and underwritten by the Keynesian welfare state in Western Europe and socialist central planning in Eastern Europe) no longer apply in the contemporary world. The contemporary socioeconomic paradigm is characterised by diversity, fragmentation, and uncertainty. The new paradigm presents significant challenges for the physical, social, and economic regeneration of large estates. It is argued here that this regeneration process represents an excellent example of 'place making', as introduced in Chapter One; that is, the promotion of the social, economic, and environmental well-being of diverse places (in this case, large estates) and the development of institutional capacity to achieve this.

In this chapter, we develop an analytical framework for assessing the process of place making in large estates. The chapter comprises five further sections: first, we consider the transition from the post-war socioeconomic paradigm in which the large estates were conceived; second, we consider the notion of place making; third, we consider one particular school of theory that has sought to interpret the role of place making, empirically and normatively, in this new paradigm – 'communicative planning' theory, the principal example of which is Healey's model of 'collaborative planning'; fourth, we consider the nature of power and governance as theorised by Bourdieu and Foucault; finally, we outline a number of dimensions for exploring, in practice, the nature of place making in large estates.

Diversity, fragmentation, and uncertainty in the contemporary world

The large post-war estates epitomise the form of the built environment that characterised the period known in Western Europe in sociocultural terms as 'Modernist' and in economic terms as 'Fordist'. This refers, in particular, to the middle of the 20th century. During this period, in the West, the old industrial scientific paradigm, based on coal and steam, was superseded by a new one, driven by oil, gas, and electricity, which facilitated mass production. At the same time, a new sociopolitical paradigm emerged in response to the inter-war challenge of mass unemployment on the one hand, and fascism on the other. This period coincided with the hegemony of central planning in Central and Eastern European countries.

The paradigm had a number of defining features (Aglietta, 1979; Lash and Urry, 1987; Hall and Jacques, 1989; Harvey, 1989; Soja, 1989; Amin, 1994), namely:

- an industrial system based on standardised mass production, supported by state-underwritten mass consumption;
- a welfare state informed by Keynesian economic principles and broad political support for full employment;
- the domination of labour-market participation by men, with women returning to their pre-war roles in domesticity and consumption;
- large-scale immigration from the former European colonies, with migrants subject to racism in the labour and housing markets;
- an exploitative approach towards the natural environment;
- a concentration of workers and consumers in towns and cities in which former slum areas were replaced by modern, system-built housing;
- an international political system characterised by West–East confrontation, and the economic and military hegemony of the United States and Soviet Union, respectively.

The development of the built environment during this period was strongly influenced by the 'Modernist' school of urban design, epitomised by Le Corbusier and the *Congrès International d'Architecture Moderne* (CIAM). The prevailing argument was that technological advances held the key to solving urban problems. The school advocated an idealised, ordered, built environment that sought to decongest city centres, increase building densities elsewhere, increase the permeability of cities to road transport, and increase parks and open space. The development of the large housing estates is hyperbolically typical of this approach. The Modernist approach to urban design was allied to an ostensibly value-free, *rational* planning paradigm. This sought to portray urban planners as apolitical technocrats working in the public interest (Chadwick, 1971; Faludi, 1973). However, in practice, this rationality was subordinated to the narrow-minded architectural thinking and interest-loaded political coalitions between local politicians and the building industry that gave rise to the large estates.

In Western Europe, the Fordist/Modernist era witnessed an unprecedented phase of economic growth and prosperity. In France, for example, the post-war years have been referred to as '*les 30 glorieuses*'. In the UK, Prime Minister Harold Macmillan famously declared that the British public had 'never had it so good'. In the domain of housing, the application of rational planning and mass production techniques contributed to the elimination of long-term housing shortages as well as ameliorating housing conditions and eradicating slum dwellings.

However, by the mid 1970s, the post-war paradigm had been undermined by a number of new developments. The most important of these was a reduction in the rate of economic growth attributed in part to the oil crisis of the early 1970s but, more fundamentally, to the long-term tendency towards over-accumulation inherent within the Fordist industrial process. It has been argued that a new social, economic, and political paradigm is emerging, the defining features of which are as follows (Aglietta, 1979; Lash and Urry, 1987; Hall and Jacques, 1989; Harvey, 1989; Soja, 1989; Amin, 1994):

- the decline of manufacturing industry as the key economic driver and its replacement by the 'knowledge-based economy' (based on the application of information and computer technology, innovation, research and design, and the pursuit of added value in the production of goods and services);
- the fragmentation of conditions of work, including the decline in collective-labour organisation and class-based politics, the polarisation of the labour market between well-paid skilled workers and 'disposable' unskilled labour, plus persistently high levels of unemployment;
- the fragmentation of consumption, including greater gender, ethnic, and environmental sensitivity, and the increasing diversity of lifestyle choices; and
- geographical fragmentation, including the polarisation of disadvantaged residents of declining urban neighbourhoods, including large estates, and 'growth' poles elsewhere.

These changes have important implications for place. First, new urban forms have arisen in response to the perceived failures of the past, including those associated with large estates. Dominant contemporary urban ideals (the compact city, the urban village, and so forth) prioritise compactness (that is, high-building densities), and social and land-use mix in order to facilitate social and economic interaction and reduce car use. Second, there has been a shift from the old paradigm of urban government, organised around the state-led delivery of services and the politics of 'collective consumption' (Dunleavy, 1980), to a new paradigm of urban *governance* (Le Galès, 2003).

In short, the political, economic, and social assumptions that underpinned the planning, development, and management of the large estates are no longer relevant. It is possible to argue that the new order of urban governance is characterised by:

(1) diversity, as a wide variety of stakeholders are potentially implicated;
(2) fragmentation, as political power is diffused between a variety of individuals and institutions; and
(3) uncertainty, as social, economic, and political change is an ever-present reality.

It is in this context that place making through collaborative planning becomes both an imperative – to increase strategic governing capacity and reduce conflict and uncertainty – and a challenge.

Place making

Healey (1997, 1998a, 1998b) defines *place making* as "the promotion of the social, economic, and environmental well being of diverse places and the development of institutional capacity to achieve this". Ideally, achievement comes through a *collective*, consensus-building decision-making process based on progression through argument and *discussion*. She therefore sets out a *normative* form of planning appropriate to an inclusive, environmentally sensitive, mixed economy. Thus, while Healey's ideas, in common with much of the theoretical literature discussed in this volume, were formulated in the context of an Anglo-centric debate, they are intended to be applicable more broadly. Indeed, it is possible to argue that the current socioeconomic paradigm has prompted a convergence amongst European states (East and West) towards a political economy based on a more pluralist form of politics, an acknowledgement of the importance of sustainable development and the mutual dependency of state and market.

The process of place making implies networking, partnerships, and institutional capacity building, the objectives of which are to develop the institutional capacity for planning in the context of diversity, fragmentation, and uncertainty. In concrete terms, Healey's agenda incorporates at least the following dimensions:

- **Integration in policy making:** A particular problem in many European countries is the separation of different 'policy communities', each having specific responsibility for a particular aspect of economic and social life (planning, housing, health, education, social services, transport) and a lack of coordination between them. This separation is referred to in France as the '*logique de guichet*'. In some countries (the UK, for example), this fragmentation of public policy has been reinforced by a highly centralised system of government. Elsewhere, the problem may be a lack (or even absence) of central government guidance and coordination. Integrated place making also implies the necessity to acknowledge the distinction between spatial policies (regeneration programmes that are implemented at a neighbourhood level, for example) and aspatial policies that may have spatial impacts, and the potential for these to be in conflict. In the context of large estates, for example, national housing policy and benefit reform are key influences on the outcomes at estate level and may even undermine local regeneration efforts.
- **Collaboration in policy making:** Integration implies a *collaborative* approach to planning. This approach implies cooperation on the development of long-term strategies for areas rather than the development of time-limited, project-specific partnerships and networks. Traditionally, these have prevailed within regeneration programmes, even in those European countries where working in multi-sector partnerships is well established.
- **Stakeholder involvement:** Networks and partnerships need to acknowledge the need for the participation of new types of stakeholders (local residents, for example) and not just the old ones (such as public authorities). In the context of estate regeneration programmes in Europe, local participation has been a decisive influence in some countries (Spain, for example), has long been encouraged by central governments in others (the UK, for example), has an uneven history elsewhere (France, for example), but has largely been absent from the (until recently) autocratic states of Central and Eastern Europe.

- **Local knowledge:** Knowledge is identified as a key resource. Collaborative planning implies the construction of mechanisms that are sensitive to cultural differences between stakeholders in ways of thinking, valuing, and communicating.
- **Building relational resources:** It is important to construct the infrastructure of positive relations between government, citizens, and business where information, knowledge, and understanding can flow. Capacity building needs to be combined with institutional reform; otherwise, the onus is placed purely on the excluded: in this instance, the residents of large estates.

In the present volume we consider to what extent these matters apply in the estates, cities, and countries under research. We refer to the way in which initiatives for particular areas mature and change, with alterations in the elements set out above, over the lifetime of projects. In so doing, we refer to the management of change and the experience of change in relational resources over time.

'Communicative' planning theory

A number of related perspectives have arisen from within planning theory in response to the new contemporary socioeconomic paradigm. These perspectives may be termed 'communicative' planning (other incarnations include 'deliberative', 'participative', and 'collaborative' planning). It has been claimed that these perspectives constitute a new paradigm in planning theory (Healey, 1996). This claim has been contested, but even its critics acknowledge that communicative planning theory corresponds to the *zeitgeist* of the turn of the Millennium (Allmendinger and Tewdr Jones, 2002). That is to say, the model has been developed in response to the diversity, fragmentation, and uncertainty of the contemporary world and is promoted as an ideal vehicle for achieving integrated place making. The model, Anglo-Saxon in origin but more widely applicable as noted above, therefore merits further consideration here.

Communicative planning theory is presented as an alternative to the ostensible (but in practice illusory) rationality of the 'technocratic' planning paradigm (Chadwick, 1971; Faludi, 1973) that resulted in the planning, building, and allocation of the large estates in a wholly 'uncollaborative' manner, the meta-narratives of the post-war era such as Marxist political economy, and the infinite relativism of Post-Modernism. The very notion of planning in an indeterminate contemporary world has been questioned (Allmendinger, 2001).

However, communicative planning theory, drawing on the Habermasian concept of 'communicative rationality', argues that social actors can achieve a collective and 'objective' understanding of the world through free and open *discourse* (under specified circumstances).

Communicative planning takes a variety of normative and empirical forms. It is simultaneously an *analytical* tool, enabling the comparison of the reality of discourse with an 'ideal typical' scenario, and a *prescriptive* model to inform real-world planning. It is also a *normative* model that specifies the value that underpins collective decision making (Allmendinger and Tewdr Jones, 2002).

The best-known example of communicative planning theory is Healey's work on collaborative planning (see Healey, 1996, 1997, 1998a, 1998b, 2002). As noted above, the notion of collaborative planning was developed in the context of circumstances that are specific to the UK. However, it is probable that the concept is applicable to a greater or lesser extent in other European countries. For example, in every case, a process of dialogue on the nature and potential of places informs planning and policy making. Of course, the precise social and political context determines the extent to which this process is inclusive, as advocated in the normative model of collaborative planning outlined below. For example, multi-sector partnership in the UK is well established but falls short of the ideal. In France, the centralised, technocratic Gaullist tradition counteracts collaborative forms. In Eastern Europe, the underdevelopment of civil society and very short history of participative policy making creates special circumstances.

The fundamental aim of collaborative planning is to set out an agenda for city planning that is *inclusive* (that is, the right of all stakeholders to a voice in the decision-making process is acknowledged), *environmentally sensitive*, and accepts the notion of a *mixed economy* (that is, the mutual interdependence of state and market is acknowledged).

Collaborative planning is, therefore, a model for the development of diverse places in an inclusive manner. Cities and their constituent neighbourhoods are experienced in different ways by different people. This observation is fundamental to the concept of collaborative planning. What cities are and what they could be are 'imagined' by people in different ways. This diversity gives rise to a multiplicity of 'images' of any given city. For example, Healey (2002) cites the following:

• Planning images of the city and neighbourhoods are often dominated by physical concepts such as the 'compact city', 'entrepreneurial city', 'urban village' or, indeed, 'large post-war housing estate'.

- Political images of the city and neighbourhoods emphasise political structures and jurisdictions.
- Economic images are not concerned with the city and neighbourhoods as places per se, but as containers of assets that may be exploited.
- Environmental scientific images envision the city and neighbourhoods in terms of a set of interrelated components of a wider eco-system.
- Residents possess a proliferation of images of the city and neighbourhoods as locales ('home', 'workplace', and so forth).

It is not, therefore, possible to conceive of a city in an 'objective' sense. What brings a city to life is the process of 'imagining' what it is and what it could be (Healey, 2002). This process is, of course, highly contested, since conflicting 'images' of the city and neighbourhood are potentially mutually exclusive. The key question for collaborative planning is whether a collective process of 'imagining' the city can provide a basis for building governance capacity around shared 'images' in a context where urban life is characterised by such diversity, fragmentation, and uncertainty: a basis that reaches a shared vision that accommodates diversity and 'difference'. In concrete terms, Healey argues for a consideration of the means to initiate proactive development strategies based on agreements around what places might look like and the opportunities and limitations of transforming them (Healey, 1998a; 1998b). Thus:

> Such an approach to planning will generate a discourse of debate about concepts of place and their meaning, combining images and symbols to express these qualities with arguments about social, economic and environmental dynamics and their expression in the lives and meanings of people and firms in particular places. These meanings will then structure the debates about specific investment and regulatory policies (Healey, 1998b, p 14).

According to Healey, it is in the arena of *governance* that competing *images* of the city jostle for position. Owing to the proliferation of images, there is a possibility of deliberation being appropriated by dominant, narrow interests. Indeed, there is a structural tendency for the form of the planning process to 'select' the hegemonic interests.

The normative, social democratic nature of collaborative planning requires a governance process that may take place in a variety of arenas, not simply the town hall or corporate headquarters; the process must keep alive a multitude of 'images' that sustain debate and participation. This conception implies *forms* that accommodate diverse groups and permit differential strategies. Collaborative planning is, therefore, process oriented:

> If there is a destination implied, it is a process dream, of a democratic society that respects difference but yet collaborates and which can live in a sustainable manner within its economic and social possibilities and environmental parameters (Healey, 1996, p 222).

The communicative planning school has been subjected to many criticisms. Allmendinger and Tewdr Jones (2002) summarise these as follows:

- The extent to which communicative planning constitutes a new theoretical paradigm is contested. A variety of competing 'world views' exists, including Post-Modern and neo-liberal perspectives.
- The model argues that argument is the primary means of accommodating diversity and neglects equally worthy methods such as bargaining, compromise, and voting.
- The model is Anglo-centric in nature and the consensus-building ethos may not necessarily be universally applicable. Indeed, it was noted above that the extent to which the normative ideals of inclusivity within the model are attainable depends on the political and social context of different countries.
- The model is superficial in that it does not acknowledge sufficiently the extent to which, beneath open public discourse, private vested interests are being pursued. That is to say, the collaborative planning model emphasises power to mobilise and pursue collective objectives rather than power to control the activities of other individuals and groups. This key issue is developed in the following section.
- The model implies equality between planners and the planned and is, therefore, a challenge to professional expertise and prestige.

Power and governance

The collaborative planning model acknowledges Foucault's argument that discourse needs to be deconstructed in order to reveal hidden values, meanings, and power relationships. However, Healey's emphasis on constructing a normative agenda has meant that the model prioritises the notion of collective *power to* rather than that of *power over*. As a result, the latter question is under-theorised within the model.

Power is not a given that is distributed equally between actors, either on housing estates or within the wider decision-making forums that influence life on the estates. If we are to understand the outcomes of decision making for estates, we must understand how decisions themselves are made and the role of the power relationship within this process. In this way we can begin to shift from a normative to a more critical framework of analysis.

Decision making is based on networks of power relationships formed between key actors that can include or exclude, increase or decrease the power of actors within the decision-making forum. Power is not a given in these networks, but is a result of relationships between individuals, as Castells declares, "Power is the action of humans on other humans to impose their will on others" (2000, p 7).

Castells suggests that the institutions of society are constructed to enforce the power relationships that emerge from power struggles. In relation to community consultation and involvement in the regeneration of large estates, for example, it is clear that institutions within this process hold power over unorganised individuals. Those individuals who are part of favoured institutions have power within the process that has an impact on others.

The above forms a useful basis from which to analyse how power is formed. First, it is important to understand the tools of power formation. Bourdieu examined the role of four forms of capital (see Table 3.1) in

Table 3.1: Bourdieu's four forms of capital

Economic capital	Financial resources available to individuals to enable them to undertake acts of consumption and access to power.
Social capital	Based on mutual ties and reciprocity. Social connections are used to exchange information that can then be used to acquire economic capital, influence, and power. A collectively owned resource.
Cultural capital	The accumulation of credential, skills, and knowledge acquired through upbringing and education that can be employed to accumulate and utilise economic capital and other forms of power.
Symbolic capital	A demonstration of an agent's aesthetic tastes. Although symbolic capital resides in the individual, its production is socially constructed and social class divisions that exist in the other forms of capital may become neutralised.

Source: Flint and Rowlands (2003)

the development of 'habitus': economic, social, cultural, and symbolic (Bourdieu, 1984). These provide the raw materials for the development of relationships and power. 'Habitus' is a way of visualising the world. Just as Healey makes her assumptions for collaborative planning, habitus creates competing views and images of the world. Habitus is not a unitary or exclusive concept: different habitus coexist within the same societies. In essence, habitus enables the creation of groups of individuals who share a similar understanding of the world. For example, habitus underpins the formation of political parties through the shared understanding of a common political goal.

Although habitus describes the relationships between individuals and how these individuals respond to and alter social structures and divisions in society arising from these relationships (Dovey, 2002; Hillier and Rooksby, 2002), habitus does not confer its own elite status and thereby power on any of the groups formed. Habitus merely creates the conditions for a group to become an elite, or to exercise enhanced power over other groups. Power relationships that form between groups are enacted through the differential use of the different forms of capital. Clearly, the possession of economic capital enables power to be gained over those whose economic capital is limited. But social ties gained in everyday life, such as school friends and colleagues (social capital), education and training (cultural capital), and the ability to fit into social trends by the way we speak or dress, or the car we drive (symbolic capital) enable us to access particular habitus groups and to enhance the position of this habitus over others within society. Habitus is socially constructed; attitudes are learned and socialised and so they are reproduced over time. Equally, habitus is not spatially uniform; different understandings of the world exist at different geographical levels and between areas.

It is the interaction with authority, power, and government that makes habitus a potent force within society. Foucault's concepts of normalisation and *governmentality,* building on his work on power, provide the framework through which the influence of habitus can be seen (Foucault, 1991). Foucault's main assertion concerned *normalisation.* He has attempted to explain how particular behaviours become the norm, the accepted way of acting or bearing oneself. In order for behaviours to be normalised, certain groups must have increased levels of power. Foucault asserted that those with power operate a 'normalising judgement' that enables them to impose dominance through different forms of penalty. The outcome is that individual citizens then take on the role of examiner to ensure that their behaviour conforms to the 'norm'. Those who lie outside the normalised judgement are considered to be 'individualised'.

'Governmentality' conceptualises the technologies of government, acknowledging the way in which power is used to construct, act upon, and regulate populations. In particular governmentality explains how those with power, primarily government authorities, identify those in need of intervention by classifying populations and their behaviours.

The concept of governmentality has been used elsewhere in urban studies to understand how populations and behaviours become classified and how government authorities identify those individuals and groups who require intervention (Foucault, 1991; Dean, 1999; Bourdieu, 2002; Flint and Rowlands, 2003). This framework requires as its basis an understanding (although not necessarily an acknowledgment) by individuals of a shared value system. The value system that is constructed creates ways of accepted living, or norms, through what Foucault termed the 'normalising gaze'. This has been used elsewhere in an attempt to understand the issues around tenure prejudice (Gurney, 1999) and, more particularly, the management and control of anti-social behaviour within communities (Flint, 2003).

As explained above, habitus helps to form groups of individuals within society who have a shared understanding; the different facets of social capital outlined by Bourdieu provide individuals and (where these facets are shared) groups with power and/or preferential access to decision making. This process helps create further power and can either promote or consolidate the position of individuals and groups within the social order. For example, financial capital can provide access to politicians; maintaining initial access can help a company reach the ear of the government. Similarly, financial capital can prevent access to power by groups whose habitus is in conflict with those making the decisions. In the context of large estates, for example, tenant groups who are in conflict with local government authorities on the running of the estates can be locked out of the decision-making forum. Power enables groups to impose their habitus as 'the norm'. For housing estates 'the norm' can be viewed as the prevailing 'image' that exists or is being pursued for the future. The role of networks is important in creating, controlling, and reproducing both habitus and power, and for providing a basis on which other individuals, groups, and networks are involved.

If we take this forward in terms of the regeneration of large estates, it is clear that there is a power relationship involved in the conceptualising, development, and delivery of policies. As Healey has suggested, there are numerous visions or images of the city or neighbourhood, and the concept of habitus helps us understand the basis on which these images are formed. Differences of economics, of social and political ties, and the differentiation in people's ability to read and understand this information create a multiplicity of visions. This differentiation applies not only to what exists, but also to what the future should hold. If we now turn our attention to Foucault's work, the notion that particular behaviours become normalised and dominant can equally be applied to prevailing discourses and policy. If we consider the problem of urban poverty since the Second World War, a series of discourses has competed for dominance in attempting to solve the problem. However, what has been clear in the case of some European countries has been the dominance of the centre over the local level. At the local level yet more dominance is obvious. And at the estate level, again, there are competing discourses about the future of the area.

This framework enables us to analyse the relative involvement of different actors in the making, shaping, and operation of large estates. The framework builds on the work of Healey; it enables us to consider which actors have a greater influence over policy and practice. This in turn facilitates an examination of the outcomes of policies and activities.

Conclusions

To conclude, the primary objective of the present volume is to explore the concept of place making – the promotion of the social, economic, and environmental well-being of diverse places and the development of institutional capacity to achieve this – in the context of the regeneration of large estates. Place making is a process driven by dialogue and the consideration of different 'images' and 'visions' of the types of place that large estates are or ought to be, plus the potential for transforming them. In an 'ideal typical' scenario, such as that presented in Healey's agenda for collaborative planning, this process would be fully inclusive. In practice, the discourse is likely to be dominated by elite groups. Healey's normative model offers a normative framework against which the empirical reality can be assessed. Bourdieu's notion of 'habitus' and Foucault's theorisation of discourse offer a means to assess why the normative model may be unattainable. A number of key dimensions of debate emerge that may inform the key questions outlined in Chapter One.

In Chapter One, we asked, "What ideas and philosophies inform policy interventions in large estates in European cities and what are the advantages and disadvantages of these approaches?". In other words, *what types of image and vision of large estates are emerging?* By definition, place making involves the definition and pursuit of 'ideal types' of place. These can be divided into two broad categories. First, there are generic images and visions that apply at a societal level, 'social cohesion' for example. In the context of large estates, a 'cohesive' estate may be one that is deemed to conform to this ideal. Second, there are images and visions that apply specifically to large estates. The most important of these is the notion of 'social mix' pursued directly or indirectly through tenure diversification and/or gentrification. There are also important questions about the intended beneficiaries of estate regeneration: for example, displacement and 'who stays', and the effect of estate regeneration on other parts of the city: 'spill over' effects. These key dimensions are considered in detail in the present volume.

In Chapter One, we also asked "Which policy interventions are important in large housing estates in European cities, how are they organised, and how effective are they?". There are essentially two issues here. First, *how do these images emerge and from whose imagination do they originate?* These questions can be addressed by consideration of a power struggle that exists along four axes. First, in some countries policy is made primarily by national governments and there are competing images that vie for position within this process. Second, in these cases, policy implementation is formed at the local level with different actors attempting to shape processes and outcomes to suit their imaginations. In other countries, policy emerges primarily at the regional or local level. The outcome of this process is, equally, a function of power relationships. Third, there may be struggles between the upper and lower power levels. In the case of the UK this struggle can be seen in the relationship between a prescriptive central government policy for regeneration and the innovation of local policy implementers that is expected to take place within these constraints. Fourth, overlaying all the above are the competing imaginations of those who live on or whose interests are situated on the estates, and those stakeholders who do not endure the day-to-day problems of these areas. These axes are explored, to different extents, in each of the chapters within this book, but specifically in respect of local resident participation and the differential involvement of stakeholders and actors.

The second issue is: *in what types of intervention can we observe the process of discourse and power at work?* Place making involves intervention in a variety of domains. In each of these, policy outcomes are a function of power relationships. In the present book, a number of specific policy areas are considered, notably knowledge management, employment, demolition, community safety and the pursuit of equality along gender lines.

References

Aglietta, M. (1979) *A theory of capitalist regulation*, London: New Left Books.

Allmendinger, P. (2001) *Planning in post-modern times*, London: Routledge.

Allmendinger, P. and Tewdr Jones, M. (2002) 'The communicative turn in urban planning: unravelling paradigmatic, imperialistic and moralistic dimensions', *Space and Polity*, vol 61, no 1, pp 5-24.

Amin, A. (ed) (1994) *Post Fordism – a reader*, London: Blackwell.

Bourdieu, P. (1984) *Distinction: A social critique of the taste of judgement*, London: Routledge.

Bourdieu, P. (2002) 'Habitus', in J. Hillier and E. Rooksby (eds) *Habitus: a sense of place*, Aldershot: Ashgate, pp 27-34.

Castells, M. (2000) *The information age: Economy, society and culture, volume II: the power of identity* (2nd edn), Oxford: Blackwell.

Chadwick, G. (1971) *A systems view of planning: Towards a theory of the urban and regional planning process*, Oxford: Pergamon.

Dean, M. (1999) *Governmentality: Power and rule in modern society*, London: Sage.

Dovey, K. (2002) 'The silent complicity of architecture', in J. Hillier and E. Rooksby (eds) *Habitus: A sense of place*, Aldershot: Ashgate, pp 267-80.

Dunleavy, P. (1980) *Urban political analysis – the politics of collective consumption*, London: Macmillan.

Faludi, A. (1973) *Planning theory*, Oxford: Pergamon.

Flint, J. (2003) 'Housing and ethnopolitics: constructing identities of active consumption and responsible community', *Economy and Society*, vol 32, no 3, pp 449-66.

Flint, J. and Rowlands, R. (2003) 'Commodification, normalisation, and intervention: cultural, social and symbolic capital in housing consumption and governance', *Journal of Housing and the Built Environment*, vol 18, no 3, pp 212-32.

Foucault, M. (1991) 'Governmentality', in G. Burchell (ed) *The Foucault effect – Studies in Governmentality*, London: Harvester Wheatsheaf, Hemel Hempstead, pp 87-104.

Gurney, C. (1999) 'Pride and prejudice: discourse of normalisation in public and private accounts of homes ownership', *Housing Studies*, vol 14, no 2, pp 163-83.

Hall, S. and Jacques, M. (eds) (1989) *New times – the changing face of politics in the 1990s*, London: Lawrence and Wishart.

Harvey, D. (1989) *The condition of post modernity – an enquiry into the origins of cultural change*, Oxford: Blackwell.

Healey, P. (1996) 'The communicative turn in planning theory and its implications for spatial strategy formation', *Environment and Planning B*, vol 23, no 2, pp 217-34.

Healey, P. (1997) *Collaborative planning: Shaping places in fragmented societies*, Basingstoke: Macmillan.

Healey, P. (1998a) 'Building institutional capacity through collaborative approaches to urban planning', *Environment and Planning A*, vol 30, no 11, pp 1531-46.

Healey, P. (1998b) 'Collaborative planning in a stakeholder society', *Town Planning Review*, vol 69, no 1, pp 1-21.

Healey, P. (2002) 'On creating the city as a collective resource', *Urban Studies*, vol 39, no 10, pp 1777-92.

Hillier, J. and Rooksby, E. (eds) (2002) *Habitus: A sense of place*, Aldershot: Ashgate.

Lash, S. and Urry, J. (1987) *The end of organised capitalism*, Cambridge: Polity.

Le Galès, P. (2003) *European cities, social conflicts and governance*, Oxford: Oxford University Press.

Soja, E. (1989) *Post-modern geographies – the reassessment of space in critical social theory*, London: Verso.

FOUR

Large housing estates in their historical context

Stephen Hall, Alan Murie and Thomas Knorr-Siedow

The principal focus of this book is on contemporary issues relating to large post-war estates. But before considering these issues we have to consider the question, "How did we get to where we are today?". The social and economic circumstances of the estates reflect changes over several decades. The objective of this chapter is to identify the underlying factors that contribute to the nature of these estates and their problems, which affect the governance and policy issues they present.

Large housing estates: origins, past and present

Predecessors to post-war housing

The origins of large housing estates in Europe lie within the poor housing conditions experienced by the working classes in certain European countries during the late 19th century. It is important to note that not all European countries were highly urbanised at this time. However, in those countries where industrialisation had been accompanied by rapid urbanisation (for example, the UK, Germany), high levels of (unregulated) new house building were unable to meet the demand for housing in the rapidly developing towns and cities. Consequently, problems such as disease, poor air quality, and overcrowding were created, which placed housing issues firmly on the political and social reform agenda (Engels, 1872; Tarn-Lund, 1971; Reulecke and Huck, 1981). In some cases, violent riots in Europe's urban areas reinforced the argument that change in the quality and quantity of mass housing was necessary.

Four strands of housing reform emerged before 1914:

- interventions to benefit public health through the regulation of water and sewerage systems and the clearance of unhealthy housing;
- the development of the garden cities, which provided an 'anti-urban' model, primarily for the (lower) middle and upper working classes;
- the development, in Austria and Germany, by builders from a philanthropic or a labour-movement-related background, of 'reform blocks'. These blocks were built for the working classes and provided a layout with open gardens, well-designed and equipped flats, and services for the residents;
- the development of quality housing estates directly related to mining or factory complexes such as the continental *Werksiedlungen* (Lepper, 1989), which provided a mix between the ambience of the garden cities and the reform blocks and the well-designed urban villages in the UK such as Bournville, built for workers at the Cadbury factory in Birmingham (Groves et al, 2003).

The architecture of this 'reform' housing was usually highly traditional, whereas the building methods deployed were often influenced by industrial processes. The new housing provided modern social amenities for residents; but although they were highly influential in the history of planning thought, none of these models had a significant quantitative impact on the housing supply. At the beginning of the 20th century, therefore, the majority of the urban working classes in Europe still lived in deplorable housing conditions.

The development of larger new housing estates was only generally realised after the First World War. The consequences of a lack of wartime investment, the destruction of parts of the housing stock, and, above all, mass migration into the industrialising towns and cities had to be addressed. Hitherto, state intervention in the housing market had been limited. However, the scale of the problem and fears of social unrest prompted governments to engage more actively in housing provision.

The period after the First World War witnessed a cultural revolution in which house building expanded rapidly, as did the number of actors involved. In the West, government authorities supported the production of modern housing, not merely to replace stock lost in the war, but also to accommodate large parts of the population. The interventions made during and after the war to control and regulate rents and tenants' rights also affected the contribution of the private sector. The situation was more difficult in Central and Eastern Europe, where borders had shifted and social and political revolutions had taken place. Government responses depended on their political position, with active interventions (red Vienna, for example) not being pursued everywhere. Hungary,

Austria, and Poland, and the Eastern parts of Germany near the new Polish border had to accommodate millions of migrants in the already overcrowded towns and cities, in addition to providing homes for their embryonic democratic societies.

Modern industrial methods of mass production were increasingly utilised to enable large groups in society to benefit from this heavily subsidised type of social housing. The scale of the 'settlements' and the blocks remained 'humane': on the estates, there were often fewer than just a few hundred flats, in blocks of three or four storeys. The majority of the housing built under these programmes was rental and cooperative housing. However, owner-occupied low-rise homes were often added to achieve a social mix. Schools, shopping facilities, and general practitioners were relocated to the estates, which were planned as self-contained neighbourhoods. Many of these estates were designed according to the principles of CIAM, which promoted the separation of land uses: residential, employment, and transport.

The new building philosophy, epitomised by the Bauhaus School, the Tudor-Walters report in Britain and the Dutch *Nieuwe Bouwen* provided an important contribution to modernism in housing. This philosophy proved highly influential in the development of the large estates after the Second World War, especially in terms of the basic principles of the spatial organisation of the neighbourhood: carefully designed flats, open access to greenery, and quality public space. The philosophy ranged from a purely humanistic approach on the one hand to technocratic dominance on the other (see Le Corbusier, 1927). Many of the estates built in the 1920s and early 1930s have proved sustainable. They remain a substantial, attractive, and rentable housing stock of socially inclusive neighbourhoods, even after 80 years.

Building the large housing estates

The post-Second World War period is of principal concern in this book. European countries emerged from the Second World War with the major tasks of rebuilding their economies as well as their housing stocks. Devastation by war and the lack of investment in housing during the wartime period left an enormous backlog and extensive housing problems. In some countries the responses to this situation emerged immediately after the war with a massive building effort to replace destroyed or damaged properties, to make up for the lack of wartime investment in housing, and to house the millions of 'displaced persons'. In addition, post-war economic reconstruction was accompanied by rapid urbanisation in several countries (for example, France). There was, therefore, in these countries, an acute imperative to accommodate a burgeoning urban population. European governments, thus, embarked on estate-based housing programmes before 1950. This policy culminated during the 1960s and 1970s in the construction of hundreds of tower blocks in British cities, the *Banlieue* projects around Paris, and massive national efforts like the Swedish 'One Million Programme'. Early experimental projects were concentrated on heavily bombed regions, such as the French Channel coast, the Western regions of the Netherlands, and the totally devastated city of Warsaw. These early projects have often been deemed to be of sufficient quality to make them sustainable. In the UK the highest quality council housing was constructed in the early post-war period. By the mid 1950s the view was held that the short-term housing crisis precipitated by the war had been addressed. There was a shift of emphasis towards slum clearance and improvement of the quality of housing rather than dealing with immediate housing shortages.

In other countries, and especially in Central and Eastern Europe, the principal post-war task had been concerned with the reconstruction of the economy and investment in the infrastructure that would facilitate economic growth. Housing investment was delayed and the first major investments in new house building only began to take off on a major scale in the 1950s. The era of house building starting in the 1950s was therefore the first wave of post-war housing development in some countries, but the second wave in others. In both cases the house building of the 1950s coincided with changes in architectural fashion and construction techniques. In Eastern and Central Europe, in particular, the adoption of industrialised techniques also affected the variety and types of dwellings that were built. The economics of industrialised building had implications for scale as well as uniformity. In other countries the adoption of new types of buildings and construction did not produce the same uniformity, but introduced a much greater proportion of medium- and high-rise properties, using different and often unfamiliar construction techniques. New estates and towns were more commonplace and larger in scale in Eastern Europe. Industrial towns like Stalinstadt (today Eisenhuettenstadt) in Germany, or Sztalinváros (today Dunaujváros) in Hungary were deliberately built far away from the existing big cities, but close to the big new socialist industries such as the steel industry.

Most Western European projects were built on a moderate scale and in a simple design. Most of these estates still impress through their mix of decent housing quality and exceptional landscaping. In contrast, in Central and Eastern European countries the state-controlled building industry adopted a more uniform and large-scale approach with little concern for high-quality provision.

The development of estates based on different architectural and urban design principles and built on a much larger scale followed, with British towns building high-rise flats as part of inner-city slum clearance programmes. In Genoa, a wall of estates was built on top of the hills surrounding the old town, and in Southern Italy large social housing estates replaced some post-war *bidonvilles*. All over Europe, the new estates were perceived to be a signal of better, modern times. The well-appointed homes were regarded as a gift from a benevolent state.

Changes in patterns of space and use

From 1960 to the mid 1970s, and subsequently in Central and Eastern Europe, over 45 million dwellings were built in estates comprising over 2,500 dwellings, some 34 million of which are to be found in Central and Eastern Europe. These numbers represent an important material difference. The significance of post-war estates for local and regional housing markets in the West varies greatly. In some localities, they constitute the dominant form of housing. However, in Central and Eastern European, this type of housing is universal (EA/UE, 1998).

The strong influence of the pre-war modernists prevailed briefly across Europe. Influenced by the works of Oskar Hansen in Poland, Le Corbusier in France, and Walter Gropius and Max Taut in Germany, the estates displayed similarities that transcended political and national boundaries. Modern urban landscapes of medium- and high-rise buildings in carefully designed open spaces prevailed; the car had not yet come to dominate urban design.

During the later 1960s and 1970s, the scale of the new estates exceeded that of recognisable neighbourhoods and often comprised tens of thousands of dwellings. Size became the dominant theme of the monumental estates that followed. Developments of twenty-plus storeys dominated.

The 'major parts of the population' (the formal term describing those aspiring to social housing in Germany, Denmark and elsewhere) were to be housed in meta-structures that were, increasingly, a product of industrial processes. Room and flat sizes were standardised, and ever more rigorous bureaucracies assisted the planners and architects to channel the users into a prescribed form of home use. The home was ascribed privacy in well-designed flats. However, social activities were externalised to the public sphere and little thought was given to the relationships between individuals and groups in the home or its immediate vicinity.

In the 1970s, the relationship between the estates and the city changed significantly. In the 1960s, estates were usually integral parts of expanding towns and cities. However, many later estates became separate entities with limited links to the existing urban fabric. These estates were planned to be self-sufficient entities in terms of amenities, but not employment.

The high-rise policy dominated Western countries for at least two decades. Since then, it has been assessed as a public policy failure, its intended benefits having been distorted by private and professional interests and fashions – by large construction corporations and design professionals, in particular (Dunleavy, 1981). In most Western countries, the failures of this policy (unpopularity, high expenses, deterioration of social life) became clear in the course of the 1970s, leading to a sharp decline in public support and a quick end to high-rise construction.

By the 1970s, the importance of the social reform agenda had been lost and many large housing estates had been reduced primarily to the means of realising a strategy for the production of mass housing. The lack of flexibility of the new estates was considered a minor issue in comparison with the gains in housing supply (Bahrdt, 1961; 1968). The 'old-fashioned' urban ideas were rejected as outdated and 'pre-modern' by planners, architects, and politicians alike, who 'believed' in the *machbarkeit* (manipulability) of modern lives. The estates were considered to provide the opportunities of a consumerist and, at the same time, private lifestyle, which was assumed to be the aspiration of the majority and so would lead to an attractive self-image of 'being modern'. This, in consequence, would force the remaining 'pre-modernists' to acquire the same values in a society that, it was thought, had eradicated poverty and social exclusion.

During the 1960s and 1970s, politicians, sociologists, and the housing industry argued that the new Western affluence would be a self-fulfilling prophecy of wealth and welfare, and was not to be called into question; the estates were the appropriate form of habitat. However, as early as 1965, the psychoanalyst Alexander Mitscherlich's critique of the 'Inhospitable City' had raised important questions. He argued that there was a two-way relationship between mankind and the built environment and he deplored the monotony of the estates. The collapse of flats at Ronan Point in London following a gas explosion, and the evidence of failure from the USA symbolised by the demolition of Pruitt-Igoe in St Louis in the early 1970s, raised doubts about high-rise flats, and restrictions were placed on their further development (Von Hoffman, 1998).

Despite the many physical similarities between the built elements of the large estates, they were perceived by the residents and the market as heterogeneous. However, the success or failure of an individual estate is affected by its position in the local housing market and cannot simply be attributed to the different forms and types of the buildings. Many of various physical forms have proved successful, while other similarly designed estates have been faced with severe problems.

Problems and perspectives of large housing estates: some examples

In Western Europe, large estates have been the focus of physical, economic and social decline, promoted by a variety of factors. Many of these causal processes are common to different European countries. However, the literature on many issues displays a strong Northern European and, especially, Anglo-centric bias. This is the product of the proliferation of research on these topics in the UK and a paucity elsewhere. Indeed, it can be argued that many of these questions have been downplayed by housing research in continental Europe, thus creating significant gaps in the academic and practitioner discourse. Therefore, many of the examples of problems cited below are sourced from the UK. Cross-references are made to other European countries where the extant literature permits.

Continuity and change

At first sight, the large housing estates in Europe look very similar. However, the housing estates we are considering were not built to a uniform design, although in some countries in Central and Eastern Europe the adoption of industrialised building methods resulted in greater uniformity of design than elsewhere. Even in these cases, housing associated with particular phases of construction or with particular locations have different qualities and reputations.

Some large housing estates have always been considered problematic. For example, in the UK different levels of subsidy, associated with different phases of policy, generated estates with houses built to different specifications. The 1950s were associated with smaller and less well-designed properties when policy targeted slum clearance rather than building for general needs. These estates were perceived as less desirable because they were built to lower specifications, and because they were perceived as housing former slum dwellers rather than the respectable, prosperous working class (see English et al, 1976; Merrett, 1979; Whitham, 1982, for example).

The different client groups of estates also strongly influence the estate trajectory. Estates built to house a particular population, low-income and workless households in particular, only became attractive to a population with similar characteristics or newcomers to the city. These estates have always been associated with a relatively high turnover, although in many cases these more transient areas have been associated with high levels of minority ethnic populations or with newcomers with lower incomes and a greater benefit dependency.

These estates had a negative reputation from an early stage. They were seen as areas that housed problematic households, and the associated stigma deterred more prosperous households from living there. The housing management process has also tended to reinforce area stereotypes and, at least in the British case, to sort the population between estates systematically according to their perceived desirability (see Phillips, 1985; Henderson and Karn, 1987, for example). These different processes of choice and management have generated estates that were disproportionately occupied by households with the least choice: those with the lowest incomes and greatest benefit dependency. Conversely, there are estates that have consistently been regarded as high quality or as adjacent to key amenities, employment, and transport links. To this extent the literature identifies continuity in reputation and role over time. Housing estates that are problematic, or that house a particular client group, have often played a similar part in the past. These continuities are often associated with differences between households in power resources and thus choice. This choice enables some to wait for better housing and facilitates transfers to other properties. However important these internal causes of negative reputation (allocations and management practices) may be, they should be distinguished from low building standards and costs, which are not so easily addressed.

Changes in the wider environment

The origins of change at estate level may be located in the wider society or in developments outside the estate, but the effect is felt locally and changes the relative attractiveness, function or position of the estate. These changes may relate to developments in the regional or sub-regional economy that alter the proximity of the estates to places of work or to transport links. For example, estates which were located close to the major manufacturing employers and which served a role in housing workers in particular sectors of the economy will be affected by changes that result in the closure of factories (Webster, 1998). Where employment terminates with factory closure there may also be a loss of heating (where the heating for an estate was connected with the factory) and sometimes even public transport. These estates may also lose the solidarity associated with housing particular occupational communities (see Bennett et al, 2000, for example).

Housing stratification and the residualisation of the social-rented sector

A major theme in housing studies since the late 1970s and early 1980s has been the residualisation of the social-rented sector and of the estates dominated by this sector. This residualisation may have occurred because of a deliberate privileging by government of home ownership through financial or other means. As home ownership has become more attractive, it has drawn middle- and higher-income groups away from the social-rented sector. The reputation and social and demographic characteristics of the estates then change, not because of any change in the estates themselves, but because their position in the hierarchy of choice and aspirations of households has changed. The estates have also been affected by privatisation (see Chapter Five) and this may mean that the residualisation of the tenure does not have the same impact at neighbourhood level. In many cases the estates no longer predominate in providing social-rented housing.

In the British context, residualisation refers to the narrowing social profile of the social housing client base and government policy towards the sector (Murie, 1983; Hamnett, 1984; Bentham, 1986; Forrest and Murie, 1983, 1990; Prescott-Clarke et al, 1988, 1994; Malpass, 1990). It has been argued that the environment in which council housing has operated has changed. For lower income groups, there have been fewer alternatives as the private rented sector has declined in size and council housing became attractive to a narrower section of the community, and as the advantages of owner occupation (reinforced by government policy) drew away demand from the higher income and social class groups among younger households (Dunleavy, 1981; Murie, 1983; Forrest and Murie, 1983, 1990; Malpass, 1990).

During the 1980s, the debate about the residualisation of social housing in the UK emphasised the interaction between housing policy and economic change. Higher unemployment increased the numbers of low-income households seeking rented housing (Forrest and Murie,

1983). Simultaneously, policy changes speeded the process of residualisation. These changes included the introduction of the Right-to-Buy scheme in 1980, and policies to increase rents, and to shift subsidies from object to subject. In a de-industrialising society such as Britain, where public sector housing has deliberately been attributed a secondary status, the sector very frequently accommodates what Byrne and Parson called a 'stagnant reserve army' concentrated in particular geographical areas, often in what they term 'system-built rubbish' (1983, p 144).

More recently, the high standing of social-rented housing has been challenged elsewhere in Europe. In Sweden, Elander (1994) argued that the challenges to the social-rented housing success story included the end of the privileged position of social-rented housing, conversion to cooperatives, rising rent levels, lowering housing standards, and social polarisation. Increasing social polarisation is found between social renting and other tenures, but also within the social-rented stock. The importance of location as well as tenure and design plus the different needs of individuals and households have stood central in this trend.

There is a growing body of evidence indicating that the social role of public and not-for-profit housing is skewed towards the lower income groups, and the trend towards a residual social-rented sector is no longer peculiar to Britain. Van der Heijden (2002), for example, presents data for six European countries showing changes (over the 1980s and 1990s) in the distribution of households in the social-rented sector according to income. Great Britain shows the strongest association between income and social renting. However, all the countries considered (except Belgium, with its very small social-rented sector) show the same trend over time. The most rapid changes are apparent in Germany and Sweden, where the percentage of low-income tenants in social-rented housing rose and the proportion from the higher income groups fell most markedly. Van der Heijden is careful to account for the changes both in terms of changes in rents, subsidies, and other housing policies and in terms of wider economic and social policy developments. He argues against any automatic assumption of convergence towards a residual model, as there is in Britain.

The residualisation theme has been taken up in the Netherlands. Schutjens et al (2002), for example, emphasise the close association between income and social renting, but otherwise highlight factors that are not associated with residualisation in the British context. They refer to the importance of minority ethnic groups in the social-rented sector and demonstrate that the age structure of the population in the social-rented sector has not polarised in the way that it has done in

Britain. This is no doubt largely because the British pattern has been significantly affected by the 'departure' of middle-aged groups through the Right-to-Buy scheme.

Borgegård and Dawidson (2000), referring to Sweden, describe how the differentiation of location and type of property (multi-family housing) and increasing income inequality appear to have affected the hierarchy of preference. They distinguished between areas and properties in a way that the finance system did not. Changes in housing policy in the 1990s have particularly impacted on low-income households in Sweden (Turner and Whitehead, 2002).

Demography, maturation, and conflict

Some of the problems associated with large housing estates relate to changing demographic structures. The lack of opportunity (or desire) to move may mean that estates move through a series of 'lifecycle' stages: an initial phase with younger families; a phase with greater overcrowding and adult households; and a phase of declining population and economic activity. In some cases (especially in Central and Eastern Europe, perhaps also in the southern countries of Europe) later phases may be associated with the sharing of accommodation since sons and daughters may find it difficult to obtain independent homes.

Some of the conflicts on estates appear to be associated with tension between the older and longer-established residents and newcomers to the estate – especially if there are disproportionate numbers of younger people amongst the newcomers. Some of the literature refers directly to tensions between different generations or to the problems associated with larger families and high child density in estates that otherwise have a high proportion of older residents (Page, 1993, 1994).

Population changes on estates may also introduce a greater degree of ethnic diversity or diversity in terms of household lifestyles. While these developments are not inevitably a cause of conflict, much of the literature on problems on estates refers to conflicts between tenants, anti-social behaviour, and managing households with problems. The increasing concentration of deprived households in these estates means that the intensity of problems has also increased and the difficulty of managing these effectively has become greater. Several influential contributions have produced plausible accounts of the housing dimensions associated with disadvantaged estates by referring to cycles of disempowerment and a downward spiral associated with spatial inequalities (Page, 1993, 1994; Power and Tunstall, 1995; Stewart and Taylor, 1995; Taylor, 1995, 2000; Young and Lemos, 1997; Power and

Mumford, 1999). In these discussions, the ability of households to move is a crucial element. The spiral of decline may be increased because more stable and affluent households move away (Andersson and Brämå, 2002), or because there are no opportunities for deprived households to move.

Design, maturation, and physical obsolescence

There is a final series of changes, which are referred to in the literature as the processes of the physical obsolescence of properties or the decline of materials. This theme becomes more relevant as estates mature and the materials used deteriorate; this process is likely to coincide with maturation in demographic terms. The properties on the estates no longer reflect what people want and no longer serve the social needs of the resident households. The properties are also deteriorating physically and have problems of dampness, infestation, and structural defects that relate to their age, their construction type, and lack of maintenance. Hausserman (1994) refers to the situation in East Germany, where housing construction had been consistently industrialised and the size structure of the building industry meant that there were no longer any small local builders who could be engaged for repair, renewal, or modernisation. Many buildings are in a very bad condition, even some that have been constructed quite recently; the dwellings have the greatest waste of energy of anywhere in Europe.

Alice Coleman's (1985) work in England adopts the arguments started by Oscar Newman's assertions concerning the relationships between housing design and criminal or anti-social behaviour (Newman, 1972). Alice Coleman suggested that high-rise public sector housing is responsible for generating a wide range of social problems. She argued that much of the high-rise industrialised public sector housing built in Britain in the 1960s was directly associated with high levels of graffiti, vandalism, litter, and excrement. She sees the design of this housing in itself as having a strong direct causal effect on these problems.

Some of the literature is particularly concerned with the undesirable nature of high-rise housing. Lawrence (1994) argues that management and maintenance problems related to this kind of housing arise repeatedly and there are continuing effects on the health and well-being of residents. van Kempen (1994, p 161) refers to several case studies of high-rise estates in the Netherlands showing that both the social climate and the satisfaction of the inhabitants with their living conditions vary considerably even between near-identical blocks.

Identical design does not imply identical problems. She refers to studies comparing high-rise blocks in the non-profit rented sector with only minor differences in design features, such as the number of storeys and the number of dwellings per block. These blocks were categorised as 'good', 'depressed', or 'bad' according to their "performance in terms of vacancy and turnover rate and the satisfaction of tenants with their living environment". From this she identifies a link between the characteristics of the occupants and the incidence of social problems and argues that these studies challenge Coleman's environmental deterministic position. It is indeed the case that high-rise estates are more likely to have an impoverished population than other post-Second World War housing projects and that high-rise blocks are over-represented among problem blocks. But the existence of trouble-free high-rise blocks at least shows that the relationship between high-rise design and the incidence of social problems is a contingent one (van Kempen, 1994, p 162).

van Kempen (1994) suggests that high-rise blocks are more likely to be associated with problems because of a mixture of factors, including the operation of the allocation system, the location of the blocks, the buoyancy of the local housing market, and the labelling process affecting estates. These processes are likely to work adversely for large post-Second World War estates in general, and in particular for those with high-rise blocks, but that will not always be the case. van Kempen (1994, p 165) emphasises that once an estate has a bad reputation, tenants and managers unintentionally work together with the local authority to reinforce the stigma of the estate. Tenants who are able to leave move out and applicants who are able to wait refuse to move in. Managers react by neglecting the upkeep of the estate or taking discrete measures to improve the situation. Often these measures prove to be counter-productive because they stigmatise the estate still further. Local authorities even adapt their allocation rules, either formally by giving the estates a low appraisal, or informally by assigning the houses on the estate only to applicants who are perceived as willing to accept.

Estates that are difficult to manage

The most substantial recent contribution to the analysis of housing management problems is by Power (1997); it is relevant to refer here to the different estates and countries appearing in her account of estates. Large-scale post-Second World War housing estates have been associated with urban unrest and riots, especially in France. The image of Les Minguettes in Lyon was associated with crime, stolen cars and joyriders, confrontations between young people and the police, and the boarding up of tower blocks in the worst affected areas (Power, 1997, p 147). The growth in low-cost home ownership had fuelled the exodus of French families from the estate, which had become heavily stigmatised. Against this background HLMs (*Habitations à Loyer Modéré* or social housing associations) began letting to newcomers from North Africa (often with large families) in an attempt to keep the number of empty units down. The over-representation of minority communities in Les Minguettes caused a collective stigmatisation of neighbourhoods and problems of co-existence between different populations (Peillon, quoted in Power, 1997, p 150). The level of empty flats rose and 'white flight' became more dramatic.

The population had almost halved and unemployment had risen. The problem was particularly acute among second-generation minorities: over half of all young North Africans were without work. Many believed the problems to be irreversible. Financially, the HLMs involved in Les Minguettes were on the verge of collapse.

In Germany the Ministry of Housing had identified estates that were developing a ghetto character. Power (1997) refers to the estate of Kölnberg outside Cologne. The problems on this estate are associated with similar factors: an unfortunate building form in which high-rise blocks dominated and hindered social contact and communication between residents, problems of prostitution, drugs, street crime, property damage, and vandalism (which affected the image of the estate); second-generation foreign youths, and stigmatisation and discrimination against the inhabitants leading to higher turnover and rising numbers of empty units. The stigmatisation of the estate accelerated its social decline (Power, 1997, p 169). Lack of provision for the large child population, serious tensions among the inhabitants, and the instability and inconsistencies of management were also identified as important factors (Power, 1997, p 177).

Power identified similar issues in relation to the Broadwater Farm estate in London. Its monolithic design and its size had contributed to its unpopularity. Robbery and violence had become serious, with disaffected youth a common problem, and conflict between tenants and the police and between black tenants and management a constant issue.

Many of the accounts of the problems on estates tend to look inwards to changes on estates rather than to refer to wider influences on the attractiveness of estates. The literature that looks inwards may identify changes on estates associated particularly with policy or the failure of policy. Although the problems on estates often began with their loss of attractiveness and consequently a shift of population from the affluent working classes to poorer and socioeconomically more unstable residents, most of the early attempts during the 1980s to find remedies were of a purely technical nature, with the politicians and builders trying to avoid facing the changed reality of the estates, which were losing their modern context and image. Socioeconomic and cultural problems on the estates were tackled later as it became clear that breaking the vicious circle would only be possible by embarking on strategies integrating change in the built environment, social and economic initiatives, and improving the internal and external image of the estates.

While most of the literature stresses the problems on the estates and discusses obsolescence and decline and an ageing and increasingly impoverished tenant population, these are not the only accounts that are possible. There is a series of accounts of policy success and good practice, and successful policy interventions to increase the attractiveness of estates in different countries (Emms, 1990; Power, 1997). These initiatives generally address not only the physical problems or management problems on the estates, but also wider issues concerning regeneration. These initiatives form part of local economic development strategies designed to increase the employment and training opportunities of residents.

One of the issues which these kinds of strategy raise, however, is the extent to which residents whose incomes rise and employability increases are more likely to leave the estates and move to more aspirational housing elsewhere. There is a strong theme in the research literature referred to throughout this chapter that, in many countries, deprived or stigmatised estates continue to be stigmatised and their social characteristics do not change even after very considerable investments have been made in regeneration activity. Either the regeneration activity has no impact on the residents, or where it is successful in increasing the income of particular households, these households move away, and the newcomers who move in to replace upwardly mobile out-migrants are likely to be households with limited choice and high levels of deprivation. Thus the social profile that regeneration activity sought to modify is reinforced. The population may have changed, but the characteristics of the estate will not appear to have done so. In this situation the function of the estate is very clearly one of catering for those with least choice, and the strategies to change the profile of the population cannot be just employment or educational strategies. The estate would have to be made more attractive relative to others so that households with improved incomes would still choose to live there and the characteristics of the estate would then change.

The Eastern estates and transition processes

The greatest 'accomplishments' of high-rise building are found in socialist countries, where the construction of large housing estates became part of the command society and the planned economy. Large housing estates formed an essential element of the top-down, centralised housing policy. In these countries, politicians and planners on the national level determined how many flats were to be built and set all their parameters. In the framework of the five-year plans, the central aims were negotiated with the sub-national administrative units (strictly controlled at the central level). The plans for these units were finalised in an iterative process – in Hungary in particular at the level of counties. Local governments had little say in the process; they were mostly consulted on the selection of the construction areas, but not on the size or other important parameters of the housing estates, the buildings or the flats. The local neighbourhoods – the districts in Budapest, for example – had no influence at all on the process of housing estate development.

In the socialist countries, wider involvement was an essential part of public policy, so that the decision makers were influenced by particular interest groups (large public construction companies and planning institutions) within the public realm, having created a strong interest coalition. Consequently, the construction of high-rise housing estates lasted much longer in the socialist countries (in most cases up to the collapse of socialism). Flats on these estates constitute a much larger share of the housing stock (20-40% of the total stock on estates of over 2,500 units, compared with 3-7% in the Western countries; the maximum share of flats in large housing estates is over 70% in some regions and cities in the socialist countries, while it is 20-25% in Western countries (EA/UE, 1998)).

The change of status of large estates (from a preferred and prestigious form of housing to a problematic one) that has occurred in the Western countries over the past 30 years has not always been experienced in the East. In some countries, including Hungary, the demand for units on large estates decreased from the late 1970s with the decrease in state subsidies and growth of alternative housing forms. In other cases (Poland and Russia, for example) the continuing shortage of housing sustained demand. Nevertheless the lack of investment in this stock over a long period is likely to mean that the physical decline of over

30 million dwellings will develop faster than rehabilitation programmes. Moreover, the transition from the former state-dominated housing system to different forms of a market orientation – including a wide variety of types of ownership – has affected the process of housing rehabilitation. Market orientation is generally seen to have hindered this process, especially in provincial cities, but in some cases privatisation has led to increased mobility and social mix.

The construction of large housing estates ended much more suddenly in Hungary than in other socialist countries. From the early 1980s onwards, the exceptional situation of housing estate construction was gradually terminated, since the special state subsidies were withdrawn and individually built units received the same amount of state support. Consequently, the demand for units on new housing estates decreased rapidly, and their construction was practically terminated by the end of the 1980s.

The 1989–90 change of the political and economic system brought about the total change of all organisational, institutional, and financial aspects of the existing large housing estates. The most important pillars of the housing estate ideology disappeared, but so did the command society and planned economy – and national-level housing policy, too. As the most visible sign of this change, housing was first transferred from central to local government responsibility in 1991. Then, by the middle of the decade, through compulsory privatisation (with the 1993 Housing Act, which contained a section on the Right-to-Buy), the responsibility was transferred to the ownership of citizens. As a result, housing estates, once dominated by state-owned rental and cooperative housing, became a collection of owner-occupied flats (now 85–100% owner-occupied). The owners of the flats were organised into condominium associations on a building-by-building basis; in the process of privatisation, the Condominiums Act (originally dating back to 1924) was applied as compulsorily determining the management form of the privatised buildings.

In parallel with these changes, the administrative setting became very different from that of the socialist period, as the level of local government became very strong (in Budapest especially at the lower, district level). One indication is that not even the normative central government subsidies are tied to specified purposes (that is to say, the 'housing normative' can be used for any other purpose if the local government so decides). Last, but not least, changes in the income and cost structures should be mentioned. While rents of the (few) remaining public rental units increased slowly, utility payments – especially the price of district heating, electricity, water and sewage – rose dramatically, resulting in a higher housing cost-to-income ratio than in Western cities and hitting the lower-income residents of the expensive-to-run large estates particularly hard.

Conclusions

This chapter has demonstrated that while there are common strands in relation to the post-war mass housing estates in different countries, and there are common problems associated with scale and building form and the management of estates, there are also some important differences. In some cases these estates form the lion's share of the social-rented sector whereas in other countries they are only part of it. In some countries they are distinctive because they form the least attractive part of the stock compared with the rest of the social-rented sector. In other countries the quality and standards of this housing are higher than in the older housing available in the private sector, and the reputation of the estates and the houses is not as damaged as in, say, the UK or France. In some countries this housing was built to house the general population and was in high demand. In others it was principally targeted at slum clearance and had a different reputation from the outset. In some cases this housing is still wholly social-rented; in other cases it has been largely privatised, and in yet other cases it has been partly privatised. The forms of privatisation have also differed. All this diversity means that while there are some lessons that can be learned between countries, the discussion presented in the remainder of the book needs to take account of these specificities associated with different national patterns of development as well as the continuities. In each of the countries and cities, even given different origins and histories, it is evident that complex, integrative regeneration and renewal policies are likely to be more effective in addressing complex problems than are one-sided physical upgrading policies. But the physical upgrading is generally necessary even if it is not sufficient. Physical and other improvements to lift the housing estate within the local housing hierarchy are necessary to achieve lasting solutions.

References

Andersson, R. and Brämå, Å. (2002) 'Social and economic mobility in large housing estates in Sweden: can area-based urban policies counteract segregation processes?', Paper presented at the European Network for Housing Research conference, 'Housing Cultures – Convergence and Diversity', 1-5 July 2002, Vienna, Austria.

Bahrdt, H.P. (1961) *Die moderne Großstadt*, Hamburg: Reinbek.

Bahrdt, H.P. (1968) *Humaner Städtebau*, Hamburg: Reinbek.

Bennett, K., Beynon, H. and Hudson, R. (2000) *Coalfields regeneration*, Bristol: The Policy Press.

Bentham, G. (1986) 'Socio-tenurial polarisation in the United Kingdom, 1953-1983: the income evidence', *Urban Studies*, vol 23, no 2, pp 157-62.

Borgegård, L.E. and Dawidson, K. (2000) 'The development of and prospects for Swedish housing policy', Paper presented at the European Network for Housing Research conference, 'Housing in the 21st Century', 26-30 June 2000, Gävle, Sweden.

Byrne, D. and Parson, D. (1983) 'The state and the reserve army; the management of class relations in space', in J. Anderson, S. Duncan and R. Huason (eds) *Redundant spaces in cities and regions?*, London: Academic Press, pp 127-54.

Coleman, A. (1985) *Utopia on trial: Vision and reality in planned housing*, London: Shipman.

Dunleavy, P. (1981) *The politics of mass housing in Britain 1945-1975*, Oxford: Clarendon.

EA/UE (European Academy of the Urban Environment) (1998) *A future for the large-scale housing estates*, Berlin: EA/UE.

Elander, I. (1994) 'Paradise lost? Desubsidisation and social housing in Sweden', in B. Danermark and I. Elander (eds) *Social rented housing in Europe: Policy, tenure and design*, Delft: University Press, pp 95-122.

Emms, P. (1990) *Social housing: A European dilemma*, Bristol: SAUS, University of Bristol.

Engels, F. (1872) 'The housing question', *Der Volksstaat*, 26 June 1872, pp 317-91.

English, J., Madigan, R. and Norman, P. (1976) *Slum clearance*, Beckenham: Croom Helm.

Forrest, R. and Murie, A. (1983) 'Residualisation and council housing: aspects of the changing social relations of housing tenure', *Journal of Social Policy*, vol 12, no 4, pp 453-68.

Forrest, R. and Murie, A. (1990) *Residualisation and council housing: A statistical update*, Bristol: SAUS, University of Bristol.

Groves, R., Middleton, A., Murie, A. and Broughton, K. (2003) *Neighbourhoods that work*, Bristol: The Policy Press.

Hamnett, C. (1984) 'Housing the two nations: socio-tenurial polarisation in England and Wales 1961-1981', *Urban Studies*, vol 21, no 3, pp 389-405.

Hausserman, H. (1994) 'Social housing in Germany', in B. Danermark and I. Elander (eds) *Social rented housing in Europe: Policy, tenure and design*, Delft: University Press, pp 53-75.

Henderson, J. and Karn, V. (1987) *Race, class and state housing*, London: Gower.

Lawrence, R. (1994) 'Rented housing design reconsidered in context', in B. Danermark and I. Elander (eds) *Social rented housing in Europe: Policy, tenure and design*, Delft: University Press, pp 139-57.

Le Corbusier, C.E.J.G. (1927) *Vers une architecture* [Towards a new architecture], Paris: Cres.

Lepper, K.B. (1989) *Werkssiedlungen in Rheinhausen 1898–1978*, Duisburg: Wilhelm-Lehmbruck Museum.

Malpass, P. (1990) *Reshaping housing policy: Subsidies, rents and residualisation*, London: Routledge.

Merrett, S. (1979) *State housing in Britain*, London: Routledge and Kegan Paul.

Murie, A. (1983) *Housing inequality and deprivation*, London: Heinemann.

Newman, O. (1972) *Defensible space: People and design in the violent city*, London: Architectural Press.

Page, D. (1993) *Building for communities*, York: Joseph Rowntree Foundation.

Page, D. (1994) *Developing communities*, Sutton: Hastoe Housing Association.

Phillips, D. (1985) *What price equality?*, London: GLC.

Power, A. (1997) *Estates on the edge*, London: Macmillan.

Power, A. and Mumford, K. (1999) *The slow death of great cities?*, York: Publishing Services Limited.

Power, A. and Tunstall, R. (1995) *Swimming against the tide*, York: Joseph Rowntree Foundation.

Prescott-Clarke, P., Allen, P. and Morrissey, C. (1988) *Queuing for housing: a study of council housing waiting lists*, London: HMSO.

Prescott-Clarke, P., Clemens, S. and Park, A. (1994) *Routes into local authority housing*, London: HMSO.

Reulecke, J. and Huck, G. (1981) 'Urban history research in Germany: its development and present condition', *Urban History Yearbook*, vol 8, p 39.

Schutjens, V.A.J.M., van Kempen, R. and Van Weesep, J. (2002) 'The changing tenant profile of Dutch social rented housing', *Urban Studies*, vol 39, no 4, pp 643-64.

Stewart, M. and Taylor, M. (1995) *Empowerment and estate regeneration*, Bristol: The Policy Press.

Tarn-Lund, J.N. (1971) *Working class housing in the 19th century Britain*, London: Lund Humphries Publishers.

Taylor, M. (1995) *Unleashing the potential*, York: Joseph Rowntree Foundation.

Taylor, M. (2000) 'Communities in the lead: power, organisational capacity and social capital', *Urban Studies*, vol 37, no 5-6, pp 1019-35.

Turner, B. and Whitehead, C. (2002) 'Reducing housing subsidy – what happened to Swedish social housing policy?', *Urban Studies*, vol 39, no 2, pp 201-17.

Van der Heijden, H. (2002) 'Social rented housing in Western Europe: developments and expectations', *Urban Studies,* vol 39, no 2, pp 327-40.

van Kempen, E. (1994) 'High-rise living: the social limits to design', in B. Danermark and I. Elander (eds) *Social rented housing in Europe: Policy, tenure and design*, Delft: University Press, pp 159-80.

Von Hoffman, A. (1998) 'High ambitions: the past and future of American low-income housing policy', in D.P. Varady, W.F.E. Preiser and F.P. Russell (eds) *New directions in urban public housing*, New Brunswick: CUPR Press Rutgers, pp 3-22.

Webster, D. (1998) 'Employment change, housing abandonment and sustainable development: structural processes and structural issues', in S. Lowe, S. Spencer and P. Keenan (eds) *Housing abandonment in Britain*, York: Centre for Housing Policy, University of York, pp 47-60.

Whitham, D. (1982) 'The first sixty years of council housing', in J. English (ed) *The future of council housing*, London: Croom Helm, pp 9-34.

Young, M. and Lemos, G. (1997) *The communities we have lost and can regain*, London: Lemos and Crane.

FIVE

Privatisation and after

Alan Murie, Iván Tosics, Manuel Aalbers, Richard Sendi and
Barbara Černič Mali

Introduction

The previous chapter gave an account of the historical development
of large housing estates, referring also to the problems of these estates
in the process of their 'natural' development. This chapter features a
separate discussion of the period of privatisation (starting in the early
1980s in Great Britain and continuing on a large scale in the 1990s in
the post-socialist countries), since this highly political process has had
a profound effect on the future perspectives of the housing estates in
these countries.

   As previously outlined, the large housing estates, which are the subject
of this book, have a range of elements in common. The estates were
built at the same time; they were built by either a local government
authority, or the state, or not-for-profit organisations; and they
represented contemporary, state-of-the-art, professional architectural
and engineering views on residential development. The estates also
had their differences: some were the first, or even the only, modern
not-for-profit housing available in a period of recovery after the Second
World War and in economies with no tradition of social-rented housing;
others were a new element in established social- and public-rented
housing provision. In these cases the estates did not necessarily offer
the most desirable dwellings or locations and this drawback often
became more apparent over time. In some cases this generation of
public and social-rented housing was targeted at different social groups
and had a different place in the policy agenda: rehousing households
from urban renewal or slum housing neighbourhoods rather than
meeting general housing needs.

   All these elements of similarity and difference existed when the
estates were built. The standing and quality of these estates, however, is
not purely attributable to these initial characteristics. The history of

maintenance and repair has affected the quality and attractiveness of the estates. At the same time the characteristics of the households living in the estates has changed and it has been argued that in some countries these estates have been more profoundly affected by the process of residualisation than other estates.

This chapter is concerned with a further element in the changing nature of these estates: the changes in patterns of ownership and control associated with privatisation. The characteristics of these large estates today – and the challenges for policy – are affected by privatisation and the different tenure structures arising through privatisation. The problems and policy solutions depend not only on the design, scale, and other features of the built environment, but also on fragmented ownership and privatisation.

This chapter draws on the experiences of four countries (the UK, Hungary, Slovenia and the Netherlands). This permits a discussion of the diversity of privatisation experience in Europe. In the UK, housing privatisation has formed part of the broader restructuring of the welfare state initiated by the Thatcher administration in the 1980s (Forrest and Murie, 1990) and continued by its successors. In Hungary and Slovenia, housing privatisation formed part of the widespread economic, social and political upheaval that accompanied the end of statist central planning in the 1990s. In the Netherlands, housing privatisation has been limited, in the context of a country in which welfare reform, generally, has been more modest.

The focus is on how privatisation has affected the contemporary situation in different countries. Particular attention is drawn to the fragmentation of control and the issues facing policy in relation to renewal and restructuring. We start by describing briefly the three types of privatisation and the four countries discussed here. We then refer to the nature of the large estates before privatisation and then discuss the processes and scale of privatisation. The consequences of privatisation are then considered in terms of who benefits, and of management. Finally, consideration is given to the impact of privatisation and the outcome for large post-war housing estates, the problems and issues that privatisation has left on these estates, and the responses that are currently being adopted in the various countries.

Types of privatisation

The privatisation of former public and social housing became a common theme in housing policy throughout Europe. Privatisation itself has taken different forms; discussions of policies that have involved elements of privatisation have referred to the movement of rents towards market levels, the contracting out of various services to private sector agencies, and the transfer of ownership in various forms. This chapter concentrates on these latter aspects. It refers to the transfer of ownership, in particular to sitting tenants or other individual owners.

We draw on three different types of experience within Europe. The first example, illustrated by the UK, is where enthusiastic and wide measures to achieve privatisation prevailed. The introduction of the Right-to-Buy scheme in the UK grew out of ideological and electoral considerations and a desire to encourage home ownership for its own sake (Forrest and Murie, 1990; Jones and Murie, 1999). Privatisation nevertheless involves consumer choice. Selectivity over what is sold is consumer-driven: almost all tenants have the Right-to-Buy, and it is not time limited.

The second type of privatisation relates to those that took place in Eastern and Central Europe and were associated with changes in political regimes in the late 1980s. These privatisations have been discussed elsewhere (Turner et al, 1992; Alexander and Skapska, 1994; Hegedüs and Tosics, 1994; Mandi, 1994; Stanovnik, 1994; Tanninen et al, 1994; Sendi, 1995; Struyk, 1996; Priemus and Mandi, 2000; Lowe and Tsenkova, 2003). They are widely presented as political shock absorbers, demonstrating how changes in political regimes have direct, tangible effects on individual households and citizens. It is also argued that privatisation in these circumstances was strongly influenced by the burden that the ownership of properties with potentially high maintenance and repair costs would have placed on new systems of local government. In these types of privatisation a Right-to-Buy was a common phenomenon (and the price paid was even lower than in the UK), but it was often only available for a relatively short time period and was then replaced with a different policy. In some cases privatisation was introduced along with restitution, whereby the people who had previous claims on land or property that had been seized by earlier regimes could reclaim it (Tanninen et al, 1994; Sendi, 1995; Struyk, 1996; Fisher and Jaffe, 2000; Lowe and Tsenkova, 2003). In this chapter we have illustrated the problems and processes associated with this type of privatisation through reference to Hungary and Slovenia. While there are considerable similarities between the two cases, there are also some differences.

The third, more cautious, approach to privatisation is illustrated by the Netherlands. Along with many other European countries the Netherlands has avoided a wholesale commitment to privatisation. Nevertheless, significant privatisation measures have been introduced, and there has been some debate and conflict over how these should be applied (Aalbers, 2004).

The policy process

Table 5.1 sets out key features of the process of privatisation in the three types and four countries referred to in this chapter.

The earliest mass privatisation is associated with the UK, where significant numbers of council houses had been sold to sitting tenants who then became homeowners well before the introduction of the Right-to-Buy in 1980 (Murie, 1976). It was the introduction of this Right-to-Buy,[1] however, which transformed the scale and coverage of privatisation; most accounts of privatisation see 1980 as the key date.

Legislation introduced a uniform national scheme that provided a right for almost all sitting tenants in local authority housing and the tenants of some housing associations to buy the property in which they lived. The legislation gave them clear entitlements in relation to the price at which they could purchase and the discount on market valuation to which they were entitled. These discounts were substantial and were further increased so that they could amount to 70% of the market value in some cases. Although there have been some subsequent modifications that reduce the maximum discount that can be obtained in some places, the Right-to-Buy provides an unambiguous entitlement to tenants. This entitlement cannot be blocked by the landlord, although stock transfer (the transfer of council housing to not-for-profit housing organisations) does affect entitlement. Where stock transfer has taken place existing tenants have a 'preserved' Right-to-Buy, but no new tenants (those with assured tenancies created after the stock transfer has been completed) have the Right-to-Buy. To this extent the entitlement under the Right-to-Buy legislation is slowly being diminished by a second form of privatisation: the transfer of ownership to housing associations. Leaving this aside, the process is activated by the tenant. Although there have been some surges in sales activity associated with changes in the detail of the Right-to-Buy, or rumours that it was to be more dramatically modified (see Marsh et al, 2003), in general the progress of the Right-to-Buy has fluctuated with housing market and economic changes (Jones and Murie, 1999).

In contrast with the UK, Hungary and Slovenia have been affected by short-term explosions of activity. In these countries a Right-to-Buy was introduced, inspired by politics and following political changes (Tosics, 2001). It was introduced as a short-timescale scheme, which

Table 5.1: Privatisation processes

	UK	Hungary	Slovenia	the Netherlands
Starting point	Public sector housing provided mainly by local authorities and comprising some 32% of all dwellings with the highest proportions in urban areas	State housing was 19% of national housing stock and 61% in Budapest	Social housing accounted for 33% of dwellings	Social rented housing was 32% of dwellings in 1990 and 37% in 2000
Policy approach	Sustained Right-to-Buy	Big bang Right-to-Buy	Big bang Right-to-Buy and restitution	Landlord-managed sales schemes
Target	Sitting tenants to become homeowners	Sitting tenants to become homeowners	Sitting tenants and former owners	Landlord-selected properties
Wider policy agenda	Previous discretionary sales and concurrent stock transfer and other privatisation measures	Transfer of state housing to local government and revitalisation of the law on condominiums	Transfer of state housing to local government and establishment of condominiums	Increased financial autonomy of housing associations, enlargement of owner-occupied housing sector
Period	Earlier variable schemes replaced in 1980 by a uniform and continuing national scheme; some regional variation in maximum discount after 1998	Uniform national scheme between 1993 and 1994 replaced by locally variable schemes within a national 'framework' regulation	Uniform national scheme between 1991 and 1993 replaced by locally variable schemes	Increase in activity from the late 1990s; further increases expected in the next few years
Discounts	High (average 50%; maximum 70%)	Very high (mostly over 70%; maximum 90%)	Very high (approximately 90%)	Low to moderate: (up to 10% for third parties; up to 30% if sitting tenants buy their own homes)
Proportion sold	1 in 3 dwellings over the 20 years after 1980	70% sold by the mid-1990s	64% sold after 2 years	4% to 5% sold by 2004

Source: RESTATE reports

was subsequently replaced by locally variable schemes. The unified national schemes operated for some two years in each case, and the brief window of opportunity that these provided, together with the much greater levels of discount, explains the much higher sales figures occurring in a short time period in these two countries when compared with the UK.

In Hungary, the Housing Act (taking effect in January 1994) introduced a Right-to-Buy under which a local government authority could only resist the sale of flats in a building if the conditions of the building were very bad (health and safety aspects), if an earlier decision had been taken to rehabilitate the area, or if the building was a listed monument. If none of these circumstances prevailed, the local government had to turn the whole building into a condominium and offer all the flats for sale, even if only one of the tenants declared a wish to buy. The prices paid were very low: in most cases (where the building had not been substantially renovated in the last 15 years) 15% of the market value; and 30% of the market value if the building had been substantially renovated in the last 15 years. In each case a further 40% discount was given if the tenant paid in cash (otherwise, the tenant paid by instalments over 35 years, on a fixed 3% interest rate, although at that time inflation was around 30% per year).

Rents for public housing in Hungary were traditionally very low, covering only 20-30% of the (low) maintenance costs, and the state-owned management companies did not carry out any comprehensive rehabilitation work. This neglect had left a legacy of disrepair and after 1990 the freshly elected democratic government did not want to deal with housing. Consequently, state ownership was transferred (at no cost) to local government. These local authorities could not afford to maintain the rental stock properly, or address the backlog of disrepair, and it was much easier for them to sell this stock. The Right-to-Buy in 1993 was endorsed by the elections in 1994 (although no political party opposed the policy). Providing real-estate ownership to the citizens was also in line with the philosophy of the transition. Finally, tenants wanted to buy their flats because they were afraid of possible rent increases. In order to facilitate sales, each building concerned was turned into a condominium and the homeowners received a share determined by the floor space of their units. The local government authority remained the shareholder for the flats where the residents did not want to buy and for those units used for commercial or other purposes.

In Slovenia, the main reasons for the privatisation of the public stock were to remove the burden of high maintenance and renewal costs from the state budget, to generate a substantial amount of cash to assist the state budget during the critical period of establishing an independent economic base, to redistribute the wealth accumulated as 'public property' during the period of socialist rule, and to establish better housing management and maintenance and the refurbishment of multi-family housing. The 1991 Housing Act transferred the entire public housing stock into the ownership of the local authorities, which were obliged to sell dwellings to the sitting tenants if they or any of their immediate family expressed a desire to purchase. In this transaction, the buyer was entitled to: a 30% discount on the total value of the dwelling; a further deduction of the amount (calculated using a correction coefficient) the tenant had been obliged to pay during the period of tenancy as a 'contribution'[2] to the social housing fund; and a discount equivalent to personal investments in the housing unit in the form of improvement.

The tenant purchaser could either pay 10% of the total amount within 60 days of signing the purchase contract, with the rest to be paid in equal monthly instalments for the next 20 years; or pay the total amount within 60 days of signing the purchase contract. This latter method of payment attracted a 60% discount on the cost of the dwelling. This privatisation model applied equally to all public rental dwellings all over the country, with the major exception of restituted housing. The conditions for the privatisation of restituted property (previously nationalised housing) differed slightly from those described above. The sitting tenants in nationalised housing had three options. They could either purchase the dwelling under the terms described above, on condition that the new landlord was willing to sell the property; or, provided nobody filed any claim for restitution, relinquish their right to the dwelling, in which case they would be entitled to a compensation of 30% of the value of the dwelling plus a loan of an equal amount with favourable terms of repayment; or stay on as tenants of the new landlord. Taking into account all the discounts and deductions, it is estimated that the average selling price for the dwellings sold off under the Right-to-Buy was a mere €100 per square metre, which is approximately 10% of the then average market value in Slovenia.

In both Hungary and Slovenia the transfer of all housing to local authorities and the establishment of condominiums for all dwellings in buildings where even one sale was completed meant that the whole stock (except for buildings that no one wanted to buy and buildings that were not available for sale because of renewal schemes, poor repair, or protection as a monument) was affected by privatisation and not just the stock purchased by sitting tenants. But the proportion of tenants who bought was also high and the brief window of opportunity within which advantage could be taken of the more generous Right-to-Buy in these countries was a key influence. While tenants triggered action – as in the UK – the pressure to take up the offer quickly before it diminished in value could be perceived as pressure from government authorities to hasten the process; the costs of delay for tenants acted as a strong pressure on uptake.

Finally, there has never been a Right-to-Buy in the Netherlands. Unlike the countries referred to above, the Netherlands' approach to the sale of properties has been more cautious (Aalbers, 2004). At no stage has the political leadership been convinced by the case for privatisation. In addition, the relationship between the state and the main providers of social-rented housing has been different from elsewhere. The most important social housing providers – the housing associations – were formerly privately regulated institutions. Although they came to function as branch offices of government in the 1950s, 1960s, and 1970s (when social housing was built in massive quantities), the associations became more independent of both central and local government in the 1990s.

Until the early 1990s, it was virtually impossible to voice the idea of selling social housing in Dutch political circles. The few attempts that were made were rather half-hearted (Boelhouwer, 1988; Frissen et al, 2001). Because so many conditions were attached to sales, they were very few. With the policy document 'Housing in the Nineties' (Ministerie VROM, 1989) the central government took its first steps towards a withdrawal from the housing market, and privatisation became more common, but only since the late 1990s has privatisation been a serious issue.

In the mid 1990s the Dutch Labour Party (PvdA) announced its plan to coerce the housing associations to sell one million of their approximately three million social housing units. After much discussion, the original Right-to-Buy idea was abandoned because the Dutch Labour Party does not hold the majority of seats in parliament and was unable to persuade other political parties to agree to the plan. Many members of parliament who opposed it were afraid that a Right-to-Buy scheme would lead to the marginalisation and residualisation of the social housing stock (the British situation was sometimes referred to as a 'worst case scenario'), while other members of parliament indicated that they did not have the power to force the housing associations into a Right-to-Buy scheme. A new plan emerged for a more moderate 'Stimulation-to-Buy' scheme that would offer subsidies to low-income households towards purchase. A majority of members of parliament supported the Stimulation-to-Buy scheme and this was included in the Promotion of Home Ownership Act (BEW), passed in 2000 and coming into force in 2001, and the 2000 Policy Document on Housing.

What has emerged from this is an arrangement of landlord-driven managed sales schemes in which the landlord chooses what to sell. Although there has periodically been pressure from the central government to adopt a more general approach to privatisation, the process has remained firmly within the control of the housing associations. The volume of sales under these schemes has been very much lower than in the other two cases, although it has risen in recent years; the Minister of Housing has frequently stressed that a 'change of attitude' is needed. Although the minister has little direct control over the independent social landlords, this change of attitude has taken place inside most of the organisations dealing with social housing. However, the properties and estates included in sale schemes have been selected by the landlords and not by the minister or the tenants.

Who benefits?

Much of the research literature associated with housing privatisation has focused on who benefits from the process. There are subtle, and even major, differences in this respect. Perhaps the most substantial body of evidence relates to the sale of council houses in the UK where the better, more attractive properties have been sold (especially houses with gardens). The purchasers tend to be the more affluent of the households who were council tenants (middle to lower income groups in relation to the population as a whole, but not including the highest or lowest income groups) and in the middle of the family cycle (see the summary of various evidence in Jones and Murie, 1999). Properties in blocks of flats, and particularly in those blocks that were built in the 1960s and 1970s, are less likely to have been bought. To some extent the Right-to-Buy in the UK has creamed off the best properties and the most affluent tenants from the state housing sector and the housing association sector, leaving a social-rented sector that is more residual in terms of property and with a narrower social profile of tenants.

In contrast, in Hungary and Slovenia the scale of uptake of the Right-to-Buy is much higher. All tenants except the very poorest have participated in the Right-to-Buy. The process has been less socially selective than in the UK and less selective in terms of property types.

This is partly because the large post-war mass housing estates in these countries provided some of the best-quality housing in the best condition, especially when compared with the run-down, older properties in the cities. Consequently, the comparative attractiveness of these properties is generally higher than those in the UK, where they fit into a much more ambiguous position in, and would often be regarded as forming the bottom end of, the housing market. Even so, give-away privatisation in Hungary generates a huge equity problem arising from the difference between the market value and the discounted selling price. Taking into account the fact that the best public housing units were allocated according to merit in the socialist period, it is estimated that 40% of investment value went to households in the top quarter of the income distribution, while only 17% went to the lowest quarter (Hegedüs et al, 1996).

In Slovenia there were two major groups of beneficiaries of public housing privatisation: the sitting tenants, who were given the opportunity to become homeowners at minimum cost; and the state, which acquired substantial financial resources in the process and also succeeded in ridding itself of the burden of housing management and maintenance. Those households living in apartments with a high market value (in the centres or in other favourable locations of major cities) benefited the most. On the other hand, the losers were the households living in restituted dwellings, whose Right-to-Buy was severely restricted. Most of these people are now tenants living under a constant threat of eviction (Sendi, 1995; Mandi, 1999).

The pattern of benefit in the Netherlands is not so clear-cut, because of the selective process of sale orchestrated by landlords. Since landlords are intent on selling properties in order to achieve other objectives and, more importantly, because many tenants have declined the offer to buy their homes (not only because the monthly mortgage payments would be much higher than the monthly rent) a sale to third parties in the Netherlands is also possible, so that the beneficiaries of privatisation are not restricted to sitting tenants.

New management arrangements

Perhaps the most important impact of privatisation for the future management and development of the large post-Second World War estates is the change in the patterns of ownership and management of the estates. In this respect the Netherlands has seen relatively little change. The process of privatisation has sometimes been undertaken along with urban renewal projects. The new mixed-tenure neighbourhoods will have differences in ownership with respect to the previous housing association estates, but the major restructuring and renewal will have already taken place and the process will have been orchestrated by social landlords. Looking even further ahead, the patterns of ownership and control are familiar in the Dutch context and there is no reason to believe that they will present particular problems in the future.

At the opposite extreme, the situations emerging in Hungary and Slovenia involve a condominium arrangement, but there are serious questions about how effectively these operate, especially in relation to the properties in the worst condition and the owners who have the fewest resources. In Slovenia, for example, the low-income homeowners are already experiencing considerable difficulties in meeting the costs associated with home ownership (Sendi, 1999, 2004). In Hungary there has been a Condominium Act in operation since 1924 (although designed mainly for new buildings) and it has not been rescinded. In Slovenia there was no Condominium Act and the legal basis for regulating the condominium system was provided by the Housing Act and the Property Code.

The situation in the UK differs from that in the Netherlands, Hungary, and Slovenia. Many of the properties sold under the Right-to-Buy, including some in the large post-war estates that are the focus of this book, were houses with gardens, and in these cases properties are sold on a freehold basis. The individual freehold owner has no obligation to cooperate or participate with other owners in any developments except those obligations established under common law. Where properties are sold in blocks of flats the situation is different, but it involves a leasehold rather than a condominium arrangement. The leasehold system means that, when individuals buy a flat within a block, they become responsible for what happens within their own flats, but there also continues to be an obligation on the part of the freeholder to maintain the common areas and the basic structure of the property.

So, in the British situation, the local authority that owned the whole block continues to be responsible (as the freeholder) for these services, and charges the leaseholders for their share of these costs. The leaseholders have to be consulted: there is a body of law that sets out what the freeholder can and cannot do. However, as long as the freeholders are working within this law, they do not require the consent of the individual leaseholders before embarking upon expenditure, and they can charge the leaseholders accordingly whether or not they have given consent.

Consequently, the local authority continues to bear a responsibility and is accountable to tenants as well as owners for the way in which they fulfil that responsibility. The local authority carries out repairs and maintenance to common areas and to the fabric of the dwellings; it is argued that this responsibility removes the likelihood of the properties falling into serious disrepair.

There are issues about how individual owners can afford the charges that derive from this, but this problem is resolved through other processes. There is legal provision for a change in this pattern of management and ownership if a sufficient number of leaseholders get together to seek to alter the arrangement under the new commonhold regulations, but in general the local authority or housing association to which stock has been transferred continues to be the freeholder and will carry out the responsibilities involved under the terms of the sale of the properties for the maintenance and repair of buildings.

In situations where it is difficult to obtain agreement from individual households living in a block to incur expenditure for the maintenance of the fabric, the leasehold system may be a better protection of the quality and condition of the property, although a leasehold arrangement may not be sufficiently sensitive to the income and resources of households. In this sense the sale of properties in the UK has not generated the subsequent problems of maintenance and repair that have become apparent in Hungary or Slovenia.

However, there are other problems that are more common across countries. There are affordability issues for some low-income owners who could afford the low purchase price, but have subsequent problems when faced with large bills for maintenance and repair (Forrest et al, 1995). More importantly, the fragmentation of ownership becomes a problem when the policy agenda is concerned with the improvement of properties rather than just maintenance and repair, or with major urban renewal. In the UK system, leaseholders can be charged for maintenance and repair, but they are not obliged to meet the costs of improvements and if a landlord embarks upon major restructuring including, for example, the demolition of properties, the landlord will have to buy the leasehold property by negotiation or ultimately through compulsory purchase. The problems faced in this situation are more comparable with the condominium-based arrangements. This is the point where the fragmentation of ownership becomes a real barrier to action. It is also evident in the UK that some tenants, and speculators operating through tenants, have identified the opportunity to make a speculative gain through this renewal process, and properties have been bought on estates scheduled for major improvement and restructuring in order to make financial gains from the process of renewal (Jones, 2003).

Impacts and outcomes

As will be evident from the discussion above, the impact and the outcomes of the privatisation process are very different in the various countries described here. Privatisation has had a very limited impact on estates in the Netherlands, and the impacts have generally been planned. The remaining estates are still predominantly rented; in several cases, privatisation has taken place alongside active restructuring both in terms of dwelling types and tenures. If the impact in the Netherlands is limited, the impact in the UK has been moderate and has varied geographically, by type of property and according to tenant characteristics. If we were talking about some other parts of the social-rented housing stock, the impact would have been more substantial, but the large post-Second World War housing estates, especially those consisting of non-traditionally built medium- and high-rise properties (flats and maisonettes), have had the lowest rates of sale of property in any parts of the council sector. However, 25 years on from the introduction of the Right-to-Buy, virtually all parts of the council housing stock have been touched by privatisation. Although the proportions of properties sold may be low, there have been some sales in almost all parts of the stock. In the large estates there is mixed tenure; there are leasehold management problems in the flatted accommodation involved. Perhaps just as important is the increased concentration of deprived households on these estates. Sales of properties have been at a higher rate in other estates and the impact of this differential is that households seeking social-rented housing are more likely to find themselves being housed in the large post-war estates. Whereas other estates may retain a social as well as a tenure mix, the large post-war estates are more likely to be affected by the general change in the profile of households in the social-rented sector.

In the 'big bang' privatisations illustrated in this chapter by Hungary and Slovenia, the impact of privatisation has been more dramatic. Before 1990 public-rental housing was almost exclusively in buildings that were wholly state-owned and this changed dramatically. There is a school of thought that housing privatisation was executed too quickly, without sufficient consideration being given to all the possible outcomes (Turner et al, 1992; Struyk, 1996; Lowe and Tsenkova, 2003). In Slovenia, those who were unable to take advantage of the Right-to-Buy (non-public-housing sitting tenants at the time) contend that the measure was unfair, since it benefited only some, while everybody had participated through the monthly contributions mentioned earlier in the creation of the public housing stock. Disputes still continue regarding the rights of the sitting tenants and those of the new landlords of restituted dwellings, and there are no indications of any viable solution to the problem being found in the near future. Coupled with the condominium arrangements and the economic restructuring that has left many households with very low incomes, the privatisation of housing has transformed ownership and management processes, but offers no general prospect of responding to the problems associated with housing quality, maintenance, repair, improvement or renewal.

Problems and responses

When the large post–Second World War estates were built in each of the countries discussed in this chapter they were generally regarded as state-of-the-art neighbourhoods. They were the result of state-of-the-art planning, and the quality and condition of properties were regarded as very high both by the professionals involved and the new tenants who moved onto the estates. In the subsequent period the standing and condition of these estates has often declined (see also Chapters One and Two). The problems they present to policy makers and to residents have been further affected by privatisation, as described in this chapter.

The present characteristics of these estates are now different from those pertaining when they were first built, and the estates also differ from each other, partly because of privatisation. The estates represent the layering of a number of processes and characteristics. First, there are those associated with their origins and initial development and their position in the housing hierarchy within cities; second are the processes of repair and improvement, and the adequacy of investment in the subsequent period. Layered on top of this are the processes of use and the changing population living in the neighbourhood; this relates in particular to the position of the housing tenure and the housing estate in the hierarchy of choice within cities and countries. Then come the changes in ownership and control associated with privatisation. It may be argued that the next layer is the policy responses that are emerging today and will develop over the next period.

The post-privatisation character of these estates is significantly different in the countries discussed in this chapter. There has been a divergence because of privatisation and the processes of investment in property associated with privatisation. In the Dutch case, privatisation may sometimes be connected to the process of the modernisation and renewal of estates. While there is a policy agenda involving the expansion of home ownership and a political impetus towards privatisation for its own sake, it is not this agenda that has driven change on the estates. In several cases estates have changed their patterns of ownership and control as part of the management of renewal and restructuring. Estates are at different stages in the process of change. Some have already been significantly modernised while others are at an early stage. Because of this time lag, they have different tenure mixes and different housing conditions. In some cases the estates have been affected by the polarisation of tenures, with the tendency for middle and higher income groups to prefer home ownership. However, because of the development of mixed-tenure estates, the increasing polarisation between tenures does not necessarily mean polarisation between estates, although polarisation within estates can ensue.

This same argument applies to a lesser extent in the UK. The large post-war housing estates are generally perceived as the least popular and least attractive options within the portfolio of social-rented housing in the UK. They have higher proportions of flats and maisonettes and are generally regarded as less attractive than the traditionally built estates of houses with gardens that form the majority of the council housing sector. While the council housing sector as a whole has been affected by residualisation and socio-tenurial polarisation, the effect has been most pronounced in the least attractive parts of the stock; consequently, it is often the large post-war estates that have the highest rates of turnover and the lowest levels of demand. It is also evident that these are the estates which privatisation affects least directly. The uptake of the Right-to-Buy is lower in these estates, so the fragmentation of ownership is less. Local authorities remain as the freeholder and have responsibilities for the maintenance of the common fabric of the dwellings. While the pressures on these estates arising from residualisation and polarisation and the damaged reputation of the estates are important, and have been made worse by the Right-to-Buy, the fragmentation of ownership is on a smaller scale than in Hungary or Slovenia. Nevertheless, that fragmentation of ownership does incorporate an additional complication when it comes to the restructuring and renewal of these estates. Privatisation was not carried out with agendas related to the quality and condition of properties in mind. It was driven by ideological and electoral factors, and the legacy in terms of the problems of managing and restructuring estates is accidental, a very different state of affairs from that in the Netherlands.

The situation in Eastern and Central European countries, as illustrated in this chapter by Hungary and Slovenia, is even more dramatic. In this case the drive to privatisation was associated with political and economic changes. If it was influenced by an explicit housing policy agenda, that was to shift the burden of repair and maintenance away from local authorities. However, the condominium arrangements that are the legacy of the policy are not operating effectively to achieve the repair, maintenance, and efficient management of these estates. This deficiency is especially true in relation to the properties that are in the worst condition, perhaps because of the poor quality of their construction, and in the estates where the residents have the lowest incomes. The condominium arrangement relies on mobilising consent between owners to carry out significant investments together. Where the repair, management, and maintenance costs are high and not likely to be fully reflected in sale prices, and where the owners have low incomes, consent is less likely to be forthcoming. At the same time the fragmented pattern of ownership presents a real barrier to many of the approaches to renewal and restructuring that have been adopted elsewhere, including in the Netherlands and the UK. Against this background the responses in Slovenia are to strengthen condominiums, to raise awareness among condominium flat owners about their home-ownership obligations, and to attempt to improve the efficiency of management and renewal. In Hungary, the Condominium Act has been amended (decreasing the 'blocking right' of the minority of owners in the case of decisions on renewal) and some subsidies have been introduced to stimulate the renovation of privatised, multi-family buildings (Tosics, 2004).

The nature, extent, and legacies of privatisation are very different and present different problems in relation to the future of these estates in the various countries considered. The immediate tasks for the agencies seeking to respond to the problems on the estates reflect this. Perhaps in the Netherlands the framework for renewal and restructuring needs very little change – until the next time major investment activity is needed. In the UK the process is much more complicated, and winning consent and support for major policy initiatives now involves negotiation with a much more diverse assortment of interest groups and stakeholders. Some situations have arisen where the Right-to-Buy significantly increases the costs and delays associated with renewal. Finally, in the cases of Hungary and Slovenia, the changed legal and ownership situations present an entirely new challenge for policy makers; without significant funding from elsewhere the problems of winning consent to major initiatives may prove insurmountable.

Notes

[1] Strictly speaking, the Right-to-Buy has not applied in Northern Ireland but a very similar house sales scheme has operated there and in this chapter reference to the Right-to-Buy in the UK includes the Northern Ireland house sales scheme.

[2] The Housing Management Act passed in 1981 required all public housing tenants to pay a personal contribution (also popularly referred to as 'participation') into the housing fund intended for the construction of 'solidarity' housing. The level of contribution, refundable after ten years, varied and was determined as a percentage of the total value of the housing unit, also taking into consideration the social status, health situation, and economic capacity of the tenant.

References

Aalbers, M.B. (2004) 'Promoting home ownership in a social-rented city: policies, practices and pitfalls', *Housing Studies*, vol 19, no 3, pp 483-95.

Alexander, G.S. and Skapska, G. (eds) (1994) *A fourth way? Privatisation, property, and the emergence of new market economies*, London: Routledge.

Boelhouwer, P.J. (1988) *De verkoop van woningwetwoningen. De overdracht van woningwetwoningen aan bewoners en de gevolgen voor de volkshuisvesting*, Delft: Delft University Press.

Fisher, L.M. and Jaffe, A.J. (2000) 'Restitution in transition countries', *Journal of Housing and the Built Environment*, vol 15, no 3, pp 233-48.

Forrest, R. and Murie, A. (1990) *Selling the welfare state*, London: Routledge.

Forrest, R., Murie, A. and Gordon, D. (1995) *Leaseholders and service charges in former local authority flats*, London: HMSO.

Frissen, J., Theunissen, V. and De Wildt, R. (2001) *Verkoop van huurwoningen in het ROA-gebied. Kansen en belemmeringen*, Amsterdam: RIGO Research and Consultancy.

Hegedüs, J. and Tosics, I. (1994) 'Privatisation and rehabilitation in the Budapest inner districts', *Housing Studies*, vol 9, no 3, pp 39-54.

Hegedüs, J., Mark, K., Sárkány, C. and Tosics, I. (1996) 'Hungary', in D. Clapham, J. Hegedüs, K. Kintrea and I. Tosics (eds) (with H. Kay) *Housing privatisation in Eastern Europe*, Westport, CT/London: Greenwood Press, pp 57-95.

Jones, C. (2003) *Exploitation of the Right-to-Buy scheme by companies*, London: Office of the Deputy Prime Minister.

Jones, C. and Murie, A. (1999) *Reviewing the Right-to-Buy*, Birmingham: CURS, University of Birmingham.

Lowe, S. and Tsenkova, S. (eds) (2003) *Housing change in East and Central Europe: integration or fragmentation?*, Aldershot: Ashgate.

Mandi, S. (1994) 'Housing tenures in times of change: conversion debates in Slovenia', *Housing Studies*, vol 9, no 1, pp 27-38.

Mandi, S. (1999) 'Impacts of privatisation and restitution on housing estates', paper presented at the international conference 20th Century Urbanisation and Urbanism', 8-10 December 1999, Ljubljana, Slovenia.

Marsh, A., Kennett, P. and Forrest, R. (2003) *The impact of the 1999 changes to the Right-to-Buy discount*, London: The Stationery Office.

Ministerie VROM (1989) (Housing Ministry) *Volkshuisvesting in de jaren negentig*, The Hague: SDU Uitgeverij.

Murie, A. (1976) *The sale of council houses*, Birmingham: University of Birmingham.

Priemus, H. and Mandi, S. (2000) 'Rental housing in Central and Eastern Europe as no man's land, special issue: Rented housing in Eastern and Central Europe', *Journal of Housing and the Built Environment*, vol 15, no 3, pp 205-15.

Sendi, R. (1995) 'Housing reform and housing conflict: the privatisation and denationalisation of public housing in the Republic of Slovenia in practice', *International Journal of Urban and Regional Research*, vol 19, no 3, pp 435-46.

Sendi, R. (1999) 'The state of large housing estates and strategies for renewal', paper presented at the European Network for Housing Research conference 'New European Housing and Urban Policies', 25-29 August 1999, Balatonfüred, Hungary.

Sendi, R. (2004) 'The refurbishment of multi-storey housing: social, legal and financial conditions. The case of Slovenia', paper presented at the conference 'Real Estate Research in Central Eastern and South Eastern Europe', 15-16 January 2004, Vienna, Austria.

Stanovnik, T. (1994) 'The sale of the social housing stock in Slovenia: what happened and why', *Urban Studies*, vol 31, no 9, pp 1559-70.

Struyk, R.J. (ed) (1996) *Economic restructuring of the former Soviet block. The case of housing*, Washington, DC: The Urban Institute Press.

Tanninen, T., Ambrose, I. and Siksiö, O. (eds) (1994) *Transitional housing systems. East-West dialogue on the new roles of actors in changing housing policies*, Dessau: Bauhaus.

Tosics, I. (2001) 'The mass give-away. Lessons learnt from the privatisation of housing in Central and Eastern Europe', *Eurocities Magazine*, vol 14, Autumn 2001, pp 15-16.

Tosics, I. (2004) 'Refurbishment of multistorey housing in Hungary: social, legal and financial consequences', paper presented at the conference 'Real Estate Research in Central Eastern and South Eastern Europe', 15–16 January 2004, Vienna, Austria.

Turner, B., Hegedüs, J. and Tosics, I. (eds) (1992) *The reform of housing in Eastern Europe and the Soviet Union*, New York, NY: Routledge.

SIX

Tackling social cohesion in ethnically diverse estates

Karien Dekker and Rob Rowlands

Introduction

One of the major fractures in contemporary civil society takes place along the line of race and ethnicity. In many Western European countries and the US, the discussion of issues concerned with a multi-cultural society focuses on the problems that result from ethnic groups' lack of integration in, and their failure to adapt to, Western society. While the assimilation of these groups is the hoped-for outcome, the reality that is increasingly perceived and presented is one of segregation and insularity. Instead of being highlighted as an advantage of modern society, ethnic and cultural diversity are now used as divisive mechanisms. The results are seen in the politicisation of issues such as immigration and asylum that split impoverished communities. As a result, many Western European countries previously lauded for their liberalism now see an increase in the votes cast for far-right political parties whose manifesto is based on race issues. This political swing has in turn resulted in more centrist governments imposing stricter immigration controls. Within countries, the position of migrants is increasingly questioned: migrants are portrayed as a social problem, a safety problem, having a retarded culture, lacking feelings of responsibility, failing to respect our values and norms, and abusing 'our' social security system (Gowricharn, 2002). This image is exemplified at its most extreme by the demonisation of the Islamic faith and its followers as potential terrorists.

One of the challenges faced in many large-scale (former) public housing estates, such as those studied in the RESTATE project, is the perceived lack of social cohesion resulting from the presence of many different ethnicities, which leads to a diversity in lifestyles that presents a challenge to social cohesion. What is more, this perceived lack of social cohesion is seen as one of the main reasons underlying the problems related to inter-ethnic conflicts, a lack of safety, problems involving the local environment, liveability, unemployment, and the like.

This chapter aims to show how social cohesion and ethnic diversity are interrelated and how urban governance arrangements can enhance social cohesion. This interrelationship is made clear in two steps. First, we outline the definition of social cohesion from a theoretical perspective, concentrating on how social cohesion and ethnic diversity are interrelated. The description of social cohesion we have used follows the five elements of cohesion outlined by Kearns and Forrest (2000). The focus on the problems that arise from a lack of social cohesion as a result of ethnic diversity may convince us that social cohesion is always positive, but social cohesion can also lead to unwanted outcomes. We do not pay exclusive attention to the positive elements of social cohesion, but also show that cohesion can lead to tensions between groups and contribute to or exacerbate social exclusion.

The second part of the chapter discusses how social cohesion in ethnically diverse areas is related to the policy-making processes applied to the estates. Social cohesion often has two goals for policy makers: first, to increase the participation of the residents not only in society as a whole, but also in policy making. Second, the goal is to increase solidarity between groups, particularly in ethnically diverse areas. We show that, in ethnically diverse areas, the existing power relationships between ethnic groups are often reproduced in social cohesion and participation, thereby failing to add significantly to social cohesion between ethnic groups. This part of the chapter is illustrated by some examples from the UK and the Netherlands. The issue of ethnicity is of particular importance in the North West European estates in the RESTATE project (that is, the Netherlands, France, Germany, Sweden and the UK).

What is social cohesion?

Providing a definition of social cohesion is a difficult task as the concept is understood in many different ways. Researchers, policy makers, politicians, and journalists all use their own variant definitions of what constitutes a cohesive society, and these definitions appear to apply differently at various spatial levels. Some elements feature in most definitions, such as the coherence of a social or political system, the ties that people have with this system, and their involvement and solidarity. Issues such as behaviour, perception, personal networks, identity, and health feature more individually.

The notion of social cohesion is difficult to comprehend; even at the estate level, what the term refers to is not always clear. Early sociologists such as Durkheim (1893), Simmel (1904), and Tönnies (1912 [reprinted 1957]) put social cohesion on the research agenda. Their concern was the division of labour in society, which leads to economic interdependency and order. Social cohesion remained a concept to which researchers and policy makers continued to turn throughout the 20th century, but which until now they have only referred to in implicit ways (see Pahl, 1991). Kearns and Forrest, for example, suggest that social cohesion is a nebulous concept carrying with it an assumption that 'everyone knows what is being referred to' (2000, p 996). Furthermore, they suggest that it is lauded by politicians and some policy makers and social commentators as *a good thing*, and that this approval is reason enough to promote it without explanation. This lack of clarity provides a problem for the researcher and the practitioner. If we do not know what constitutes social cohesion, how can we know whether it exists in our cities and on our estates?

Is cohesion good? There is an unwritten, often unspoken, implicit assumption that cohesion is always positive. But there are negative consequences of cohesion. Community is hailed as a positive thing to promote inclusion, but communities can be closed and hostile. The growth of *gated communities* exemplifies how communities can become cohesive in the face of the fear of crime and presence of undesirable people (Atkinson and Flint, 2003; Blandy and Lister, 2003); this phenomenon may represent social cohesion, but it is not the kind that governments promote explicitly and publicly, nor does it offer many benefits to society at large. Equally, the cohesion promoted by gangs within a neighbourhood can make the area unattractive and intimidating to those who do not feel they belong within the area they claim.

Despite these negative aspects, government authorities at both central and local level continue to devise and implement policies designed to revive, create, and sustain social cohesion within often extremely diverse communities. The ethnic composition of residents on the estates in the UK and the Netherlands can be highly diverse; today, non-native groups are sometimes in the majority. Racial tensions are perceived as a threat to social cohesion. The governments' focus has turned from socioeconomic values to the adaptation of the population to moral, social, and religious values. In both countries, concern over ethnic segregation within equally deprived urban neighbourhoods, such as the RESTATE estates, is growing, as is made clear in the report of the Community Cohesion Review Team (Home Office, 2001) in its response to disturbances in some Northern English towns in 2001. In the post 9/11 world, enhancing social cohesion is seen as a means of dealing with these issues and keeping the so-called Islamic threat under control.

Levels of social cohesion

There are two levels at which social cohesion is seen to be of consequence for estates. The impact of these two levels is very different and has profound consequences for the trajectory of the estates and the development and implementation of policies designed to bolster or alter these trajectories.

At the *macro* level, social cohesion refers to the interaction that takes place across a city or region and is concerned with the society:

> a cohesive society 'hangs together'; all the component parts fit in and attribute to society's collective project and well being; and conflict between societal goals and groups, and disruptive behaviour, are largely absent or minimal (Kearns and Forrest, 2000, p 996).

The increasing levels of diversity, instability, and uncertainty that have accompanied the post-modern world have made cohesion more difficult, or at the very least have increased the chances of social friction and fracture along social, economic, and cultural divides. Across cities, there has been a process of growing fragmentation and increasing segregation of different groups focused primarily on income and race. Housing market processes, particularly state housing allocation practices, have been a key to this growing segregation (Rex and Moore, 1967; Henderson and Karn, 1987; Murie, 1997; Lee and Murie, 1999), but this is linked to people's ability to afford housing and therefore to the job market opportunities available. For example, Sassen (2001) has highlighted how lower-skilled, lower-paid workers are being forced to the peripheries of cities, further from their place of work and the economies and lifestyles they are servicing. Race plays a significant part in this process and adds another layer of differentiation, fragmentation, and segregation to the equation. The question here revolves around the impact on marginal and residualised housing estates within this context and their position within the city.

At a *micro* level, we are concerned with a different set of cohesive qualities that go beyond the structural issues of the macro level. At the micro level, cohesion is concerned with the interaction between residents on estates and the extent to which their lives can exist first in harmony and second with a growing level of synergy and assimilation. In the UK, in the recent increase in concern over social cohesion, the term has often been expressed as *community cohesion*. At estate level, social cohesion thus refers to:

> the degree to which the residents share values and norms, a certain degree of social control, the existence and availability of networks (informally shaped in friendships, or formally in the sense of participation in organisations, associations, and neighbourhood activities), the existence of trust between residents, and the willingness to find solutions to problems collectively. (authors' translation, De Hart et al, 2002, p 12).

The challenge of community cohesion is growing. In the UK, the perceived need for cohesion is clearly the result of racial tensions. The reports that followed disturbances in the Northern English towns of Burnley, Oldham, and Bradford in 2001 identified the lack of interaction between individuals of different cultural, religious, and racial backgrounds as a common causal factor (Home Office, 2001; Oldham Independent Review, 2001; Ousley, 2001; Burnley Task Force, 2002). *Community cohesion* is identified here as an important factor in promoting a strong and healthy society and establishing a greater sense of citizenship (Home Office, 2001). It is evident from the above that policy makers see social cohesion as the solution to racial tensions:

A cohesive community is one in which:

- there is a common vision and a sense of belonging for all communities;
- the diversity of people's backgrounds and circumstances is appreciated and positively valued;
- people from different backgrounds have similar life opportunities;
- strong and positive relationships are being developed between people from different backgrounds in the workplace, in schools, and within neighbourhoods (Home Office, 2004).

This development has highlighted the shift from a lack of cohesion between estates and neighbourhoods to the potential for growing fragmentation within estates. While policy is easier to design and implement with the agreement of residents in areas that are marginalised, but perceived as cohesive, the role for policy makers is increasingly more challenging. If place making is to be an inclusive process based on consensus (see Chapter 3), the increased fragmentation of communities within a narrow spatial area raises new challenges. How can communities that are increasingly divergent in themselves be expected to shape a common future for these estates?

These macro and micro levels do not operate in isolation. Individual actors bridge the levels by creating their own networks. There is therefore a distinction to be drawn between internal group cohesion and external cohesion between groups. Both kinds of cohesion can be either weak or strong (Duyvendak, 1997; Schuyt, 1997), or they can go together.

Care should be taken not to overemphasise the importance of ethnicity. Throughout history, one of the main critiques of far-right political parties in Europe has been their use of race to explain structural social and economic problems. The needs of each individual are related to that individual's specific characteristics, which brings up the question of the adequacy of using only race and ethnicity as a dividing mechanism (Amin, 2002). By racialising all problems, other facets of commonality between individuals are ignored. These facets include gender, age, education, class, and consumption; they cut across ethnic lines and are shared with other groups. For example, young people may have similar interests (such as music or school), which may be a stronger bonding topic than their differences based on race. Similarly, women of most backgrounds have similarities such as combining childcare with other activities. These shared interests are more important than their different ethnic backgrounds.

Housing estates and social cohesion

The debate about community on housing estates, especially among politicians, has been dominated by the issues related to a deficiency of cohesion (Home Office, 2001; Groves et al, 2003; Morrison, 2003). Although there are signs that communities in some areas may appear less cohesive, in many cases it could be argued that the concern is about a perceived rather than a demonstrable lack of social cohesion on estates. The perception is often that of the state and its associated organisations and is based on the form of social cohesion they want to see in society. In particular, there is a preoccupation with formalised notions of cohesion, including community participation in decision making, rather than with more organic and informal signs of cohesion. Equally, many governments do not want to see communities that are mono-ethnic; the notion of cohesion is based on particular *definitions*

Table 6.1: Domains of social cohesion

Domain	Description
Common values and a civic culture	Common aims and objectives; common moral principles/codes of behaviour; support for political institutions and participation in politics
Social order and social control	Absence of general conflict and threats to the existing order, absence of incivility; effective informal social control, tolerance, respect for differences; inter-group cooperation
Social solidarity and reduction in wealth disparities	Harmonious economic and social development; redistribution of public finances and of opportunities; equal access to services and welfare benefits; ready acknowledgement of social obligations and willingness to assist others
Social networks and social capital	High degree of social interaction within communities and families; civic engagement and associational activity; easy resolution of collective action problems
Place attachment and identity	Strong attachment to place; intertwining of personal and place identity

Source: Kearns and Forrest (2000)

and *observations* of what it may constitute. In the UK, for example, community cohesion has been adopted as a proxy for race equality, with other issues of cohesion pushed to the periphery. It is therefore important to consider who has defined the cohesiveness of communities we study, and redefine a more objective approach. The framework above enables us to achieve this.

Kearns and Forrest (2000) have developed a framework that outlines the different domains of social cohesion that can be usefully applied to the understanding and analysis of social and community cohesion at the estate level.

Using the framework above is by no means the only method of analysing social cohesion. The framework is, however, comprehensive in that it includes all the main elements involved in building cohesive communities. Furthermore, it has been adopted by the UK government as a framework for the implementation of its own community cohesion policies (Local Government Association et al, 2001). Here we outline what each of these elements mean for analysing social cohesion on large housing estates.

Common values and a civic culture

Common values are perhaps the most outward manifestation of social cohesion. A system of shared values has been used to define the creation and operation of communities. This sharing provides citizens with common aims and objectives and thus a means of constructing normal ways of behaving towards each other. Supposedly, the liveability increases on large housing estates when the residents mutually agree on public behaviour. On a higher scale level, it is suggested that citizens support larger political institutions and identify with them (see, for example, Tannsjö, 1995; Commission of the European Communities, 1997; Hebert and Page, 2000).

However, in discussing cohesion against a background of increasing disparity of income and opportunity, the debate has sometimes been clouded by a moralising discourse (Murray, 1990; Pahl, 1991). Cohesion is often referred to in terms of a shared moral code of behaviour. In the UK, this association has resurfaced in terms of ethnicity, with senior government ministers calling on black and minority ethnic groups to embrace so-called British culture as a way of becoming cohesive. This refrain marks a change from the multi-cultural ethos that has been promoted in recent years. In the Netherlands, the same development is taking place; values and norms are a major issue in politics and policy making. The Prime Minister has even made the topic his personal priority target, aiming to persuade non-Westerners to adopt Western modes of behaviour. Policy makers tend to be pragmatic rather than politically correct. Cohen, Mayor of Amsterdam, sees religion (specifically, Islam) as a good basis for cohesion and the empowerment of the poor (Cohen, 2002).

Social order and social control

At one level, social order means that there is a general absence of conflict, because people have similar routines, demands, and reciprocities in everyday life. Social order also involves social control, enhancing the feeling of safety in urban neighbourhoods. Tönnies' *Gemeinschaft* is relevant here, since people still lead their lives in narrow domestic worlds in spite of all the discussions about such worldwide processes as globalisation. Most people feel part of their neighbourhood or small group; they feel excluded from larger groups, or they themselves exclude other groups, attitudes that eventually lead to conflict. Ideally, there are no conflicts between groups in a cohesive society, because there is mutual respect and tolerance (see, for example, Jackson, 1986; Benoist and Sunic, 1994; Horne, 2001). However, this mutual trust, respect, and tolerance should be firmly rooted in legal, institutional, and formal sanctions against racial and cultural hatred (Amin, 2002; Cliteur, 2004).

Cohesion is envisaged as a passive state in which competing views of the city are resolved amicably. Sometimes, however, the use of the power of the majority has proved to be effective. There is, for example, considerable evidence of residents on housing estates taking their own action to force change. The success of the change on the Central Estates in Birmingham is widely attributed to tenant protests, including a rooftop demonstration on the house of the then leader of the City Council. The protests instigated a programme of renewal on the estate, including a change of landlord through housing stock transfer. Arguably, such action constitutes a threat to the existing order. A government seeking to promote community interaction can be faced with a challenge to the way in which action on the estates is implemented.

Existing power relationships are reportedly under constant challenge on the RESTATE estates. A recent study on empowering muted communities and hard-to-reach groups within communities in England declared that there was a need to "get behind the 'usual suspects'" in order to "promote involvement". Taking this step is essential in promoting inclusivity and preventing so-called community leaders from dictating the agenda (Mullins et al, 2004; Temple and Steele, 2004).

The Dutch case of Hoograven provides an example of the consequences where participation is based around the 'usual suspects'. *Hoograven aan Zet* [Hoograven's Turn] is a project within the Big Cities Policy. Its aims are to increase social cohesion through the active participation of residents in neighbourhood activities. Although many different groups were involved at the start of the project – the point at which goals were set and funds distributed – those groups and individuals who were previously inactive still failed to become participants in the new project. Elderly native people and a group of Moroccan men were included, while youngsters and women had very little influence. As a consequence, the projects organised for youngsters are characterised by their top-down approach; there are no projects for immigrant women.

Solidarity and the reduction of disparities

Building social solidarity and reducing disparities, particularly of wealth, are often seen to meet national or city level concerns. It is argued that people organise systems of financial redistribution through taxes, social security benefits, services and other benefits in kind because of feelings of solidarity. In the 20th century this redistribution was largely organised by the state. Whether such redistribution is the result of altruism or a necessity to facilitate the capitalist system has been debated elsewhere. Nevertheless, the continuing debate about the future of the post-war welfare state in many Western European countries has seen a shift in the process and means of application of this redistribution. The reduction of disparities in income has become an issue reaching beyond the mere redistribution of wealth. The UK government, for example, has made reducing the gap between rich and poor an explicit function of social policy. But the role of the state has been reduced and the individual who has the means, the skills, and the energy to take advantage of this reduction has become greatly empowered.

In the event, the estate level is of particular importance since inter-ethnic relations have a neighbourhood dimension, linked to the cultural identities and socioeconomic situations that together form the local way of life. This everyday form of social solidarity implies the recognition of and interest in the well-being of other residents (see, for example, Davoudi and Atkinson, 1999; Blokland, 2003). In estates with high levels of deprivation, competition for scarce opportunities (jobs, money) is harsh and ethnicity easily feeds jealousy against 'the other', harbouring such ideas as 'they are always given the best jobs' or 'they all live on welfare benefits'. Interest in each other's well-being is not present in such situations (Amin, 2002). It is clear that this situation exists in urban areas in both the UK and the Netherlands. Such assertions have been used by the far-right British National Party in the UK as a focus for their policies, as highlighted in the June 2004 parliamentary by-election in Hodge Hill, one of the RESTATE case study estates. Furthermore, there is no reference to the reduction of disparities in the criteria adopted by the UK government for successful community cohesion.

Social networks and social capital

Social networks can provide support, based as they often are on family, kin or friends. Networks can also provide support for work and other opportunities. A network helps a person to 'get by and get on' (see, for example, Arrow, 2000; Scheepers and Janssen, 2001). Some authors state that social networks can also produce social capital, associational activity, and community organisations (see, for example, Putnam, 1995; Portes and Landholt, 1998; Taylor, 2000).

Unfortunately, social networks are most frequently formed by people with similar characteristics. The sociocultural (including ethnic) or socioeconomic diversity of the population can and has been shown to be a negative factor within social networks and an exclusionary mechanism. As Fischer (1982) points out, people of the same race, religion, and national origin often tend to be part of the same network, a pattern highlighted by more recent studies (Morrison, 2003; Dekker and Bolt, 2005). A physical concentration of ethnic groups can therefore easily lead to homogeneous ethnic social networks concentrated on the neighbourhood. Segregation then enhances internal group cohesion (van Kempen, 2001).

Associational activity – the extent to which individuals within communities and neighbourhoods participate in activities together – is a key indicator of social networks and social capital. Tenant and resident associations are the more visible and obvious forms of this type of associational activity. Other forums should not, however, be overlooked. Schools, faith groups, sporting and social clubs all provide an opportunity for interaction. In a world where individuals find formalised political involvement of decreasing importance, involvement in these other arenas are perhaps more realistic.

We should exercise caution when using associational activity as an indicator of social capital and social networks because of two almost polemic effects. First, we have to account for the 'busybody' effect – the people who talk to many residents and think they speak for everyone. But second, are we to say that more affluent communities, where there may be little interaction between the residents, are (a) uncohesive, and so (b) problematic by definition?

Place attachment and identity

Kearns and Forrest's (2000) final element is one of *place attachment and identity*. Although this is evident at the national level, with national pride following sporting successes, for example, it is the neighbourhood level that concerns us most here. When people feel attached to a place and identify with it they may also develop common values and norms and be more willing to participate in networks and build social capital. Place attachment and identity may also enhance feelings of belonging ('I am part of this area') and safety. One of the dangers here is that people live in very small worlds and identify with them without identifying with larger contexts, thereby excluding those who live elsewhere, and feeling unsafe in other, often unfamiliar areas (see, for example, Puddifoot, 1995; Orchard, 2002; Uzzell et al, 2002). The results of a survey of the residents living on four estates in the UK revealed that the majority of the residents identified with a single street or block of flats as their neighbourhood. It is therefore not difficult to imagine why wider community cohesion may be difficult to achieve around spatially defined communities.

There is a need here for a critical examination to discover whether there is a synergy between personal identity and place identity. If community cohesion is intended to be built spatially, it is important to understand whether people not only identify with that spatial area, but also socially embrace others who live within it. The results of a survey in two post-Second World War housing estates in the Netherlands show a strong negative relationship between place attachment and identity and ethnic diversity; native Dutch people in particular feel less attached to their neighbourhood when they perceive ethnic diversity as a problem (Dekker and Bolt, 2005).

Each of these elements of social cohesion can be observed in varying degrees within the estates in the RESTATE project and between these estates and their cities.

Policies aiming at social cohesion in ethnically diverse estates

Social cohesion is believed to help overcome the problems created as the result of differences between ethnic groups:

> Local community and a shared sense of space are both said to constitute the local glue for agreement and understanding within a mixed community (Amin, 2002, p 15).

If so much good is expected from social cohesion, we need to ask how policies can achieve it in areas accommodating complex ethnic groups. First, however, we show how social cohesion forms part of urban policies in the Netherlands and the UK.

It is important to note before we start how policies can address this issue, and that social cohesion may never be perfect (Gowricharn, 2002). Individualisation, secularisation, increased numbers of ethnic groups, transnational communities and immigration lead to societal changes that stand in the way of total social cohesion. Moreover, the diversity in lifestyles that results from these societal developments prevents a society from being uniform. In this kind of modern society differences need to be respected. Furthermore, rather than being a negative influence on civic society, these differences might be productive and foster an organic solidarity. Differences are not the problem; the difficulty lies rather in the way in which differences are conceptualised and reacted to.

Social cohesion as part of estate regeneration

If we consider the policies being implemented on the estates in the UK and the Netherlands, it is clear that social cohesion forms part of the ideal image that has been created by politicians and policy makers both in terms of policy documents and in the ways in which the population is involved in policy development. In the UK, the Labour government has attempted to mainstream community cohesion into urban areas following the disturbances in Northern towns in 2001. The community cohesion pathfinders who have been put in place have refocused policy initiatives, particularly regeneration.

In the Netherlands, social cohesion is not included in the list of the goals of the Big Cities Policy, although it has several elements which relate to social cohesion: discussing values and norms at various places, enhancing the identity of cities and neighbourhoods through characteristic buildings, and city marketing. 'Our Neighbourhood's Turn', in particular, aims to increase liveability, social cohesion, and safety in urban neighbourhoods.

Clearly, cohesion is a central element of regeneration within estates. The aim of the programmes is supported in many cases by the involvement of the community; their consensus is vital to the delivery of programmes. Social cohesion within the estates is, therefore, a policy goal. Central and local governments remain concerned about the lack of involvement of black and minority ethnic groups and consider how these groups could be more fully involved; an example in the UK was afforded by the process of local authority housing stock transfer (Mullins et al, 2004).

The possibility arises, however, that divided cities enable governments to implement programmes while retaining control over public expenditure. Competitive funding programmes foster an incohesive city by pitting one poor community against another poor community, and in some respects lead to fragmentation of the community, particularly along racial and ethnic lines.

Participation as a stimulus for social cohesion

An important starting point for social cohesion in ethnically diverse neighbourhoods is participation in diverse aspects of society and the recognition of heterogeneity. Differences in cultural background can lead to tensions between groups (or within them) and loss of trust. People gain responsibility for their lives through participation in work, education, voluntary networks or political decision-making networks. Empowerment and involvement in local improvements is an important step to this end (Madanipour, 1998). Public organisations and policies play a decisive role because they provide inhabitants with the necessary resources and conditions through urban policy.

If governments want to enhance social cohesion in ethnically diverse neighbourhoods, they should design policies that enhance feelings of belonging, civic culture, and the existence of networks. In addition, the current orthodoxy in much research and policy is that societal cohesion builds from the bottom up through social organisations. Consequently, if a government wishes to influence social cohesion, it should start by supporting social organisations in neighbourhoods and incorporating community organisations in policy-making processes. It is important that involvement strategies are well designed and implemented. Enhanced involvement requires extending the reach into the community, making structures open to new participants and, importantly, approaching the community on its own terms rather than those of the organisations.

The latter point highlights the need to reassess the power relationships between the groups concerned in the process. Two factors are of significance in this regard: first, the need to recognise the networks that exist within estates. *Community* as it is found in estates such as those studied in the RESTATE project grows organically; at the heart of a 'community' is a series of individual networks. In the UK there has been a growing recognition of minorities within minorities, groups such as women and younger people who are hidden behind, or not spoken for by, formalised networks. Thus, although involvement strategies are often well intentioned, they are sometimes not well designed and are poorly implemented. In this way *existing power structures are enhanced*: active people are again enabled to use more funds, while those who stay home get nothing. The reason often given in both the Dutch and the English cases, either implicitly or explicitly, is that there was no time to organise their inclusion, as the whole process had to be completed quickly because of central government time constraints.

The second point requiring us to reassess the power relationships between the groups concerned is the need to harness the informal processes of community, cohesion, and participation. Formalised approaches such as public meetings and elected associations only have a limited role in securing participation and it is clear that only a minority of residents will participate on these terms. A number of social landlords in the UK have demonstrated how informal approaches can be exploited. For example, several social landlords in England use *estate walkabouts* to address residents' concerns on their own terms. At the same time, the personal networks of staff members in organisations can be used to increase reach into the community. In Hoograven, activities to develop cohesion and wider participation were organised by the residents. Clearly, in this case, participation and involvement have been a stimulus for social cohesion. Unfortunately, owing to time constraints imposed from the top, the input from non–involved residents was not increased in this project. Therein lies a requirement to view these processes in the longer term and within timeframes that do not fit with the life of one initiative.

Considerations in dealing with ethnic groups in participation

Local policy makers should promote actions that enhance social cohesion in such a way that all groups are included in the policy-making process. In diverse urban areas in North West Europe, particularly on the large housing estates, promoting inclusion can be a problem. Usually, the longstanding original white residents participate in policy making, whereas the newcomers of foreign origin do not. The question whether the residents are all represented can be answered with a resounding 'No'. On the other hand, service providers find it difficult to deal with the many voices coming from within communities, so they favour one voice (Taylor, 2000). It is perhaps understandable that organisations working in these areas face resource constraints, so they take the easiest route. The points mentioned below refer to an ideal type of participative policy-making process in ethnically diverse areas. Naturally, there will still be many positive results even when not all requirements are met.

A governance process that takes the ethnic diversity of the population into account attends to the following points (Healey, 1997; Hebert and Page, 2000; Allen and Cars, 2001; Forrest and Kearns, 2001; Mullins et al, 2004; Temple and Steele, 2004):

- The process has a bottom–up approach. The different groups should decide on their common norms to be used in governing. Effective and acceptable neighbourhood governance structures should be designed from the bottom up by those involved so as to incorporate these common norms.

- The role of language is of particular importance in areas of diverse ethnic population and must receive due consideration. First, participation is difficult for those who do not speak the local language well. Furthermore, it is important to remember that some words may have different meanings in different languages. Second, informal methods of communication are explored to facilitate communication across the neighbourhood. And finally it is important to foster trust between all participants through having a neutral party produce translations.

- The process of thinking through and negotiating changes in governance structures is continuous; the population composition is always changing, and interaction between people will develop ever-changing norms related to governance. The steering of governance processes is under constant review.

- The focus is on the negotiation process itself rather than the output it achieves. According to Healey (1997, p 288), a good governance process "recognizes the ranges and variety of stakeholders ... their social networks, the diversity of their cultural points of reference and their systems of meaning". The governance process, in which all groups are involved, is therefore more important than the official outcome of the policy or 'counting the beans' (Power, 1997).

- The process fosters a vibrant civic culture with an extensive local network of formal and informal cross-communal linkages that nurture social capital, mutual trust, and cooperation. Both formal and informal networks and interventions can facilitate and enable the diversity of the ways to organise and the goals to achieve.

- The process shares responsibilities, power, and financial resources and provides practical and moral support so that all groups can use these resources to empower themselves and participate in decision making.

- The governance arrangements are open, transparent, and accountable so as to include all members of the community. Any person may ask what is going on and whether they can be involved.

- The governance arrangements take account of the problems a diverse population composition poses in representation. Each group has its own culture with a set of meanings and ideas about the roles of men and women in general and participation in particular.

Expectations about how to participate and responsibilities are as diverse as the people taking part in the process. It may not be clear whether an individual represents a group or participates in order to achieve an individual goal (Dekker and van Kempen, 2004).

- The process takes into account the variety of images different parties and individuals hold of how the estate should look (Healey, 1996). Power relationships formed between groups decide which image is strived for and translated into policy. Different forms of capital are decisive for the degree of power of that group or individual.

The role of the individual staff members of several English social landlords has been paramount in driving forward the process of engaging hard-to-reach groups. Against a background of supportive management, staff can use their own networks to seek involvement deep within communities. In one organisation, a tenant participation officer who was herself a refugee has been able to tap into the experiences of other members of similar communities and thus enhance that organisation's communication with these groups.

However, although the practical responsibilities of staff are often devolved effectively, that cannot always be said for the financial resources. In Hoograven, for example, the urban district office (*wijkbureau*) and the local administration are responsible for the financial affairs of all seven partial projects, so the project managers must ask the urban district office to sanction the expenditure of any large sums. This necessity leads to some irritation within the projects. Moreover, as the urban district office can decide how the money is spent, they have the authority to hire an external project manager from this budget. Similarly, the assumption that organisations own staff members' personal networks can make these networks vulnerable in the long term and in some cases undermine the credibility of the individuals' own efforts.

The issues come back to resources and the emphasis that should be placed on long-term sustainable involvement strategies. Furthermore, as with all group actions, consultation and involvement needs to be followed by action. The Hoograven example illustrates how a project may score highly on issues of continuous negotiation and creating a vibrant civic culture. In the beginning, differences in command of the local language were taken into account; later on in the project, the rhetoric capacities of the participants became more important. Certain groups of the community were excluded from the project at an early stage and this shift led to their further exclusion, so that their situation deteriorated, while the capacity and inclusion of those who did participate increased. The gap between those who did and those who did not take part in the project widened, leading to the failure to reach the goal of social cohesion for the community.

Conclusion

The focus in this chapter has been on the relationship between social cohesion and the ethnically mixed population composition of large housing estates. Certainly, in North West Europe an increasing share of the population is of non-native origin, presenting a challenge to social cohesion. Different groups are shaped on the basis of ethnicity. Moreover, each group is characterised by its own identity that takes different spatial forms and so has its own conception of what the neighbourhood should look like. As a consequence, there is a whole spectrum of images of the wished-for neighbourhood that come together in the same space.

In general, social cohesion is a positive factor, which may help overcome the differences between groups. Social cohesion is a goal to be pursued to help the regeneration of the estates. It can lead to positive outcomes such as mutual support between residents, friendships, clean public spaces, and so forth. However, it is important to consider whose cohesion it is that is being pursued, since too much cohesion within one group can easily lead to the exclusion of another group. If it is predominantly white middle-class cohesion, it may exclude non-Western minority ethnic groups or low-income households. Also, if social cohesion takes shapes that are similar to cultures of poverty, social cohesion is not a positive thing and should not receive support.

Social cohesion is a policy goal addressed in both the UK and the Netherlands through participative governance processes. Again, it is important to consider whose cohesion is being pursued; identifying which groups are involved is essential in designing the policies that shape the estate. Minority ethnic groups are often less involved in the policy process than natives.

One of the reasons for the lower participation of ethnic communities is their different notions of citizenship when compared with natives. Citizenship relates to the expectations that people have of themselves and the authorities in the policy-making process. Minority ethnic groups will have a different input in these processes because of their different civic and historical backgrounds. A governance process that aims to enhance social cohesion for all residents should be sensitive to these different kinds of input given by ethnic communities.

Aiming to involve *the* ethnic community is not sufficient. As in all groups, those with power – often men of a certain age – become involved, while the women and young people stand on the sidelines. Problems of representation are created and a cohesive society for all will not be achieved. Note should therefore be taken of how powers are divided within ethnic groups.

The future of social cohesion in ethnically mixed large housing estates lies in accepting the fact that they are increasingly multi-ethnic and will not form one big cohesive community. Rather, the estate community consists of several separate communities that are partially overlapping. Cohesion then takes the shape of mutual respect for differences based on commonly agreed rules about society's organisation. In order to include all groups, democratic principles that allow all groups in the estate to become active in shaping their own lives should be followed rather than principles based on religion, prejudice, or a national history.

References

Allen, J. and Cars, G. (2001) 'Multi-culturalism and governing neighbourhoods', *Urban Studies*, vol 38, no 12, pp 2195-209.

Amin, A. (2002) 'Ethnicity and the multicultural city', *Environment and Planning A*, vol 34, no 6, pp 959-81.

Arrow, K.J. (2000) 'Observations on social capital', in P. Dasgupta and I. Serageldin (eds) *Social capital: A multifaceted perspective*, Washington, DC: World Bank, pp 3-5.

Atkinson, R. and Flint, J. (2003) 'Fortress UK? Gated communities, the spatial revolt of the elites and time-space trajectories of segregation', paper presented at the Housing Studies Association Autumn Conference, 'Community, Neighbourhood, Responsibility', 9-10 September 2003, Bristol, UK.

Benoist, A. and Sunic, T. (1994) 'Gemeinschaft and gesellschaft: a sociobiological view of the decay of modern society', *Mankind Quarterly*, vol 35, no 3, pp 263-70.

Blandy, S. and Lister, D. (2003) 'Gated communities: (Ne)Gating community development?', paper presented at the Housing Studies Association Autumn Conference, 'Community, Neighbourhood, Responsibility', 9-10 September 2003, Bristol, UK.

Blokland, T. (2003) 'Unravelling three of a kind: cohesion, community and solidarity', *The Netherlands Journal of Social Sciences*, vol 36, no 1, pp 56-70.

Burnley Task Force (2002) *Report of the Burnley Task Force*, chaired by Lord Anthony Clarke of Hampstead, Burnley: Borough Council.

Cliteur, P. (2004) *Tegen de decadentie*, Amsterdam: De Arbeiderspers.

Cohen, J. (2002) *Cleveringalezing.* (Retrieved 13 August 2004, from www.zorgwelzijn.nl/)

Commission of the European Communities, (1997) *Training, and youth. Accomplishing Europe through education and training,* Brussels: Study Group on Education and Training.

Davoudi, S. and Atkinson, R. (1999) 'Social exclusion and the British planning system', *Planning Practice and Research,* vol 14, no 2, pp 225-36.

De Hart, J., Knol, F., Maas-De Waal, C. and Roes, T. (2002) *Zekere banden, sociale cohesie, leefbaarheid en veiligheid,* Den Haag: Sociaal en Cultureel Planbureau.

Dekker, K. and Bolt, G. (2005) 'Social cohesion in post-war estates in the Netherlands: differences between socioeconomic and ethnic groups', *Urban Studies,* vol 42, no 13.

Dekker, K. and van Kempen, R. (2004) 'Urban governance within the Big Cities Policy', *Cities,* vol 21, no 2, pp 109-17.

Durkheim, E. (1893) *De la division du travail social,* Paris: Presses Universitaire de France.

Duyvendak, J.W. (1997) *Waar blijft de politiek? Essays over paarse politiek, maatschappelijk middenveld en sociale cohesie,* Amsterdam: Boom.

Fischer, C.S. (1982) *To dwell among friends, personal networks in town and city,* Chicago, IL, and London: The University of Chicago Press.

Forrest, R. and Kearns, A. (2001) 'Social cohesion, social capital and the neighbourhood', *Urban Studies,* vol 38, no 12, pp 2125-43.

Gowricharn, R. (2002) 'Integration and social cohesion: the case of the Netherlands', *Journal of Ethnic and Migration Studies,* vol 28, no 2, pp 259-73.

Groves, R., Middleton, A., Murie, A. and Broughton, K. (2003) *Neighbourhoods that work,* York: Joseph Rowntree Foundation.

Healey, P. (1996) 'The communicative turn in planning theory and its implications for spatial strategy formation', *Environment and Planning B,* vol 23, no 2, pp 217-34.

Healey, P. (1997) *Collaborative planning: Shaping places in fragmented societies,* Basingstoke: MacMillan.

Hebert, Y. and Page, M. (2000) 'Research initiatives in citizenship education. Research in focus', *Education Canada,* vol 40, no 3, pp 24-26.

Henderson, J. and Karn, K. (1987) *Race, class and state housing,* Aldershot: Gower.

Home Office (2001) *Community cohesion: A report of the Independent Review,* London: Home Office.

Home Office (2004) *Community & race: Community cohesion.* (Retrieved: 14 September 2004, from www.homeoffice.gov.uk/)

Horne, C. (2001) 'The enforcement of norms: group cohesions and meta-norms', *Social Psychology Quarterly*, vol 64, no 3, pp 253-66.

Jackson, P.I. (1986) *Black visibility, city size, and social control*, Washington, DC: American Sociological Association.

Kearns, A. and Forrest, R. (2000) 'Social cohesion and multilevel urban governance', *Urban Studies*, vol 37, no 5-6, pp 995-1017.

Lee, P. and Murie, A. (1999) 'Spatial and social divisions within British cities: beyond residualisation', *Housing Studies*, vol 14, no 5, pp 625-40.

LGA (Local Government Association), DLTR (Department for Transport, Local Government and the Regions) and CRE (Commission for Racial Equality) (2001) *Draft guidance on community cohesion*, London: DLTR.

Madanipour, A. (1998) 'Social exclusion and space', in A. Madanipour, G. Cars and J. Allen (eds) *Social exclusion in European cities: Processes, experiences and responses,* London: Jessica Kingsley, pp 75-89.

Morrison, N. (2003) 'Neighbourhoods and social cohesion: Experiences from Europe', *International Planning Studies,* vol 8, no 2, pp 115-38.

Mullins, D., Beider, H. and Rowlands, R. (2004) *Empowering communities, improving housing: Involving black and minority ethnic tenants and communities*, London: Office of the Deputy Prime Minister.

Murie, A. (1997) 'The social rented sector, housing and the welfare state in the United Kingdom', *Housing Studies*, vol 12, no 4, pp 437-62.

Murray, C. (1990) *The emerging British underclass*, London: Institute for Economic Affairs Health and Welfare Unit.

Oldham Independent Review (2001) *One Oldham, one future*, panel report, chaired by David Ritchie, Oldham: Oldham Metropolitan Borough Council.

Orchard, V. (2002) 'Culture as opposed to what? Cultural belonging in the context of national and European identity', *European Journal of Social Theory*, vol 5, no 4, pp 419-33.

Ousley, H. (2001) *Community pride not prejudice. Making diversity work in Bradford*, Bradford: Bradford Vision.

Pahl, R.E. (1991) 'The search for social cohesion: from Durkheim to the European Commission', *European Journal of Sociology*, vol 32, no 2, pp 345-60.

Portes, A. and Landholt, P. (1998) 'The downside of social capital', *The American Prospect*, vol 7, no 26, pp 18-22.

Power, A. (1997) *Estates on the edge: The social consequences of mass housing in Northern Europe*, Basingstoke: MacMillan.

Puddifoot, J.E. (1995) 'Dimensions of community identity', *Journal of Community and Applied Social Psychology*, vol 5, no 5, pp 357-70.

Putnam, R.D. (1995) 'Bowling alone: America's declining social capital', *The Journal of Democracy*, vol 6, no 1, pp 65-78.

Rex, J. and Moore, R. (1967) *Race, community and conflict*, Oxford: Oxford University Press.

Sassen, S. (2001) *The global city: New York, London, Tokyo*, Princeton, NJ: Princeton University Press.

Scheepers, P. and Janssen, J. (2001) 'Informele aspecten van sociaal kapitaal: ontwikkelingen in Nederland 1970-1998', *Mens en Maatschappij*, vol 76, no 3, pp 183-201.

Schuyt, K. (1997) *Sociale cohesie en sociaal beleid, drie publiekscolleges in de Balie Amsterdam*, Amsterdam: Stichting Uitgeverij De Balie.

Simmel, G. (1904) *On individuality and social forms, selected writings*, Chicago, IL: University of Chicago Press.

Tannsjö, T. (1995) 'The secular model of the multi-cultural state', *Inquiry*, vol 38, no 1-2, pp 109-17.

Taylor, M. (2000) 'Communities in the lead: power, organisational capacity and social capital', *Urban Studies*, vol 37, no 5-6, pp 1019-35.

Temple, B. and Steele, A. (2004) 'Injustices of engagement: issues in housing needs assessments with minority ethnic communities', *Housing Studies*, vol 19, no 4, pp 541-56.

Tönnies, F. (1912 [reprinted 1957]) *Community and society*, New York, NY: Horper Torch Books.

Uzzell, D., Pol, E. and Badenas, D. (2002) 'Place identification, social cohesion, and environmental sustainability', *Environment and Behavior*, vol 34, no 1, pp 26-54.

van Kempen, R. (2001) 'Social exclusion: the importance of context', in H.T. Andersen and R. van Kempen (eds) *Governing European cities. Social fragmentation, social exclusion and urban governance*, Aldershot: Ashgate, pp 41-70.

SEVEN

Social mix and social perspectives in post-war housing estates

Roger Andersson and Sako Musterd

Introduction

It seems to be received opinion that large housing estates, especially in Western Europe, attract many immigrants and households in a weak social position. Politicians and researchers alike express the view that these estates are not only homogeneous in terms of housing characteristics, but also socially, in the sense that concentrations of poor people are found there. Many think that the homogeneous stock is capable of 'producing' these concentrations and, moreover, that social homogeneity tends to have the effect of diminishing further the social opportunities of those who live there. This situation would create a seedbed for a 'place making' type of policy, which puts forward the concept of a more mixed environment as the ideal kind of place that policy makers should strive to develop.

Place making involves the participation of new types of stakeholders (local residents, for example) and not just the traditional ones (public authorities, for example). The new role of the residents in estate regeneration requires them to have enhanced capacities, which are expected to be associated with an enhanced socioeconomic status. A population with fewer poor people would be capable of enhancing the role of residents in estate regeneration, but would simultaneously lead to a wider diversity of 'ideal images' of the estate (see Chapter Three). In this chapter, we concentrate on some crucial assumptions underlying these ideas.

The assumptions regarding the relationship between housing mix, social mix, and social perspectives have clearly been insufficiently tested. Of course, there are some highly problematic post-war housing estates on which a homogeneous population can indeed have very few social career perspectives, and there may be social 'traps', making it difficult for people to leave certain neighbourhoods. Some of these estates may also be characterised by other problems such as high crime rates and collective social tensions, which occasionally may even lead to urban riots. We can find examples of these estates across Europe. Local specialists and the population in general know where they are to be found. Not surprisingly, such estates are frequently stigmatised.

Nevertheless, academics should not draw conclusions too quickly on the basis of these individual cases. The fact that there are some particular estates that show many problems does not automatically imply that all post-war housing estates are problematic. Neither is it implied that all 'other' housing complexes are free from problems. van Kempen and Musterd (1991), for example, have shown that different blocks of flats with similar physical characteristics, and with similar locations in a city, function very differently owing to the fact that the populations of these flat blocks differ. This type of research suggests that the physical structure – whether homogeneous or not – may not be the crucial explanatory factor.

However, it may nevertheless be the case that the social composition of the blocks is indeed a crucial factor. It is currently suggested that homogeneous physical structures result in homogeneous social profiles and that these have negative impacts on people's social perspectives. Although we investigate these relationships with a critical eye, it makes sense to study these assumptions in today's urban reality. In this chapter we report our study addressing the questions about the relationship between the (physical) housing mix and social opportunities, and the social mix and social opportunities.[1] Before we describe our empirical analysis in which we investigated the associations mentioned, we first take a closer look at the populist and political debate that triggers actions and ideas with regard to the association between housing and social mix and social perspectives in several European countries.

Housing and social mix policies in Europe

Many European politicians and other actors concerned with urban social issues seem to have a predilection for area-based interventions expressed in mixed housing strategies aimed at producing a social mix of the population at the neighbourhood level. Neighbourhood diversification aims have been stated explicitly in countries such as the Netherlands, the UK, France, Germany, Sweden, and Finland. In the Netherlands the call for more diversified neighbourhoods is already deeply entrenched in efforts to create 'balanced' communities. However, the current debate has a closer link with the integration of immigrants, which is considered problematic. This started with a call for income mix in 'differentiated cities', but recently turned into a debate driven by race and ethnicity-related xenophobic suggestions to disperse the poor, and implicitly or explicitly spread immigrants across a wider area to avoid strong concentrations (see Ostendorf et al, 2001; Van Beckhoven and van Kempen, 2003; Musterd, 2003). Mixed neighbourhoods are also increasingly the targets sought in the UK. In the Department of the Environment, Transport and the Regions (DETR) report on 'The state of English cities' (Robson et al, 2000), for example, it was argued that tenure mixing and social mixing are regarded as appropriate policy strategies to overcome the risk of negative neighbourhood effects.

In France, the *politique* aimed at *mixité sociale* is one of the key principles of housing policy. This *politique* is also rooted in the fear of urban 'ghettoisation'. Tenure diversification as a means of achieving a social and perhaps an ethnic mix is again frequently applied. Since public housing is considered to cause increasing segregation because of the narrow social range of tenants and because of the spatial concentration of public housing estates, efforts have been made to rebalance the housing mix. These efforts are supported by a recent Act on 'Solidarité et renouvellement urbain' which sets compulsory minimum percentages of public housing that should be reached in each municipality, with a financial penalty for those municipalities that neglect to take the necessary steps to reach such a goal (Jacquier, 2001).

In Sweden, social mix has been a housing policy goal since 1974-75 but, according to Borevi, analysing the 1970-2000 period, this goal has in practice never been allowed to prevail over freedom of choice for the individual (Borevi, 2002, p 302). Social mix has, however, been a key philosophy in the present area-based urban policy (The Metropolitan Development Initiative), and since the 1970s it has had a key role at a rhetorical level, presupposing negative effects of poor socially homogenous neighbourhoods with a high density of immigrants (Andersson, 2001).

In Finland, there is also a lively debate about the potential effects of homogeneous or heterogeneous housing areas and the related social effects (Kaupinen, 2002). The long periods of moderate inequality these countries experienced before the final decade of the 20th century may explain the high level of intensity of the debate today. In both contexts, the majority of politicians believe that mixed housing would be of benefit to the population as a whole, or at least to the relatively less affluent.

In fact, the basic philosophies of these European policies differ very little from those expressed in the US policies aimed at improving the lives of the poor, such as the 'Moving to Opportunity' programme and HOPE VI. Both the US and several European countries aim at more social spatial mix, since it is believed that this would enhance people's opportunities to bring about better social perspectives for themselves and their children.

The very different historical institutional context and the position of the local housing markets probably explain why this issue is not – as yet – on the agenda in other European regions.

However, we notice that these ideas, debates, and policies tend not to be based on either firm empirical or theoretical support. Most actions are based on certain crucial assumptions. Therefore, in the study reported in this contribution we tested some of these assumptions on the basis of detailed longitudinal data. The focus is on large housing estates in comparison with other housing complexes. We investigated their social characteristics, and paid special attention to the assumptions made, related to whether they were socially homogeneous or heterogeneous (mixed), and what the relationships were with the social perspectives of their inhabitants.

Large housing estates: definitions and data sources

Identifying large housing estates

In most countries the notion of a large housing estate refers specifically to certain aspects of the scale of buildings and thereby to population density (see also Chapter One). Murie et al (2003) have provided us with a background to, and outlined the development of, this housing phenomenon. It is clear that the concept of a large housing estate bears connotations of 'inflexibility', 'mono-functionality', 'monotony', 'high-rise', 'post-war', 'monolithic design', 'mass housing' and 'satellite towns', indicating that large housing estates can be identified by a combination of the type of production method used, housing and area design, scale and location. However, not all these characteristics can or should apply to all countries and cities; the prevalence of high-rise buildings, for instance, is not typical of all large housing estates (see also Power, 1997).

The 'large housing estate' notion is thus difficult to comprehend; it is in any case context-dependent in the sense that building styles, scale, and density vary between cities and countries. Any quantitative study of the phenomenon needs the operationalisation of the concept; some aspects of the notion will doubtless be lost in this process through the lack of adequate statistical information.

Data

In the data available for the Swedish study, it was not possible to take the height of the buildings or the number of dwellings per apartment block or per area directly into account. We did, however, have information at our disposal about the number of residents per neighbourhood and we had information about the distribution of inhabitants between building types (single-family/multi-family housing). The neighbourhood concept used was the SAMS (Small Area Market Statistics) classification developed by Statistics Sweden.

Housing estates

On the basis of this information we made a tentative classification of all areas in Sweden, starting by identifying housing estates dominated by multi-family architecture according to Table 7.1. Table 7.2 shows that only 18 areas have more than 10,000 people residing in multi-family housing. These areas comprised close to 3% of the total population of Sweden in 2000. We label these 'very large multi-family neighbourhoods'. Another 76 areas have between 4,000 and 10,000 residents in multi-family housing. These areas, comprising 5.7% of the Swedish population, are labelled 'large multi-family neighbourhoods'. We also identified a third, somewhat smaller, type of neighbourhood, labelled 'semi-large multi-family neighbourhoods' where the number of people residing in multi-family housing is between 2,000 and 4,000. Taken together the three types of areas accommodate about 1.3 million people (16.4% of the total population).

The sixth type consists of neighbourhoods dominated by single-family houses, the overwhelmingly dominant type of residential area in the SAMS classification system, accounting for more than 60% of the total population.

In Sweden, as elsewhere in Europe, the city cores contain multi-family housing; they have neither the physical nor the social image that would justify the label 'large housing estate'. We have therefore narrowed the concept further by adding 'year of construction' to the identification in a more appropriate operationalisation of the concept. Although some estate-like suburban neighbourhoods were constructed in the 1950s and early 1960s, we chose to select the 'Million Homes Programme' (MP) period as a relevant delimitation of large housing estates, since the MP features the typical locational and structural characteristics of what is normally regarded as a large housing estate in the Swedish context. The MP period was from 1965 to 1974, but

Table 7.1: Neighbourhood classification, first step

Label	Definition
Very large multi-family neighbourhoods	Number of inhabitants in multi-family housing >10,000
Large multi-family neighbourhoods	Number of inhabitants in multi-family housing 4,000-10,000
Semi-large multi-family neighbourhoods	Number of inhabitants in multi-family housing 2,000-3,999
Small multi-family neighbourhoods	Number of inhabitants in multi-family housing 1,000-1,999
Very small multi-family-dominated areas	Number of inhabitants in multi-family housing <1,000
Single-family housing areas	All other areas

Source: GeoSweden00 Database

Table 7.2: Number of areas and inhabitants in 2000 according to neighbourhood structure

Label	Number of areas	Number of inhabitants	% of all inhabitants	Accumulated (%)
Very large multi-family neighbourhoods	18	250,766	2.9	2.9
Large multi-family neighbourhoods	76	497,412	5.7	8.6
Semi-large multi-family neighbourhoods	220	686,406	7.9	16.4
Small multi-family neighbourhoods	620	1,018,984	11.7	28.1
Other multi-family-dominated areas	1,218	807,383	9.2	37.3
Single-family housing areas	6,826	5,482,731	62.7	100.0
Total	8,978	8,743,682	100.0	

Source: GeoSweden00 Database

we adjusted the final year to 1976 to take account of the fact that changing planning practice and building techniques as a response to criticism of the MP took several years. Table 7.3 shows the outcome of a cross-tabulation of the multi-family classification of areas with year of construction, and provides a basis for our final classification of Swedish neighbourhoods, in the sense that the three tinted fields constitute separate categories in the subsequent analysis (see Table 7.4).

Table 7.3: Identification of Million Homes Programme large housing estates: number of inhabitants per neighbourhood type in 2000

Label	Unknown	Construction period				Total
		Before 1946	1946-1964	1965-1976	1977-2001	
Very large MP housing estates	28,824	76,793	33,034	52,208	59,907	250,766
Large MP housing estates	87,599	45,845	129,250	134,558	100,160	497,412
Semi-large MP housing estates	147,539	53,846	157,520	191,785	135,716	686,406
Small housing estates	209,434	92,148	241,897	241,489	234,016	1,018,984
Other multi-family-dominated areas	133,569	93,547	214,827	164,003	201,437	807,383
Single-family housing areas	640,874	1,089,159	988,571	1,283,933	1,480,194	5,482,731
Total	1,247,839	1,451,338	1,765,099	2,067,976	2,211,430	8,743,682

Source: GeoSweden00 Database

The sources used (property registers and population registers) did not provide us with complete information about the construction year for all houses. About 139,000 individuals lack a precise SAMS code; these individuals represent 1.5% of the Swedish population, and they are not included in this analysis at all. Another 17% of all individuals with a SAMS code reside in houses of unknown construction date. It is highly likely that lack of information is a much bigger problem for older properties than for new construction. Hence, the majority of people allocated to the first column in Table 7.3 should in fact be in the second column.

In short, adding in the MP differentiation results in a classification of nine types.

Categories 2, 4, and 6 in Table 7.4 constitute the large MP housing estates; these are first compared with the other categories in terms of demographic profile (gender, age, and country of origin). We then proceed with our analysis of the degree of social mix characterising the nine categories of neighbourhoods and, finally, we address the issue of social opportunity and link these two last issues to policy goals and strategies.

Table 7.4: Final neighbourhood classification scheme

Final classification	Number of inhabitants	%
1 Very large non-MP multi-family neighbourhoods	198,558	2.3
2 Very large MP multi-family neighbourhoods	52,208	0.6
3 Large non-MP multi-family neighbourhoods	362,854	4.1
4 Large MP multi-family neighbourhoods	134,558	1.5
5 Semi-large non-MP multi-family neighbourhoods	494,621	5.7
6 Semi-large MP multi-family neighbourhoods	191,785	2.2
7 Small multi-family neighbourhoods	1,018,984	11.7
8 Very small multi-family-dominated areas	807,383	9.2
9 Single-family housing areas	5,482,731	62.7
Total Sweden	8,743,682	100.0

Source: GeoSweden00 Database

Table 7.5: Gender composition by neighbourhood type in 2000

Neighbourhood type	Men	Women	Total
Very large multi-family neighbourhoods	47.7	52.3	100.0
Very large MP housing estates	48.5	51.5	100.0
Large multi-family neighbourhoods	47.8	52.2	100.0
Large MP housing estates	49.3	50.7	100.0
Semi-large non-MP multi-family neighbourhoods	47.7	52.3	100.0
Semi-large MP housing estates	48.6	51.4	100.0
Small non-MP multi-family neighbourhoods	47.7	52.3	100.0
Very small multi-family neighbourhoods	47.9	52.1	100.0
Single-family housing areas	50.4	49.6	100.0
Total Sweden	49.5	50.5	100.0

Source: GeoSweden00 Database

Demographic and ethnic structure of the housing estates

The RESTATE national background reports provide considerable information about the demographic profile of the large housing estates covered by the project. Some reports state that an ageing process can be ascertained (Węcławowicz et al, 2003, p 47; Pareja Eastaway et al, 2003, pp 49, 98; Aalbers et al, 2003, p 111; Erdősi et al, 2003, p 50) but this tendency does not seem to prevail where there is a substantial influx of new households, as in Kanaleneiland-Noord in Utrecht, for instance (Aalbers et al, 2003, p 129) and Råslätt and Tensta in Sweden

Table 7.6: Age composition by neighbourhood type in 2000

Neighbourhood type	Age groups						
	0-20	20-29	30-49	40-49	50-64	65+	Total
Very large multi-family neighbourhoods	16.5	19.1	19.9	12.6	17.2	14.7	100.0
Very large MP housing estates	22.4	16.7	17.9	12.7	15.8	14.6	100.0
Large multi-family neighbourhoods	19.7	18.1	17.0	12.9	14.9	17.5	100.0
Large MP housing estates	26.1	16.9	15.6	13.1	15.7	12.6	100.0
Semi-large non-MP multi-family neighbourhoods	18.3	18.6	14.7	11.4	16.6	20.4	100.0
Semi-large MP housing estates	24.1	18.9	14.5	11.6	16.0	14.8	100.0
Small non-MP multi-family neighbourhoods	18.5	19.3	14.2	11.3	16.5	20.1	100.0
Very small multi-family neighbourhoods	17.5	19.0	14.5	11.4	16.5	21.2	100.0
Single-family housing areas	27.4	8.8	13.7	14.0	20.5	15.6	100.0
Total Sweden	24.3	12.5	14.2	13.2	18.9	16.9	100.0

Source: GeoSweden00 Database

Table 7.7: Country origin by neighbourhood type in 2000

Neighbourhood type	Sweden	Rest of EU15 and Switzerland, Norway, Iceland	Rest of Europe including Russia	Western Asia	Rest of Asia	Africa	North America and Oceania	South and Central America	Total
Very large multi-family neighbourhoods	83.8	5.4	2.4	3.5	1.3	1.8	0.7	1.2	100.0
Very large MP housing estates	66.9	6.2	3.3	11.0	1.9	7.7	0.5	2.5	100.0
Large multi-family neighbourhoods	80.7	5.6	3.6	4.3	1.7	1.9	0.4	1.8	100.0
Large MP housing estates	65.1	6.8	5.9	11.6	2.9	4.1	0.3	3.3	100.0
Semi-large non-MP multi-family neighbourhoods	82.1	5.1	5.0	4.2	1.3	1.0	0.3	1.0	100.0
Semi-large MP housing estates	72.6	5.4	7.7	8.2	2.1	2.2	0.2	1.5	100.0
Small non-MP multi-family neighbourhoods	83.4	4.6	4.7	3.8	1.3	1.0	0.2	1.0	100.0
Very small multi-family neighbourhoods	86.4	4.5	3.7	2.6	1.0	0.7	0.2	0.7	100.0
Single-family housing areas	93.0	3.6	1.5	0.7	0.6	0.2	0.2	0.3	100.0
Total Sweden	88.9	4.1	2.6	2.1	0.9	0.6	0.2	0.6	100.0

Source: GeoSweden00 Database

(Andersson et al, 2003, pp 39 and 85). An ageing process is, in a way, quite natural in the sense that such a process characterises most European countries and that the estates under consideration were often built several decades ago. New residential areas tend to have younger populations than older estates.

The gender balance does not vary much between the different neighbourhood types in Sweden. The share of people aged under 20 on the MP large housing estates corresponds approximately to the national average (24%), which is a much higher share than for similarly large but non-MP estates. In this particular time period, people over 64 years of age were underrepresented on the MP estates, especially on the large estates (4,000-10,000 people). Finally, all three types of MP housing estates have a much higher presence of immigrants, especially of people originating from the Western part of Asia, Africa, and Latin America.

Meanwhile, the Swedes are clearly clustering in single-family housing neighbourhoods.

The issue of social mix, on the agenda in Swedish housing policy since the early 1970s, has therefore become a racial issue where the debate has concentrated on the clustering of immigrants who are 'different' from the native population (Eriksson et al, 2002). Policies aiming at social mix are normally underpinned by the idea of achieving a different ethnic mix, but official documents speak primarily about class as the primary factor producing and reproducing segregation in cities (for an overview and criticism, see Andersson, 1999). In order to assess the extent to which the class structure of large MP housing estates indeed differs from other types of neighbourhood, we constructed an income-based classification taking the decile composition of male incomes in all neighbourhoods into account. The classification principles are explained below.

Social mix in housing estates

Definition of social mix

The level of social mix is based on the yearly work-related income of all males aged 20-64. Data for 1995 were used. Income deciles were calculated and clustered into three categories: decile 1-3 (that is, the 30% who had the lowest incomes in 1995), decile 4-7 (comprising the next 40%) and decile 8-10 (comprising the top 30%). SAMS areas were then classified according to the following rules:

- Group 1 was excluded from the income classification, because it was the category for sparsely populated areas.
- Group 2 consists of all SAMS areas where the sum of deviations for the three income groups is less than 15% (for example, if 26% of all male income earners in SAMS area x belong to the lowest three deciles, 38% to the middle deciles, and 36% to the highest deciles, then the following outcome is obtained: Abs $(30 - 26)$ + Abs $(40 - 38)$ + Abs $(30 - 36)$ = $4 + 2 + 6 = 12$. Hence, in this particular example the area is regarded as being highly mixed.
- Group 3 contains areas where the sum of deviations is between 15 and 25 and there are more low-income than high-income residents: these areas are called mixed low-income areas.
- Group 4 refers to areas where the sum of deviations is between 15 and 25 and where areas have more high-income than low-income residents: mixed high-income areas.
- Group 5 refers to all areas having a sum of deviations exceeding 25 and mainly low-income residents.
- Group 6 consists of all areas exceeding a score of 25 with mainly high-income residents.
- Consistency checks have been carried out. Most of the known traditionally poor neighbourhoods are in group 5, although a few have been classified as group 3.

Housing estates and social mix: empirical evidence

If we consider the association between housing types and social mix, some interesting facts appear (Table 7.8).

Contrary to many observers' belief, a majority of very large and large MP and non-MP estates can be classified as either highly mixed or mixed income areas. All three types of MP large housing estates contain a higher share of low-income areas, but if account is taken of scale (measured here as number of residents) clearly the semi-large MP estates stand out as the poorest. This type of estate is also the only one where a majority of neighbourhoods are either of a low or a mixed low-income type. A possible explanation for this is the fact that the large estates in Gothenburg and Malmö, where we find the highest concentrations of deprived neighbourhoods in Sweden, are often split into smaller statistical units.

The overall conclusion must be that multi-family neighbourhoods are very seldom high-income areas but also that by no means all large housing estates are marked by socially homogeneous populations.

Table 7.8: Income homogeneity in different types of neighbourhoods: percentage of all residents in 2000

Neighbourhood type	Areas with less than 10 persons	Male income homogeneity					Total
		Highly mixed areas	Mixed low income areas	Mixed high income areas	Low income areas	High income areas	
Very large multi-family neighbourhoods	0.0	77.9	1.4	11.0	9.6	0.0	100.0
Very large MP housing estates	0.0	49.1	17.0	7.9	25.9	0.0	100.0
Large multi-family neighbourhoods	0.0	65.8	21.8	5.3	7.1	0.0	100.0
Large MP housing estates	0.0	50.5	23.7	1.9	23.9	0.0	100.0
Semi-large non-MP multi-family neighbourhoods	0.0	53.6	23.2	3.1	19.5	0.6	100.0
Semi-large MP housing estates	0.0	35.8	27.4	1.3	34.8	0.6	100.0
Small non-MP multi-family neighbourhoods	0.0	49.1	27.8	2.4	20.4	0.4	100.0
Very small multi-family neighbourhoods	0.2	45.3	29.3	3.7	20.5	1.1	100.0
Single-family housing areas	0.1	45.5	11.7	16.2	4.7	21.7	100.0
Total Sweden	0.1	47.9	16.6	11.5	10.1	13.8	100.0

Source: GeoSweden00 Database

Housing estates and social opportunity

Many large housing estates are socially mixed, but what about social careers? Before we discuss that issue we consider the relationship between social mobility and residential mobility. We know that approximately half the population of the larger estates in Stockholm has moved out within the last five or six years (Andersson and Bråmå, 2004). Many of the movers have been able to take some steps in a social career and have moved on to another area, which they regard to be more attractive. We also know that new residents entering the estates have a much lower level of labour market integration than out-migrants and stayers. These differences between immigrants, stayers, and movers led us to the decision to focus on stayers. We calculated the percentage of all neighbourhood stayers aged 25-59 in 2000 who, for the 1995-2000 period, were employed both in 1995 and in 1999.

Table 7.9 shows that the percentage of all neighbourhood stayers employed in 1995 and 1999 in the selected age groups is generally quite high, although it varies with residence. People living in the MP estates seem to be more likely to have been out of work for either or both these years than do people resident elsewhere. The effect is greater for people with a short school education although, as can be seen in Figure 7.1, lower levels of employment in MP estates are noticeable for all educational categories.

Scale and housing type do not seem to tell us much about employment trajectories or employment prospects. The noticeable effects are most obviously connected to the MP areas and can probably be attributed to the prevailing stigmatisation and bad reputation that such areas have in most Swedish cities. We are not talking about neighbourhood effects as such – although such effects may occur – but we are probably looking at the outcome of a selection process (which occurred before 1995) where people with less choice, in particular immigrants, were either directed to these neighbourhoods by institutional actors or faced a housing market situation where they could enter only those neighbourhoods where vacancies appeared more often.

Social mix and social opportunities

As previously suggested, it is possible that it is the social mix levels and not the physical structures that are responsible for reduced social perspectives. To investigate this possibility further, we calculated the association between social mix and social opportunities (being (un)able

Table 7.9: Change in employment status 1995-99 for people aged 25-59 (in 2000) residing in the same neighbourhood 1995-2000

| Neighbourhood type | Employed 1995-99 | Change in employment 1995-99 | | | Total |
		Employed 1995 Unemployed 1999	Unemployed 1995 Employed 1999	Unemployed 1995-99	
Very large multi-family neighbourhoods	88.6	3.4	5.3	2.7	100.0
Very large MP housing estates	79.3	4.4	8.2	8.0	100.0
Large multi-family neighbourhoods	86.5	3.6	6.3	3.6	100.0
Large MP housing estates	81.7	4.4	7.6	6.3	100.0
Semi-large non-MP multi-family neighbourhoods	84.6	3.9	6.4	5.1	100.0
Semi-large MP housing estates	81.7	4.2	8.3	5.7	100.0
Small non-MP multi-family neighbourhoods	83.6	4.1	6.7	5.6	100.0
Very small multi-family neighbourhoods	84.8	4.0	6.1	5.0	100.0
Single-family housing areas	90.3	2.8	4.4	2.6	100.0
Total Sweden	88.7	3.1	5.0	3.3	100.0

Source: GeoSweden00 Database

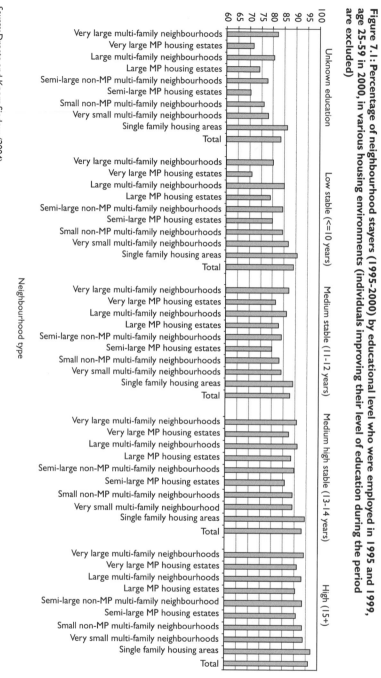

Figure 7.1: Percentage of neighbourhood stayers (1995-2000) by educational level who were employed in 1995 and 1999, age 25-59 in 2000, in various housing environments (individuals improving their level of education during the period are excluded)

Source: Droste and Knorr-Siedow (2004)

Figure 7.2: Percentage of individuals who remain employed in the period 1991-99 per social mix environment and per educational attainment level for 1991-95

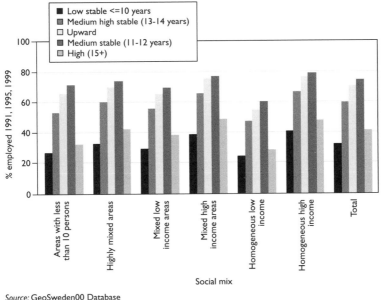

Source: GeoSweden00 Database

to stay in employment) (Figure 7.2). The results show us the percentage of individuals who were able to stay in employment during the 1990s while living in a different social environment and while characterised by different levels of educational achievement in the first half of the 1990s. The reason why we looked at the longer 1990–99 period was related to the fact that we could then include educational performance in the first half of the 1990s and measure its effects on social opportunities. Indeed, a clear relationship between employment opportunities and education can be seen; however, there is also a systematic effect of the social environment, in the sense that the effect occurs for each educational attainment level. We may notice that those who live in homogeneous low-income neighbourhoods have the lowest chance of remaining employed throughout the period under investigation, but that chances are also much lower than for those who live in mixed low-income environments. Those who improve their educational level are difficult to deal with in these types of analysis through the mere fact that being engaged in educational programmes increases the risk of not being employed. The reader should not view the weak performance of those moving educationally upward as evidence for declaring that education does not pay off.

Those who live in a more affluent homogeneous environment have the highest chances of remaining employed; this also holds true for people in these areas who have only moderate educational attainment levels.

Conclusions

Housing mix and social mix ideologies rank high in current social policies in European cities, as we have shown in our short overview of recent urban policy practices. However, the question is, are such ideologies legitimised? Here we have shown that the association between housing mix and social mix is not very strong. Multi-family neighbourhoods are very seldom high-income areas, but it is also true that by no means all large housing estates have exclusively socially homogeneous and socially weak populations. Scale and housing type do not seem to tell us much about employment trajectories or employment prospects. That is not to say that there is no relationship between physical and social structure. There is a concentration of immigrants and of socially weak households in the areas dominated by the Million Homes Programme. These areas are stigmatised and many of them have a poor reputation. Their population structures are probably the outcome of a selection process where people with less choice, in particular immigrants, are either directed to these neighbourhoods by institutional actors, or they are faced with a housing market situation where they can only enter those neighbourhoods where vacancies often appear because the mobility rates are higher there. Nevertheless, there are also MP areas with a more mixed population.

When we turn our attention to the social dimension it can be shown that the social environment has a systematic effect. Those people who live in homogeneous low-income neighbourhoods have the lowest likelihood of having remained employed throughout the period under investigation, and chances are much lower than for those who live in mixed low-income environments.

These findings suggest that some physical structures (the MP structures) relate to social opportunities, but not all large estates can automatically be regarded as problematic. A clear association, with greater differences between the social categories than we could show for the physical housing categories, could be found between social structures and social opportunities. These opportunities need not, however, be caused by the composition of the area; the causal relationship could be the other way around: households with a certain social level may settle, or may have to settle, in areas with a specific social character. Moreover, the analyses regarding the relationship between physical structure and social opportunity refer only to the 1995-99 period (when the economy was in an upswing), while the analyses regarding the relationship between the social structure and social opportunities refer to the longer 1991-99 period (with downward and upward shifts in the economy). These economic fluctuations may potentially have affected the outcomes of the analyses. Our final words have therefore not yet been spoken. Housing theory and housing practice should be based on robust research outcomes before conclusions are drawn. Our aim was to contribute to the body of robust research, but we have to admit that further investigation of the impact and kind of association between physical and social compositions and social perspectives is still required.

Notes

[1] We do so using the GeoSweden00 Database. This database is also used in Chapter Nine by Bråmå and Andersson. There they clarify both the character and the destinations of out-migration flows.

References

Aalbers, M., Van Beckhoven, E., van Kempen, R., Musterd, S. and Ostendorf, W. (2003) *Large housing estates in the Netherlands: Overview of developments and problems in Amsterdam and Utrecht*, Utrecht: Urban and Regional research centre Utrecht, Faculty of Geosciences, Utrecht University.

Andersson, R. (1999) 'Divided cities as a policy based notion in Sweden', *Housing Studies*, vol 14, no 5, pp 601-24.

Andersson, R. (2001) 'Spaces of socialisation and social network competition – a study of neighbourhood effects in Stockholm, Sweden', in H.T. Andersen and R. van Kempen (eds) *Social exclusion, social fragmentation and urban governance*, Aldershot: Ashgate, pp 149-88.

Andersson, R. and Bråmå, Å. (2004) 'Selective migration in Swedish distressed neighbourhoods: can area-based urban policies counteract segregation processes?', *Housing Studies*, vol 19, no 4, pp 517-39.

Andersson, R., Molina, I., Öresjö, E., Pettersson, L. and Siwertsson, C. (2003) *Large housing estates in Sweden: Overview of developments and problems in Jönköping and Stockholm*, Utrecht: Urban and Regional research centre Utrecht, Faculty of Geosciences, Utrecht University.

Borevi, K. (2002) 'Välfärdsstaten i det mångkulturella samhället', series: Skrifter utgivna av Statsvetenskapliga föreningen i Uppsala, 151, doctoral thesis, Uppsala: Acta Universitatis Upsaliensis, Department of Political Science, Uppsala University.

Erdösi, S., Geröházi, É., Teller, N. and Tosics, I. (2003) *Large housing estates in Hungary: overview of developments and problems in Budapest and Nyíregyháza*, Utrecht: Urban and Regional research centre Utrecht, Faculty of Geosciences, Utrecht University.

Eriksson, U., Molina, I. and Ristilammi, P.M. (2002) *Miljonprogram och media. Föreställningar om människor och förorter*, Norrköping/Stockholm: Integrationsverket and Riksantikvarieämbetet.

GeoSweden00 Database, Institute for Housing and Urban Research, Uppsala University.

Jacquier, C. (2001) 'Urban fragmentation and revitalisation policies in France: a new urban governance in the making', in H.T. Andersen and R. van Kempen (eds) *Social exclusion, social fragmentation and urban governance*, Aldershot: Ashgate, pp 321-46.

Kaupinen, T.M. (2002) 'The beginning of immigrant settlement in the Helsinki metropolitan area and the role of social housing', *Journal of Housing and the Built Environment*, vol 17, no 2, pp 173-97.

Murie, A., Knorr-Siedow, T. and van Kempen, R. (2003) *Large housing estates in Europe: General developments and theoretical backgrounds*, Utrecht: Urban and Regional research centre Utrecht, Faculty of Geosciences, Utrecht University.

Musterd, S. (2003) 'Segregation and integration: a contested relationship', *Journal of Ethnic and Migration Studies*, vol 29, no 4, pp 623-41.

Ostendorf, W., Musterd, S. and De Vos, S. (2001) 'Social mix and the neighbourhood-effect: policy-ambition and empirical support', *Housing Studies*, vol 16, no 3, pp 371-80.

Pareja-Eastaway, M., Tapada-Berteli, T., van Boxmeer, B. and Garcia Ferrando, L. (2003) *Large housing estates in Spain: Overview of developments and problems in Madrid and Barcelona*, Utrecht: Urban and Regional research centre Utrecht, Faculty of Geosciences, Utrecht University.

Power, A. (1997) *Estates on the edge: the social consequences of mass housing in Northern Europe*, London: MacMillan.

Robson, B., Parkinson, M., Boddy, M. and Maclennan, D. (2000) *The state of English cities*, London: Department of the Environment, Transport and the Regions (DETR).

van Beckhoven, E. and van Kempen, R. (2003) 'Social effects of urban restructuring: a case study in Amsterdam and Utrecht, the Netherlands', *Housing Studies*, vol 18, no 6, pp 853-75.

van Kempen, E. and Musterd, S. (1991) 'High-rise housing reconsidered: some research and policy implications', *Housing Studies*, vol 6, no 2, pp 83-95.

Węcławowicz, G., Kosłowski, S. and Bajek, R. (2003) *Large housing estates in Poland: overview of developments and problems in Warsaw*, Utrecht: Urban and Regional research centre Utrecht, Faculty of Geosciences, Utrecht University.

EIGHT

On physical determinism and displacement effects

Sako Musterd and Wim Ostendorf

Problems and questions

Housing estate restructuring tends to target specific areas that need to be restructured. Usually the areas involved are clearly delineated spaces. A main topic of social science research, which aims to evaluate restructuring policies, is also targeting these areas, concentrating on the direct impacts of the physical restructuring processes in the areas themselves. There appears to be a long tradition of area-based regeneration in many Western European countries, while in Central and Eastern Europe the process of regeneration started much more recently. In England, Estate Action, City Challenge, and the Single Regeneration Budget programmes are examples; there is also a debate in France about the relative merits of area-based action (*Développement Social des Quartiers*; *Grand Projet de Ville*), although conurbation-wide intervention strategies are also discussed (*Contrats de Ville*). Usually the results of evaluations of such area-based programmes, undertaken soon after the restructuring, are positive because of the physical upgrading of the area.

With respect to the social upgrading of an area, the results are less clear: sometimes social upgrading does take place, but often only because new residents have replaced the original inhabitants. Evaluation after a number of years often results in a more negative picture: new physical decay and new social downgrading have again become manifest. However, in addition to any drastic social or physical effects there may be in the areas under consideration, the restructuring can also have quite serious short-term or long-term effects on other areas. These effects are often neglected in evaluation studies.

Such effects need not be entirely negative, however. Some people may have moved from the area under consideration to better housing and a better environment. The income or household situations of those involved, who had to move as a result of the restructuring process, could have developed in a way that made the household ready to move anyway. However, the reverse may also be true. Highly problematic households (the long-term unemployed, anti-social tenants) may have been pushed towards the next weakest segments of the housing market. Their move to these areas will result in a reduction of the social level of the areas in which they settle. Such an effect is particularly disappointing when the main aim of the restructuring process was of a social nature, because the upgrading of the area under consideration is then compensated by the downgrading of adjacent areas, undermining the total balance. In connection with this issue of pushing the problem on to another neighbourhood, the question to be addressed is: to what extent is the resolution of the perceived problem looked for in the right direction?

This chapter helps answering the question posed in the first chapter of this book: "What types of image and vision of large estates are emerging?". The question of the beneficiaries of estate regeneration and the effects on other parts of the city (spillover effects) is closely related to the images and visions of large estates, as described in Chapter Three. The displacement effect problem is strongly related to the basic assumption of physical determinism that underlies many restructuring efforts, that is, the idea that physical intervention will resolve the social problems of those who have lived in the physically targeted estates. In other words, displacement effects embody part of the relationship between physical intervention and social impact and should therefore be taken into account when evaluating restructuring.

This contribution addresses these two related issues through three questions:

- What do the literature and experience teach us about the relationship between social and physical problems and solutions?
- What do the literature and experience teach us about the negative and positive impacts of displacing people from the restructured housing estates?
- What empirical indications can be found regarding the displacement effects of the recent restructuring projects in Amsterdam, the Netherlands?

The answers to these questions put forward in the following three sections may help to adjust the level of expectations with regard to housing restructuring processes and contribute to the debate about what may be the proper policies in various physical and social contexts.

In the fourth section we present some empirical illustrations, specifically derived from the City Monitor of Amsterdam, to illustrate the (lack of) relationship between physical and social problems. This will be followed by some conclusions.

Physical interventions to solve social problems

As suggested in the introduction, it is not exceptional for policy makers to believe in physical determinism and use the instrument of physical restructuring to resolve social problems. In fact, the suggestion that there is a link between the physical and social condition of an area is increasingly supported via two policy trends that seem to prevail in Europe today. One refers to the emphasis on the use of 'integrated' policy programmes. Although this concept is vague, many policy makers derive from it the belief that they should deal with physical, social, and economic interventions simultaneously. This kind of integration suggests that there are strong relationships between these dimensions, which can easily result in the development of physical plans to resolve social problems. The second policy trend that supports the linking of physical and social issues is area-oriented targeting. The suggestion here is that most problems are capable of being resolved within a specific area. If these problems are predominantly social, physical measures will also still be directed to these areas.

Abundant examples illustrate the suggested link between the physical and social conditions of housing estates. The most obvious examples refer to the – partial – demolition of estates even though they were physically still of good quality. Such demolition has happened all over the world. The most infamous estate – demolished as an answer to social problems only 18 years after completion – was the Pruitt-Igoe complex in St Louis (US); but the large-scale demolitions in places such as Vaulx-en-Velin, Lyon; Castle Vale, Birmingham, UK; and Bijlmermeer in Amsterdam, have not passed unnoticed. Perhaps Bijlmermeer will even reach the top of the list of 'powerful' interventions in post-war housing. Approximately 30 years after they were built more than half of all the 13,000 high-rise dwellings in that area, all of good quality, will have been demolished; several more will have been reconverted and renovated.

These kinds of strategy are not exceptional. They had already seen the light of day in the 1970s and 1980s, when physical structures were frequently blamed for the existence of many social problems. As soon as the first 'modern' functionalist housing estates were built they were subjected to severe criticism, and by association were rapidly linked to social problems of all kinds. Coleman (1985), for example, made a strong impact on the debate with her book, *Utopia on Trial*. She stated explicitly that there was a direct relationship between the number of storeys of an apartment block and the presence of social problems. Before her, Oscar Newman (1972) had also argued that there was a direct relationship between high-rise estates and the crime levels to be encountered on them.

These viewpoints did not remain without criticism. It could, for example, be shown that the association between apartment blocks and crime disappeared after controlling for the presence of young children. In general, the link between physical characteristics (number of storeys, number of entrances per building, and so forth) and social characteristics (vandalism, graffiti, unemployment, and so forth) is strong, but most probably caused by a third set of intermediary variables, such as the housing allocation strategies of local government authorities (putting 'problem families' into unpopular neighbourhoods). In such cases these intermediary variables ought to be surveyed, and the policies connected to them analysed and changed, rather than embarking on extensive physical improvements. Nevertheless, those who took pleasure in showing that tough physical interventions – the demolition of estates, for example – were required to resolve the social problems on the estates ('salvation through bricks') gratefully accepted the basic ideas of academics such as Coleman and Newman. Not surprisingly, rather mechanistic urban decay theories in which the type of development, the design, and management played a large part, gained firm support in that context (see Prak and Priemus, 1985).

Eva van Kempen and Sako Musterd (1991) have shown that only in the second half of the 1980s and in the 1990s did critical views receive more attention. It could be shown that social problems also existed in low-rise housing; and that identical apartment blocks with similar locations were functioning either well or poorly, largely depending on who was living in them. More attention was also paid in research to developments in both well-functioning and poorly functioning apartment blocks, whereas previously the focus had often been limited to the 'problem estates', which was methodologically unjustifiable. The wider urban contexts and the (lack of) tension in the housing market were also included in new research. The overall conclusion from this and related research was that the differences between the apartment blocks in terms of social problems could not be ascribed to the physical structures or to the management. Occupancy differences were found to account for some of the problems and differences in the occupancy rates of identical apartment blocks could be explained by the structure of the housing market and to the history of occupancy.

However, support for large-scale housing restructuring, aimed particularly at the post-war high-rise estates, has continued up to the present day. This continuation may partially be understood by the fact that physical interventions, through demolition or otherwise, do not always aim to bring back the former residents or resolve the social problems in the metropolitan area. In other words, it may be argued that many renewal efforts are actually only aimed at elevating or gentrifying the area under consideration. If that were indeed the objective, displacement would be a logical outcome of such efforts (see next section). However, this strategy is seldom expressed openly as a deliberate policy. On the contrary: in certain eras such as the 1980s, substantial efforts were made in several countries to improve the opportunities for the 'sitting tenants', to resolve the social problems 'on site', and to raise the social level at that very location. Urban renewal strategies were targeted at 'renewal for the neighbourhood', which implied that the policies were directed at the residents who lived in these areas. These socially driven efforts – the restructuring of the Amsterdam Bijlmermeer may serve as an example – may indeed have prevented the extensive displacement from these neighbourhoods that would certainly have occurred if the restructuring process had been left to the private sector. However, the social upgrading of the neighbourhood resulting from the input of huge amounts of public money may only have been moderate (Musterd, 1991, p 37). This seems to have contributed to the feeling expressed by some that the outcomes had not been successful. Politicians wondered disappointedly why the social problems were still there, even after so much money had been 'put into the neighbourhood'. Their disappointment revealed that they had actually expected there to be a relationship between intense, publicly funded physical renewal and social renewal. That there clearly was none may have been one of the reasons for changing the type of policy occasionally from 'for the neighbourhood' to 'for the city', or to raise the efforts aimed at physical changes. Both responses allowed for a continuation of policies aimed at solving social problems through physical interventions.

The points mentioned above can be illustrated by the current discussion regarding urban restructuring in the Netherlands: the Big Cities Policy. This policy is based on domains or 'pillars'. The economic pillar receives the most direct Big Cities Policy funds while the physical pillar in effect receives the largest sums of money. Actually, there are two sorts of pillar: the physical pillar on the one hand and the social and economic pillars on the other. Their coexistence enables us to reveal the tensions in the debate about the key character of the problems and of the solutions for them. Urban restructuring decisions are linked to the physical dimension. Buildings may be dilapidated in technical terms, or in terms of standards by which they may be judged to be unfit for human habitation. This dilapidation could be a reason to demolish or restructure the units and to create better alternatives. The problems may also be labelled 'social problems': this classification applies when we find large numbers of unemployed people or residents who in other ways do not participate well in society. In addition to the unemployed, these problem residents include drug addicts, (petty) criminals, low-skilled and poorly educated people, and so on. The physical and social dimensions may occur simultaneously. The solutions defined for the social or physical problems may be either socioeconomic or physical. On the basis of these ideas it makes sense to distinguish between three types of combinations of problems and solutions, as shown in Table 8.1. One combination does not seem to be logical from the outset: trying to solve a physical problem with socioeconomic policies is hardly logical. The other three policies, however, may well be possible.

From our point of view the most logical combinations are those marked with an 'X'. In such a direct intervention, physical problems are approached via physical solutions; the case study of the Budapest Havanna estate in the RESTATE project might serve as an example here (Szemzö and Tosics, 2004). Interventions were aimed at improving public spaces and introducing a CCTV system. The other type of direct intervention consists of tackling social problems through social measures; as illustrated by the Stockholm case in the RESTATE project (Öresjö et al, 2004). The Dutch experience, however, can be characterised as an indirect intervention and is represented by 'O'. That combination is complicated, and is referred to as 'salvation through bricks'. Various assumptions are required to defend a policy intervention in which physical change takes precedence, while the problems have

Table 8.1: The association between types of problem analyses and types of policy solutions

		Problem analysis	
		Socioeconomic	Physical
Solution	Socioeconomic	X	
	Physical	O	X

Source: own research

been defined as social. These assumptions relate to the idea that the physical structure has a large impact on people's well-being and mental health and that it is precisely these conditions of well-being and mental health that are the crucial parameters conditioning the social problems that arise, such as unemployment, criminality, and deviant behaviour. It is often difficult to support these assumptions; nevertheless, they form a crucial element of the Dutch Big Cities Policies and the related restructuring policy.

Displacement through housing restructuring

The restructuring of housing, or urban renewal, has resulted in displacement for as long as this process has taken place. There is every reason to state that the social consequences of this displacement were more severe in the past and for the working class than in the present and for the middle or upper classes. This assertion relates to the part that immediate residential environments, such as estates and neighbourhoods, play in the everyday life of their residents. A short overview of the changing importance of these direct environments will make this point clear.

Until 1850 or 1900 the local residential environment, usually referred to as the neighbourhood, formed the territorial framework within which almost all inhabitants used to spend their daily lives. Within the neighbourhood, one found work, housing, social relationships and, as far as time allowed, recreation. Frankenberg (1969, pp 249, 255) describes examples of such neighbourhoods. This local orientation was an unavoidable consequence of the very limited opportunities for mobility in those days: a lack of free time and a lack of means of transport made it impossible to move out of one's own neighbourhood. The dispersal of population and services at the neighbourhood level therefore depended completely on the dispersal of jobs (Vance, 1966). Within such neighbourhoods one found employer and employee, doctor and patients, poor and prosperous, young and old. In other words, these local communities were evenly balanced and characterised by a heterogeneous composition in social respects. Communities were also quite stable, based on the presence of families and firms with strong local roots. This stability also resulted in a local identity in cultural respects based on the traditions of generations. Such neighbourhoods used to form well-integrated functional units. The basis for integration was local autonomy and the resulting strong mutual dependencies and functional relationships between the residents in almost all aspects of life. The presence of different social classes did not form any impediment to this integration. The coordination of interaction was self-evidently based on the functional mutual dependencies. That is not to say that mutual feelings were invariably warm and sincere. But the mutual dependency and the fact that meeting each other was unavoidable resulted in the evolution of 'local rules', which avoided the occurrence of open conflicts (Frankenberg, 1969). The strength of this integration implies that breaking up such communities as a result of urban renewal would result in strong social effects and strong feelings of displacement.

However, the situation of neighbourhoods as functional units has changed completely during the last hundred years. The continuously increasing opportunities for moving in time and space – shorter working hours, faster and private means of transport, and more money to pay for transport – opened up opportunities for many households to increase the distance between their place of residence and their place of work. This move enabled them to pay more attention to their individual preferences regarding housing. This process resulted in new forms of socio-spatial differentiation. Population categories with specific social characteristics, especially regarding income, the presence of children, and cultural identity, concentrated in residential environments that fitted their preferences and their (financial) resources, resulting in urban social areas, such as 'gold coasts', middle-class neighbourhoods, and working-class neighbourhoods. This process started in cities, but in later phases also applied to metropolitan regions, giving rise to suburban areas housing families and urban areas with smaller households, fitting in with lifestyles that aimed at familism in suburban areas or careerism in urban areas (Bell, 1968).

In this situation the functional unit is no longer the neighbourhood or the estate, but the metropolitan region. The 'ideal' neighbourhood is no longer heterogeneous or balanced, but homogeneous with respect to a certain category of household. Selective migration adds to this homogeneity. And the increasing variety of households with regard to income and number of jobs within the household, the presence or absence of children, and cultural and ethnic background, sharpen this differentiation between neighbourhoods. The neighbourhood is also no longer an experience for the complete lifetime of the residents, but a choice for a particular phase of the lifecycle. In this connection Stein (1960) even speaks of the eclipse of the community. Neighbourhoods are therefore less stable and more sensitive to change than previously observed. Urban neighbourhoods with predominantly rented accommodation can change particularly quickly; suburban neighbourhoods with a large proportion of owner-occupiers tend to be more stable.

In this situation, the neighbourhood is a place where a household finds fitting accommodation in a location that suits their specific characteristics. Similar kinds of household will be found there, not other kinds, but 'our sort of people'. This homogeneity is appreciated, because it helps create smooth social relationships and prevent conflict in a situation that is not based on mutual dependencies. Small social distances make social relationships easier and help people to anticipate successfully the norms and values of others. Social integration is not based on a functional unit, but is now based on homogeneity in a social respect: that is, on similarity in terms of social characteristics (Ostendorf and Vijgen, 1982).

Returning to the issue of the social consequences of urban renewal for the neighbourhoods of today, it is important to realise that not all neighbourhoods are the same. Long-established working-class neighbourhoods with strong ties of family and kinship do show a particularly strong social integration and a relatively weak orientation to the outside world (Bott, 1957). Breaking up such communities for the sake of urban renewal results in strong social effects; people will be relocated, but their patterns of social interaction will disappear (Young and Wilmott, 1957). But most neighbourhoods are very different from such communities. A much stronger orientation towards and relationship with the world outside the neighbourhood, especially for the middle class with a cosmopolitan orientation, has resulted in a steady decline of social ties within the neighbourhood; as a consequence, social integration in the neighbourhood has become less intense. Neighbourhoods have developed into communities of limited liability. This decline justifies the view that the need to move to another neighbourhood has less social impact than in earlier days; and also that social impact is greater for working-class people than for the middle and upper classes. But that is not to say that the social consequences have become of no significance. Research shows that even today a move to another neighbourhood results in a decrease in social relationships and activities within the neighbourhood (van Beckhoven and van Kempen, 2002).

In line with this argument is the situation where vulnerable people in particular, that is those in the weakest position on the labour and housing markets, can become the victims of urban restructuring. In the first place they are often among the few who are more dependent on their neighbourhood than others; and second, they are less able to pay for the housing that becomes more expensive after restructuring.

Consequently, they have to move to another place. The policy documents that accompany the restructuring process usually claim that the restructuring is aimed primarily at improving the lives of those who are already living on the estate involved. Moreover, it is often stated that most of the residents will be able to return to the renewed neighbourhood. For those who cannot do so, or cannot afford the new rents, special support programmes are said to be available to help them settle in an adequate new housing situation. These expressions of policy can be found everywhere in the Western world. They refer to the social nature of housing policies.

However, the more critical literature on urban restructuring often suggests that the restructuring processes are rarely based on enlightened social motives, such as preserving social relationships in the neighbourhood, but that the aims and objectives of the major suppliers in the process, such as bank presidents and property managers, are the real initiators (see Logan and Molotch, 1987). This will more often be the case in situations where the private sector is dominant rather than those in which the public sector takes the lead.

However, even in these cases, restructuring activities may easily result in the need for the displacement of part of the population. Because the renewed neighbourhoods are most likely to have become more expensive in terms of the monthly payments households need to pay, there will be a tendency for those from the weaker social strata to be overrepresented in the category that has to move elsewhere. These processes of displacement of the socially weaker households, often regarded as 'displacing the poor' (or worse, displacing the 'problems'), have strong parallels with what happens in cities when gentrification processes take off, with all kinds of social sorting processes as a result. The gentrification of an area will result in an influx of financially better-off people in the areas concerned. Consequently, the service structure will change. The changes will result in a displacement of the poor, who simply cannot afford the more expensive housing and services available in the neighbourhood; but many other characteristics of the neighbourhood may also change through displacement.

Schumacher and Leitner (1999) provide a clear example of these 'other' effects that may accompany new investments in existing areas. Their focus was on criminal activity. They looked at the differential levels of investment in downtown Baltimore and noticed that the huge investments in the city's renewal projects, including along the waterfront at the Inner Harbor, helped discourage criminal activity in these areas, but simultaneously served as the mechanism for wide-scale shifts in criminal activity. The increased presence of security personnel, improved street lighting, and increased pedestrian traffic in the inner city worked as 'push' factors. Hotspot analysis revealed that new concentrations of criminal behaviour had emerged outside the areas of re-investment. The authors conclude:

> Those living outside of the redeveloped areas of Fells Point and the Inner Harbor have largely not benefited from these programmes. Furthermore, the possible displacement of criminal activity into these neighbourhoods suggests that they may have even been harmed (albeit indirectly) by these redevelopment projects.

Overall, the literature on upgrading and gentrification is rather negative as regards the effects these processes have on the population who had previously lived in the area concerned. This negative opinion is clearly expressed by Atkinson (2002) who, in a literature review of this topic, concluded:

> The overwhelming evidence from existing research on the neighbourhood impacts of gentrification concern its negative influences and there is a strong cumulative weight to this evidence – particularly with regard to population displacement of the most physically vulnerable and deprived households.

However, not everyone shares this conclusion. Hamnett (2003), for instance, argues that gentrification is best explained as the social and spatial manifestation of the transition from an industrial to a post-industrial economy based on financial, business, and creative services, with associated changes in the nature and location of work, in the occupational class structure, earnings and incomes, and the structure of the housing market. With respect to the extensive gentrification-induced displacement in London, he states that it may be more appropriate to view this process as one of replacement, not displacement.

   Evidently, considerable attention is being paid to displacement in urban renewal and restructuring processes. That is not to say, however, that extensive geographical studies have been carried out aimed at arriving at a full understanding of the social–spatial effects of restructuring. There are several cross-sectional and even some longitudinal studies that have followed those displaced, but these just focus on the (dis)satisfaction or social opportunities of displaced people

(Lyons, 1996; Atkinson, 2000; Kleinhans and Kruythoff, 2002). However, it is not known whether, or how quickly, new spatial concentrations of socially deprived households develop. In contrast with the feelings of displacement and loss of community in old working-class neighbourhoods, the majority of residents displaced nowadays harbour no negative feelings regarding their displacement. Many simply take the opportunity, often financially supported, to move to a (slightly) better house in another environment. Moreover, some of those who have to be displaced, because of demolition, for example, will have improved their own financial situation and so will aim for better and more expensive housing opportunities. However, nothing is known about the new sifting and sorting processes that are going on in social terms or about the development of new concentrations of socially weak households in the 'social problem areas'. The claim is often made that all the displaced people will become dispersed, and so poverty will be de-concentrated. However, we are not aware of any evidence in the literature to support this statement. Urban theory leads us to believe that housing market processes and demand and supply interactions will rapidly result in new concentrations of residents who find themselves at the lower end of the socioeconomic ladder. Therefore, the urban nomads, or 'restructuring nomads' as they are sometimes labelled, will probably pop up again in areas that in their turn will be found at the new bottom end of the housing market. In other words, dispersal per se will not resolve the problems of the population involved; resolving the problems of disadvantaged population categories demands more than just moving these people on to another neighbourhood.

Displacement through restructuring: empirical indications in the municipality of Amsterdam

The Amsterdam experience of urban restructuring shows an increasing anticipation of problems of displacement by involving the residents in the process in some respects. In the 1960s, urban renewal did not lead to any form of collaboration with the residents. Urban renewal meant a complete destruction of the housing stock and offering the residents alternative housing in other neighbourhoods. This form of urban renewal was criticised for not being to the benefit of the residents involved. As a reaction to this experience, urban renewal in the 1970s took the interests of the residents as the fundamental point of departure. Urban renewal then concentrated completely on housing for the urban poor. In neighbourhoods with poor housing conditions, urban renewal realised the construction of new buildings and, at a later stage, the improvement of existing houses, not for new residents, but for the underprivileged residents already living in that area ('building for the neighbourhood'). In line with that objective, urban renewal was aimed at maintaining the inexpensive social housing stock.

Towards the end of the 1980s it was realised that this emphasis on poor residents and their housing provision did not really improve the city and that this form of urban renewal did not prevent the downgrading of the city. A new form of urban renewal, 'urban revitalisation', was therefore introduced with different objectives: not housing needs, but the reinforcement of the urban economy was the most important aim. In addition to this urban revitalisation, a policy of social renewal was put into place.

This policy concentrated on the improvement of social cohesion within neighbourhoods, but was soon replaced by the Big Cities Policy. Based on the framework of this policy, the urban restructuring of the Bijlmermeer, which started in the early 1990s, is now taking place. The Big Cities Policy concentrates on urban neighbourhoods where a relatively large proportion of the population has a low income, and aims to decrease that proportion. The idea of the policy is to change the composition of the population via the housing stock of the neighbourhood: low-cost accommodation has to be demolished and replaced by more expensive houses in order to create a mix of dwellings and to attract more well-to-do households to the neighbourhood. At a later stage this aim changed somewhat from attracting new well-to-do households to offering better opportunities to the existing residents of the neighbourhood to enable them to continue to be housed within the same area; that is, the need for them to go to another neighbourhood to find other accommodation was avoided (van Kempen, 2000). Apart from this ambition to make the housing stock more differentiated, the image of the Bijlmermeer is changing completely. The construction of the Bijlmermeer was based on the ideas of Le Corbusier: a 'modern', 'functional' or even 'radiant' city for 'the new man' in the form of high-rise apartment blocks with a complete separation of living, working, traffic, and recreation. There was no private space, such as individual gardens or individual parking lots, but common amenities, such as parks and parking garages. The restructuring seeks to create the opposite scenario: no separation of functions, single-family houses with private gardens and individual parking spaces. In this process of urban restructuring, extra attention is paid to achieving the collaboration of the residents. Although this collaboration can never be expected to be perfect, and will always be open to improvement, it seems fair to expect that there will be no significant displacement. Evaluation has confirmed this.

There are no strong indications of serious effects of restructuring for those leaving the neighbourhood under consideration. Most people have been treated with care and are quite satisfied. They have been able to improve their housing situation and/or were already considering a move; that has now been made possible owing to the framework of measures related to the process of restructuring that aimed to compensate those who had to leave the area. That is not to say that all the movers are happy. Many complain, but their complaints do not relate to essential issues and are judged to be unavoidable (Kleinhans and Kruythoff, 2002). Nevertheless, there are indications that the people who have left the neighbourhood are those in a relatively weak position on the housing market: the movers were, in particular, one- and two-person households rather than families, and those dependent on rented accommodation (Kleinhans and Kruythoff, 2002). These people were apparently unable to buy accommodation in the restructured area, where the share of owner-occupied housing increased as a result of the very aim of the policy to make the housing stock more mixed: replacing rented housing with owner-occupied housing. Dignum (2002) also emphasises the weak position of the movers on the housing market. Families stay, while small households, renters, and foreigners from non-Western countries move. Apparently, these movers are unable to afford the higher prices in the restructured parts of the Bijlmermeer; they find accommodation in other parts of Amsterdam, often with a high proportion of rented housing and frequently near the areas of restructuring. In short, it seems fair to say that in the process of restructuring, the interests of those who have to move have not been lost from sight, but, on the other hand it also seems clear that a social downgrading of other areas in the city, where the movers have settled, compensates a social upgrading of the area that is restructured.

This downgrading of areas near to the urban restructuring projects may be illustrated with the help of the City Monitor of Amsterdam.[1] Figure 8.1 shows Daalwijk, an area in the Bijlmermeer, where on one or two estates the relative concentration of unemployed people has increased during the restructuring of the housing stock in adjacent areas (that is, the demolition of high-rise apartment blocks, and the building of low-rise and often owner-occupied accommodation). Daalwijk accommodated the highest concentration of unemployed people in the municipality of Amsterdam between 1996 and 2000. In this period unemployment in Amsterdam decreased; unemployment also decreased in Daalwijk, but clearly at a slower pace. So, the location-

Figure 8.1: Concentration of unemployed people in Daalwijk, Bijlmermeer, Amsterdam in 1996, 1998 and 2000

Source: Own research

quotient of Daalwijk increased between 1996 and 2000 (Table 8.2). Since the year 2000 part of Daalwijk (the central part) has also been restructured and this area no longer shows a high concentration of unemployed (Figure 8.2). The location-quotient has now decreased (Table 8.2).

Figure 8.2: Concentration of unemployed people in Daalwijk, Bijlmermeer, Amsterdam in 2002

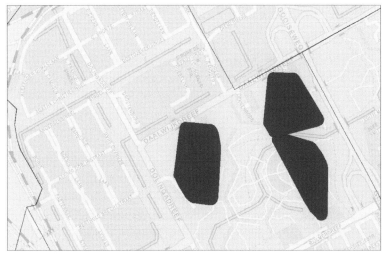

Source: Own research

Table 8.2: Percentage of unemployed people in the municipality of Amsterdam and in Daalwijk, and the location-quotients for Daalwijk (1996-2002)

Year	% Unemployed Amsterdam	Daalwijk	Location-quotient Daalwijk
1996	16.1	38.3	2.38
1998	14.6	36.8	2.52
2000	11.2	28.3	2.53
2002	9.2	22.7	2.47

Source: own research

In short, the restructuring of the area has brought the increasing concentration of poverty to a halt. At the same time the proportion of families living there has increased. But what has happened to the ethnic mix in this area? To answer this question we have to go back in time. The spacious and comfortable high-rise apartments of the Bijlmermeer, mostly developed as social housing, were intended for middle-class families from the older parts of Amsterdam. However, the developments that followed the completion of the first homes showed a different picture. The families from Amsterdam preferred individual and low-rise single-family housing in the new towns and suburbs. The population flow into the Bijlmermeer grew much more slowly than had been expected, resulting in low occupancy rates. Instead of families, the vacant apartments attracted a relatively large number of one-parent families, single people, and people without children. The Bijlmermeer became an area where people settled if they could not find anywhere else to live.

This process intensified enormously in the early 1970s. Preceding the independence of Surinam, many Surinamese came to the Netherlands in order to preserve their Dutch nationality. Many of them had low education levels and were highly dependent on affordable housing. Since the Bijlmermeer was one of the few places where they could easily find a home, many of them settled there; they were soon followed by immigrants from the Dutch Antilles.

Then, in the middle of the 1980s, other groups such as refugees, migrants, illegal immigrants, and so on, settled in the Bijlmermeer area. As a result the proportion of native Dutch people in the Bijlmermeer fell and continued to decrease. In Daalwijk in 1996 only about 10% of the population was of Dutch origin, while the corresponding percentage for Amsterdam as a whole was 58% (Table 8.3). As expected, the most important ethnic category in Daalwijk is

Table 8.3: Percentage of native Dutch people in the municipality of Amsterdam and in Daalwijk, and the location-quotients for Daalwijk (1996-2002)

Year	% Dutch		Location-quotient Daalwijk
	Amsterdam	Daalwijk	Daalwijk
1996	57.6	10.7	0.19
1998	56.5	9.6	0.17
2000	54.7	9.4	0.17
2002	52.7	8.2	0.16

Source: own research

the Surinamese, forming some 38% of the population (the proportion of Surinamese in the whole of Amsterdam is about 10%). The obvious expectation is that restructuring will lead to an increase in the proportion of the population with a Dutch background; the results of a study by Dignum (2002) also suggest this. But this increase is not taking place: the proportion of residents of Dutch origin is still continuing to decrease even after the restructuring (Table 8.3). In other words, restructuring the Daalwijk area has resulted in a slight upgrading in socioeconomic terms, but it has not stopped the exodus of the native Dutch population. The combination of these two factors points to the presence of a Surinamese middle class and to the success of the Big Cities Policy in offering this middle class a housing career in the same area. However, this does not apply to the native Dutch population; the restructuring process does not seem to have appealed to them.

Conclusions

In this chapter we have introduced three related questions: what can we learn from the literature regarding (1) the impacts of displacing people from the restructured housing estates, and (2) the relationship between the social and physical character of problems and solutions; and what empirical indications can be found regarding displacement effects of recent restructuring projects in Amsterdam? These three questions will help to answer the first main question raised in this book: "what types of images and visions of the large estates are emerging?". Let us briefly summarise the answers given to these questions.

Öresjö (1999) points to the strategy of large-scale restructuring projects to avoid concentrations of poor households in the most problematic areas (read: the areas with high ethnic concentrations). The intention was *to attract more middle and higher income people to settle in polarised areas.* Despite protests against the demolition of the apartment blocks and the ensuing involuntary removal of low-income groups, the restructuring proceeded. Later research showed that the main effect was that social problems became relocated, but not resolved. Problematic households did not improve their behaviour in their new surroundings. This example serves to make the point that, in the process of urban restructuring, displacement effects are unavoidable. Adequate accommodation cannot be offered to everybody in the same area. Households who have to leave the area are often in a weak position on the regional housing market. Their new accommodation will therefore be found at the bottom end of the regional housing market; as a result, new or growing concentrations of disadvantaged people will arise elsewhere and poverty will not be eliminated. However, two additional points have to be mentioned here. First, the problem of displacement: this problem depends heavily on the intensity of the relationship between the displaced household and the original, now renewed, neighbourhood. When this relationship is important, displacement has greater social impact. In most cases, however, the relationship between household and neighbourhood is not very strong. Nowadays, neighbourhoods no longer have the all-encompassing role that they had in the past. During their lifetimes, people have become used to changing their neighbourhood, and the impact of a change of neighbourhood as a result of urban restructuring is less damaging. A second reason limiting the social effects for displaced people is found in the influence that residents often have in the process of urban restructuring. The authorities care of the interests of the residents involved and as a result many residents take the opportunity to consolidate or even improve their housing situation. This is the case in the Netherlands, but the process of urban restructuring might be more neglectful elsewhere.

The findings in this chapter show that the emerging vision that large housing estates are able to exist without social problems, and that this vision should be realised through physical intervention, lacks adequate empirical support. The Dutch situation, in particular, is strongly characterised by this vision of physical determinism to resolve social problems indirectly through the physical improvement of the housing stock instead of opting for the more direct way through programmes that stimulate the raising of education levels or access to the labour market.

The Amsterdam experience with urban restructuring underlines the insights just mentioned. Urban restructuring does not lead to the resolution of social problems, but merely their relocation: in particular, it is the people in a relatively weak position who leave the area of urban restructuring and move to other disadvantaged neighbourhoods. But although displacement effects take place, the impact of displacement can be relatively mild if sufficient accompanying measures are taken.

Note
[1] The City Monitor is an instrument to create concentration maps of phenomena, starting from six-digit postal code data; the Monitor is developed by the Department of Human Geography, Planning, and International Development Studies of the University of Amsterdam and the Department of Research and Statistics of the Municipality of Amsterdam.

References

Atkinson, R. (2000) 'Measuring gentrification and displacement in Greater London', *Urban Studies*, vol 37, no 1, pp 149-65.

Atkinson, R. (2002) *Does gentrification help or harm urban neighbourhoods? An assessment of the evidence-base in the context of the New Urban Agenda*, Glasgow/Bristol: Economic and Social Research Council Centre for Neighbourhood Research.

Bell, W. (1968) 'The city, the suburb, and a theory of social choice', in S. Greer, D. McElrath and D. Minar (eds) *The New Urbanisation*, New York, NY: St Martins Press, pp 132-68.

Bott, E. (1957) *Family and social network*, London: Tavistock.

Coleman, A. (1985) *Utopia on trial: vision and reality in planned housing*, London: Shipman.

Dignum, K. (2002) *Doorstroming of verstopping? Dynamiek in de Amsterdamse bevolking en woningmarkt*, Amsterdam: Het Amsterdamse Bureau voor Onderzoek en Statistiek.

Frankenberg, R. (1969) *Communities in Britain: Social life in town and country*, Harmondsworth: Penguin.

Hamnett, C. (2003) 'Gentrification and the middle-class remaking of inner London, 1961-2001', *Urban Studies*, vol 40, no 12, pp 2401-27.

Kleinhans, R. and Kruythoff, H. (2002) *Herstructurering: in het spoor van de vertrekkers*, Utrecht: DGW/NETHUR.

Logan, J. and Molotch, H. (1987) *Urban fortunes: the political economy of place*, Berkeley: University of California Press.

Lyons, M. (1996) 'Gentrification, socioeconomic change, and the geography of displacement', *Journal of Urban Affairs*, vol 18, no 1, pp 39-62.

Musterd, S. (1991) 'Neighbourhood change in Amsterdam', *Tijdschrift voor Economische en Sociale Geografie*, vol 82, no 1, pp 30-9.

Newman, O. (1972) *Defensible space. Crime prevention through urban design*, New York, NY: MacMillan.

Öresjö, E. (1999) 'Problems and opportunities in a large-scale suburban housing estate: the case of Råslätt, Jönköping, Sweden', in E. Öresjö (ed) *Large scale housing estates in Northwest Europe: Problems, interventions and experiences*, Delft: Delft University Press, pp 153-61.

Öresjö, E., Andersson, R., Holmqvist, E., Pettersson, L. and Siwertsson, C. (2004) *Large housing estates in Sweden: Policies and practices*, Utrecht: Urban and Regional research centre, Faculty of Geosciences, Utrecht University.

Ostendorf, W. and Vijgen, J. (1982) 'Segregatie en sociale integratie. De spreiding van bevolking binnen dynamische stadsgewesten', *Geografisch Tijdschrift XVI*, no 4, pp 368-79.

Prak, N.L. and Priemus, H. (eds) (1985) *Post-war public housing in trouble*, Delft: Delft University Press.

Schumacher, B.J. and Leitner, M. (1999) 'Spatial crime displacement resulting from large-scale urban renewal programs in the city of Baltimore, MD: a GIS modelling approach', Geocomputation conference series, (www.geovista.psu.edu/).

Stein, M.R. (1960) *The eclipse of community, an interpretation of American studies*, New York, NY: Harper and Row.

Szemző, H. and Tosics, I. (2004) *Large housing estates in Hungary: policies and practices*, Utrecht: Urban and Regional research centre, Faculty of Geosciences, Utrecht University.

van Beckhoven, E. and van Kempen, R. (2002) *Het belang van de buurt. De invloed van herstructurering op activiteiten van blijvers en nieuwkomers in een Amsterdamse en Utrechtse buurt*, Utrecht: DGW/NETHUR.

van Kempen, E. and Musterd, S. (1991) 'High-rise housing reconsidered: some research and policy implications', *Housing Studies*, vol 6, no 2, pp 83-95.

van Kempen, R. (2000) 'Big Cities Policy in the Netherlands', *Tijdschrift voor Economische en Sociale Geografie*, vol 91, no 2, pp 197-203.

Vance, J.E. jr. (1966) 'Housing the worker: the employment structure as a force in urban structure', *Economic Geography*, vol 42, no 12, pp 294-325.

Young, M. and Willmott, P. (1957) *Family and kinship in East London*, Harmondsworth: Penguin.

NINE

Who leaves Sweden's large housing estates?

Åsa Bråmå and Roger Andersson

Introduction

Debate and research on large housing estates are integrated and embedded in wider discourses on the role of neighbourhoods, communities, urban change, poverty, and segregation. The problems associated with the large estates are similar to those being discussed in relation to 'deprived neighbourhoods' in more general terms: why they exist; how they are produced and reproduced; and what effects they might have on people growing up and living there.

The issue of selective migration figures prominently in these debates, especially in North Western Europe, and is often seen as a contributing factor in the processes of decline and deprivation. The situation in Eastern Europe is somewhat different, partly because in Eastern European cities a higher proportion of the urban population lives on the large housing estates, a fact that might reduce the risk of residualisation and stigmatisation. Whether this situation will persist is discussed in other chapters in this book; one might hypothesise that rising economic standards in these countries will increase the demand for single-family housing and housing environments other than those presently found on the large estates. If neighbourhoods become less popular for various reasons, selective migration can indeed be expected to occur.

Murie, Knorr-Siedow and van Kempen state with reference to this phenomenon that the "spiral of decline may be increased because more stable and affluent households move away …, or may be increased because there are no opportunities for deprived households to move away" (2003, p 29). They continue by arguing that the "danger with these kinds of accounts is that they imply an inevitability to processes of decline and give too little attention to human agency, individual and collective action designed to improve estates or to address particular problems".We would like to argue, first, that we believe that individual and collective action are indeed important and can make a difference for neighbourhoods and residents; second, that knowledge about the demographic and structural position and change of different types of neighbourhood normally improves the capacity to act and to decide on what measures to take regarding particular problems.

Relatively little is known about the character of the out-migration from large housing estates. Who stays and who moves? And where do the out-migrants move to? The phrase 'middle-class leakage' has sometimes been used to describe the out-migration flow (Friedrichs, 1991). But it might be unreasonable to assume that all out-migration can be described in these terms, at least if it is to be understood as the out-migration of the well-to-do households who leave the estates for other kinds of residential area and other types of housing. Research on the migration flows from large Swedish housing estates indicates that much of the outflow is directed towards other similar residential areas (Andersson, 2000b).

By definition, the concept of place making, as described earlier in Chapter Three of this volume, involves the definition of 'ideal types' of places. There are specific images of the intended beneficiaries of estate regeneration. A clearer picture of the character of the out-migration flows from the estates is important in order to understand how different policy measures might affect them. If, as in the Swedish case, urban policy is to a large extent directed towards helping localised individual residents, how is this approach likely to affect the estates, given the kinds of out-migration flow that can be observed there?

Chapter Seven, which uses the same database and neighbourhood division as used in this chapter, analyses all Swedish neighbourhoods and shows that not all larger estates are socially homogeneous and characterised by concentrations of poverty. However, it also shows that many estates that are part of the so-called Million Homes Programme (MP)[1] are indeed characterised by high concentrations of immigrants and low employment rates. Andersson and Musterd (in Chapter Seven) also suggested that their population structures are probably the outcome of a selection process where people with less choice, in particular immigrants, are either directed to these neighbourhoods by institutional actors or face a housing market situation where they can enter only those neighbourhoods where vacancies appear, more often due to the fact that mobility rates are higher there.

This chapter clarifies both the character and the destinations of the out-migration flows. We concentrate on the four estates selected for the Swedish RESTATE project. Two of these, Tensta and Husby, are located in the region of Stockholm, while the other two (Råslätt and Öxnehaga) are in Jönköping, a medium-sized city in the South Central part of Sweden. The study focuses on the individuals who were living in the estates in 1995 and tracks where they were residing five years later. The destinations of the out-movers are analysed in terms of different kinds of neighbourhoods, and the out-movers are compared with the stayers using logistic regression, thereby describing the basic demographic and socioeconomic characteristics of those who leave in comparison with those who tend to remain for longer periods of time. A multinomial technique has been used; the out-movers are divided into two categories based on whether they have moved to a similar neighbourhood (that is, between different housing estates) or to another kind of residential area, and they are then compared with the stayers, the default category. This comparison enables us to investigate not only the differences between stayers and out-movers, but also between those out-movers who remain in the same segment of the housing market and those who move upwards in the housing market hierarchy.

The data material used, the GeoSweden00 Database[2] is a longitudinal set of information comprising information on all individuals who were residing in Sweden during the period 1990–2000. In total, the database contains more than 10 million people. For each person, and for each year, we have demographic and socioeconomic information as well as a neighbourhood code, which makes it possible to trace an individual's movements between different neighbourhoods on a yearly basis. The geographical division into neighbourhoods is based on the SAMS[3]-area division, which reflects what might be considered 'natural' neighbourhoods quite well, at least in the urban areas. In the rural parts of Sweden the SAMS areas are usually larger.

Selective migration in European large housing estates: some RESTATE evidence

Since the early 1980s, the issue of selective migration has been strongly related to the residualisation debate, first in the UK but also in Sweden and the Netherlands (Murie, Knorr-Siedow and van Kempen, 2003, p 26); the Right-to-Buy policies and tenure conversions put into practice in several countries have also led to great concern in relation to this issue.

Inner-city gentrification processes have often been studied from the perspective of who leaves and who enters such neighbourhoods

(Millard-Ball, 2002). The large housing estates could be said to represent areas where the gentrification process is reversed. That is not to say that all those who stay do so involuntarily, or that those who migrate are necessarily well-established, more resourceful households. There could be many reasons why people stay put, or conversely leave a certain neighbourhood; they may be locked in neighbourhoods that might be characterised as highly dynamic. In discussing the situation on the British estates, Hall et al (2003, p 25) state: "They are easy to get into for those who have not got choice but they are not easy to get out of because the facilities that they provide do not form a good platform for the development of employment or housing careers."

The national background reports produced in the RESTATE project include little information on the empirical assessment of who stays and who leaves the estates, although several countries refer to the topic as important. Knorr-Siedow and Droste (2003, pp 77, 116) note in their analysis of the Berlin estates that selective migration is to some extent concerned with the overall supply/demand balance on the housing market, but also with the emergence of certain types of problems (alcoholism, noise, vandalism). Like Berlin, Lyon has also experienced selective migration related to vacancies on the large estates. Chignier-Riboulon et al (2003, pp 45-47) stress the importance not only of social problems and the supply surplus but also of the lack of small dwellings on the large estates: "The lack of small flats is linked to the high rate of young people leaving the estate ..." (p 47). This deficiency is often mentioned with reference to the Swedish estates. In Spain, out-migrants are often thought to be the children of the first generation of settlers from rural Spain. The young, having obtained a reasonable level of education, left the estates because "they had more opportunities outside" (Pareja-Eastaway et al, 2003, p. 82). Some reports, for instance the British (Hall et al, 2003, p 82), the Dutch (Aalbers et al, 2003, pp 77-79) and the Slovenian (Černič Mali et al, 2003, p 45), discuss turnover rates and note that, at least historically, these have been higher on the large estates than elsewhere – in the Amsterdam Bijlmer, much higher. In many cases the influx of recent immigrants seems to be of concern in relation to the issue of who stays and who leaves. Even on the Milanese estates, where the percentage of immigrants is still low compared with most of the other RESTATE cities, "these numbers seem to symbolise new trends, which might cause anxiety and create tension in a neighbourhood that was previously socially and culturally very homogeneous" (Mezzetti et al, 2003, p 43). On the Havanna estate in Budapest, the ethnic component (in this case the presence of Roma families) is also thought to have triggered the out-migration of high-income households in particular (Erdösi et al, 2003, p 43).

Brief descriptions of the estates

This section is based on the two Swedish RESTATE teams' background report on large housing estates in Sweden (Andersson et al, 2003).

The Jönköping estates

Råslätt is a clearly demarcated suburban area situated about 5 km south of the city centre of Jönköping. The estate is owned by one of the municipality's housing companies and consists of 30 uniformly built six- to eight-storey buildings, initially containing 2,657 flats and now reduced to about 2,200. The first apartment block was finished in 1968 and the last in 1972. The estate is divided into two sections joined in the middle by a complex containing a commercial building (1972), a medical and social care centre (1974), a church (1975) and a recreation building, which is integrated with one of Råslätt's three primary schools (1975). In addition to the centrally located facilities, there are schools, nursery schools, kiosks, a sports field with artificial lighting, a mini-farm, allotments, and the like.

Geographically, Råslätt is isolated from the rest of the urban environment and constitutes a small community of its own. The estate is situated at the edge of the densely populated area of Jönköping. The grounds surrounding Råslätt have the physical features of the countryside; the estate is bordered by areas of single-family houses. At the same time Råslätt is, to a certain extent, the centre of this part of the municipality. The inhabitants of the housing areas located nearby use the commercial and public services and also the primary schools in Råslätt. The public transport is very good: the travelling time between the centre of Jönköping and Råslätt is 15 minutes by bus. Of the two Jönköping estates, Råslätt is the most representative of the MP on the basis of large-scale physical structure. In the local perspective, Råslätt contains almost 10% of all the apartment blocks in Jönköping. In the national debate about the MP, Råslätt, together with other housing estates with the same characteristics, became the symbol of housing policy failure, exemplifying how politicians and planners have failed in their social housing policy (Franzén and Sandstedt, 1981).

Öxnehaga is situated between Jönköping and Huskvarna, about 3 km to the west of the former Huskvarna town centre and 10 km east of Jönköping city centre. Öxnehaga is less typical than Råslätt as a large housing area from the MP period. There are some areas with cooperatives and single-family houses in the southern and the northern parts of the estate. Öxnehaga is located on a hillside with a view of Lake Vättern. At the beginning, this outlook made the area attractive. Later, the reputation of the blocks of flats degenerated significantly; this decline resulted in part from the inferior housing standards and in part from the problems that arose in the organisation and management of the housing service. The area was renovated in several stages between 1985 and 1994. The total number of dwellings in Öxnehaga is 2,041; of these, 1,393 are rented flats in apartment blocks, and 99 flats provide sheltered accommodation for the elderly. In 2001 the housing estate had 5,300 inhabitants.

The Stockholm estates

About 10 km north-west of downtown Stockholm we find the Tensta housing estate. Together with its (nationally and internationally) better-known adjacent neighbourhood Rinkeby, it forms the southern part of *Järvafältet* (the Järva Field). The planning principle guiding the general plan for the southern part of Järva was to form large but concentrated housing estates around a centre with subway connections and different kinds of services. The estates were planned to be dispersed throughout a large green park, leaving extensive green spaces between the blocks. These were organised in right-angled patterns. High-rise buildings were placed adjacent to the highway running alongside the estate (E18), but in terms of what was considered to be high-rise at the time, their six storeys were quite modest. Elsewhere, the apartment blocks were lower, but placed more closely together. Traffic separation was another key feature. The subway, of course, was underground. The ground level was planned for cars. People walking and cycling did so on separate paths. The entire concept of the general plan presupposed high ambitions in the detailed planning and construction process in order to achieve variations in building styles. However, the design failed in many ways. Tensta has close to 6,000 dwellings, two thirds of which are either one- or two-bedroom apartments. Two thirds of the dwellings are owned by public housing associations, and most of the remaining apartments are cooperative housing.

The Husby housing estate is part of the Kista district authority in the north-western part of the city of Stockholm. The borough of Kista consists of three residential districts: Akalla, Husby, and Kista. As in Tensta, the entire area used to be a greenfield area, forming the northern part of the Järva Field. It was planned in the beginning of the 1970s, but completed just after the MP period: Husby in 1975, Akalla in 1976, and Kista in 1977. All three residential parts of Kista are connected to the Stockholm subway system, and each has its own station, located in the shopping centre, where many types of administrative and public service facilities are also to be found. Most buildings in Husby have five storeys, but the central part is more densely built and has some high-rise blocks. Some buildings have recently had an extra storey added to them in an attempt to provide more housing for students in Kista and with the underlying idea that the area would benefit from more social mixing. Today the area has about 12,000 residents, with most of them living in rented housing.

Quantitative analysis of out-migration flows

The empirical part of this chapter addresses two sets of questions. The first set concerns the extent of the out-migration and the destinations of the out-movers in terms of different kinds of residential areas. How many of the 1995 residents had left five years later? And how many of the out-movers were living in a similar residential area in 2000? In order to answer these questions we analysed where the 1995 residents were living in the year 2000. The classification of destinations in different types of residential areas was based on a cluster analysis of all residential areas in Sweden.

The second set of questions can be found in the title of this chapter: who leaves the estates? Or, more precisely, what are the demographic and socioeconomic characteristics of those who stay in comparison with those who move to another kind of residential area and those who move to similar neighbourhoods? In order to answer these questions we used multinomial logistic regression, with a dependent variable that had three options: stayers; out-movers to similar neighbourhoods; and out-movers to other kinds of neighbourhood. The division into neighbourhood types was based on the results of the cluster analysis.

Clustering procedure

In order to separate the large housing estates from other types of neighbourhood, we carried out a cluster analysis of all Swedish neighbourhoods (SAMS areas), using a simple k-means procedure. All areas with fewer than ten inhabitants were excluded from the analysis, as were all individuals who did not have a neighbourhood code (about

5% of the population).We ended up with about 8,700 neighbourhoods, with on average about 1,000 residents (see Table 9.1). Five variables were used in the clustering calculation: the percentage of all residents living in rental multi-family dwellings; the percentage living in single-family home ownership; the percentage born abroad; the percentage of the population aged 20-64 years who were employed; and the average work-related income (recoded into deciles).The final cluster centres of the four resulting clusters are shown in Table 9.2.

The difference between the two ownership clusters (1 and 2) is also geographical; while the high-income cluster consists mainly of urban and suburban residential areas, the low-income cluster consists mainly of rural areas.The mixed housing, mid-income cluster (3) is in fact dominated by cooperative housing, which is the third main tenure form in Sweden, following rented housing and home ownership. Cluster 4 includes the large housing estates in the urban fringe, but also, in some cases, the more attractive rental areas in the city centres. All four case study areas,Tensta and Husby in Stockholm, and Råslätt and Öxnehaga in Jönköping, can be found in Cluster 4.

Table 9.1: Results of the cluster analysis of Swedish neighbourhoods

Cluster	Description	Number of residential areas	Number of residents
I	Home ownership, high income	2,828	2,748,815
2	Home ownership, low income	3,059	2,181,519
3	Mixed housing, mid-income	1,435	1,727,144
4	Rental, low income	1,381	2,013,229
Total		8,703	8,670,707

Source: GeoSweden00 Database

Table 9.2: Cluster centres for the four neighbourhood clusters

Cluster	% rental	% home-owners	% born abroad	Employment rate	Work-related income (decile)
I	4.55	84.65	6.60	78.64	9
2	5.56	80.86	5.26	71.76	4
3	20.92	17.34	9.96	70.93	5
4	79.04	4.77	17.80	65.25	3

Source: GeoSweden00 Database

Table 9.3: Outcome of the cluster analysis: a comparison of the two cities

		Stockholm[a]		Jönköping[b]	
Cluster	Description	Number of residents	% of residents	Number of residents	% of residents
I	Home ownership, high income	582,112	34.3	38,938	34.3
2	Home ownership, low income	29,836	1.8	26,854	23.7
3	Mixed housing, mid-income	397,589	23.4	17,901	15.8
4	Rental, low income	686,171	40.5	29,854	26.3
Total		1,695,708	100.0	113,547	100.0

Notes: [a] County of Stockholm; [b] Municipality of Jönköping
Source: GeoSweden00 Database

The two housing markets in the study differ quite substantially (see Table 9.3). While the two ownership clusters (1 and 2) dominate in Jönköping, accommodating nearly 60% of the residents, less than 40% of the Stockholm residents lived in these two clusters. The difference is the result, as can be expected, of the very low share of Cluster 2 (rural home ownership) neighbourhoods in Stockholm.

Out-migration rates and destinations

Table 9.4 shows the stability of the four housing estates measured as a percentage of the 1995 inhabitants who were living in the same area five years later, and the destinations of the out-movers in terms of the different neighbourhood types from the cluster analysis. All four estates had a lower share of stayers than the average for each housing market, which was 66.6% in the County of Stockholm and 64.6% in the Municipality of Jönköping. For two of the estates, Tensta and Öxnehaga, the stability was relatively high; this can be explained at least in part by the larger share of non-rental dwellings in these areas,[4] since turnover is generally higher in the rental segment.

In all four estates, the most common destination for the out-movers was a similar residential area. On the Stockholm estates, around 15% of the 1995 residents had moved to another Cluster 4 neighbourhood. In Jönköping the figures are somewhat lower, but considering the relatively small size of the rental cluster in Jönköping, 12-14% could

Table 9.4: Residence in 2000 for individuals who lived in the four estates in 1995 (%)

	Tensta	Husby	Råslätt	Öxnehaga
Same area	63.8	59.6	58.7	63.8
Other rental, low income (Cluster 4)	16.8	14.1	13.8	12.1
Home ownership, high income (Cluster 1)	6.0	5.7	6.5	7.6
Home ownership, low income (Cluster 2)	0.9	1.1	6.8	6.6
Mixed housing, mid-income (Cluster 3)	5.9	12.5	4.8	6.0
Other[a]	6.6	6.9	9.3	3.9

Note: [a] includes deceased, emigrants and movers to residential areas with less than ten inhabitants

Source: GeoSweden00 Database

be considered to be quite high. The importance of the geographical context can also be seen in the differences between the two housing markets in the number of residents who have moved to the rural ownership cluster. But since most moves generally take place in a very local context, the differences in the immediate surroundings of the estates are also important, as can be seen in the high proportion of moves from Husby to the cooperative housing cluster; Husby's two neighbouring areas Kista and Akalla are both Cluster 3 areas. In terms of the geography of destinations, about two thirds of the out-migrants from the four estates remain within the respective municipality.

The regression models

We used multinomial logistic regression to address the question of who moves and who stays. We analysed the four case study areas of Tensta, Husby, Råslätt, and Öxnehaga separately. The base population consisted of those individuals who were living in these estates in 1995 and who were then between 20 and 64 years old. A division of the residents was made, based on the results of the cluster analysis, using information on where people were residing in the year 2000. The population was divided into three categories: 1) people who were living in the same neighbourhood; 2) people who were living in another Cluster 4 neighbourhood; 3) people who were living in another cluster (that is, Clusters 1-3). This categorisation was used as the dependent variable of the regression.

The independent variables used were chosen to reflect differences related to the lifecycle as well as to ethnic and socioeconomic factors. Residential mobility has been a lively research topic for many decades (Rossi, 1955; Brown and Moore, 1970; Quigley and Weinberg, 1977; Cadwallader, 1992); most researchers recognise the profound importance of lifecycle positions in relation to migration frequencies, choice of tenure, residential area, and migration destinations. Apart from age, household type is highly related to the lifecycle, and both variables must be included in any model that is used to analyse intra-urban migration. Two lifecycle-related variables were therefore included in the model: age and family status. Age was coded into three 15-year intervals (20-34, 35-49, 50-64), compromising accuracy in the interests of having the manageable number of categories needed for reliable results to be obtained from the model. 'Family status' shows the type of family arrangement and/or the position of the individual in the family. We used a simplified version of the variable in the regressions, with only four categories: couple, single parent, living with parent(s), and single. As a result of the coding of the original variable, the 'couple' category refers to married people, with or without children, *and* unmarried people living as a couple *with* children. For the same reason, the 'single' category includes singles without children as well as unmarried couples *without* children.

A number of recent studies of the housing conditions and housing careers of immigrants have revealed differences between the majority population and various minority groups (Friedrichs, 1998; Murdie and Borgegård, 1998; Drever and Clark, 2002; Bolt and van Kempen, 2002; Magnusson and Özüekren, 2002). Immigrants, especially those who have recently arrived, often experience inferior housing conditions in comparison with the majority population. When immigrants move they usually do so between dwellings in the rental sector and less frequently into home ownership. While some researchers prefer to leave open the question of whether this limitation is the result of differences in preferences or prescribed restrictions, most seem to view it as the result of various institutional factors that reduce the available options for immigrants who try to advance in the housing market. For instance, it is often the case that one must be a citizen, or have stayed a specific number of years in a country, in order to obtain a mortgage or other type of loan. In relation to refugees in particular, many different institutional arrangements are applied that affect where they live and which segments of an urban housing market they can access (Robinson et al, 2003). This ethnic dimension is dealt with by including a country-of-birth variable in the model. The variable has three categories: Sweden; other European countries (including the former Soviet Union); non-European countries. Of course, the important dimensions of the ethnic component of residential segregation are not fully captured in this categorisation, but it is an improvement on the 'native' versus 'immigrant' dichotomy that is normally used.

Furthermore, socioeconomic resources are of vital importance in people's decisions of when to move and where to live. Not only disposable income but also income security is of vital importance. Some housing companies, including municipal housing associations, have from time to time tried to apply certain mechanisms to avoid high concentrations of poor and/or unemployed people. One such mechanism is to deny people who live on social welfare benefits the right to become tenants in certain areas. Benefit dependency or unemployment is often an obstacle in applying for a loan, since a regular income is usually a prerequisite for qualification. Four variables reflecting socioeconomic differences were included in the regression model: education; employment; benefit dependency; and disposable income. The education variable allocates years of education into three categories (<10 years; 10-12 years; >12 years), while the employment variable simply distinguishes between the employed and the unemployed. Benefit dependency is a dichotomous variable: people living in a family on social benefits are coded as dependent, regardless of the amount of benefit the family receives.

The model also includes a variable referred to as 'length of residence', which distinguishes between those residents who in 1995 had lived in the neighbourhood for less than three years, and those who had lived there for a longer time. The variable was included in order to capture whether, *ceteris paribus*, those who had lived longer in the same place were less inclined to move than those with a shorter period of residence. All independent variables refer to conditions in 1995.

Results

The results of the regressions are summarised in Table 9.5. The effects of the various parameters are presented as odds ratios. As mentioned earlier, two kinds of movers are compared with stayers, the default category.

For moving to another type of residential area, age, country of birth, family status, and length of residence were the most important variables. The age variable was significant in all four residential areas, showing that younger residents are more inclined to move than older residents.

Table 9.5: Results of the regression model; effects are presented as odds ratios

	Moving to another cluster				Moving within Cluster 4			
	Tensta	Husby	Råslätt	Öxnehaga	Tensta	Husby	Råslätt	Öxnehaga
Constant	0.114	0.111	0.103	0.032	0.133	0.120	0.222	0.083
Age								
20-34	**2.883**	**3.013**	**4.509**	**5.181**	**2.855**	**2.330**	**3.387**	**2.123**
35-49	**2.092**	**2.192**	**2.683**	**1.520**	**2.000**	**1.679**	**1.719**	1.411
50-64	1.000	1.000	1.000	1.000	1.000	1.000	1.000	1.000
Gender								
Men	0.984	0.960	0.903	**1.322**	1.135	1.090	0.958	1.340
Women	1.000	1.000	1.000	**1.000**	1.000	1.000	1.000	1.000
Country of birth								
Sweden	**1.672**	**2.117**	**1.704**	**3.951**	1.146	**1.499**	0.890	**1.624**
Rest of Europe	1.077	**1.493**	1.073	**3.838**	1.158	0.981	0.669	2.349
Outside Europe	**1.000**	**1.000**	**1.000**	**1.000**	1.000	**1.000**	**1.000**	**1.000**
Family status								
Couple	**0.762**	**1.260**	**0.650**	**0.592**	**0.575**	**0.497**	**0.419**	**0.372**
Single parent	0.803	1.151	**0.418**	1.621	1.070	1.018	0.587	1.287
Living with parent(s)	0.908	0.991	**0.604**	1.170	1.254	1.174	0.680	**4.568**
Single	**1.000**	**1.000**	**1.000**	**1.000**	**1.000**	**1.000**	**1.000**	**1.000**
Length of residence								
<3 years	**1.215**	**1.701**	**1.707**	**1.795**	**1.702**	**1.904**	**1.667**	**1.809**
3+ years	**1.000**	**1.000**	**1.000**	**1.000**	**1.000**	**1.000**	**1.000**	**1.000**
Education								
<10 years	**0.646**	**0.534**	0.697	0.803	**0.734**	**0.691**	**0.535**	0.818
10-12 years	0.902	**0.717**	1.021	1.034	0.985	0.898	0.963	0.855
>12 years	**1.000**	**1.000**	1.000	1.000	**1.000**	**1.000**	**1.000**	1.000
Employment status								
Unemployed	**0.757**	**0.693**	0.820	0.929	**0.817**	0.849	0.908	**1.496**
Employed	**1.000**	**1.000**	1.000	1.000	**1.000**	1.000	1.000	**1.000**
Social benefits								
No	**1.614**	**1.334**	**1.632**	1.026	0.910	1.013	0.894	1.116
Yes	**1.000**	**1.000**	**1.000**	1.000	1.000	1.000	1.000	1.000
Disposable income								
1st quartile	0.807	1.145	0.850	1.376	**1.409**	**1.749**	1.149	1.311
2nd quartile	0.847	0.901	0.742	1.373	**1.413**	**1.317**	1.188	1.315
3rd quartile	0.941	1.040	0.771	1.148	**1.292**	**1.265**	0.842	1.229
4th quartile	1.000	1.000	1.000	1.000	**1.000**	**1.000**	1.000	1.000

Note: **Bold** = significant at the 5% level
Source: GeoSweden00 Database

This tendency to move was particularly strong for the youngest age category (those aged 20-34). The effect was greater on the Jönköping estates than in Stockholm; the difference might be explained by the lower prices on the Jönköping housing market than in Stockholm, making it easier for young people to leave the rental segment of the housing market for other forms of tenure.

The regressions also revealed a significant difference between Swedish-born and non-European residents. Those born in Sweden were more likely to leave Cluster 4 for other kinds of residential area than those born outside Europe. Furthermore, in two cases (Husby and Öxnehaga) people born in other European countries were more likely to leave than were non-Europeans.

In all four areas the family status variable revealed a significant difference between singles and couples. The latter category was found less likely to move on three of the estates. In Råslätt the same kind of differences were found between singles and all other categories. In Husby, on the other hand, couples were found to be *more* inclined to move than singles. This tendency might be explained by Husby's proximity to the two Cluster 3 neighbourhoods, Kista and Akalla, where a large part of the housing stock consists of cooperatively-owned terraced housing, which might attract couples with children.

Length of residence was significant on all four estates showing, as expected, that residents with a shorter period of residence were more likely to move than those with a longer residence. Gender was not found to be very important. There was a small, but significant difference between men and women in Öxnehaga, where men seemed more likely to move than women. Apart from that, there were no significant differences between men and women.

The socioeconomic variables were not found to be as unanimously influential as the demographic and ethnic variables were. In Öxnehaga, none of the socioeconomic variables was found to be significant. In Råslätt, only benefit dependency was significant. On the two Stockholm estates, Tensta and Husby, all the socioeconomic variables except disposable income were significant. There, the education variable showed that those with a lower level of education were significantly less likely to move than those who were highly educated. Unemployment was shown to reduce the tendency to move, as was benefit dependency. Again, the difference between Stockholm and Jönköping might be explained by the lower prices in Jönköping. In Stockholm a house-seeker probably needs to be established on the labour market with a regular income to qualify for a loan, whereas in

Jönköping a student, for example, might be able to buy a home in the cooperative housing sector.

In the other out-moving category – moving to another residential area within Cluster 4 – age was again one of the most important variables. Except in Öxnehaga, the two younger age categories were significantly more likely to move than was the oldest age category. In Öxnehaga, however, only the difference between the oldest and youngest categories was significant. Apart from age, only two parameters showed the same tendency in all four housing estates. Those with a short period of residence were found to be more likely to move than those with long-term residence, and couples were found to be less likely to move than singles. In Öxnehaga, people who were 'living with parents' were significantly more inclined to move than even the singles were. Since the parents (found mostly in the 'couple' category) were less likely to move, these movers can only be interpreted as nest-leavers.

The country-of-birth variable was less easy to interpret than in the other out-moving category. Only on two of the estates, Husby and Öxnehaga, did the same differences between Swedish-born and non-Europeans appear that were found in the case of moving to other types of residential area. That is to say, residents born in Sweden were significantly more likely to move than non-Europeans. As for the 'rest-of-Europe' category, on one estate (Öxnehaga) these residents were found to be even more likely to move than were those born in Sweden. In Råslätt, on the other hand, the only significant effect associated with this variable was that this category was *less* likely to move than the non-Europeans. These differences are probably capable of being explained by differences within the categories concerning the actual country of birth ('cultural distance'), duration of residence in Sweden, and other factors not included in the model.

As mentioned above, there were significant differences between Swedes and non-Europeans in Husby and Öxnehaga for moving within Cluster 4. This, together with the fact that these estates also showed the largest differences between non-Europeans and native Swedes with respect to moving to other kinds of neighbourhoods, suggests a greater overall propensity for Swedes to leave these estates for other residential areas rather than to the other two estates. We have no clear answer as to why this is the case. One possibility is that it might indicate processes of 'white flight' in Husby and Öxnehaga. While Testa and Råslätt have been considered 'immigrant dense' (in their specific contexts) for a long time, both Husby and Öxnehaga had comparatively low shares of immigrants in 1990. And while all four estates experienced an increase in the proportion of immigrant residents between 1990 and 1995, the effects might have been more noticeable in Husby and Öxnehaga, thus accelerating the out-migration of Swedish-born residents in the following years.

All in all, however, the vague and partly contradictory results for the country-of-birth variable indicate that this factor is not as important when it comes to moving between different housing estates as it is for leaving the housing estates for other types of residential area (we return to this point in the conclusions section).

Of the socioeconomic variables, education seems to be the most important. The results indicate that a low level of education reduces the tendency to move on all the estates except Öxnehaga, where the effect of this variable was not significant. Disposable income was significant on the two Stockholm estates but not in Jönköping. Both in Tensta and Husby, residents in the highest income quartile were, surprisingly, the least likely to move. Employment status was significant on two estates, Tensta and Öxnehaga, but with results in opposite directions. In the Tensta case unemployed residents were *less* inclined to move, while in Öxnehaga unemployed residents were *more* inclined to move. The benefit-dependency variable was not significant for any of the estates.

The explanatory power of the regression models as expressed by the Cox and Snell R2 values was generally higher in the Jönköping estates (Råslätt 0.153; Öxnehaga 0.212) than in Stockholm (Tensta 0.095; Husby 0.104).

Conclusions

On all four estates, therefore, the person most likely to leave the estate, regardless of the destination, is a young person (20-34 years old in 1995), who is single rather than living as a couple, who has not been living in the estate for very long (less than three years in 1995) and who has a relatively high level of education. Considering only the effects of these parameters, the probability of moving within Cluster 4 for this type of person is between 56% and 24%, and of moving to another cluster between 44% and 23% (see Figure 9.1). Consequently, the person least likely to move is older (50-64 in 1995), living as one of a couple, has lived on the estate for more than three years, and has a relatively low level of education. For this type of person the probability of moving within Cluster 4 is only about 3-5%, and of moving to another cluster between 2% and 7%.

But there the similarities between the movers to other clusters and

Figure 9.1: Probabilities of moving out of the estates for the most likely and least likely movers

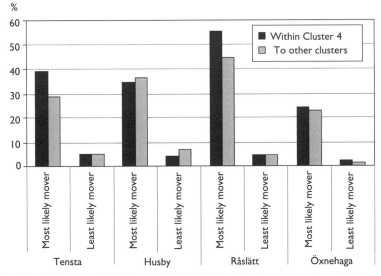

Note: Most likely to move = 20 to 34-years-old, single, lived less than three years on the estate, high level of education. Least likely to move = 50-64-years-old, living as couple, lived three years or more on the estate, low level of education,

Source: GeoSweden00 Database

the movers within Cluster 4 end. In the case of leaving the low-income, rental-dominated cluster for another type of residential area, the factors of being employed and, in particular, not being dependent on social benefit also seem to increase the chances of moving, at least on the Stockholm estates. For a young single person with a short period of residence, as in the 'most likely mover' example above, being unemployed and dependent on social benefit reduces the probability of moving to another cluster from about 40% to around 25%.

The fact that the disposable income variable was found not to be significant, while employment and benefit dependency were (at least in some cases), indicates that it is not income *per se*, but rather income *security* that is influential on the chances of advancing on the housing market from the rental sector to cooperative housing or home ownership. In the case of moving within Cluster 4, on the other hand, there were very few indications that being well-endowed in terms of socioeconomic resources increases the chances of moving. In contrast, the disposable income variable, where significant, indicated that high-income residents were the least likely to move between different areas within Cluster 4. High-income households probably choose a destination outside this cluster when they decide to move.

Apart from this, the most obvious disparity between the two types of move was the difference in the significance of the country-of-birth variable. Being born in Sweden, particularly compared with being born outside Europe, proved to be one of the most important factors in explaining who moves to other types of residential areas, even when socioeconomic differences were controlled for. Again, considering the 'most likely mover' from the example above, being born in Sweden increased the probability of moving by between 11 percentage points (from 28-39% for Tensta) and 31 percentage points (from 23-54% for Öxnehaga). For the Cluster 4 movers, this was only true for two estates, Husby and Öxnehaga, and the effects were much lower. The disparity found here is in line with results from other studies on the mobility of immigrants in Sweden (Andersson, 2000a; 2000b; Magnusson and Özüekren, 2002). While native Swedes often leave the rental-dominated residential areas for other kinds of neighbourhood as a step in a 'normal' housing career, immigrants remain to a greater extent within the rental segment of the housing market.

Although the out-migration rates on the estates were not exceptionally high, the results of the quantitative analysis seem to indicate that, for many residents, the estates are perceived as a temporary solution. But the out-migration seems to consist of two rather different kinds of flow. One flow is directed away from the rental-dominated, low-income areas towards other kinds of neighbourhoods. Two conditions seem to be of special importance to match the features characterising this flow: income security and being born in Sweden. The other flow is directed towards other similar neighbourhoods, and can be seen as part of a circulation within the rental sector. In this flow we find the less well-established movers, often unemployed and/ or living on social benefits.

Policy implications

Although contemporary Swedish urban policy has, to some extent, been influenced by the lock-in perspective – leading to the emphasis on area-based solutions to the problems of deprived neighbourhoods – the bulk of research evidence points in the direction of the gateway role that these (transient) neighbourhoods have in the major Swedish cities. Thus, area-based approaches tend to be ineffective *with respect to their overall political goal in Sweden,* namely to 'break segregation'.

The policy and its shortcomings *vis-à-vis* the anti-segregation goal are illustrated in Figure 9.2. The vertical axis represents *per capita* income and the horizontal axis represents all neighbourhoods in a city, ranked

Figure 9.2: Economic segregation: a schematic view

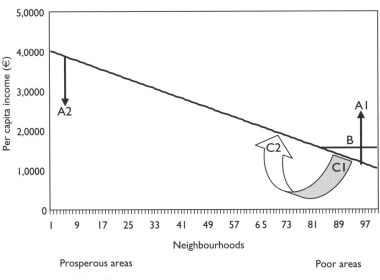

Source: Andersson (2004, p 8)

from left to right according to the average income level of their residents. Class segregation is in this case illustrated by the gradient of the line connecting each neighbourhood's income value. Measures that reduce the gradient can subsequently be expected to reduce the level of residential segregation by class.

Such a change could come about either by raising the average income level more in poor neighbourhoods than in prosperous areas or, in theory, by reducing the level of income in prosperous areas more than in poor areas. A1 and A2 above, illustrate developments that would alter the gradient: that is to say, reduce economic segregation. However, there is nothing that can be identified in Swedish urban policy that would have this type of redistributive effect in relation to urban segregation. If there were such processes, they would doubtless contribute to the resolution of some of the problems currently under discussion in relation to the large housing estates.

A breakthrough in segregation could be achieved if the income level were to increase in the poorest neighbourhoods without affecting the remaining parts of the city. This situation is illustrated by B. In this case, no 'absolutely poor' neighbourhoods would exist: that is, the tail of the income-related gradient would be cut off, but segregation would nevertheless remain in its basic form. The B case scenario could be said to represent the level of ambition in Swedish metropolitan policy fairly well, although it has not been stated explicitly in such terms in any published document.

Our acquaintance with the areas affected by the state interventions leads us to the view that this, however, would not be the most probable outcome of the area-based interventions. C1 and C2 represent two further, more realistic scenarios. C1 signifies that an individual estate or neighbourhood may manage to 'escape' from a poor position by some type of gentrification process, but that this area will be replaced by some other area joining the group of poor neighbourhoods (this is the *displacement* scenario, 'moving the problems on': see Burgers and Vranken, 2003). From the perspective of a particular poor estate, C1 is indeed something to be welcomed, not least by the residents, housing associations, and local administrators. C2 represents the movement of individuals, not of areas; this is the scenario which so far seems to be best supported by the empirical data (Andersson and Bråmå, 2004). As expressed by Murie et al (2003), the "spiral of decline may be increased because more stable and affluent households move away". The C1 and C2 scenarios concern the confusion often embedded in area-based policies, namely that whether interventions are aimed primarily at the socioeconomic position of individuals or of neighbourhoods is not made clear. A certain policy may be quite effective with regard to individuals but nonetheless fail with respect to the position of the neighbourhood.

We would like to emphasise that this discussion should not be used as an argument for ending area-based policies; we only wish to make it clear that area-based policies have limitations in relation to the ambitious goal to 'break segregation'. Area-based policies have indeed had positive effects on many of the large estates (improving labour market integration, schools, public spaces, cultural life, and so forth) but as yet we have seen no evidence of breaking segregation or of targeted neighbourhoods being able to change their relative position *vis-à-vis* other residential areas. And, in our opinion, the relative position is most decisive for the type of migration pattern that develops in a neighbourhood.

Returning to the model of the possible futures of the large housing estates in the context of Swedish urban policy, the main challenge seems to be to reduce out-migration, especially the 'middle-class leakage', since this is the driving force behind the production and reproduction of segregation. As we said earlier, one possible outcome of the area-based urban policy is some kind of gentrification process which alters the position of an estate (see the C1 alternative in Figure 9.2). At the neighbourhood level, this reduction of out-migration means increased stability. Individuals who manage to improve their socioeconomic conditions, whether as the result of a successful urban policy or not, remain on the estate. A part of the flow is reduced, and this affects the estate, possibly even the character of the in-migration flow. But even if that is not changed, the in-migration rate is reduced, and some of those who would otherwise have moved there will probably move to another, similar, neighbourhood instead.

However, since a large part of the out-migration, as we have seen, seems to be housing-career related, this C1 scenario does not seem very likely as long as these residential areas fail to provide any opportunities for a housing career within the neighbourhood. And for that to be possible, a more varied housing stock would be needed in terms of apartment size, house type, and tenure form. As reported in Chapter Seven, Swedish neighbourhoods, including many multi-family apartment block areas, are indeed quite mixed in terms of social and ethnic composition. Therefore, the large estates (except for Öxnehaga) on which we have concentrated in this chapter do stand out as being quite different from what is normally found in the country.

But the existence of two relatively different kinds of out-migration flow also points in another policy direction, namely measures that aim at a reduction of the migration flow between similar housing estates. If the urban policy includes some kind of measure directed towards the neighbourhood rather than the people who live there (which is usually the case) it might lead to a reduction of the out-migration directed towards other similar housing estates. An increased stability of this kind might not be visible (not initially, at least) in macro-level descriptions of the estate in terms of socioeconomic status, but the residents would doubtless notice a difference. The increased stability would probably promote a greater sense of community and place attachment among the residents, and possibly provide a chance to break the spiral of decline. And, as we have seen, once people have remained in the same neighbourhood for about four to six years, the probability of their moving is reduced considerably. So, in the longer perspective, this situation might also lead to the C1 scenario, if those who have lived there for a few years decide to stay even when their socio-economic conditions have improved.

Whether increased stability in a neighbourhood at the bottom of the hierarchy results in another neighbourhood taking its place depends on the extent of the difference in attractiveness between the housing estates. If there is a distinct hierarchy within the rental-dominated segment, the replacement scenario will probably apply. If there is no such hierarchy, the effect might be that the gateway character of certain estates will spread over a larger number of residential areas, and so the effects in each area will be reduced.

Notes

[1] The Million Homes Programme (or One Million Programme) was initiated by a Social Democratic government in the early 1960s. The aim was to produce one million new dwellings in ten years' time (1965-74). This aim was accomplished. We use the abbreviation MP (Million Programme) to denote this housing construction programme.

[2] The GeoSweden00 Database was also used by Andersson and Musterd in Chapter Seven. That chapter focuses on the relationship between the (physical) housing mix and the social opportunities, and the social mix and social opportunities.

[3] SAMS stands for 'Small Area Market Statistics'. The SAMS areas were constructed by Statistics Sweden for commercial purposes, based on information about housing stock and household characteristics, so that continuous geographical areas sharing the same characteristics were identified.

[4] About 25% of the housing stock in Tensta is cooperative housing. And, unfortunately from an analytical perspective, the Öxnehaga SAMS area contains not only the housing estate but also a homeownership neighbourhood, where about one third of the population resided in 1995.

References

Aalbers, M., van Beckhoven, E., van Kempen, R., Musterd, S. and Ostendorf, W. (2003) *Large housing estates in the Netherlands: Overview of developments and problems in Amsterdam and Utrecht*, Utrecht: Urban and Regional research centre Utrecht, Faculty of Geosciences, Utrecht University.

Andersson, R. (2000a) *Segregerande urbanisering? Geografisk rörlighet i Sveriges storstadsregioner, Hemort Sverige*, Norrköping: Integrationsverket.

Andersson, R. (2000b) *Rörligheten i de utsatta bostadsområdena, Hemort Sverige*, Norrköping: Integrationsverket.

Andersson, R. and Bråmå, A. (2004) 'Selective migration in Swedish distressed neighbourhoods: can area-based urban policies counteract segregation processes?', *Housing Studies*, vol 19, no 4, pp 517-39.

Andersson, R., Molina, I., Öresjö, E., Pettersson, L. and Siwertsson, C. (2003) *Large housing estates in Sweden: Overview of developments and problems in Jönköping and Stockholm,* Utrecht: Urban and Regional research centre Utrecht, Faculty of Geosciences, Utrecht University.

Bolt, G. and van Kempen, R. (2002) 'Moving up or moving down? Housing careers of Turks and Morrocans in Utrecht, the Netherlands', *Housing Studies,* vol 17, no 3, pp 401-22.

Brown, L.A. and Moore, E.G. (1970) 'The intra-urban migration process: a perspective', *Geografiska Annaler B,* vol 52, no 1, pp 1-13.

Burgers, J. and Vranken, J. (eds) (2003) *How to make a successful urban development programme. Experiences from 9 European countries,* UGIS Working Paper, Antwerpen-Apeldoorn: Garant.

Cadwallader, M. (1992) *Migration and residential mobility. Macro and micro perspectives,* Madison: The University of Wisconsin Press.

Černič Mali, B., Sendi, R., Boškič, R., Filipovič, M., Goršič, N. and Zaviršek Hudnik, D. (2003) *Large housing estates in Slovenia: overview of developments and problems in Ljubljana and Koper,* Utrecht: Urban and Regional research centre Utrecht, Faculty of Geosciences, Utrecht University.

Chignier-Riboulon, F., Commerçon, N., Trigueiro, M. and Zepf, M. (2003) *Large housing estates in France: overview of developments and problems in Lyon,* Utrecht: Urban and Regional research centre Utrecht, Faculty of Geosciences, Utrecht University.

Drever, A.I. and Clark, W.A.V. (2002) 'Gaining access to housing in Germany: the foreign-minority experience', *Urban Studies,* vol 39, no 13, pp 2439-53.

Erdösi, S., Geröházi, É., Teller, N. and Tosics, I. (2003) *Large housing estates in Hungary: Overview of developments and problems in Budapest and Nyíregyháza,* Utrecht: Urban and Regional research centre Utrecht, Faculty of Geosciences, Utrecht University.

Franzén, M. and Sandstedt, E. (1981) *Grannskap och stadsplanering. Om stat och byggande i efterkrigstidens Sverige,* doctoral dissertation, Uppsala: Acta Universitatis Upsaliensis.

Friedrichs, J. (1991) 'Middle-class leakage in large new housing estates: empirical findings and policy implications', *The Journal of Architectural and Planning Research,* vol 8, no 4, pp 287-95.

Friedrichs, J. (1998) 'Ethnic segregation in Cologne, Germany, 1984-1994', *Urban Studies,* vol 35, no 10, pp 1745-63.

GeoSweden00 Database, Institute for Housing and Urban Research, Uppsala University.

Hall, S., Lee, P., Murie, A., Rowlands, R. and Sankey, S. (2003) *Large housing estates in United Kingdom: Overview of developments and problems in London and Birmingham*, Utrecht: Urban and Regional research centre Utrecht, Faculty of Geosciences, Utrecht University.

Knorr-Siedow, T. and Droste, C. (2003) *Large housing estates in Germany: Overview of developments and problems in Berlin*, Utrecht: Urban and Regional research centre, Faculty of Geosciences, Utrecht University.

Magnusson, L. and Özüekren, S. (2002) 'The housing careers of turkish households in middle-sized Swedish municipalities', *Housing Studies*, vol 17, no 3, pp 465-86.

Mezzetti, P., Mungano, S. and Zajczyk, F. (2003) *Large housing estates in Italy: Overview of developments and problems in Milan*, Utrecht: Urban and Regional research centre, Faculty of Geosciences, Utrecht University.

Millard-Ball, A. (2002) 'Gentrification in a residential mobility framework: social change, tenure change and chains of moves in Stockholm', *Housing Studies*, vol 17, no 6, pp 833-56.

Murdie, R.A. and Borgegård, L.E. (1998) 'Immigration, spatial segregation and housing segmentation of immigrants in metropolitan Stockholm, 1960-1995', *Urban Studies*, vol 35, no 10, pp 1869-88.

Murie, A., Knorr-Siedow, T. and van Kempen, R. (2003) *Large housing estates in Europe: general developments and theoretical backgrounds*, Utrecht: Urban and Regional research centre, Faculty of Geosciences, Utrecht University.

Pareja-Eastaway, M., Tapada-Berteli, T., van Boxmeer, B. and Garcia Ferrando, L. (2003) *Large housing estates in Spain: Overview of developments and problems in Madrid and Barcelona*, Utrecht: Urban and Regional research centre Utrecht, Faculty of Geosciences, Utrecht University.

Quigley, J.M. and Weinberg, D.H. (1977) 'Intra-urban residential mobility: a review and synthesis', *International Regional Science Review*, vol 2, no 1, pp 41-66.

Robinson, V., Andersson, R. and Musterd, S. (2003) *Spreading the 'burden'? A review of policies to disperse asylum seekers and refugees*, Bristol: The Policy Press.

Rossi, P.H. (1955) *Why families move: a study of the social psychology of urban residential mobility*, Glencoe: The Free Press.

TEN

Demolition of large housing estates: an overview

*Fatiha Belmessous, Franck Chignier-Riboulon, Nicole Commerçon
and Marcus Zepf*

Introduction

Since the 1990s, the question of demolishing and rebuilding large housing estates has emerged as a central theme of urban policies linked with social housing. According to Christine Lelévrier and Jean-Claude Driant (Lelevrier, 2002), demolition characterises certain operations (which may be on a small or large scale) undertaken with state support and designed to improve the housing stock.

As a result of the generally poor quality of buildings erected after the Second World War, their poor image, and the various difficulties concentrated within them (especially socioeconomic problems, reduced quality of life, and antisocial behaviour) the policies deployed have very often led to a decision to demolish large estates. Of course, the situations vary throughout Europe, for historical and political reasons. But, in general terms, the same questions are being asked about the rationale for demolition and rebuilding.

We first consider the rationale and objectives for demolition and rebuilding, in both a theoretical and practical context, before we discuss the implications of this practice for low-income households. The rationale for demolition is linked to so many different factors in different European countries, the various situations are neither strictly compared, nor the cases listed. This chapter, therefore, is derived from the large housing estates in the RESTATE project, although some other examples are given. General tendencies are considered and an analysis offered of why some large housing estates – even after having been physically improved – remain problematic areas and sometimes still have to be demolished. The political context of the socioeconomic and spatial questions is considered in order to illuminate the main goals of the European countries in terms of rebuilding, before exploring how demolition and rebuilding is experienced and what are now the main results of these policies.

Theoretical reasons for demolition

The current debate on demolition originates from the 1990s. The majority (sometimes even 100%) of the accommodation in most of the deprived urban neighbourhoods in the countries of Western Europe (the Netherlands, Germany, the UK, and France, for example) is in the social-rented sector, although some private-sector estates are also problematic (for example, the Bron Terraillon estate in the east of Greater Lyon belongs to the private-rental sector). These housing districts are characterised by a concentration of difficulties such as increasing numbers of deprived households, including a large proportion of some minorities such as Arabs in France or Moroccans in the Netherlands. Moreover, these neighbourhoods generate feelings of insecurity and declining well-being; their image continues to deteriorate in spite of past public policies or, in some cases, even of their good physical quality (such as in Sweden). In most cases, subsidies have allowed the updating of physical housing quality through refurbishment, the maintenance of local public services, a continued supply of affordable housing (through housing benefit), or improvements to the urban environment. In certain specific cases, particular policies were implemented to transfer stock to registered social landlords, or to facilitate the privatisation of some social-rented areas in Spain and France.

Nevertheless, in the early 1990s, the manner in which this situation was countered changed and demolition has become a useful tool of new policy in many European countries, although demolition has also been used in the past to renovate urban sectors of derelict houses (in the UK, the Netherlands, and Spain) or to destroy unoccupied dwellings (Chignier-Riboulon, 1999). Thus, within the old terminology of 'renewal', new policies have been developed: the diversification of dwellings offered in former social-rented areas (the Netherlands), redevelopment (the UK), mass demolition (Germany and the Netherlands), and the reconstruction of small housing units, for example.

What are the reasons for demolition? One must remember that the question of the future of large housing estates cannot be discussed without reference to the broader issue of urban change. The large estates are often perceived to be a general obstacle to urban restructuring or a threat to the social cohesion within the city (Baudin and Genestier, 2002).

The arguments put forward to explain demolition have to be considered with care, because they are specific to each estate and each country and accord with the relevant social, economic, political, and cultural history. However, we can at least build a framework in which some common tendencies to justify this practice are noted. These arguments here concern Western European countries in particular: France, Germany, the UK, the Netherlands.

Those in favour of demolition argue that these buildings have achieved their original objectives (to enable people to live in a decent dwelling) but have long since reached the end of their useful lives. These buildings are now considered to be obsolete and too expensive to maintain. The rehabilitation option would have cost the landlord too much and perhaps the result would not have been effective (Union HLM, 2001).

Some estates were rehabilitated during the 1980s but the current policy puts a premium on the demolition of these types of buildings – particularly in France and in some parts of Germany – to avoid the need for further rehabilitation ten years on. This decision may also be considered as an acknowledgement of the failure of previous policies. In this group of estates, we have many large housing estates built as functional towns according to Modernist principles (high density; separation of home, work, transport, and recreation functions). Thus, their inability to adapt to traditional and emerging urban forms leads to their demolition.

Examples of this argument are put forward with respect to high-rise estates built in East Germany and France. The development of this housing stock is very problematic, and has been linked to an increase in crime and feelings of insecurity. Demolition is considered as a suitable solution to decrease the crime rate (Coleman, 1985). In France, gradual demolition of concrete apartment blocks took place in Vaulx-en-Velin and in the peripheral estates of Paris (Aubervilliers, for example). In the UK, a formal programme (Design Improved Controlled Experiment) was launched in 1999 to improve 'radically' the design scheme on some estates (Hall et al, 2004).

Another frequently used argument concerns the residents' misuse of the large housing estates. The housing design could no longer be adapted to the current housing demands of households and it became unpopular with both the sitting tenants and possible newcomers. The problems concern essentially the higher density, and the lack of private areas and 'liveability'. Currently, people typically prefer individual houses with a garden, or apartments in blocks of reasonable height (three or four storeys), which include private spaces. In urban renewal, the development of these areas implies the change of the urban structures by creating, for example, new roads or public spaces to open up the area. The town planners then try to integrate these places with the whole of the city by diversifying and laying out public, semi-public, and private spaces.

As a result of the suburbanisation of middle-class households and the concentration of low-income people on the estates, some estates have become financial burdens for landlords (Union HLM, 2001). Massive vacancy rates and/or rent arrears have provoked economic problems in the neighbourhood, such as the increasing costs of keeping up empty dwellings and cleaning common areas. Thus, maintaining these dwellings in an appropriate state has become too expensive. For example, in Le Mas du Taureau, a neighbourhood in Vaulx-en-Velin, one of the Eastern suburban communes of Greater Lyon, some high-rise buildings suffered an incredible vacancy rate[1] of almost 60% in the 1990s. Gradually, the landlords tried to empty entire buildings and demolish them to avoid losing money. In East Germany, where the rise of vacancies has provoked important economic problems, demolition has afforded the opportunity either to improve the dwellings or to demolish some of the housing stock. In Marzahn North, for example, the housing companies have to face vacancies of over 15% on average. In some buildings, vacancies run at over 30% (Knorr-Siedow, 2003).

Despite the implementation of various policies, many estates have become the focus for conditions of rising social and spatial segregation (Haussermann, 2000). In Germany, owing to the current employment crisis with between 3.5 and 4 million people out of work, reductions in unemployment benefits have led to a reduction in rent-paying capacity and an increase in poverty on many large housing estates (Droste and Knorr-Siedow, 2004). The economic problems have led to a rise in the number of segregated housing estates. In France, as in Germany, the current debates about the welfare state and the reform of the pensions system and the reduction in benefits and pensions will have a great impact on the housing estates, particularly on the aggravation of the precarious material situation of their residents (and also the landlords and the local authorities). By demolishing some dwellings within an integrated programme, other land uses, ranging from housing to service activities, may be introduced to the estates, which would involve the participation of various public and private entities, and public and private financial resources. The housing stock on many estates is characterised by an overrepresentation of social-rented dwellings. Breaking up this homogeneity contributes to a differentiated and attractive housing stock, thereby creating more attractive neighbourhoods.

These policies, including demolition, are designed to prevent and combat segregation and, at the same time, provide opportunities for middle-income households to obtain affordable dwellings. But often the pursuit of a social mix through a greater variety of housing is clearly encouraged (see also Chapter Eight). These policies assert that such operations are capable of changing the social composition of an area (we refer to the urban renovation during the 1970s in the centres of many European big cities), while they fail to address the principle problem which arises after the rebuilding, namely locating new housing for the displaced residents (Abbé Pierre Foundation, 2004).

Reasons for demolition in practice

At the European level, we concentrate on a few countries representative of the variety of policies at stake. Some countries have undertaken very few demolition and reconstruction programmes compared with others. Belgium and Italy, for example, still prefer to renew their social housing stock. Thus, in 2000 the Lombardy Region in Italy launched a new social programme with the major aim of moving away from the traditional approach of maintaining the social housing stock. The new approach affects the social mix by renting affordable dwellings to specific social groups (students, police, and guest workers) and by creating public spaces. This programme has therefore necessitated the coexistence of a mix of actors and public and private resources (Zajczyk et al, 2004).

At the opposite end of the spectrum is the policy adopted in Germany, which has to cope with reunification problems and in particular the difficulties linked with two political and socioeconomic models and, thus, two housing models. In the East, one person in six lives on a large estate.[2] These estates have accumulated all the problems that occur in these types of neighbourhood; now, one million apartments are vacant. In 1993, a programme evaluation came to the conclusion that, despite high investment in the rehabilitation of large housing estates (€150 million), some neighbourhoods have not shaken off their negative image (Droste and Knorr-Siedow, 2004). After more than two decades of rehabilitation in the West and one decade in the East, the residents on some estates found that the estates had become acceptable after they had been improved. But others have remained problematic and are still in permanent need of subsidies to remain or become quality dwellings. It is generally accepted that some estates should be demolished. A large programme of demolition has been set up – the Stadtumbau Ost Programme (August 2001) – and, in 2001, 249 neighbourhoods were selected for demolition. These buildings include 350,000 apartments (Droste and Knorr-Siedow, 2004). The objectives of the programme are the demolition of empty apartments and the improvement of the remaining stock and the waste area resulting from demolition. Droste and Knorr-Siedow (2004) note in their report, however, that this priority given to housing will preclude wider efforts to tackle social exclusion.

In the UK, governments since the 1970s have given priority to encouraging owner-occupation. The 'Right-to-Buy' programme has resulted in the sale of the better quality properties on the more attractive estates to the more affluent tenants (see also Chapter Five). This programme has changed the social composition of these areas. In 1988, the Housing Action Trust model was turned into physical housing regeneration, involving a substantial demolition and rebuilding programme (Evans and Long, 2000). Since the beginning of the 1990s, the UK has chosen to develop a demolition programme[3] as part of a wider estate regeneration scheme (DETR, 1999). These demolitions are targeted at the worst properties, on the worst estates, where the worst problems appear (unpopular estates, hard to let, hard to manage), mainly in old industrial cities and inner London Boroughs, where refurbishment is too expensive.

The Netherlands case is another interesting example since this country went further than most other West European countries with respect to the social-rented housing sector; in 1997, 37% of the total housing stock belonged to the social-rented sector. Demolition has been chosen since the second half of the 1990s, particularly within the Big Cities Policy framework, as a solution to address deprivation problems in the old post-Second World War neighbourhoods. In Rotterdam, the housing associations started to demolish the Hoogvliet-Noord estate, considered one of the most deprived areas in the city, at the beginning of the 1990s. Following the demolition of 2,000 houses, a further 4,800 will be removed to make room for new buildings of higher quality (Burgers et al, 2001). In the Big Cities Policy II, the aim was to attract well-to-do households by offering better opportunities to the existing residents of the neighbourhood, enabling them to find attractive accommodation in the same area and avoiding the need for them to go elsewhere to build a housing career (Musterd et al, 2003).

In France, since the first main demolition project in 1986 at La Courneuve (which involved 367 apartments in a 15-storey building), on average about 4,000 to 5,000 apartments are demolished each year (although the available data are not authoritative). Since 2003, this policy of demolition has operated on a much larger scale and has been set down in law.[4] The legislation provides for the demolition within five years of 200,000 apartments in the social housing stock which have been identified as in a state of 'disrepair', the rebuilding of 200,000, and the rehabilitation of a further 200,000. This spectacular physical measure is intended to resolve the 'social crisis' and transform these neighbourhoods into better places in which to live.

Beyond this programme, which was approved unanimously by the Chamber of Deputies, a few questions remain. Will the state keep its financial promises in a difficult economic context where property and land prices continue to rise? Even though the grants enabling the massive demolition programme are already committed, little consideration has been given to the rehousing of the present inhabitants. In any case, more than 100,000 new social housing apartments are required to be built per year to satisfy the present demand in addition to the rebuilding required after the 200,000 projected demolitions.

Today, this new orientation towards demolition is considered more pragmatic and less ideological. The social-rented dwelling stock is too large because households do not want to live in this type of dwelling in a neighbourhood with a poor image. Demolition is perceived as an opportunity to adapt housing supply to housing demand. Demolition is a tool to extend the opportunities for choice available to each household within the city and make all residential environments accessible for potential residents. By differentiating the housing stock, the city's well-to-do residents are retained because a housing career within the city or within the neighbourhood becomes possible. However, some commentators, particularly in France, fear that new exclusions will take place in relation due to the bad image of the social-rented sector and the orientation of policies to middle- and higher-income households. These commentators do not want to see a market solution catering only for the well-to-do. They consider demolition to be an easy option and, at the same time, an opportunity to eliminate a symbol of urban crisis and political failure, but with no real consideration of social perspectives (Belmessous, 2001).

Theoretical goals of urban regeneration

The goals of demolition and the goals of rebuilding large housing estates are closely linked because of the increasing housing demand in European cities. These cities often have to face an increasing demand for social housing from the poor and migrant people searching for accommodation. The extension of the EU may increase the problem. Thus, the main question of rebuilding policies is: how and where should social housing be rebuilt? This general question is related to the aims of urban policies in other fields: for example, the social policy of integration (immigrants) and social cohesion; and the economic effects of housing policies (the relationship between social housing estates and free-market housing estates), which are often linked to general economic goals such as the competitiveness of urban spaces.

The adoption of a more holistic view of the different types of interaction between social, economic, and spatial issues which can have an impact on the policies of urban renewal, and especially the question of how and where to rebuild social housing estates, therefore seems necessary in order to understand the theoretical goals of rebuilding social housing estates.

To establish a comparison between the different European countries, it is important to take into account the national political context of the social, economic, and spatial questions with regard to the rebuilding goals. Some aspects of the political context are more or less common to most European countries through the phenomena affecting the global and European context in general (globalisation of the economy, standardisation of the European legal system, general social evolution, and so forth). Other aspects tend to be specific to the national political context as a result of historical evolution (the centralistic political system in France, for example), or cultural aspects.

The social aspect

The increasing social problems of the segregation and concentration of migrant and poor residents in the large housing estates in many European countries in the late 1970s and 1980s led to new political goals related to the question of rebuilding. One of the major aims is to obtain improvements in the security and well-being of residents, and the quality of the built environment. In the Netherlands the policy of *menging* (mixing) sought territorial solutions for the social problems and in particular those of the minorities. The *Nota Stedelijke Vernieuwing* (Memorandum on urban renewal) (Ministerie VROM, 1997) announced the objective of establishing a more 'heterogeneous' population in the cities. New housing units are therefore to be integrated within the social housing estates or at their borders; these should then be sold to middle-class people (Jacquier, 2003).

In the UK, the social aspect of 'multi-sector partnerships' became an important issue in the 1990s; the context was the reconciliation of social and economic objectives. The 'City Challenge' and 'Single Regeneration Budget' programmes had the goal of strengthening the role of the local stakeholders in order to exploit the competencies of local residents and business interests (Hall et al, 2004)

In Sweden, the social aspects seem to be more important than the physical aspects when it comes to elaborate programmes to regenerate large housing estates: the goal is "to stop social, ethnic and discriminating segregation in the metropolitan regions, and to work for equal and comparable living conditions for the people living in the cities" (Andersson et al, 2004, p 11).

The economic aspect

Since the 1980s, the economic context has changed in many European countries with a housing demand that is increasingly determined by the dynamics of the market. Consequently, the demand for housing on the large estates started to decline. The changed demand implies 'new' strategies such as demolition programmes, even if these policies are not strictly 'new' (in the UK and France, for example). In Eastern Europe the 1990s are defined by the end of the socialist system. Hungarian, Polish, and ex-East German households have had a greater choice from different types of housing, and an extensive debate has taken place on the renewal of the old housing stock.

In other European countries (for instance, the Netherlands and the UK), policy makers have concentrated on market-oriented solutions. In the UK, for example, the policies of regenerating large housing estates are strongly oriented to the transfer of housing stocks from public to quasi-private ownership. Since the 1990s several political programmes have been set up to enhance the privatisation processes ('Housing Action Trust', 'Large Scale Voluntary Transfer', 'Estate Renewal Challenge Fund'). One of the major goals of this privatisation process seems to be better management of the housing stock and fundraising to improve housing conditions (Hall et al, 2004).

The economic context of labour has also changed and the high unemployment rate on many European large housing estates may have a strong influence on the vacancy rate on these estates.

The spatial aspect

Building very large estates was a state response to a very strong demand in the 1950s, 1960s, and early 1970s. Throughout these decades there were large population flows to the cities. However, policy makers, architects, and city planners were also influenced by ideological interpretations. The large estates were seen as the genesis of a new society (Kaës, 1963; Chombart de Lauwe, 1965). There was diversity in housing and in social respects on most of the estates. However, residents never really accepted this type of urbanism, or if they did, only for a short time. Thus, in France, an early survey carried out in 1983 showed that more than 85% of households would prefer to live in an individual house with a garden (Bachmann and Leguennec, 1996, p 506).

Since the 1990s, a general massive rejection of this type of urbanism has been the result of its poor image, the concentration of poverty, and the availability of other forms of housing. Currently, household demand seems to be increasingly oriented to the refurbished city centres, renovated neighbourhoods, areas round the historic city centre and individual houses on suburban greenfield sites. This process is older in Western Europe, but is a recent and massive trend in East Germany (Droste and Knorr-Siedow, 2004). The new policies seek to adjust supply to demand by building small housing units (the UK, France) or by adding more expensive blocks of apartments within former social-rented large estates (the Netherlands). The general consensus is to meet the demand for dwellings, inside or outside the very large estates, and demolition is a useful tool to regulate the market and change the image of neighbourhoods in decline inside the city.

Goals of urban regeneration in practice

The theoretical goals described above are based on the political programmes drawn up in the different European countries to find solutions for the different types of problems (social, economic, and spatial problems) related to the rebuilding of social housing estates. After the formulation of the goals of the political programmes, the public and private actors at local level have to implement the actions to meet them. Between these two steps (formulation of the goals and their implementation) there is often the transformation of initial goals into more practical goals that are better related to a particular context (political, social, economic, and spatial distinctiveness) at the local implementation level. But behind the formal goals of a political programme, other more practical goals can be discerned. In fact, in many cases, there are significant differences between the practical goals and the theoretical goals, which often seem more ambitious and noble (or maybe less realistic) than the practical goals. Three types of practical goals may be distinguished, which, in fact, derive from the theoretical goals described above.

Comparison of the different aspects of rebuilding (social, economic, and spatial) in relation to the political programmes in different European countries and the theoretical goal reveals the general problems that are common to many of these countries.

Sometimes even the programmes themselves present a certain number of similarities. One of these general problems is the transformation process from the centralistic management of renewal policies (initiated and organised by the state government) to a more decentralised management (see also Chapter Eleven). But the housing sector is only one of several political sectors affected by the general tendency of decentralisation.

Another goal that seems to be common in several European countries is to integrate social housing policy into the general urban marketing strategies in order to enhance the image of the social housing sector. This type of practical goal refers to the global context of the increasing competition between European cities. Finally, there is the common political goal of European local governments to reinforce democratic practices in order to avoid the crises in the political system of representative democracy. Residents' participation as exemplified by their engagement in the planning processes of rebuilding social housing estates is an important component in the re-establishment of confidence between the political leaders and civil society.

The management goal

The process of administrative transformations resulting from the transfer of legal competence from the state to local government authorities (decentralisation), and the increasing influence of private actors in the former public sectors (privatisation), seem to be general tendencies in many European countries. In the social housing sector, especially in the rebuilding of social housing estates, the theoretical goal is to attract non-governmental or private investors in order to raise funds for the realisation and the management of new housing estates. However, in most cases fundraising is very difficult because of the low returns from rents in social housing estates. Most potential private financiers of housing are more interested in rebuilding housing estates destined for the free market.

It seems that a more practical goal for the local actors involved in the rebuilding of social housing estates is to set up a new type of public–private partnership to manage the 'burden' of the social housing estates equitably. Some local actors have lost all illusion of a resolution of poverty on social housing estates. For these parties, the practical goal is to find a new system of financial partnership assuring permanent investment in the deficits of the social housing sector. The question is: how can local authorities afford heavy social costs in a new decentralised context in which they obtain fewer subsidies from the state government?

The marketing goal

One of the major practical goals of the demolition and rebuilding of social housing estates is to improve the poor image of the large housing estates. In many European countries these estates symbolise poverty, crime, and poor living conditions. Even if in some cases rehabilitation might cost less, the local authorities would prefer to demolish part of an estate and rebuild it in order to change the area and try to remove its stigma. This practical goal is related to the struggle of local authorities to reach a higher ranking in international competition for the social and economic attractiveness of European cities (Bonneville et al, 1991).

The democratic goal

The participation of the different stakeholders, particularly the residents of the housing estates, is an important goal within the political programmes of urban regeneration. However, the integration of the inhabitants in the decision-making system of planning is difficult. Often the inhabitants are ill-equipped to take a full part in the debates on the project (due to lack of time, lack of technical knowledge, lack of interest, and so forth). As a consequence, they can rarely influence the conception of the rebuilding project. Many local actors are aware of this problem and point out the necessity of a long-term learning process for the inhabitants to achieve the skills of a real stakeholder. There have been some approaches from this direction (mainly in the UK and in Switzerland) referred to as 'empowerment' (Albrechts, 2003).

But it seems that there is a more practical goal behind the efforts of ensuring participation that is not oriented to the outcome of the planning project. That goal is focused on the current crisis of democracy and especially the crisis affecting the political system of representational democracy. The gap between political leaders and society is evident from the weak participation of voters when elections are held. It seems that the participation process can have the aim of testing other forms of communication between society and political representatives such as hybrid forms of democracy (Albrechts, 2003): mixing representative democracy and participation democracy. So the practical goal of planning participation processes can have strong political goals to re-establish confidence between political leaders and representatives of society (Friedmann, 2002).

Demolition and the question of housing for people on low incomes: a confrontation

Dwellings on large estates were mainly built to provide housing for low-income households. At least in France, Sweden, the Netherlands and the UK many large estates offer low-rent dwellings in the private or social-rented sector to this type of household. But demolition reduces the supply of affordable dwellings and problems therefore arise for low-income households. What can be said about the confrontation between demolition and the housing demand of low-income households?

The current trends

The current situation is characterised by a few general trends that create conditions of social and geographical exclusion for lower-income households. On the one hand, market-oriented policies were the main driving force during the 1990s. Thus, most of the new apartment blocks were built for higher-income households and, in the context of gentrification taking place in many parts of cities, low-income households rarely interest developers. On the other hand, state involvement in housing for people of low social status is in retreat. New strategies aim to reduce public expenditure and encourage home ownership. Liberalism strives for less public funding for housing, including social housing. Some experts therefore consider the primacy of market-oriented policies as a new form of exclusion (Lapierre, 2000). The social distance between the middle and upper classes and the poor is gradually increasing; if the large estates are improved by demolition, renovation, or other policies, the housing question remains. Finally, policies create social fragmentation within large estates: some districts are improved, and then become attractive for higher socioeconomic classes; others remain in decline; the worst are demolished. Demolition does not therefore seem to resolve the housing problems and housing demands of low-income households.

Developments in housing demand: housing prices increase more rapidly than incomes

In the last decade, private rents and house prices have increased markedly. In the same period, the polarisation between the real incomes of the most prosperous and the poorest households increased strongly in England (Hall et al, 2004) and in France (Fitoussi et al, 2004); in the ex-socialist countries the evolution is faster than in the West. In the UK, the endlessly upward spiral of housing prices prompts important social questions; young or low-income households find it impossible to buy even a relatively cheap apartment. In France, too, the last Abbé Pierre Foundation report (2004) makes it clear how difficult it is for the poor to find accommodation. Social housing becomes an important issue in the provision of a solution, especially in France. Political parties, residents' associations, trades unions, and humanitarian associations regularly launch public debates about this question.

According to the Abbé Pierre Foundation report mentioned above, the number of households seeking a social-rented dwelling in France is currently more than one million, compared with about 885,000 in 1996. At the same time, the building of social-sector apartment blocks has been in decline. In France, the construction of social-rented dwellings fell from 80,000 in 1994 to 44,000 in 2002 (Chignier-Riboulon et al, 2003). The situation in the agglomeration of Lyon reflects the national trend: more than 40,000 households were seeking accommodation in the social-rented sector in 2003, according to the Greater Lyon Urban Community, compared with 29,000 in 1998 (Chignier-Riboulon et al, 2003). Moreover, in the last few years housing benefit payments for low-income households have decreased. The construction of social-rented apartments has declined and residential mobility in the social-rented sector has decreased; there is a link here with the higher prices on the housing market.

Demolition and the lack of dwellings for low-income households: a state response and a common refusal – the French case

Politicians, professionals, and academics are all concerned about the current crisis in the social-rented sector. New dwellings are often built for middle-income households. In the city of Lyon, the only site which will contain more apartments in the future than there are at present is the urban project of Les Minguettes; there, 700 dwellings will be demolished and 780 new dwellings constructed, 60% of which will be in the social-rented sector.

In France, the socialist government and parliament passed an Act in 2000 designed to mix social classes within cities and disperse social-rented apartments within all the communes of an urban agglomeration; the aim is for 20% of the dwellings in each commune to be in the social-rented sector by 2020. Those municipalities which do not wish to integrate these measures with their local policies will be fined. The idea may be well intentioned, but unfortunately, this type of policy is difficult to implement. Popular vision associates social difficulties with social dwellings, and social dwellings with large estates, even if they incorporate private renting and home ownership. So, where should the new social-rented apartments be built?

The question can be answered in two ways. On the one hand, the social image of this type of housing is so poor that many politicians, especially those in the right-wing parties, disagree with the new legislation. The legislation is a political risk, since most homeowners do not want social-rented housing units in their neighbourhood. According to the residents or their associations, the introduction of social-rented apartments represents a decline in their quality of life and they fear that the prices of private houses will fall. The present residents are anxious about delinquency, loss of well-being, educational problems for their children, and so forth, and so, they set up associations to try to prevent such future developments.

On the other hand, the cost of land in attractive neighbourhoods within or on the edge of a city is so high that building social-rented apartment blocks there would be very expensive. This applies particularly to the Mediterranean coast (Daligaux, 2003), and within the greater urban agglomerations such as Paris or Lyon. One of the current answers to the problem is to organise programmes based on smaller groupings of social-rented housing units to avoid the negative reactions of the other inhabitants and to facilitate social inclusion; however, the unit cost would be greater as a result of this approach.

Conclusion

Large housing estates were constructed in the context of the Fordist paradigm to provide new large stocks of housing after the Second World War in the cities and towns into which new populations were moving for work. Years later, as a result of social and economic change, the turnover of inhabitants on the large housing estates has led to the confinement there of residualised populations, mainly unable to afford accommodation in the private housing sector and the concentration of the present socioeconomic problems in an environment with a poor image.

Demolition and rebuilding have finally appeared as a way to reintegrate large housing estates within the city and to resolve the social and economic problems associated with them. But, essentially, the current housing market conditions, financial difficulties, and liberalism weaken or even undermine the major goal of demolition and rebuilding. Consequently, in spite of the goodwill exemplified by the new policies, the social housing question has not been resolved by the demolition and rebuilding solutions and is still a matter of debate.

The most important problems are generally avoided: where should the people evicted from the demolished apartments live? In which part of the city should the new buildings be built: within the neighbourhood, or within another commune containing fewer large social housing estates? As long as there is no clear answer, many local authorities will attempt to improve their marketing image by using demolition as an easy lever to add value to their land in introducing private actors from the free market. But, in doing so, the social perspectives have not been taken properly into account.

Notes

[1] It must be noted that this vacancy rate is also linked to the riots of 1990.

[2] The large social housing sector included 240 estates of 2,500 apartments or more (that is, 1.6 million residents).

[3] The number of local authority dwellings demolished increased from 4,000 in 1991/92 to 7,700 in 1996/97; 87% of the estates demolished have been or have yet to be redeveloped, mainly (90%) for housing purposes.

[4] Act: 2003-710 Trend and Scheduled Programmes for Town and Urban Renovation. See Table 11.1 for the first ten projects.

References

Abbé Pierre Foundation (2004) *L'état du 'mal-logement'*, annual report, Paris: Imp. Artésienne.

Albrechts, L. (2003) 'Public involvement: the challenges of difference', *NSL Network City and Landscape: DISP Journal*, vol 155, no 4, pp 18-28.

Andersson, R., Öresjö, E., Holmqvist, E., Pettersson, L. and Siwertsson, C. (2004) *Large housing estates in Sweden: Policies and practices*, Utrecht: Urban and Regional research centre Utrecht, Faculty of Geosciences, Utrecht University.

Bachmann, C. and Leguennec, N. (1996) *Violences urbaines*, Paris: Albin Michel.

Baudin, G. and Genestier, P. (2002) *Banlieues à problèmes, La construction d'un problème social et d'un thème d'action publique*, Paris: La Documentation Française.

Belmessous, F. (2001) 'En quête de legitimation d'une pratique courante: la démolition des logements collectifs sociaux', *Les Cahiers du CRDSU*, no 30-1, pp 20-1.

Bonneville, M., Buisson, M.-A., Commerçon, N. and Rousier, N. (1991) *Villes européennes et internationalisation*, Lyon: CNRS.

Burgers, J., Dukes, T., Hoes, J., Musterd, S., Staring, R. and van Kempen, R. (2001) *The Netherlands: The cities of Amsterdam, Rotterdam and the Hague*, Amsterdam/Rotterdam/Utrecht: University of Amsterdam, Erasmus University, Utrecht University.

Chignier-Riboulon, F. (1999) *L'intégration des Franco-maghrébins*, Paris: L'Harmattan.

Chignier-Riboulon, F., Commerçon, N., Trigueiro, M. and Zepf, M. (2003) *Large housing estates in France: Overview of developments and problems in Lyon*, Utrecht: Urban and Regional research centre Utrecht, Faculty of Geosciences, Utrecht University.

Chombart de Lauwe, H. (1965) *Des hommes et des villes*, Paris: Payot.

Coleman, A. (1985) *Utopia on trial: Vision and reality in planned housing*, London: Shipman.

Daligaux, J. (2003) 'Les DTA en recherche d'un équilibre', *Etudes foncières*, no 104, pp 30-38.

DETR (Department of the Environment, Transport and the Regions) (1999) *Business planning for local authority housing with resource accounting in place*, consultation paper.

Droste, C. and Knorr-Siedow, T. (2004) *Large housing estates in Germany: Policies and practices*, Utrecht: Urban and Regional research centre Utrecht, Faculty of Geosciences, Utrecht University.

Evans, R. and Long, D. (2000) 'Estate based regeneration in England: Lessons from housing action trusts', *Housing Studies*, vol 15, no 2, pp 310-17.

Fitoussi, J.P., Laurent, E. and Maurice, J. (eds) (2004) *Ségrégation urbaine et intégration sociale*, rapport du Conseil d'analyse économique, Paris: La Documentation Française.

Friedmann, J. (2002) *The prospect of cities*, London, Minneapolis: University of Minnesota Press.

Hall, S., Murie, A., Rowlands, R. and Sankey, S. (2004) *Large housing estates in the United Kingdom: Policies and practices*, Utrecht: Urban and Regional research centre Utrecht, Faculty of Geosciences, Utrecht University

Haussermann, H. (2000) 'Die Krise der "sozialen Stadt"', *Aus Politik und Zeitgeschichte*, pp 10-11.

Jacquier, C. (2003) *Rapport de synthèse des politiques intégrées de développement urbain, Royaume*. Paris: DIV.

Kaës, R. (1963) *Vivre dans les grands ensembles*, Paris: Editions ouvrières.

Knorr-Siedow, T. (2003) 'L'intégration urbaine à Berlin', *Cahiers de l'IAURIF*, no 123, pp 151-63.

Lapierre, U. (2000) 'Logement et marché: le principe d'exclusion', *Etudes foncières*, no 88, pp 16-19.

Lelevrier, C. (2002) 'Habitat et politique de la ville', in M. Segaud, J. Brun and J-C. Driant (eds) *Dictionnaire de l'habitat et du logement*, Paris: Armand Colin, pp 220-4.

Ministerie VROM (1997) *Nota stedelijke vernieuwing*, Den Haag: Ministerie van VROM.

Musterd, S., Ostendorf, W., Van Antwerpen, J. and Slot, J. (2003) *Measuring neighbouring trajectories in understanding processes of social exclusion: Amsterdam, the Netherlands*, Amsterdam: University of Amsterdam/Municipality of Amsterdam.

Union HLM (2001) *Démolition HLM, projets à trois ans et perspectives*, internal report.

Zajczyk, F., Mugnano, S., Borlini, B., Memo, F. and Mezzetti, P. (2004) *Large housing estates in Italy: Policies and practices*, Utrecht: Urban and Regional research centre Utrecht, Faculty of Geosciences, Utrecht University.

ELEVEN

Building partnerships in Spanish and Italian regeneration processes

Silvia Mugnano, Montserrat Pareja-Eastaway and
Teresa Tapada-Berteli

Introduction

In Chapter Three, it was argued that the political paradigm on which the large estates were built – characterised by *dirigiste* state-led provision of many public goods and services, including housing – had been superseded by a new paradigm characterised by the participation of a wider array of stakeholders – government, business and civil society – between whom power was (unevenly) distributed. In other words, the system of 'government' that evolved during the certainty engendered by economic growth following the Second World War had been displaced by a new, flexible form of multi-agency 'governance' more attuned to the uncertainties of a period of social, economic and political change.

The focus of this chapter is a comparative study of contemporary urban governance practices – that is, the multi-agency, decision-making dynamics that provide the context within which the large estates currently develop – taking into account four different local scenarios in Spain and Italy. These scenarios are: Community Development Plans (CDPs) in Sant Roc and Trinitat Nova (Barcelona, Spain), the Villaverde-Usera Investment Plan (VUIP) (Madrid, Spain) (see Pareja Eastaway et al, 2003, 2004 for a complete description of the Spanish case studies) and Paolo Pini Hospital in Comasina (Milan, Italy) (see Mezzetti et al, 2003, and Zajczyk et al, 2004 for a complete description of the Italian case study). This chapter presents our analysis of the main issues, the implications, conditions, and difficulties in building the praxis of urban governance, with the main focus on the players' involvement in the process of partnership in the case study estates.

Our analysis provides a set of variables that could account for the positive or negative outcomes of certain partnerships. In spite of the specific characteristics of these four scenarios, the comparison of different models of partnership has allowed us to identify some of the explanatory variables and mechanisms underlying the process of the players' involvement.

Two features have to be taken into account in the comparison of these projects: first, Spain and Italy belong to the South of Europe; second, the four programmes are on different local scales. Sant Roc and Trinitat Nova form part of a regional programme at neighbourhood level; VUIP covers two districts of the city; and a local micro-project has started for the revitalisation of the neighbourhood of Comasina.

With the the first feature, the analysis in this chapter makes clear the importance of the local dimension in relation to the mechanisms and strategies of building and maintaining partnerships, despite the considerable influence of Esping-Andersen's (1990) categorisation of the three worlds of welfare capitalism, which classifies Italy and Spain as the 'Latin particularistic-clientelist-subsidiary regime'. Although Italy and Spain present similar socioeconomic and demographic trends, we maintain that the local dimension should be taken into account in the process of urban governance.

Concerning the second feature, although the projects are completely different, here we look into the managerial structures behind the partnership cases. The aim of this chapter is to demonstrate the transferability of managerial structures and their variables, which in the end determine the success or failure of these partnerships. The number of players involved in each case is basically limited by the different tiers of government and types of residents' associations concerned. Despite the lack of involvement of other participants such as developers or private companies in our examples, the results might be usefully applied to those cases in which more agents are involved.

This chapter is divided into two parts: the first deals with the theoretical issues related to governance, paying special attention to the implementation of the governance concept in the urban arena. We focus on partnership as a form of urban governance practice. The second part is an exploration of the specific practices of urban governance in the partnership process related to the four case study estates. The focus is on how players – that is, government authorities, stakeholders, associations, and other institutions – participate and influence the policies of regeneration. In these sections we have followed the definition of partnerships set out by the European Foundation for the Improvement of Living and Working Conditions (EFILWC 1998; 1999; 2002a; 2002b; 2003).

Finally, we present our conclusions, taking into account the knowledge obtained through comparison of the different scenarios. The explanatory Boxes 11.1, 11.2, and 11.3 present the specific features of each case synthetically.

Theoretical discussion of the concept of urban governance and partnership

As noted above, the main idea underlying the concept of governance is the replacement of traditional forms of normative practices of government by a multi-agency approach. The increasing attention paid to the governance perspective has been facilitated by the changing context within which it has taken place. This changing context has, in part, been prompted by epoch-making social, economic and political changes, as noted earlier, but also, in the European context, has a particular formal, institutional imperative. Since the creation of the EEC in 1957 and especially as soon as the Maastricht Treaty's

---

Box 11.1: Description of Community Development Plans (CDPs), Catalonia, Spain

Background: The Integral Plan to Counteract Poverty and Social Exclusion (PPSE).

Objective: Creation of a framework to achieve the improvement of citizens' quality of life through an area-based approach to intervention.

Specific projects: Trinitat Nova (1996) and Sant Roc (1998, 2003).

Scenario level: Neighbourhood.

Actors involved: Regional and local government, residents' associations, neighbourhood associations.

Organisation: The CDP in Trinitat Nova distinguished four main areas of intervention: urban planning, economic, educational, and sociocultural. The present CDP in Sant Roc (2003) has been set up around three working areas: socioeducational and health; promotion of the economy; labour integration and living together, public spaces and housing.

Funding: Regional and local government.

Box 11.2: Description of Investment Plan in Villaverde-Usera (VUIP), South of Madrid, Spain

Background: *Movimiento por la Dignidad del Sur (MDS)* [Movement for the Dignity of the South].

Objective: The main objective of the €108 million investment plan of Villaverde-Usera was to combat the social imbalance characterising the City of Madrid.

Other projects: VUIP was a predecessor of the Puente and Villa de Vallecas Investment Plan, spanning the period 2000-05 and currently constituting work in progress. Four investment plans have already been approved: they concern the Carabanchel, Vicálvaro, San Blas, and Tetuán Districts. All except the Tetuán District are located in the southern periphery of the city.

Scenario: The two districts.

Actors involved: Regional government, Regional Federation of Neighbourhood Associations.

Organisation: The VUIP is based on seven working fields:
- relocation;
- infrastructure – trains;
- unemployment and development;
- education;
- economy;
- infrastructure – motorway (M-40) and other roads;
- 'lineal' neighbourhood.

In addition, a follow-up commission was also created.

Funding: Regional government.

convergence criteria were put into effect, the relationship between various levels of government and the traditional responsibilities assumed by the state have changed (the 'process of Europeanisation') (Marks, 1992; 1993; Scharpf, 1994). The multi-level governance approach stresses the changes in European governance without claiming the decline of the national state role and the importance of the policy networks at the various levels. Furthermore, most nation states have

---

Box 11.3: Description of Paolo Pini, Comasina, Milan, Italy

Background: Until 31 December 1998 Paolo Pini was a mental hospital.

Objective: Transformation of the mental hospital into a multi-activity centre.

Specific activities: The creation in 1998 of a Social Cooperative (Olinda) within the hospital space.

Scenario: The mental hospital within the neighbourhood of Comasina.

Actors involved: The enterprises created and administered by Olinda: the bar–restaurant Jodok, *La Falegnameria* (Carpentry), Olinda Multimedia, and a youth hostel.

Organisation: The cooperative and the association decided to work together to collect ideas, playing an apparently passive part, since their aim was to attract people with initiatives and proposals for this space and to enable them to implement their plans.

Funding: EU, regional, provincial, and local funds.

---

been involved in a *process of decentralisation:* the transfer of responsibilities from central to local government. The new role of the local government authorities (regions, councils, and cities) has a direct impact on the processes concerning the different strata of the implementation policies and becomes a central issue in the debate on governance.

Within this new multi-level decision-making structure, the last few decades have also been characterised by the *revitalisation of the local democracy approach.* As Burns stresses (2000), local governments have long been considered to be examples of an "irresponsible, inaccessible, inefficient, and unaccountable bureaucratic system" under the control of councillors perceived by their electorate to be 'unrepresentative'. Nowadays the actors' involvement is synonymous with neighbourhood action (neighbourhood councils, committees, and working groups) on large-scale issues (the environment, traffic congestion, and so forth) or on a micro-level scale (demands for green areas in the neighbourhood, for instance).

The concept of urban governance can be visualised as a synthesis of transformations taking shape in an attempt to relate the *governance* paradigm to a precise territorial context (Rhodes, 1997). This approach involves the integration of the economic, political, social, and technological changes that have taken place in European cities within a single interpretative grid. As Le Galès maintains, *urban governance* is:

> the ability to integrate and to give form to local interests, organisation and social groups, and, on the other hand, in terms of its ability to represent them to the outside, to develop more or less unified strategies for relating to the market, to the state, to the other levels of the government (1998, p 79).

As noted in Chapter Three, Healey's notions of 'collaborative planning' and 'place making' represent a normative model of urban governance that assumes that the capacity for governance can be created through a process of dialogue that is open to a wide range of players (Healey, 2002). Such a dialogue appears within different processes; partnership, as it is considered in this chapter, is, among other things, a relationship in which dialogue is explicitly or implicitly expressed.

The label of *urban governance*, as Elander (2002) points out, covers a wide variety of fields such as social welfare, environmental protection, education, and physical planning. What is worth noting, however, is that *urban governance* is innovative in terms of co-regulation, co-steering, co-production, cooperative management, and public–private partnership on national, regional and local levels (Kooiman, 1993). Furthermore, partnership is a practice that has become commonplace all over Europe. In this sense, "each government should ensure the right of all members of its society to take an active part in the affairs of the community ... and encourage participation in policy making at all levels" (United Nations Centre for Human Settlements (UNCHS), 1996, p 121).

Following Geddes (1998), the EFILWC defines partnerships as having the following characteristics:

- a formal organisational structure for policy making and implementation;
- the mobilisation of a coalition of interests and the commitment of a range of different partners;
- a common agenda and multi-dimensional action programme to fight unemployment, poverty and social exclusion and to promote social cohesion and inclusion (EFILWC, 1998, p 12).

Partnership, according to Elander (2002), belongs to a broader family of ideas within the concept of 'network' used in urban policy making and implementation. Partnership is often seen as cooperation and a coalition strategy that policy makers of different sectors establish at different levels. Indeed, neighbourhood development programmes usually require vertical and horizontal private–public partnerships that include not only relationships between central government departments and between central and local government departments, but also between government departments and local non-governmental organisations or between the EU and local non-governmental organisations. Although the potential combinations of interplay between participants is nearly infinite, mechanisms allowing such combinations might have common features. However, what is worth noting is that these relationships do not always carry the same strengths or flaws. It is difficult not only to define the partnership concept, but also to make it operative and to analyse how different typologies of partnership can be implemented in different local contexts. Within this perspective, the EFILWC model (2003) signifies an interesting attempt at an innovative evaluation tool for investigating to what extent local, national, and supranational players are collaborating in planning at the local level.

On the basis of the EFILWC (2003) series of handbooks dealing with building and maintaining partnerships, particular attention is paid in this chapter to four main dimensions through the analysis of four particular cases, presenting their similarities and differences and facilitating the identification of the elements that could be considered as prerequisites for building partnerships. Table 11.1 is a summary of the variables belonging to each dimension.

Table 11.1: Dimensions of partnership

Creation of partnerships: political and social context	Actors' involvement and partnerships	Development of organisational structures and procedures	Establishment of multilevel links for partnership funding
Existence or absence of a policy strategy; the peculiarities of the *contingent circumstances;* forms of conflict between agents	Identification and recognition of actors; participation; leadership; accountability	Synergies between actors; expertise; follow-up by agents	Financial agreements among actors; flexibility

Source: EFILWC, 2003

The analysis of case studies, although they belong to completely different arenas, reveals the variables capable of contributing to a partnership's success or failure. We have selected a variety of partnership scenarios which might help to forecast the potential outcome of a partnership and to correct or improve undesirable situations.

Creation of partnerships: the political and social context

The creation of a partnership may reflect the existence of a policy framework that stimulates and sets up the necessary legal, political, and financial means to develop a multi-agency approach to urban governance and, thus, the management of large estates. For example, the Integral Plan to Combat Poverty and Social Exclusion (PPSE) (approved in Catalonia in 1995) constitutes the philosophical and political background for the creation of Community Development Plans (CDPs). The PPSE requires a multi-dimensional procedure in urban governance in the CDPs. The PPSE facilitates, on the one hand, coordination in different fields such as urban planning and social welfare, and on the other hand, the involvement and participation of different levels of government and other players.

However, a partnership may appear in the absence of such a structure as the result of a demand to meet certain special needs. In the cases of Madrid and Milan, the lack of a previous political framework did not prevent the establishment of partnerships as a result of citizens' demands, in the first case organised under the *Movimiento por la Dignidad del Sur* (*MDS*) [Movement for the Dignity of the South], and as an *ad hoc* solution for a specific situation in the case of Paolo Pini.

The composition of the sociodemographic environment in a particular scenario strongly influences the degree of involvement and identification of the different players in new partnership projects oriented to the improvement of the residents' quality of life. The strength of this influence is related to the *contingent circumstances* affecting urban governance in general and the creation of partnerships in particular. For at least part of the explanation, the hypothesis underlying the current analysis relates the distinct contingent circumstances which characterise the neighbourhood to the various characteristics of the players involved. According to Judd (2000), these contingencies include the structure of the local and regional government authorities, the degree of cohesion among business elites, the strength of non-profit and neighbourhood organisations, and the cultural factors arising from ethnic, racial, and identity-based movements. In addition, the general context of which the city forms a part must also be included.

As for the sociodemographic composition, the weakness of the social fabric and the presence of non-integrated groups in sociocultural and political systems confirm forms of *asymmetric conflict* among agents (Borja, 2003). These agents reveal hesitation and an inability to build room for negotiation and to generate valid intermediaries to be accepted by all. In Sant Roc, the lack of a cohesive society or any confidence in a positive change for the neighbourhood produced a fragmented initiative which has resulted in an unclear response from the other partners, the local and regional government authorities.[1] The case offered by Trinitat Nova or the South of Madrid represents a situation involving forms of *symmetric conflict* between agents (Borja, 2003). On the one hand, a well-organised neighbourhood association took up a position with clear-cut interests and enough flexibility to negotiate and accept limitations. On the other hand, the representatives of the local and regional government authorities agreed to negotiate and satisfied all the requirements of a partnership until the final key words came up for discussion: responsiveness, adaptability, and hands-on control involving the residents in the development of the process.

Actors' involvement and partnerships

In order to guarantee a partnership's long-lasting and proper functioning, the first steps taken must include the identification and recognition of the other partners, together with the process of learning to cooperate and to discuss together. Once the individual partners have been separated out, the negotiation of a common strategy becomes essential for the development of the following steps.

During this stage of the process, openness, transparency, exchange of information and accountability are necessary elements for establishing lasting partnerships with civil society (EFILWC, 2003). The importance of creating networks among agents limits the strength of corporatism and attitudes which reinforce the collective instead of working for the network, allowing reciprocity and self-support in local initiatives (Alguacil, 2000). These elements are essential to the establishment of the basic level of trust necessary for the development of a successful partnership.

In Trinitat Nova, the result of the two diagnoses carried out in the neighbourhood before the implementation of the CDP – a compulsory requirement for starting a CDP – has been not only the provision of available information, but also the identification of potential players who could be involved. These include the residents and the local and regional government authorities. These parties should all be involved in continuous discussion and feedback.

The strongly social and ideological MDS in Madrid was initially organised around petitions for the demolition of Torregrosa, a rundown district in which drug smuggling had created serious social distress. MDS capitalised on the situation to draw further attention to wider problems resulting from the abandonment of the south of the city (Walliser, 2003). Residents' associations and other social bodies organised themselves under the umbrella of a single institution that was already in existence: *Federación Regional de Asociaciones de Vecinos de Madrid* (*FRAVM*) [the Regional Federation of Neighbourhood Associations of Madrid]. This institution gathered together all the proposals to be discussed with the representatives of the various authorities.

The first summer festival in Paolo Pini Hospital in Comasina enabled the creation of networks of people, organisations, and institutions interested in the project. Some patients were then still living in the hospital; the reconversion started once it was closed down.

The concurrence of stakeholders' and residents' interests is evident in Trinitat Nova, the South of Madrid, and Comasina. The design of a strategy and opportunities for negotiation with other partners are clear. In Sant Roc, the lack of a clear diagnosis of the neighbourhood's problems that all the actors could agree upon has been mentioned as the main reason for the failure of the CDP (DEHISI, 2001).

The need for strong leadership, particularly in the early stages of the process, is cited as a requirement for building partnerships (EFILWC, 2003). In Trinitat Nova, the previous presence of a powerful residents' association contributed to its leadership role in the implementation of the CDP and the strategy designed for the interventions. This strength derives from the fact that there is only one association bringing together all the residents in the area. Blanco and Rebollo (2003) discuss other qualities attributed to the association which help to explain its key role; they mention the association's capacity for self-criticism and the recognition of its own weaknesses and limitations which laid the ground for its readiness to heed the advice of experts – academics and an influential technical expert trained as a sociologist, Marco Marchioni.

In Madrid, the MDS worked as a catalyst allowing ideas and demands to emerge from the sociopolitical context. However, it was the FRAVM which acted as spokesperson, playing a leading part in the organisation and management of the implementation process of the VUIMP and acting as an intermediary between the participants in the process: the various levels of government and civil society.

The leadership role in Comasina was essentially taken by a social cooperative[2] (Olinda) created within the structure of the hospital that not only helped by giving support to the patients in the closing-down process, but also made a huge effort to reopen the vast spaces occupied by the hospital and its grounds for the benefit of the neighbourhood of Comasina and other people living nearby.

The urge for intervention in Sant Roc[3] and the lack of a coordinated response from the inhabitants warranted a strong input for setting up a coordinated plan following a traditional top-down approach. But one of the CDP's requirements was the best possible participation of citizens and their willingness to take part in the project. That requirement led to many calls on residents' representatives for their participation under the auspices of their various associations. The combination of the two approaches epitomises a situation which could be described as 'bottom-up from above'. However, the failure of the previous CDP generated a certain lack of confidence in the neighbourhood about the chances of success a new CDP might have. Moreover, Sant Roc, in contrast with Trinitat Nova, the South of Madrid, and Comasina, is a fragmented society and the organisations and associations that have emerged reflect such a pattern. As for accountability, the EFILWC (2002a) continues to campaign for the importance of partnership as a possible mechanism for social inclusion. Partnership can be used as a real tool for allowing social censure mechanisms to be uncovered and eliminated.

Strong pressure emanating from the need to justify the funding that had been provided by the public administration culminated in a diagnosis that was not agreed upon and, consequently, in a fragmented vision of the problems and perspectives of the neighbourhood.

Development of organisational structures and procedures

The organisation and management of partnerships varies according to the various scenarios in which they take place. As Elander (2002) points out in referring to partnership creation, the implementation of the urban governance concept is left to loosely defined partnerships including a wide array of players. The freedom this practice creates contributes decisively to the players' determinant influence on the process.

Following Hastings' classification (1996) of synergies affecting the partnership process, the cases of Trinitat Nova and the Paolo Pini Hospital are closer to a 'policy synergy' than a 'resource synergy': both exemplify a joint approach, combining the different perspectives of each partner, which results in new solutions, while their differences in culture and objectives remain unchanged. The partnership process is not merely a question of the coordination of the spending of resources, looking for a more efficient use of the money invested; the process also seeks a broader goal, to forge an innovative set of policies or solutions.

In Sant Roc, and to a certain extent in the South of Madrid, efforts are oriented towards the improvement of effectiveness in the expenditure of resources through the partnership (Hastings' 'resource synergy' process), probably because creating an arena where the exchange of perspectives could offer an innovative approach or policy as an outcome might be impossible (Hastings' 'policy synergy'). Since residents are involved in both cases, this model goes further than merely extracting added value in strictly financial terms. However, the residents' committees' lack of understanding reduces from the outset the opportunities for joint action in the case of Sant Roc. The hands-off approach of the regional government of Madrid[4] and the passive part played by the municipality makes the VUIP a Plan in which the MDS and its embodiment, the FRAVM, represent the main actors, without any real commitment from the authorities.

The availability of expertise, not only from the management perspective but also from the technical point of view, represents an essential element in the process. The transformation of relatively abstract concepts into everyday practice is usually delegated to an ad hoc organisation that is also responsible for the implementation of the project. This organisation connects the players not only vertically (connecting the government to the residents and vice versa), but also horizontally (connecting the people living and working in the neighbourhood).

The 'Community Team'[5] is responsible for the coordination, programming, and planning of the activities and projects of the CDP in Trinitat Nova. In Sant Roc, the local government authority engaged the external company VINCLE (Services to the Person and to the Community), which is responsible for implementation and management. The FRAVM in Madrid and Olinda in Paolo Pini have corresponding roles. In each case there is an observable institution that links the partners, managing and coordinating the set of activities proposed under the umbrella covering the various partnerships.

Comparison of the cases in terms of the supervision and control of activities reveals differences, although the projects have developed similar tasks: the residents' association supports and controls the work of the Community Team in Trinitat Nova, while the MDS in Madrid forms the framework within which the FRAVM works. The regional and local government authorities perform this function in Sant Roc, while an absence of control and guidance characterises the Paolo Pini case. The concept of governance at this stage has encountered two dissimilar trends. On the one hand, local democracy directly affects the performance of the CDP in Trinitat Nova and the VUIMP in Madrid, not only during the process of setting up priorities and projects, but also in their implementation. In the micro-project of Comasina, the organisation of players with no direct intervention by the government authorities clearly guarantees their accountability. In these cases, the initial and successive agreements drawn up by the partners guarantee an effective system for managing the process. On the other hand, however, the opportunities in Sant Roc to use the partnership as a channel for different citizens' groups to influence policy making are very limited.

Establishment of multi-level links for partnership financing

Urban governance and the management of large estates exemplifies through partnerships the shift from an exclusive reliance on public funds to a more open scenario where various partners are invited to co-finance and participate in projects. The determination of priorities in the process of intervention is unavoidably affected by budgetary constraints. The creation of partnerships often requires the players involved to draw up agreements and make compromises with respect to the partnerships' funding. In some cases, the interaction among these players is basically related to the synergies they produce in their efforts to augment the available finances. According to this view, partnerships may or may not include specific features in relation to the players' finances. In addition, the deferment of activities is related to some extent to the capacity to source additional funding and at the same time to justify the effective use of the money invested.

CDPs are incorporated and formalised in a 'Neighbourhood Contract' or 'City Contract': a legal instrument setting out the specific actions, common diagnoses, objectives, programmes to be developed, partners, technical and other participatory bodies, sources of finance, and evaluation criteria (EFILWC, 2002a).[6] Usually, the municipality and the regional authority to which the neighbourhood belongs provide an annual budget for the development of CDPs. These receive 50 per cent funding from each government authority. However, other bodies might also contribute to a CDP's finance: the *Federació d'Associació de veins d'habitatge social* (*FAVBIC*) [Federation of neighbours' associations living in social dwellings in Catalonia], for example, receives an annual grant from central government[7] in order to develop social programmes in certain neighbourhoods. Moreover, once a CDP has been established in a particular neighbourhood, the opportunities to find other funding sources depend on its management and on further agreements drawn up with other players or bodies. Of course, the stronger the players' partnership, the easier it is for them to attract external resources.

Follow-up of the process takes place through the annual review of the 'Neighbourhood Agreement', which mainly sets out the amount of funding available for the following year. This review does not necessarily guarantee the quality or effectiveness of the results, although it is obviously cheaper for the administrations concerned.

The VUIP in Madrid is mainly financed by a single partner, the regional government or *Comunidad de Madrid*. The social movement (MDS) that initiated the process reached an agreement with the regional government on the amount[8] to be invested over six years (1998–2003) in order to diminish the social imbalance with respect to the rest of the city. This case features a striking innovation in its project management (Cazorla et al, 2001), influencing the adjustable distribution of money over the six-year period. Such flexibility is a key element which facilitates the adaptation of the specific dynamics of the investment plan to the availability of resources. The follow-up of this programme was undertaken by a specially convened committee within the MDS.

The VUIP has been considered as best practice for other districts in Madrid. Performance in accordance with this plan serves as a guarantee for players who may be involved in further programmes. A clear example is the future involvement of the local government in subsequent plans.

Multi-level links are evident in the Paolo Pini case: several EU, regional, provincial, and local resources have contributed to its funding, confirming the collaborative urban governance process underlying this partnership. The project is presented in collaboration with other local players (the Lavorint Association (a training organisation), for example). The OPEN project (1998–99) provided an opportunity for the renewal and refurbishment of the carpentry house. This, however, was just one of many partnerships and funding forms of the project.

During this year, Olinda established through several cultural events a broad network linking various players (NGOs, local government, national government, EU) operating with varying levels of involvement in the realisation of the project. Other forms of partnership were established with commercial organisations interacting with the structure (providing food for the bar-restaurant, for example). In the Paolo Pini case there is also a well-established relationship with the central government.[8] This relationship was developed by different institutional and non-institutional players in different ways: through forms of financing or through the transfer of human resources, for instance. What characterises this experience is the fact that the private–public partnership model is not traditional, in the sense that it is not based on the 'public finance/private delivery' paradigm, but on the hypothesised collaboration between the private and public sectors for programming, designing, and managing the interventions.

Conclusions

In this chapter the practices and mechanisms of partnership have been explored through four different urban governance contexts: CDPs in Sant Roc and Trinitat Nova (Barcelona, Spain); the VUIP in the south of Madrid (Madrid, Spain); and the Paolo Pini project in Comasina (Milan, Italy). As has been shown, the transfer and implementation of the broad concept of governance to specific territorial contexts has to cope with the diversity and complexity characterising them.

Partnership is highly influenced by external factors such as the existence of any previous political strategy, the social context, and the multi-level dimension together with internal factors that are more related to the nodes in the networks such as leadership and participation and organisational structures and procedures. The combination of these aspects impacts strongly on the potential failure or success of the partnership.

The following three partnership scenarios have been identified in the research:

- An *interactive partnership* scenario: this refers to the situation in which the local context both welcomes the implementation of the programme and offers the preconditions allowing the programme to operate. This situation is also helped by a positive interplay among the players and a visible, stable, and structurally organised network. In addition, the leadership role is clearly defined (VUIP, CDP Trinitat Nova).

- A *top-down partnership scenario*: the policy conditions (instruments, programme, and so on) facilitate and develop forms of partnership, but a positive response from the local context is lacking. In this case, players are not formally recognised and problems may appear in the course of acknowledging the nodes in the networks (CDP Sant Roc).
- A *bottom-up partnership scenario*: there is a vibrant local commitment to action, but there is no positive response from the policy level that would provide a stable policy framework. This deficiency leads to a widespread dispersion of resources and the loss of the local perspective (Comasina).

From the residents' perspective, identification with the neighbourhood and confidence in its future should be included in the positive variables to be considered which directly affect the players' involvement. In addition, the players' recognition of their common interests provides a shared scenario in which problems and priorities can be distinguished. In contrast, if understanding between the neighbourhood and the stakeholders is lacking, different priorities emerge, thereby creating a lack of confidence in accountability in the partnership process.

As the case studies have shown, two aspects have to be taken into account in a partnership's creation: contingent circumstances and the policy framework under which the partnership process operates. Contingent circumstances might stimulate or obstruct the promotion and functioning of a partnership. In the case of Sant Roc, for example, contingent circumstances such as the lack of cohesion among the different committees of the neighbourhood have prevented a smooth functioning of the CDP; the absence of a municipal policy strategy in Milan is dispersing vital local energies in the Comasina case. Trinitat Nova and VUIP exemplify a better combination of elements: there is an interactive flow between the two dimensions. While the local players have developed a high level of confidence in the programme through their clear and shared vision of the situation, the programme itself has empowered the stakeholders and residents.

From the central government perspective, the provision of the necessary means to improve the knowledge of the different groups living together on the same territory and to stress the need for their mutual comprehension becomes one of its main tasks. The provision of a stable framework for negotiation and the creation and distribution of funds are also included in the government's main responsibilities. In addition, the creation of a powerful feedback link based on the effectiveness of the process during the implementation phase is essential for the wider establishment of good practice. The delegation of management tasks to a locally based ad hoc institution is appropriate, provided that a clear mechanism of evaluation of the process is also included.

As for the implementation policy, the main issue is still represented by the transferability of urban governance practices. Only the capacity to adapt to specific circumstances and contexts will improve the success of partnership responses to precise conflicts and problems.

Notes

[1] Currently, efforts are being made to improve the coordination of government's responses.

[2] Social cooperatives are cooperatives which employ disadvantaged workers and engage disadvantaged people as active cooperative members (implemented in 1991).

[3] In Trinitat Nova and Sant Roc, 'concrete cancer' affected some of the buildings, which meant demolition and new construction to relocate inhabitants.

[4] The regional government ensured the effectiveness of the VUIP by providing qualified personnel such as engineers, sociologists or architects to set up the different projects. However, the establishment of priorities is the responsibility of the working groups related to the MDS.

[5] At the moment, three people are working full-time in the Community Team.

[6] See Chapter Two for an evaluation of neighbourhood contracts in Catalonia.

[7] Specifically from the Ministry of Labour and Social Services. In 2000, the amount received was around €350,000 (for all neighbourhoods associated with FAVIBC).

[8] €108 million.

[9] *Presidenza del consiglio dei Ministri, Dipartimento degli affari sociali, Ministero del Lavoro e della Previdenza sociale.*

References

Alguacil, J. (2000) *Calidad y praxis urbana. Nuevas iniciativas de gestión ciudadana en la periferia de Madrid,* Colección Monográficos, no 179, Madrid: Centro de Investigaciones Sociológicas.

Blanco, I. and Rebollo, O. (2003) *El Plan Comunitario de la Trinitat Nova (Barcelona): Un referente de la planificación participativa local,* (www.pangea.org/trinova/).

Borja, J. (2003) *La ciudad conquistada,* Colección Alianza Ensayo, Madrid: Alianza Editorial.

Burns, D. (2000) 'Can local democracy survive governance', *Urban Studies,* vol 37, no 5-6, pp 963-73.

Cazorla, A., Cano, J.L. and De los Rios, I. (2001) *La orientación por proyectos como estrategia de gestión para fomenter la cooperación social en el desarrollo,* (www.unizar.es).

DEHISI (2001) *Estudi de necessitats socials al barri de Sant Roc,* Barcelona: Generalitat de Catalunya.

EFILWC (European Foundation for the Improvement of Living and Working Conditions) (1998) *Partnership, participation, investment, innovation – meeting the challenge of distressed urban areas,* conference report, 17-19 June, Dublin, Ireland.

EFILWC (1999) *Local community involvement – a handbook for good practice,* Luxembourg: Office for Official Publication of the European Communities (OOPEC).

EFILWC (2002a) *Integrated approach to activate welfare and employment policy – Spain,* Luxembourg: OOPEC

EFILWC (2002b) *Integrated approach to activate welfare and employment policy – Italy,* Luxembourg: OOPEC.

EFILWC (2003) *Social inclusion: Local partnership with civil society, foundation,* Luxembourg: OOPEC.

Elander, I. (2002) 'Partnership and urban governance', *International Social Science Journal,* vol 172, June 2002, pp 191-204.

Esping-Andersen, G. (1990) *The three worlds of welfare capitalism,* Cambridge: Polity Press.

Geddes, M. (1998) *Local partnership: A successful strategy for social cohesion?,* Dublin: EFILWC; Luxembourg: OOPEC.

Hastings, A. (1996) 'Unravelling the process of "partnership" in the urban regeneration policy', *Urban Studies,* vol 33, no 2, pp 253-68.

Healey, P. (2002) 'On creating the city as a collective resource', *Urban Studies,* vol 39, no 10, pp 1777-92.

Judd, D. (2000) 'Strong leadership', *Urban Studies,* vol 37, no 5-6, pp 951-61.

Kooiman, J. (ed) (1993) *Modern governance,* London: Sage Publications.

Le Galès, P. (1998) 'La nuova political economy delle città e delle regioni', *Stato e Mercato*, vol 52, April, pp 53-91.

Marks, G. (1992) 'Structural policy and multilevel governance in the EC', in A. Sbragia (ed) *Euro-politics*, Washington DC: The Brookings Institution, pp 191-224.

Marks, G. (1993) 'Structural policy and multilevel governance in the EC', in A. Cafruny and G. Rosenthal (eds) *The state of the European community, vol 2: the Maastricht debates and beyond*, Harlow: Longman, pp 391-410.

Mezzetti, P., Mugnano, S. and Zajczyk, F. (2003) *Large housing estates in Italy: Overview of developments and problems in Milan*, Utrecht: Urban and Regional research centre Utrecht, Faculty of Geosciences, Utrecht University.

Pareja-Eastaway, M., Tapada-Berteli, T., van Boxmeer, B. and Garcia Ferrando, L. (2003) *Large housing estates in Spain: Overview of developments and problems in Madrid and Barcelona*, Utrecht: Urban and Regional research centre Utrecht, Faculty of Geosciences, Utrecht University.

Pareja-Eastaway, M., Tapada-Berteli, T., van Boxmeer, B. and Garcia Ferrando, L. (2004) *Large housing estates in Spain: Policies and practices*, Utrecht: Urban and Regional research centre Utrecht, Faculty of Geosciences, Utrecht University.

Rhodes, R.A.W. (1997) *Understanding governance: Policy networks, governance, reflexivity and accountability*, Buckingham: Open University Press.

Scharpf, F. (1994) 'Community and autonomy: multi-level policy making in the European Union', *Journal of European Public Policy*, vol 1, no 2, pp 219-42.

UNCHS (1996) (United Nations Centre for Human Settlements) *Habitat Agenda and Istanbul Declaration: Second United Nations Conference on Human Settlements*, Istanbul, Turkey, 3-14 June 1996, New York, NY: United Nations Department of Public Information.

Walliser, A. (2003) *Participación y ciudad*, Madrid: Instituto Juan March de Estudios e Investigaciones.

Zajczyk, F., Mugnano, S., Borlini, B., Memo, F. and Mezzetti, P. (2004) *Large housing estates in Italy: Policies and practices*, Utrecht: Urban and Regional research centre Utrecht, Faculty of Geosciences, Utrecht University.

TWELVE

Local participation in Spain and the Netherlands

Ellen van Beckhoven, Brechtje van Boxmeer and
Lídia Garcia Ferrando

Introduction

As a result of the shifting role of governments across Europe, noted in Chapter Three and elsewhere in this book, civil society and local participation have become more important in public policy, including estate regeneration policy. Regeneration programmes with a more explicit and organised role for local participation are clearly becoming more common. Nevertheless, local participation is still more the exception than the rule in the everyday politics of western societies (Font, 2003), suggesting that the notions of 'place making' and 'collaborative planning' remain normative ideals rather than empirical realities.

As noted in Chapter Three, the role of citizens and communities is important in determining the nature of places and in the process of 'place making'. This chapter makes a comparative analysis of local participation in the regeneration processes of large housing estates. The issues that are discussed in the theoretical literature with respect to local participation are set against the empirical situation revealed in the Netherlands and Spain. The juxtaposition of the Netherlands and Spain allows an examination that includes elements of the traditional dichotomy between Northern and Southern Europe. The analysis of forms of local participation on large housing estates in these two countries also highlights certain differentiations between a mature, long-established democratic system (the Netherlands) and a (relatively, if not absolutely, as democracy is an even more recent phenomenon in Central and Eastern Europe) new one (Spain). This factor, which is elaborated later, has some influence on the extent to which the voice of residents is acknowledged in urban policy. This chapter makes clear which is more important in shaping local participation: national factors (including national policy approaches), or neighbourhood characteristics.

The most recent literature suggests that there are two main reasons for undertaking international comparative research in the social sciences: the furtherance of explanatory and predictive theory; and the understanding and transfer of policy from one country to another (Couch et al, 2003). We consider the first reason to be the more important, but since we present recommendations for estate regeneration policy in the conclusions, the paper may also contribute to the understanding of policy transfer.

In the next section, local participation is placed in a broader context and is related to the concepts of urban governance and collaborative planning. In this theoretical section, an inventory of factors and developments that are important in the analysis of local participation is presented. In the third section, an overview is given of what is taking place in Europe with respect to local participation. In order to create an empirical framework in which to place the Spanish and Dutch cases, other European countries are briefly discussed in relation to the theoretical factors identified.

After this overview, we consider Spain and the Netherlands in more depth. In the fourth section, some of the countries' important differences and similarities are discussed. The focus is on how these dimensions may influence the formation of local participation. We then present an analysis of the practice of local participation in the two countries by describing the situation on two large housing estates in Utrecht and two in Barcelona. Finally, we put forward our conclusions.

Participation in a broader context

Participation in a theoretical perspective

Two sets of influences promoting local participation are discussed here. The first concerns the consequences for society of macro changes, noted in Chapter Three, such as the shift from a welfare to a post-welfare 'mode of regulation', an economic shift from Fordist to a post-Fordist 'mode of accumulation', and the shift from a 'providing' state to an 'enabling' state. The planning theory literature concentrates on a shift from rationalist, analytical policy processes to more interactive, deliberative and collaborative modes (that is, collaborative planning). Within this framework, the trend from government to governance represents an endeavour to make the new paradigm more governable.

The concepts of governance and collaborative planning are central to this discussion.

The second set of influences towards local participation discussed here derives from a micro-level approach and is related to the belief that local participation produces more effective policy outcomes. In addition to the main arguments for and against developing local participation mentioned in the literature, the willingness of residents to participate is also discussed in this section.

Urban governance

In Europe, (local) government has traditionally been the main player in urban and estate-based projects. However, in the 1990s urban government encountered a movement leading towards more differentiated forms of governance. More sectors were becoming involved in governing activities and decision making: local government became urban governance. Since some responsibilities have been transferred to the marketplace and civil society, public matters are no longer the exclusive responsibility of the state (Kooiman, 1993). Following a first move to involve the private sector, the voluntary and community sectors have also recently been involved (Kearns and Paddison, 2000). According to Docherty et al (2001), the current ascendance of local participation in urban governance can be seen as a response by government authorities and citizens to a lack of confidence in the ability of the state and the market to create socially cohesive and economically successful cities. Local participation is one element of the shift from government to governance and is seen as an important condition for successful urban processes (Andersen and van Kempen, 2001).

Local participation was already present in traditional governments. Walliser (2003) draws a distinction between informal and formal participation. *Informal* participation takes place around different types of interaction between players or as a result of protests and demonstrations that result in negotiations. *Formal* participation, on the other hand, is organised via formal government strategies. This latter form of local participation has become increasingly important in urban governance and the management of large estates.

Collaborative planning

It was argued in Chapter Three that, in the new socioeconomic paradigm of the late 20th and early 21st century, governing cities has become more complicated as a result of the growing complexity of social life and increased social differentiation. Cities have become complex, diverse entities and different people experience them in different ways. This observation is fundamental to the concept of collaborative planning (see Healey, 1997; 1998a; 1998b; 2002). Collaborative planning develops a normative model of planning appropriate to an inclusive, environmentally sensitive, mixed economy. The concern is with 'place making': the promotion of the social, economic, and environmental well-being of diverse places and the development of institutional capacity to realise that well-being (see Chapter Three). In a normative situation, place making is achieved through a collective, consensus-building, decision-making process based on progression through argument and debate. The agenda for city planning should be inclusive; all stakeholders should have the right to a voice in the decision-making process. A focus on 'place' at the neighbourhood, city, and regional levels has the potential to strengthen the 'voice' of those 'living in the city' (Coaffee and Healey, 2003). In the analysis of local participation, several questions must be borne in mind: who, for example, is involved in the discussion on 'place making'? Who is excluded? Who makes the decisions, and why?

Local participation: why and why not

From a micro-level point of view, local participation is concerned with the belief of policy makers that local participation produces more effective policy outcomes. The involvement of residents can improve policy, since residents can bring significant knowledge resources to the table. A simple example is their knowledge as to what will and what will not work locally: what facilities would be used and what would rapidly be daubed with graffiti and be abandoned (Taylor, 2000). Residents can be crucial in both the diagnosis of the systematic causes of problems and in deciding who should be engaged in resolving them (Wilkinson and Applebee, 1999).

Another important objective encouraging policy makers to involve residents in drawing up policy is to develop more democratic policies in which citizens are heard and are empowered (Font, 2003). Related to this, local participation is also expected to bridge the gap between the electors and the elected (creating political trust). In some cases, having politicians with an open attitude and citizen-centred policies can be a marketing strategy to 'sell' policy to the electorate. Local participation also often encourages the acceptance of policy implemented within an area.

Furthermore, local participation can be developed in order to create or increase human and social capital. Local involvement is collective action – involvement in influencing, planning, managing, and working in local activities and services; it develops the skills and confidence needed if social exclusion is to be dealt with effectively (Taylor, 2000).

Local participation also has its downside from the policy makers' point of view. Two reasons can be discerned for opposing the involvement of residents. The first is related to the possibly undemocratic representation within the participation process. Many forms of urban governance (including local participation) are not open to all the stakeholders (that is, the whole neighbourhood population); governance can be closed to those who are not involved (Elander and Blanc, 2001). The question of whether the participating residents represent the whole neighbourhood has become a classic debate (Font, 2003). The second reason for policy makers to oppose local participation is related to their expectation that the demands of participants will be unrealistic. Participants may have no appreciation of technical difficulties and might not take the arguments of other sectors into consideration. Involving citizens then takes too much time and delays policy making.

Policy makers may, however, be unwilling to give residents a voice. As we see in the next section, the government's motives in involving residents and the political willingness to share power result in different forms of local participation.

Propensity of residents to participate

Apart from the fact that residents deserve the opportunity to participate, they also have to be willing and able to do so. Besides a lack of interest, local participation can also be affected by residents' lack of knowledge of how to participate. In addition to personal factors such as educational level, the provision of information is also important.

According to Olsen (cited by Schlozman et al, 1995), the will to influence policies is the most important motivating element leading citizens to take part in participatory mechanisms. However, politicians are held to account by the electorate and so they must have the last word on any accepted policy (Font, 2003).

A study of local participation by Docherty et al (2001) refuted the idea that willingness to participate is mainly explained by 'compositional factors' of the population, such as the level of education and socioeconomic class (the notion that highly educated people are more active, for example). An important factor in explaining the level of participation is the residents' level of confidence that their neighbourhood is improving. The mutual trust between the citizens and the local government authority is also a stimulating factor in local participation (Ángels and Gallego, 2002).

Finally, the focus of a restructuring project in the neighbourhood can affect local participation. The aims of the interventions can vary from improving the social structure, to attracting other residents, or improving the physical structure, for example. Later in this chapter we show how these factors have influenced the success of local participation in the four case studies.

Organisational forms of local participation

Organisational forms of local participation can be categorised by type of representativity, level of citizens' power, and top–down or bottom-up orientation. These organisational forms may co-exist in each particular participation process. They help us analyse local participation in practice and they are discussed in the context of the case studies.

Associative and individual participation

Wuthnow (1998) argues that patterns of local participation have changed; to some extent, organisations and clubs have been replaced by looser, more individual forms of participation. In 'associative participation', representatives of residential associations or other groups or organisations are involved in the participation process. In 'individual participation', individuals who are not linked with any particular association represent personal interests. Although some participation processes are characterised by a combination of individual and associative (or group) participation, many are still dominated by group representatives.

Share of power

Power determines who participates and in what ways. One of the obstacles to participation is the reluctance of local politicians to share power with local lay people. The political will to share power is therefore important for the type of local participation found in the policy-making process (Del Pino and Colino, 2003). Arnstein (1969) developed a framework for outlining the key stages leading towards citizen control. In her model, she ranked eight forms of participation on a participation ladder, varying from a low level of citizens' power to the highest level, where citizens are in control ('citizen control'). On the lowest two rungs of the ladder, those with power are simply manipulative and one cannot speak of local participation (these forms are referred to as 'manipulation' or 'therapy'). Further up the ladder, residents are informed, or asked for their opinions ('informing' and 'consulting' respectively). On the top four rungs, residents are involved in the decision-making process increasingly as equal partners: they acquire an advisory role ('placation'), are involved in 'partnerships', acquire 'delegated power', and finally are in control. On the top rungs of the ladder, decisions match the wishes of the whole community increasingly closely.

The ladder has recently been adapted. By relating the concept of the ladder to real initiatives in the British context, Burns and colleagues (1994) discovered more steps higher up the ladder above Arnstein's first six rungs. The main change, however, concerns the gaps between the rungs. These are not equally spaced; climbing the first few rungs (up to 'consultation') is far easier than climbing the higher rungs. Furthermore, the number of rungs has now been extended; there are 14 in the new model instead of eight. Successive studies of local involvement agree that, in most participatory programmes, communities have remained on the margins of power, even when they are relatively well organised (Hastings et al, 1996; Taylor, 1998, 2000). Fewer examples are therefore found of forms of local participation that could be placed higher on the ladder.

A higher level of participation does not automatically result in more effective or more democratic policy. Without specific resources, residents' power may not give the expected or desired results. According to Wilcox (1998), different levels of participation are appropriate in different circumstances to meet the expectations of different interests. In a democracy, residents' responsibility also has limits; the elected politicians take ultimate responsibility. Therefore, to avoid situations in which residents expect more power than they can realistically acquire and to aim at effective and democratic policy, the limits of residents' powers and responsibilities need to be made clear to all stakeholders from the start.

Top-down and bottom-up

In many cases, local participation is initiated by local, regional, or national government authorities. Their aim is to enhance the position of the authorities and gain the confidence and support of the public (Stoker, 1997). However, government authorities can also initiate local participation to strengthen the 'voice' of the residents in decisions concerning their 'place' and meet other objectives as stated above (to increase human and social capital, for example).

In a bottom-up form of local participation, residents put themselves forward to make their voices heard. They ask the policy makers for more power in decision-making processes. In practice, these two forms of local participation (top-down and bottom-up) are expected to have different organisational forms and produce different results.

Participation in the European context

According to Font (2003), local participation is still more often the exception than the rule in the everyday politics of western societies. Nevertheless, the numbers of cases with a more explicit and organised role for citizen consultation are clearly increasing. This section gives an overview of the situation with respect to local participation in Europe; we can then place the Spanish and Dutch cases in an empirical framework. Some international experiences are briefly discussed in relation to the theoretical factors identified in the previous section.

In the Netherlands, local participation in regeneration policy has been stimulated by the central government's Big Cities Policy. The government authorities in other countries such as France, the UK, and Sweden also encourage local participation. In Spain, on the other hand, the government has only recently begun to do so. According to Szemzö and Tosics (2004), in the young democracy of Hungary, the idea of actively involving citizens in any form of public life is also relatively new. In general terms, government stimulation of local participation is encountered less frequently in the relatively young democracies than in the older democracies.

During the past decade, local participation has been a central objective of regeneration schemes in different places across Europe and for different motives. Much has been achieved, although significant obstacles have also been encountered. Reaching an acceptable level of representativity seems to be difficult; socially excluded groups, for example, are rarely involved in participation processes. The Swedish government tries to improve representativity by stimulating the participation of socially excluded groups such as immigrants. As discussed in section 2 of this chapter, developing participation can be important in contending with social exclusion. In Sweden, integration forms an important philosophy underlying regeneration policies, and local participation in the form of consultation is one of the instruments to realise this integration. In practice, however, as in other countries, language problems form an obstacle in generating participation *en masse* in Sweden (Öresjö et al, 2004).

The level of political trust also influences the level of participation. Öresjö et al (2004) showed that in Sweden, as in the Netherlands, expectations about policy plans play a crucial part. If people begin to distrust renewal policies or become frustrated by them (if they receive fewer decision-making powers than they expected, for example), these policies seem to have less chance of being successful. The broad acceptance by residents of a specific project seems to be crucial.

Furthermore, it can be seen that, although participation is becoming an important issue in the policy-making process across Europe, the political will to share power is often limited to the 'information' or 'consultation' form of power-sharing and only rarely involves a form higher up the participation ladder (such as 'partnership' or 'delegated power'). In France, as in many other countries, 'information' is the most common form of local participation in the regeneration processes of large housing estates. In Lyon, for example, the residents' observations and suggestions are noted during meetings. Although this note taking may seem to be a form of consultation, according to Belmessous and colleagues (2004) the residents' comments have little influence on policy; the policy makers have already made the decisions beforehand. Trinitat Nova in Barcelona (discussed further below), where local participation shows forms of co-decision, can be seen as an exception, not only in Spain, but also in the European context.

Spain and the Netherlands: different countries, different issues

The juxtaposition of Spain and the Netherlands allows an examination of the traditional dichotomy between Northern and Southern Europe. In addition, the analysis of the forms of local participation implicitly includes some differentiation between a relatively recently established democratic system (Spain) and an old democracy (the Netherlands). In this section, some of the important ways in which Spain and the Netherlands resemble or differ from one another are discussed. The focus is on how these dimensions influence the shape of local participation.

Institutional frameworks compared

Role of governmental levels

Ever since the Second World War, the Netherlands national government has played a leading part in public policies, including housing (Salet, 1999). In the 1980s, however, the role of the national government changed. In the Netherlands, national government has gradually retreated from many areas of responsibility, including housing policy. The responsibilities of the local government authorities in this field have therefore become more important. Other parties, especially housing associations, have also become responsible for housing. In the Netherlands there is a regional level of government in addition to the national and local governmental levels. The role of regional authorities is rather limited and is nowhere comparable to those of more federalised states such as Spain or Germany (see Aalbers et al, 2004, for example).

In comparison with the Netherlands, Spain is a relatively new democracy. Following Franco's death in 1975, Spain changed from a dictatorship to a constitutional monarchy, and three levels of government were created: central, regional, and local. Many responsibilities have been decentralised from central government to regional government, which consists of 17 Autonomous Communities. In contrast with the Netherlands, the regional government in Spain is an important level of government. This institution has, amongst other things, responsibilities in urbanism and housing.

The role of the local government also differs in the two countries. Although in Spain local government's responsibilities have increased as a result of the decentralisation process, in comparison with the Netherlands the responsibilities of Spanish local authorities are nevertheless relatively small and their budgets are rather limited. In general, local government is seen as the most appropriate governmental level at which to set up initiatives for local participation (Del Pino and Colino, 2003). Because the responsibilities and resources of local governments in Spain are fewer than in the Netherlands, there are fewer opportunities for initiating local participation in comparison with the opportunities available to Dutch local government authorities.

Welfare state and political consensus

The development of the welfare state in Spain has only been very modest, while in contrast the Dutch welfare state is generous. Citizens living in a welfare state that is relatively undeveloped are more likely to take the initiative to participate in order to meet needs that the authorities have not provided (Bruquetas et al, 2002). In Spain, therefore, more bottom-up forms of local participation may be expected than in the Netherlands.

Akkerman (2003) describes the Netherlands as a country with a strong consensual tradition. In Spain, on the other hand, the level of consensus is much lower. According to Walliser (2003), this lower level of consensus can explain why nowadays Spanish politicians have more influence on public policy than politicians in the Netherlands, where urban policy in particular has a more technical character. In Spain, politics play a considerable part in urban policy and therefore local participation has an important political dimension (Bruquetas et al, 2002). In the Netherlands, on the other hand, urban policy and local participation are less influenced by politics, which may result in a more stable environment in which to develop participation processes.

Participation compared

Spain is a relatively young democracy with a short political tradition of formal local participation. Informal participation, however, has a longer history. In Spain, between the late 1960s and the early 1980s, urban crises and political change resulted in the most significant urban mobilisation in Europe since 1945 (Castells, 1986). Residents' associations played a major part in these large social movements. Having fulfilled their clear objectives (decent dwellings and an attractive built environment, for example) in the 1970s and 1980s, the residents' associations became less important. Although their power has been decreasing, local government authorities still use residents' associations as their principal partners in dialogue (Pindado, 2000). In Catalonia (the Autonomous Community of which Barcelona is the capital), where participation processes have increasingly featured a leading role for individual citizens, the role of associations is still important (Font, 2003).

In contrast with Spain, there has never been any urban social movement to this extent in the Netherlands; residents' associations have always had a minor role. Residents' associations can therefore be expected to play a more important part in local participation processes in Spain than in the Netherlands.

Against a background of declining legitimacy of local politics in the 1990s, more instruments of local participation were developed in the Netherlands (discussion groups for example). In Spain, the idea of involving residents in policy making is more recent. Accordingly, in the Netherlands more formal instruments are used to stimulate and organise local participation.

Local participation in large housing estates in Utrecht and Barcelona

Four case studies were carried out to facilitate the analysis of local participation at the neighbourhood level. This section focuses on the involvement of residents in regeneration projects on the large housing estates of Hoograven and Kanaleneiland in Utrecht (the Netherlands), and Trinitat Nova and Sant Roc in Barcelona (Spain). The developments and problems in the four neighbourhoods and the policies implemented are briefly described. In order to filter the local factors influencing local participation, the level and organisation of participation are prominently featured.

Large housing estates

The four housing estates discussed in this chapter were built in the 1950s and 1960s; they are characterised by a mixture of medium-rise and high-rise apartment blocks. Trinitat Nova and Sant Roc are peripheral neighbourhoods in Barcelona. Trinitat Nova was built to accommodate immigrants from rural areas in other parts of Spain; Sant Roc was designed to rehouse people relocated through slum clearance. The central government kept its investments at a low level, and builders and public developers sought to maximise their gains. Consequently, poor materials were used and a chaotic urban environment was created. With respect to ownership, it can be said that most dwellings in both areas are 'officially protected houses': public dwellings with a postponed ownership.[1]

Kanaleneiland and Nieuw-Hoograven in Utrecht, both located relatively near the city centre, were built as part of an extensive national programme designed to resolve the post-Second World War housing shortage in the Netherlands. In many cities a large number of dwellings had to be built as quickly as possible, so 'efficiency' became the keyword. In these post-war neighbourhoods, most of the dwellings belong to the social-rented sector.

At present, the estates in all four case studies are confronted with both physical and social problems. Although every neighbourhood is different, in all four cases some of the 'classic' problems of the large housing estates (see also Chapter One of this book) can be found: vandalism; drug abuse; the anti-social behaviour of gangs and groups of youths;

unemployment; poor educational levels; and the obsolescence of the housing stock. (See Aalbers et al, 2003, for further information on the Utrecht neighbourhoods, and Pareja-Eastaway et al, 2003, on the Barcelona cases.)

By the end of the 1960s the residents in both neighbourhoods in Barcelona had started to organise themselves in order to campaign for better living conditions; initially, many facilities were lacking and construction deficiencies became apparent. The government responded to the protests by putting plans into effect to improve the neighbourhoods. In contrast with Trinitat Nova and Sant Roc, the history of the Utrecht neighbourhoods shows no patterns of informal local participation; plans to improve the area have mainly been initiated by the national and local government authorities.

The neighbourhoods also differ with respect to the composition of the population. Both Kanaleneiland and Nieuw-Hoograven have changed from homogeneous neighbourhoods with a native population into heterogeneous areas with a range of different cultures. In Sant Roc the population has never been homogeneous. Recently, however, the population has become more heterogeneous as a result of the arrival of many immigrants. In Trinitat Nova, on the other hand, the population has always been homogeneous.

Utrecht: policies, organisation, and participation

Policies

In 1995, the national government in the Netherlands introduced the Big Cities Policy (BCP). The philosophy behind this policy is to create a 'complete city' by integrating three policy fields ('pillars'): physical, economic, and social. The horizontal coordination of the various policy areas involving urban issues is essential to this integrated approach. Recently, the policy has been extended by adding safety as a fourth pillar. Breaking up the homogeneity in some designated areas[2] is considered an important measure to create a neighbourhood that is attractive and differentiated (in both physical and social respects). This objective can be realised by replacing parts of the housing stock by new buildings with a higher value. Other interventions include the improvement, merging, and sale of (social-) rented dwellings.

Local participation is an important element of the BCP. In order to improve the social situation on the designated estates, the residents need to become more involved with their living environment and with each other. They should therefore organise themselves, or at least see to it that they secure for themselves a say in the regeneration plans. In the Netherlands, improving the social structure is an important reason for involving citizens. Another reason for stimulating local participation is the growing gap between the electorate and the politicians; this became apparent in the Netherlands towards the end of the 1990s. Against this background, in common with other local authorities, Utrecht initiated the 'neighbourhood approach'; local authorities have become more active on the neighbourhood level (by organising evening meetings for the dissemination of information or discussions about planned policy interventions, for example).

Organisation

In 2001, the plans for the physical restructuring of Utrecht in the framework of the national BCP were documented in the 'DUO agreement' (*De Utrechtse Opgave* [Utrecht's Task]). This agreement sets out the powers and responsibilities of all partners in the restructuring process, including the residents.[3] The extent to which residents can influence plans (citizen power) depends on how well they are organised. A residents' association is often involved in the form of 'placation' (see Arnstein, 1969); they can give advice. The opinions of other residents are gathered through surveys or interviews organised by the housing association or by the local government authority ('consulting'). Since local politicians in Utrecht seem to prefer associative participation, the question of representativity arises; do the participating residents represent the whole neighbourhood accurately? Although in the opinion of the local politicians they do, social workers and people working at the neighbourhood level often take the opposite view (see Aalbers et al, 2004).

Level of participation

There are several citizens' associations in Kanaleneiland: in addition to a tenants' association and a homeowners' association, there are also ethnic associations. The associations do not cooperate with each other, and each has its own opinions about the regeneration plans. This weak association structure in Kanaleneiland, which can also be seen in Nieuw-Hoograven, makes it difficult for local government or housing associations to involve these lay associations in the regeneration process. This weak association structure is related, among other things, to a lack of mutual respect between the different residents' groups. Difficulties related to language or culture also play a part.

Another factor influencing the level of participation is related to residents' expectations about the organisation and execution of the restructuring process. Before the DUO agreement was set up, residents living in the neighbourhoods undergoing reconstruction were invited to work in focus groups on a plan of requirements. This procedure was also followed in Nieuw-Hoograven. All the people who were affected by the interventions (residents, entrepreneurs, for example) were invited to think about one particular aspect, such as safety. However, because several of the plans put forward were unrealistic or unaffordable and therefore not considered practicable, the participating residents became disappointed; they thought their opinions should be taken more seriously. To prevent such situations recurring, residents' power is now clearly defined in the DUO agreement.

Residents may also become frustrated through the poor internal management of a particular project. In Nieuw-Hoograven, a large regeneration project has suffered enormous delays because the parties involved (local government, developers, and the housing association) found it difficult to come to agreement (about finances, for example). This delay has resulted in a situation in which the residents and entrepreneurs have lost confidence in the local government authority and their willingness to participate in the project has declined.

Finally, the inadequate provision of information can cause anxiety among the neighbourhood's residents. In both Kanaleneiland and Nieuw-Hoograven, residents fear that the increasing housing costs brought about by the intervention will oblige them to leave the neighbourhood. The local government and the housing associations both wish to increase the proportion of dwellings in the owner-occupied sector and the proportion of more expensive dwellings in the social-rented sector. Many households complain about the lack of information on this issue, and the uncertainty reduces their willingness to participate.

Barcelona: policies, organisation, and participation

Policies

In Spain, there is no central policy or general integrated approach regarding the physical regeneration of neighbourhoods. Urban regeneration mainly consists of the demolition of the most dilapidated dwellings and their replacement with newly built dwellings. These processes only take place in areas where rehabilitation would be more expensive than new construction.

In the second half of the 1990s, the local and regional government authorities directly responsible for the dwellings decided to implement certain urban regeneration and renewal projects in the neighbourhoods of Trinitat Nova and Sant Roc in Barcelona.

In Sant Roc, many different cultures live side by side: gypsies, recently arrived immigrants, and others. The gypsies in the regeneration area live for the most part in separate apartment blocks. This division contributes to a situation in which residents are subjected to social exclusion. In addition to replacing technically deficient dwellings, the regeneration project aims to break up the concentration of gypsy families in some apartment blocks by relocating these families and spreading them over the entire regeneration area. The government has provided funds to implement a social programme dealing with the integration of these families into the new apartment blocks.

A Community Development Plan (CDP) (*Plan de Desenvolupament Comunitari*) has been set up in both neighbourhoods. The CDP is financed by the regional government and aims to prevent social exclusion and improve the residents' quality of life (Direcció General de Serveis Comunitaris, Servei de Plans i Programes, 2002). In the CDP, the involvement of residents is not seen as an aim in itself, but as a strategy to achieve the CDP objectives. Finally, a CDP can be seen not only as a programme, but as a general model that incorporates local participation as an important aspect in the transformation process. The CDP concept aims to increase social activity in all aspects of daily life and expand the use of the economic resources of the region as an instrument to counteract social exclusion (Rebollo, 2001).

Organisation

A CDP covers several fields, including education, economic development, and communication. In each field, a workgroup is set up including residents and specialists. These workgroups are responsible for developing projects to resolve the various problems defined at the start of the CDP. The Technical Committee, a group of professionals commissioned by the government, is responsible for the coordination of the whole process. To encourage the integral approach, meetings are organised for the various workgroups, together with open meetings for all residents.

Policy concerning physical regeneration does not stimulate local participation. Nevertheless, the residents on both estates have intervened in the decision-making process of the regeneration to a certain extent. In Trinitat Nova, the public authorities' decision to intervene in the poor physical state of the dwellings occurred at the same time as the CDP was set up. It was the residents of Trinitat Nova, not the regional government, who took the initiative to set up the CDP. The residents' association is an important player in both the CDP and the physical regeneration; the association commissioned a company specialising in urban planning to represent residents' interests and petitions in the design of a Special Plan for Interior Regeneration (PERI) (*Plan de Especial de Reforma Interior*). Some ideas that have been included in the PERI were indeed proposed by the residents. The coordinators of the CDP are also closely associated with the residents' association. Residents of Trinitat Nova participate in the regeneration project through mechanisms and networks established by the CDP, such as the Regeneration Workgroup. The residents' position on Arnstein's participation ladder is quite high, located on the step of 'placation' and maybe even 'partnership'.

The regeneration programme in Sant Roc only affects that part of the neighbourhood where the physical condition of the dwellings is the worst. The CDP, on the other hand, is implemented over the entire neighbourhood. In the course of the last ten years, several programmes[4] (comparable to the CDP) have been implemented to improve the social situation in Sant Roc, but these programmes were unsuccessful and ended in an unsatisfactory situation (Garriga and Carrasco, 2003).

In the regeneration process in Sant Roc, the residents received information about the physical interventions at public meetings on the regeneration and relocation process ('information'). The government also held further discussions about relocation with representatives of the residents' association. Participation is limited, however, to the lowest levels: 'information' and 'consultancy'.

Level of participation

In Trinitat Nova, the residents have much more decision-making power than in Sant Roc and a high participation level has been reached (the population is about 8,000 and roughly 500 residents participate). The CDP has extended and reinforced social networks and created various projects. One of the success factors producing the high level of participation and the positive results of the CDP is the bottom–up organisation of the programme. The CDP in Trinitat Nova has gone further than the 'formal policy' set up by the regional government; it surpasses the objectives and projects put forward by the administrative programme.

In both the physical regeneration project and the CDP, local participation in Sant Roc is lower than in Trinitat Nova. Several explanations can be given for this (see Pareja-Eastaway et al, 2004). First, it can be said that the CDP in Sant Roc has a top-down organisation; the decision to start the process was an administrative one and not an initiative of its residents, as it was in Trinitat Nova. Second, the CDP in Sant Roc is managed by an independent company commissioned by the public authorities and not by the residents or by an organisation closely linked with the residents' association, as is the case in Trinitat Nova. Furthermore, participation in Sant Roc has been affected by a lack of political trust. The residents have lost confidence as a result of the poor coordination between the different levels of government involved in the territory (local and regional),[5] and the frustrating situation left behind by the previous failed programmes. Finally, Sant Roc has a weak and disintegrated association structure[6] and shows a lack of social cohesion among the different collectives, which affects participation badly. In Trinitat Nova the strong social cohesion is a positive factor in local participation. Although residential organisation was relatively weak at the start of the CDP process, it has contributed to a strong association structure in the neighbourhood and has played an important part in the CDP and the regeneration process.

Summary

The following tables provide a summary. Table 12.1 is an overview of: (1) the roles of local participation in the implemented policies; (2) the

Table 12.1: Overview: policy and organisation

	Utrecht	**Barcelona**
Role in policy	Important item in national and local policy; aim: – improving social structure; – building political trust	Not important item in urban policy; Important in CDP as a strategy to prevent social exclusion
Organisation	– Previously mainly through focus groups – Currently documented in the DUO agreement (advisory role for residents' associations, discussions, information meetings, neighbourhood councils, surveys, interviews)	*Trinitat Nova:* – workgroups in CDP – residents contracted professionals as interlocutors with local government *Sant Roc:* – meetings and negotiations

Source: RESTATE reports

aims of stimulating local participation; and (3) the instruments used to organise local participation. Table 12.2 summarises the factors influencing local participation in the four case studies.

Evaluation and conclusions

This chapter has concentrated on local participation in regeneration processes on large housing estates. The issues that have come to the fore in the theoretical literature with respect to local participation have been set against practice in the Netherlands and Spain. In this final section, an analysis is presented of whether national factors or neighbourhood characteristics have more influence on shaping local participation.

A major difference between the two countries is the fact that Spain is a younger democracy than the Netherlands. In relatively young democracies, the idea of involving residents in decision making is unfamiliar. In contrast with the Netherlands, estate regeneration policy in Spain does not stimulate local participation; the right of residents to have a voice in discussion and decision making concerning their city or neighbourhood is only acknowledged to a certain extent. The longer tradition of local participation in Dutch policy making results in the availability of more participation instruments in the Netherlands than in Spain.

However, the presence of formal instruments at the local level does not automatically imply a high level of participation. It seems that an instrument may be more successful in one neighbourhood than another. The difference between Trinitat Nova and Utrecht demonstrates this. In Trinitat Nova, the residents themselves developed instruments to enable them to participate. They used these instruments more successfully than did the residents in Utrecht, where policy makers made their instruments for them. Apparently, other local factors influence the use of available instruments.

The differences at a national level discussed here do not seem to have much influence on levels of participation. Local participation is affected more by local variables.

The first local variable is the association structure within a neighbourhood. Weak association structures, no associations, or associations lacking cooperation form a barrier to the development of local participation (as in Nieuw-Hoograven and Sant Roc). On the other hand, in neighbourhoods with a strong association structure, the residents' association can play an important part in the regeneration process. Second, the composition of the neighbourhood population

Table 12.2: Factors influencing local participation

Organisation of the restructuring process

	Nieuw-Hoograven	Kanaleneiland	Trinitat Nova	Sant Roc
Position on participation ladder	Placation Consulting Information	Placation Consulting Information	Partnership Placation Consulting Information	Consulting Information
Expected power versus real power	Disappointment	Not applicable	Not applicable	Not applicable
Bottom-up versus top-down	Top-down	Top-down	Bottom-up	Top-down
Management of regeneration process	External	External	Internal	External

Neighbourhood characteristics

	Nieuw-Hoograven	Kanaleneiland	Trinitat Nova	Sant Roc
Association structure	Weak	Weak	Strong	Weak
Social cohesion	Weak	Weak	Strong	Weak
Political trust				
– trust in local government and other actors	Low	Low	Not applicable	Low
– opinion regarding previous/ present programmes	Negative	Not applicable	Not applicable	Negative
Level of participation	Low	Low	High	Low

Source: RESTATE reports

can be cited as an important variable. As can be seen in several European contexts, the absence of strong social cohesion on an estate can result in a low level of local participation and in difficulties in achieving representativity. The third local variable is the level of political trust. In a neighbourhood where residents are disappointed with the results of (previous) restructuring projects, or have been left in a state of uncertainty about these projects, both their trust in the local government and their willingness to participate may decrease. Finally, the organisation of the restructuring process also plays a part in the level of local participation. It seems that the expectations that residents have of their powers influence their willingness to participate. When residents expect to have more power than is actually the case, they may become less willing to participate. It is therefore important to inform residents accurately about their level of power in policy making at the beginning of a participation process. Apparently, a bottom-up process and a management model in which the project managers are directly connected with a residents' organisation have a positive effect on local participation.

It can be concluded that neighbourhood characteristics account better for the level of participation than national differences do. This finding has important implications for urban and estate regeneration policy. If it is designed to stimulate local participation, urban policy should take variables at the neighbourhood level into account. This assertion is particularly true for regeneration policies focusing on neighbourhoods that are confronted with different kinds of problems, as the large housing estates in many European cities are. When restructuring these neighbourhoods (both socially and physically), instruments enabling residents to participate should be developed at a very local level, taking into account the extent of social cohesion, the composition of the neighbourhood population, the association structure, and the extent of residents' confidence in national or local policy.

Notes

[1] Residents pay a relatively small amount of money each month for about 25 years before becoming owners of the dwellings. An officially protected dwelling (*Vivienda de Protección Oficial* (VPO)) starts as a publicly owned dwelling and finally becomes a dwelling in the owner-occupied sector.

[2] Within the framework of this national policy, Dutch cities could designate specific neighbourhoods that need extra attention. Like

Kanaleneiland and Nieuw-Hoograven in Utrecht, these neighbourhoods often belong to the post-war urban housing stock and are characterised by a socioeconomically weak population.

[3] In each restructuring project, residents: (1) can give (unasked and qualified) advice; (2) can signal problems; (3) can test plans/visions; (4) can influence decisions; (5) have the right to take part in discussions; and (6) have the right to receive information.

[4] In 1990: an intensive administrative programme; in 1995: work sessions with professionals in the neighbourhood, and in 1998: PLADICO (the first Community Development Plan [CDP] in Sant Roc).

[5] However, after recent elections the same political party is governing at the local and regional level, which may influence coordination positively.

[6] Recently four residents' associations – Sant Roc, La Union, Maresme and La Concordia – have merged.

References

Aalbers, M., van Beckhoven, E., van Kempen, R., Musterd, S. and Ostendorf, W. (2003) *Large housing estates in the Netherlands: Overview of developments and problems in Amsterdam and Utrecht*, Utrecht: Urban and Regional research centre Utrecht, Faculty of Geosciences, Utrecht University.

Aalbers, M., Van Beckhoven, E., van Kempen, R., Musterd, S. and Ostendorf, W. (2004) *Large housing estates in the Netherlands: Policies and practices*, Utrecht: Urban and Regional research centre Utrecht, Faculty of Geosciences, Utrecht University.

Akkerman, T. (2003) 'Political responsiveness and public participation', in J. Font (ed) *Public participation and local governance*, Barcelona: Institut de Ciencies Polítiques i Socials (ICPS), Universitat Autonoma Barcelona, pp 85-102.

Andersen, H.T. and van Kempen, R. (2001) *Governing European cities: Social fragmentation, social exclusion and urban governance*, Aldershot: Ashgate.

Ángels, M. and Gallego, A. (2002) 'Civic entities in environmental local planning. A contribution from a participative research in the metropolitan area of Barcelona', *GeoJournal*, vol 56, no 2, pp 123-34.

Arnstein, S. (1969) 'A ladder of citizen participation', in P. LeGates and F. Stout (eds) (1996) *The City Reader*, London: Routledge, pp 242-52.

Belmessous, F., Chemin, C., Chignier-Riboulon, F., Commerçon, N., Trigueiro, M. and Zepf, M. (2004) *Large housing estates in France: Policies and practices*, Utrecht: Urban and Regional research centre Utrecht, Faculty of Geosciences, Utrecht University.

Bruquetas, M., Moreno, F.J. and Walliser, A. (2002) *Urban development programmes: The Spanish cases*, UGIS 2002. Retrieved: 1 February 2004, from www.ufsia.ac.be/ugis

Burns, D., Hambleton, R. and Hoggett, P. (1994) *The politics of decentralisation – revitalising local democracy*, Basingstoke: Macmillan.

Castells, M. (1986) *La ciudad y Las Masas. Sociología de los movimientos sociales urbanos*, Madrid: Alianza Editorial.

Coaffee, J. and Healey, P. (2003) 'My voice, my place – tracking transformations in urban governance', *Urban Studies*, vol 40, no 10, pp 1979-99.

Couch, C., Fraser, C. and Percy, S. (2003) *Urban regeneration in Europe*, Oxford: Blackwell.

Del Pino, E. and Colino, C. (2003) *Las nuevas formas de participación en los gobiernos locales*. Retrieved: 13 January 2003, from www.enredalicante.org/

Direcció General de Serveis Comunitaris, Servei de Plans i Programes (2002) *Memòria 2002*, Barcelona: Generalitat.

Docherty, I., Goodlad, R. and Paddison, R. (2001) 'Civic culture, community and citizen participation in contrasting neighbourhoods', *Urban Studies*, vol 38, no 12, pp 2225-50.

Elander, I. and Blanc, M. (2001) 'Partnerships and democracy: a happy couple in urban governance?', in H.T. Andersen and R. van Kempen (eds) *Governing European cities: Social fragmentation, social exclusion and urban governance*, Aldershot: Ashgate, pp 93-124.

Font, J. (2003) *Public participation and local governance*, Barcelona: Institut de Ciencies Polítiques i Socials (ICPS), Universitat Autonoma Barcelona.

Garriga, C. and Carrasco, S. (2003) *Els gitanos de Badalona, una aproximació sociològica*, Barcelona: Diputació de Barcelona.

Hastings, A., McArthur, A. and McGregor, A. (1996) *Less than equal: Community organizations and estate regeneration partnerships*, Bristol: The Policy Press.

Healey, P. (1997) *Collaborative planning: Shaping places in fragmented societies*, London: MacMillan.

Healey, P. (1998a) 'Building institutional capacity through collaborative approaches to urban planning', *Environment and Planning A*, vol 30, no 11, pp 1531-46.

Healey, P. (1998b) 'Collaborative planning in a stakeholder society', *Town Planning Review*, vol 69, no 1, pp 1-21.

Healey, P. (2002) 'On creating the city as a collective resource', *Urban Studies*, vol 39, no 10, pp 1777-92.

Kearns, A. and Paddison, R. (2000) 'New challenges for urban governance', *Urban Studies*, vol 37, no 5, pp 845-50.

Kooiman, J. (ed) (1993) *Modern governance*, London: Sage.

Öresjö, E., Andersson, R., Holmqvist, E., Pettersson, L. and Siwertsson, C. (2004) *Large housing estates in Sweden: Policies and practices*, Utrecht: Urban and Regional research centre Utrecht, Faculty of Geosciences, Utrecht University.

Pareja-Eastaway, M., Tapada-Berteli, T., van Boxmeer, B. and Garcia Ferrando, L. (2003) *Large housing estates in Spain: Overview of developments and problems in Madrid and Barcelona*, Utrecht: Urban and Regional research centre Utrecht, Faculty of Geosciences, Utrecht University.

Pareja-Eastaway, M., Tapada-Berteli, T., van Boxmeer, B. and Garcia Ferrando, L. (2004) *Large housing estates in Spain: Policies and practices*, Utrecht: Urban and Regional research centre Utrecht, Faculty of Geosciences, Utrecht University.

Pindado, F. (2000) *La participación ciudadana en la vida de las ciudades*, Barcelona: Ediciones del Serbal.

Rebollo, O. (2001) 'El Plan Comunitario de la Trinitat Nova: una experiencia de participación ciudadana', *Revista Mientras Tanto*, vol 79, February 2001.

Salet, W.G.M. (1999) 'Regime shifts in Dutch housing policy', *Housing Studies*, vol 14, no 4, pp 547–57.

Schlozman, K., Verba, S. and Brady, E. (1995) 'Participation is not a paradox', *British Journal of Political Science*, vol 25, January, pp 1-36.

Stoker, G. (1997) 'Local political participation', in R. Hambleton, H. David, C. Skelcher, M. Taylor, K. Young, N. Rao and G. Stoker (eds) *New perspectives on local governance: Reviewing the research evidence*, York: Joseph Rowntree Foundation, pp 157-96.

Szemzö, H. and Tosics, I. (2004) *Large housing estates in Hungary: Policies and practices*, Utrecht: Urban and Regional research centre Utrecht, Faculty of Geosciences, Utrecht University.

Taylor, M. (1998) 'Combating the social exclusion of housing estates', *Housing Studies*, vol 13, no 6, pp 819-32.

Taylor, M. (2000) 'Communities in the lead: power, organisational capacity and social capital', *Urban Studies*, vol 37, no 5-6, pp 1019-35.

Walliser, A. (2003) *Participación y ciudad*, Madrid: Centro de Estudios Avanzados en Ciencias Socials.

Wilcox, D. (1998) *The guide to develop trust and partnerships*. Retrieved: March 2004, from www.partnerships.org.uk/

Wilkinson, D. and Applebee, E. (1999) *Implementing holistic government: Joined-up action on the ground*, Bristol: The Policy Press.

Wuthnow, R. (1998) *Loose connections. Joining together in America's fragmented communities*, Cambridge, MA: Harvard University Press.

THIRTEEN

Fighting unemployment on large housing estates: an example from Sweden

Lars Pettersson and Eva Öresjö

Introduction

> In one estate in the city we had a lot of rich people, and at the same time we had a lot of poor people in another estate. In one estate the employment rate was high, and in another estate the employment rate was low. The situation in the poor estate could be characterised as the opposite of that in the rich estate. The tension between different estates in the city created destructive forces in the everyday lives of the citizens. This could be seen for example in the elementary school, when children were losing their faith in the future. This problem motivated the municipality to take the initiative and start the Integration Programme in Jönköping with the purpose of bringing together all possible efforts in order to change the situation (Peter Persson, city council member).

This was the explanation given at an Integration Conference in Jönköping on 25 April 2002 by city council member and stakeholder for the RESTATE project, Peter Persson, as to why an Integration Programme in the municipality of Jönköping was initiated. The issue highlighted in the statement has a number of general aspects that apply to the large housing estates that are in focus in the RESTATE project.

The problem of low employment in segregated estates has been treated in different ways in different countries and in different metropolitan areas. The policy tools differ between cases, and different methods have been used at various points in time. The focus in this chapter is primarily on an employment project in Jönköping in Sweden, and the analysis is based on evaluation studies made by the authors at different times (Pettersson, 2003; Vindelman and Öresjö, 2001). We compare the results of the policy initiatives in Jönköping with other forms of policies described in the different country reports in the RESTATE project. In this way the experiences from Jönköping are analysed in a European perspective in order to provide more general observations. (The reason why no other RESTATE case study has been analysed in detail is simply that the Swedish experiments with employment projects focusing directly on large housing estates appear to be more advanced and that no such information in similar detail is available from the other estates.)

We start our analysis from a theoretical perspective that focuses on *insiders* and *outsiders*. The population is subdivided according to closeness to the labour market. The title of this chapter stresses the link between integration and employment. This captures the essence of the political agenda in Sweden on this topic. Descriptive statistics show there is a relationship between employment and ethnicity, which also covariate in space (SOU (Swedish Government Official Reports), 1998). These problems (segregation and unemployment) are agglomerated in large housing estates in Sweden, as well as in the rest of Europe (Power and Tunstall, 1995). Employment is one of the most important factors that can contribute to integration and therefore forms part of the aims for inclusion (see the discussion of collaborative planning in Chapter 3). During the past three decades there have been a number of policy initiatives made by the national government, the local authorities, and the housing companies in Sweden in an attempt to turn around the situation in the large housing estates . The targets for these policies have been physical renewal, improved housing management, infrastructure and communication, and local community development (Öresjö, 1996). Nevertheless, these have not been entirely successful. The polarisation between urban areas has in fact increased during recent years in terms of unemployment and low employment, and income differences (SOU, 1998; Integrationsverket, 2002). Current policies in Sweden focus very much on how employment can break the marginalising effects of spatial segregation (SOU, 2004).

According to the empirical analysis in this chapter, *outsiders* should be divided into subgroups. In particular a group of people may be identified who are not employed, but actually who have the means to compete on the labour market. Due to asymmetric information for employers about the skills of people belonging to this group, these outsiders will not be likely to get a job on a free market although they do have a relatively high level of education and skills. One such group in Sweden consists of immigrants living in large housing estates.

Why is employment important?

Even if the economy of a country as a whole performs very well, it is likely that parts of the labour market (geographical as well as population groups) will experience difficulties. The focus in this study is on people who are outside the labour market but who attempt to enter it. In particular, the emphasis is on policies that aim to integrate immigrants and people outside the labour market by providing them with employment. We refer to this as the process of turning *outsiders* into *insiders* (see also Blanchard and Summers, 1986; Lindbeck and Snower, 1988).

According to the *insider-outsider theory*, there is a risk that the number of outsiders in the economy will increase during times of depression. This can be explained by the difficulties outsiders face when they try to enter a labour market that is determined by the behaviour of insiders who are defending their positions as insiders.

Changes in social norms could also have an influence on the number of people outside the labour market. Higher levels of non-employment could possibly be explained by a drift in social norms in favour of attitudes that are more tolerant towards people who live on welfare and who are not working. Lindbeck (1995) argues, for example, that social norms in favour of non-employment might be established in an economy where subsidies and welfare benefits are extensive. A change in the social norms may occur in a recession, when more people become dependent on public assistance. As time goes by, it is likely that more people will adopt a new way of living without working, which was previously not accepted as 'good behaviour'. This means that countries, regions, cities or estates with high employment rates will also be likely to have social norms in favour of working lifestyles, and vice versa.

The so-called 'job-search theory' and related models can serve as a basic explanation as to why individuals may become long-term unemployed. In such models the individual's decision to accept or reject a job offer (or to enter the process of searching for a job) is dependent on the expected benefits of undertaking additional efforts compared with the expected costs (Martensen, 1986; Muffels and Vriens, 1991; Zaretsky and Coughlin, 1995). It is most reasonable to assume that the efforts individuals will use on searching for a job will be dependent on their expectations of being acknowledged as applicants in the ordinary labour market. It is a realistic assumption that if an applicant for a job has no prior experience with the national labour market and no references, then the expected probability of that person being hired (or called to a job interview) would appear to be low. This means that the expected benefits from searching for a job are low among many immigrants and other outsiders in the economy.

Performance on the labour market has been studied in numerous analyses (Löfgren and Wikström, 1991; Calmfors, 1993; Ackum Agell et al, 1995). A recent published overview of labour market policy in Sweden is found in Ackum Agell and Lundin (2001). A special issue with the labour market as the central theme was published by the Swedish journal *Ekonomisk Debatt* (2001).

From these studies it is possible to make the following observations:

(1) the problem with persistent unemployment is significant for some groups of the population;
(2) the length of time individuals have been unemployed appears to have significant importance with respect to the probability of finding a job, and
(3) various forms of selection mechanisms appear to fuel persistent unemployment for groups of the population.

Ekberg and Rooth (2001) show that persistent unemployment is a more substantial problem among immigrants in Sweden than among the native population.

The labour market can be described in a simple way by dividing the population of working age into different groups with respect to their status on the labour market (see Figure 13.1). The first group of people have a job and are employed. The second group consists of the short-term unemployed: people who are between two jobs or are applying for a job after they have finished their studies. A third group of people comprises those who are long-term unemployed. This group of people has been unemployed for a long time, often because of structural reasons (which means that there is a demand on the labour market but for people with other types of education or located in other places than where the unemployed live) or sometimes also because of recession in the business cycle. This group is still included in the labour force, in contrast to the fourth group of people, who are 'genuine' outsiders. This group does not have a strong tie to the labour market. It is common to find immigrants in this group who never have been hired on a long-term contract, and there are also other people who do not have a job because of health reasons, for example, or because they have taken early retirement.

It is common that people whose chances of employment are slim need some type of major change or injection (such as targeted education) if a period of long-term unemployment is to be ended. Education or migration is usually assumed to break long-term unemployment. Where the unemployed migrate to regions where there is a high demand for labour and/or take up education related to labour demand, one can assume that unemployment levels will be reduced.

Economic growth and decline influence the large housing estates and the people who live there. This is, for example, shown in Öresjö et al, 2004, where the number of vacancies on the large housing estates in Jönköping and Stockholm correlates with economic growth. Power and Tunstall (1995) show the same problem for the UK economy. The presence of vacant flats, changes in unemployment and employment levels, and migration in the large housing estates are dependent on the economic performance of urban regions. Since groups of people with low rates of employment tend to agglomerate on large housing estates, there is a spatial element in the distribution of problems related to the particular phenomena.

The case of Jönköping

In the municipality of Jönköping, a city in the central south of Sweden, a project aiming to introduce long-term unemployed immigrants into the labour market was carried out between 1996 and 2002. The project focused on immigrants living in four large housing estates, Råslätt,

Figure 13.1: The labour market and the population

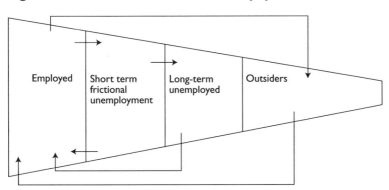

Source: Pettersson (2001)

Österängen, Öxnehaga and the south part of Huskvarna, and was part of the Integration Programme of the municipality. Immigrants were offered employment for a 12-month period, for which they had to apply. In order to qualify, the individuals had to have been outsiders on the labour market and, for example, had to have received social assistance. They also had to be motivated to search for employment.

The project's method was to identify persons who qualified for the project and then give them the opportunity to make formal applications for the jobs offered. The applicants matching the requirements of the jobs offered were interviewed (approximately half of the applicants) and after this the 'best man/woman for the job' rule was applied in order to match supply and demand. The hiring process was carried out in a collaboration between the local office for labour market administration, the social service department in the municipality and the employers.

One important aspect of the project was to establish a situation where outsiders get an opportunity to not be sorted out by the usual allocation mechanisms that might stress ethnicity. Thereby outsiders should get a better chance to receive references, and obtain access to contact networks in the labour market, which are important with respect to getting new jobs in the future. In this way persistent unemployment can be reduced and positive economic effects, as well as integration effects, should be realised in the long run.

One main problem for many of the outsiders featured in this analysis was a lack of recent experience in the labour market. In some cases they had been employed before in Sweden, but not in the recent past. A majority of all applicants for the project did not have any working experience at all on the Swedish labour market.

The project has been organised into six phases, and around 70 to 90 people have been employed in each phase. During the first phases of the project, the jobs were located in the large housing estates. Since then, there have also been jobs located in other parts of the city, outside the areas where the employees lived. The jobs offered by the project have been within the local authority as well as in some private firms, for example in an elementary school, in restaurants, in a nursery school, caring for the elderly and housekeeping. One important aspect is that the jobs should not 'crowd out' any regular employment. This is something that is difficult to evaluate, and the persons employed in the project have often been regarded as an 'extra resource'. The project and the jobs offered by the project have been financed by the local authority together with funding from the local office for labour market administration.

After being employed in the project, around 60% of participants have moved on to other forms of employment and around 10% have entered different forms of education programmes, for example, training for teaching at elementary school, for nursing and for working in restaurants. This performance has been fairly consistent over time with some difference in distribution. In general, more people have moved on to other forms of employment during periods of economic recovery and more people have entered education during times of recession.

The evaluation

The first three phases of the employment project have been evaluated by the authors. Three issues that are stressed in these evaluation studies are of particular concern for this study:

- In what way are the isolated effects from the project important with respect to turning outsiders into insiders?
- What are the most important social effects for individuals employed in the project?
- What will the outcome be when language skills in Swedish are not the most important requirement?

The first issue was answered by an experimental study (Pettersson, 2003). The performance of the group of people who were employed in the project (the experiment group) was compared with a reference group. The reference group consisted of people who applied to the project and were interviewed but did not get employment. The second and third issues are analysed in a survey targeting the total population of employees and employers/tutors, covering the first three phases of the project.

Table 13.1 characterises the experiment and reference groups, respectively. As can be seen, the two groups look very much the same, except for the high share of women in the experiment group. The high proportion corresponds to the general position with regard to outsiders on the estates. This is also the situation on the national level. Data from Swedish statistics show that the employment rate for women is significantly lower than for men among immigrants in Sweden (Pettersson, 2003). The lowest employment rate is found among women from Arabic countries. These women had an employment rate of around 25% in 1999, while the average for the whole Swedish economy was around 70% in the same year.

A majority of the people who were hired in the project originated

Table 13.1: Experiment group and reference group for the employment and integration project in Jönköping (2000-01)

Variables	Experiment group	Reference group
Number of persons employed by the project	71	70
Number and percentage of females	56 (78%)	42 (60%)
Average age	39 years	39 years
Percentage with origin from Europe	38%	27%
Percentage with origin outside Europe	62%	73%
Average number of children per household	1.93	1.75
Percentage of married couples	72%	77%
Percentage of households receiving social assistance before the project	61%	70%
Percentage of households receiving social assistance 3 months after the project	34%	42%
Average time living in Sweden	10.2 years	9.9 years
Percentage of population with high (university level) education	30%	23%
Percentage of people who never had been employed in Sweden	68%	62%
Percentage of people who had good knowledge in the Swedish language	49%	Not available

Source: Pettersson, 2003

from countries outside Europe. On average they had spent around 10 years in Sweden, and 68% had never had a job in Sweden. This means that those who were hired by the project could be regarded as outsiders on the labour market. Before they received employment in the project, all participants were unemployed or not part of the labour force. This is also reflected by the high share of households that received social assistance.

After the project around 70% of the people in the experiment group went on to other jobs or started education programmes. The change in their situation is reflected in the decrease in dependency on social assistance. The evaluation of the project also confirms that the public sector benefited from the shift in monetary flows. Instead of receiving subsidies, this population group paid taxes and thereby the project appears to be a successful policy strategy. A cost-benefit analysis of the project showed that a break-even point was reached after three years (Pettersson, 2003). In this analysis, the gap in performance between the experiment group and the reference groups was used.

The evaluations of the project (Luthander, 1999; Johansson, 2000;

Vindelman and Öresjö, 2001) show a great impact on participants' self-esteem and their future possibilities of getting a job. Quite a number of people point out the importance of having a job as a model for the children and that they have had renewed trust, energy and inspiration to start new activities. Several people stated that it was the first time they felt part of Swedish society, despite having lived in Sweden for many years. This positive effect was also spread to the surrounding family members, relatives and others in a similar situation. Examples of various statements made by participants are set out below.

> "It was like living in a black hole looking towards the bright future – very positive. I learnt about my own capabilities and the value of my education from my native country in Sweden. Now I know how to complete my studies (which skills I need, etc.)."

> "I haven't had a job for six years. I felt lost, lonely and depressed. I was afraid of being with people. With the job I got self-confidence and my family got joy of life. I got to know Swedish society and developed the language. I also got new friends."

> "My five-year-old kid asks every day about my work. He is proud of his father working. I didn't think about small kids like him being concerned about if you have a job or not."

> "The fact I got a permanent job has influenced others to start looking for a job, too. Through the project we have discovered there is a lot to learn, and gain success by trying over and over again."

As part of the employment process in the project, great care and attention was given to getting the right person in the right position, whereas demands for 'perfect' Swedish were removed. The experience of this approach has been positive. It is through daily confrontation with the language that it develops, but simultaneously it put high demands on the tutors in the workplace.

> "To learn a new language demands that you are in touch with people. A workplace is maybe the best environment for a foreigner to improve his Swedish."

"I have improved my Swedish, increased my vocabulary. I learnt about cultural differences in society and increased my knowledge about different traditional festivals and Swedish customs. Today I know many Swedes and know how they think and what they like as well as how they would react if something odd is occurring."

"Language difficulties and cultural differences have caused some tensions and misinterpretations. Some have been difficult to sort out in a positive manner." (Interview tutor)

The evaluations of the employment project in Jönköping show that people tend to continue to be insiders to the same degree as when the project ended (Pettersson, 2003). Our conclusion is that one can expect the effect to last at least as long as a regular business cycle, in general four to five years. It is possible that the effects are more long term. Our interpretation is that the outsiders often need some type of stimulation to become insiders. This is also what the theory indicates. Concerning the people who were employed in the project in Jönköping, a substantial number went on to jobs in the manufacturing sector, or became employed by other parts of the city. This means that when outsiders received references, job experience and contact networks, they also improved their opportunities to become employed in other sectors of the economy.

The results from the different evaluations appear to be consistent. In relation to other labour market policy efforts from the 1990s in Sweden, the results from the Jönköping project must be regarded as significant. Ackum Agell and Lundin (2001) show that there are few policy programmes where more than 50% of participants have become insiders after the programme, which can be compared to around 60-70% in the Jönköping case. Standard economic theory can be applied in order to explain this phenomenon. The opportunities for this particular type of policy may be motivated by the presence of asymmetric information, meaning that employers lack perfect information about employees' skills in the labour market. If there are outsiders who actually can provide a marginal revenue product (MRP) (contribution to total revenues from the last one employed) that is at least in parity with the wages and costs of labour, there is an opportunity for this type of policy to be efficient.

The problem is depicted in Figure 13.2. In the figure there are a given number of people who do not have a job, that is, outsiders. The dotted line represents the MRP that employers expect the outsiders

Figure 13.2:A labour market with information asymmetry

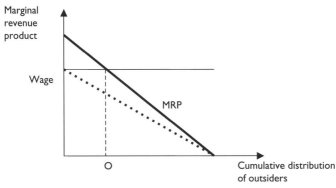

Source: Our own construction

to have. However, there are a number of outsiders that actually have a higher MRP (O) than the wage on the labour market. The actual MRP relation includes the information asymmetry effect and is depicted by the steepest line in the figure. The free market will not reach an efficient equilibrium if this type of information asymmetry is present, and hence, employment will be too low.

Information asymmetry can be assumed to be significant for immigrants, since they usually do not have CVs with experience from the national economy; for example they may have educational degrees from universities and other educational institutions that are not familiar to employers.

A European perspective

In order to be able to reflect more generally on the experiences from the Jönköping case we must also acknowledge the situation in other countries. There were significant differences in national labour market performance in Europe during the 1990s. Countries like the Netherlands, Portugal and Spain increased their employment rate, while at the same time countries like Sweden and Finland sharply decreased their employment rate between the years 1990 and 2000. Table 13.2 shows the development for 'open unemployment' and non-employment (defined as the 1-employment rate). Open unemployment is defined as the share of the labour force that is registered as unemployed. The non-employment figure reveals the extent to which people of working age (15-64 years) do not have a job in different countries.

Table 13.2 does not reveal information on all aspects of the labour

Table 13.2: Open unemployment and non-employment in European countries for persons aged 15-64 years, 1990 and 2000 (%)

Country	Open unemploy- ment 1990	Open unemploy- ment 2000	Non- employ- ment 1990	Non- employ- ment 2000
Belgium	7.3	6.6	48.6	41.4
Denmark	8.5	4.5	26.1	24.5
Finland	3.2	9.9	26.6	35.6
France	9.2	10.1	43.2	42.1
Germany	6.2	8.1	37.8	35.9
Ireland	13.2	4.4	53.0	37.0
Italy	9.9	11.0	50.1	51.1
Luxemburg	1.6	2.4	41.5	38.2
the Netherlands	7.7	2.7	41.5	27.8
Norway	5.3	3.5	28.2	22.8
Portugal	4.8	4.1	36.0	33.1
Spain	16.1	14.1	55.2	48.8
Sweden	1.8	5.9	17.2	27.0
UK	6.8	5.6	29.0	29.0
OECD Europe	8.1	8.9	41.3	41.7
European Union	8.3	8.4	40.9	38.9

Source: OECD (2001)

market. For example, there might be differences with respect to the proportion of part-time workers in the different countries. Furthermore, there may be other types of discrepancies, such as sick leave, early retirement, etc., that influence the demand and supply for labour and the number of hours worked in the different countries.

The question of employment is central in all the case studies included in RESTATE report 3, *Policies and practices*, either as a problem which exists in society as a whole, or more as a problem of socioeconomic polarisation of towns and cities. In the first group of cases we find Italy, Poland, Slovenia and Spain, where the economic and employment problems in the large housing estates are characterised as originating at the national level. Spain and Italy had the highest non-employment rates in the EU for persons aged between 15 and 64 years in 2000. Ten years earlier, in 1990, the situation was the same, except that Ireland shared this distinction (see Table 13.2).

In Slovenia, the labour market has been drastically changed during the last 15 years. During the socialist era in Slovenia, the country did not report any problems due to unemployment or low employment rates. Slovenia was a country of immigration for jobseekers from other republics of Yugoslavia. Due to the economy's adjustment to new markets and new ownership relations, unemployment has become one of the most important economic and social problems. In Slovenia as well as in Spain, the focus of labour market policy is at the national level in order to reduce high unemployment.

In Poland, the economic and employment problem in the Warsaw housing estates has its roots in the national economic problem, and particularly in the importance of the capital. Warsaw is considered to be among the cities that are most attractive for investment, particularly by foreign investors in Poland. As a result Warsaw has led the way in transformation, compared with the regions, which have not benefited from the changes. So the unemployment issues are of different character, even in the worst housing estates of Warsaw, compared with those of some rural areas of Northern Poland.

In Hungary, where the unemployment rate is one of the lowest among the countries considered, local policies addressing the issue of unemployment almost never address a spatial unity; rather their focus is on selective initiatives for special groups.

In France, the Netherlands, Sweden, the UK and Germany the relationship between employment levels and the economy and rehabilitation of the large housing estates is different, with some similarities and some dissimilarities between the various countries. Among the similarities is the fact that all the projects have been initiated at the local level on the housing estates, projects which include language training, self-employment and new jobs action, business advisory services, courses and education for the unemployed, matching of the unemployed with local companies, and so on.

The dissimilarities are connected with differences in the history of the countries as well as the developments in employment and the economy during the last decade. In Germany, the labour market is undergoing radical changes. Eventually this could lead to a change in the large housing estates. In France, the open unemployment rate and the non-employment rate for persons aged between 15 and 64 years have been high both in 1990 and 2000. In the Netherlands the improvement of the employment rate has been very pronounced during the second half of the 1990s, while the opposite situation has influenced development in, for example, Sweden.

Even the question of ethnicity is different, in spite of all the projects that aim at language knowledge training. Countries like the UK and the Netherlands have a comparatively longer experience of immigration than the Nordic countries. Traditionally, Sweden was perceived as a homogeneous country, socioeconomically as well as ethnically. Today there is a large diversity with respect to ethnic, cultural, religious and linguistic plurality, which is greater and more pronounced than ever. This explains why questions of inter-ethnic interaction (or ethnic segregation) and questions about non-employment among immigrants tend to dominate the Swedish debate about large housing estates. A core question is to find opportunities for immigrants to enter the job market, rather than to provide employers with workers.

Comparing the international experiences with the case of Jönköping, we are able to make some statements. A high level of employment in a country, region or estate can be assumed to reflect a high level of competition, and thus one would not expect to find a large number of outsiders who could be competitive on the labour market. At the same time, a substantial decrease in employment in a country, region or estate can be assumed to reflect a large number of people outside the labour market who have had problems becoming insiders. Nevertheless, this group of outsiders may have a comparatively high level of MRP. The presence of a minimum wage regime and control of wage levels will drive development towards these situations.

According to the theoretical considerations presented in the first part of our study, we conclude that the policies used in the estates in Amsterdam in the Netherlands are comparable with the Jönköping case. These programmes have also proved to be successful. In both these cases the policies target groups of outsiders who might be expected to have a comparatively high level of MRP and to be competitive on the labour market. These cases use individual approaches and small-scale specialised programmes oriented towards groups of outsiders for whom asymmetric information could be assumed to be a significant problem.

Conclusion and summary

General statistics at the national level show that there are substantial differences between countries in Europe with respect to labour force participation and unemployment. In the 'small open economies' in the North of Europe one finds a higher level of employment compared to the Mediterranean basin and the East of Europe. Unemployment and people who are outsiders in the job market and in society are likely to be clustered in large housing estates. This problem is acknowledged in the different case studies in the RESTATE project.

The evaluations of the employment project in Jönköping show that micro-level policies can be successful both from a labour market and an integration perspective. It is important to recognise fundamental conditions in the local market, and one must be careful concerning policy transfer to other countries and markets. Our conclusion is that the phase of the business cycle is a most important factor for determining the success of this particular form of policy. During periods when the demand for labour is expanding there should also be an increasing number of job opportunities. This means that the type of project represented in the case of Jönköping can be assumed to work well during times of recovery. When the economy is in recession, however, it is likely that outsiders will face more problems entering the labour market.

The particular type of policy effort can also be assumed to work well in advanced welfare states like the Swedish economy with high employment. Outsiders who lack references, recent job experience and contact networks are likely to need some type of support in order to become competitive on the labour market.

It is important to acknowledge the search process and the problem with asymmetric information. If an employment project is to be successful in the long run there must some explanation as to why people do not get a job on a free market. If asymmetric information is present, then there may be an opportunity for the particular type of policy analysed in this chapter. Otherwise outsiders can only be employed by means of subsidies in the long run, because their MRP will be lower than their wage in a competitive labour market.

References

Ackum Agell, S., Björklund, A. and Harkman, A. (1995) 'Unemployment insurance, labour market programmes and repeated unemployment spells in Sweden', *Swedish Economic Policy Review*, vol 2, no 1, pp 101-28.

Ackum Agell, S. and Lundin, M. (2001) 'Erfarenheter av svensk arbetsmarknadspolitik', *Ekonomisk Debatt*, vol 29, no 4, pp 239-50.

Blandchard, O. and Summers, L. (1986) 'Hysteresis and the European unemployment problem', in S. Fisher (ed) *NBER Macroeconomics Annual*, Cambridge, MA: MIT Press, pp 15-78.

Calmfors, L. (1993) 'Centralisation of wage bargaining and macroeconomic performance: a survey', *OECD Economic Studies*, vol 21, winter, pp 161-91.

Ekberg, J. and Rooth, D-O. (2001) 'Är invandrare oprioriterade inom arbetsmarknadspolitiken?', *Ekonomisk Debatt*, vol 29, no 4, pp 285-92.

Ekonomisk Debatt (2001), vol 29, no 4, (Special issue with the labour market as the central theme).

Integrationsverket (2002*) Förort i Fokus - interventioner för miljoner. En kunskapsöversikt'*, Integrationsverkets rapportserie, no 1, Norrköping: Integrationsverket.

Johansson, E. (2000) *Jobb istället för bidrag, Hundrajobben*, Arbetsrapport, Högskolan Karlskrona/Ronneby: Institutionen för fysisk planering.

Lindbeck, A. (1995) *The Swedish experiment*, Stockholm: SNS Förlag.

Lindbeck, A. and Snower, D. (1988) *The insider-outsider theory of employment and unemployment*, Cambridge, MA: MIT Press.

Löfgren, K-G. and Wikström, M. (1991) *Lönebildningen och arbetsmarknadspolitiken*, Umeå: Umeå Economic Studies, Umeå University.

Luthander, E-L. (1999) *Utvärdering av projektet jobb istället för bidrag*, Högskolan Karlskrona/Ronneby: Institutionen för fysisk planering.

Martensen, D.T. (1986) 'Job search and labour market analysis', in O. Ashenfelter and R. Layord (eds) *Handbook of labour economics*, Amsterdam: North Holland, pp 849-919.

Muffels, R. and Vriens, M. (1991) 'Labour-market behavior of long-term unemployed: a multidisciplinary approach', *Journal of Socio-Economics*, vol 20, no 4, pp 325-45.

OECD (Organisation for Economic Co-operation and Development) (2001) *OECD Employment Outlook June 2001*, Paris:OECD.

Öresjö, E. (1996) *Att vända utvecklingen, Kommenterad genomgång av aktuell forskning om segregation i boendet*, rapport nr. 57, SABO Utveckling: Stockholm.

Öresjö, E., Andersson, R., Holmqvist, E., Pettersson, L. and Siwertsson, C. (2004) *Large housing estates in Sweden: policies and practices*, Utrecht: Urban and Regional research centre, Faculty of Geosciences, Utrecht University.

Pettersson, L. (2001) *Location, housing and premises in a dynamic perspective*, Jibs dissertation series, nr 10, Jönköping: Jönköping International Business School.

Pettersson, L. (2003) *Ekonomisk utvärdering av 100-jobben*, projekt 'Jobb istället för bidrag 100-jobben' omgång 3, Jönköping: Jönköping International Business School.

Power, A. and Tunstall, R. (1995) *Swimming against the tide. Polarisation or progress on 20 unpopular council estates, 1980-1995*, London: Joseph Rowntree Foundation.

SOU (Swedish Government Official Reports) (1998) *Tre städer. En stadspolitik för hela landet. Slutbetänkande från Storstadskommittéen*, Stockholm: SOU.

SOU (2004) *Egenförsörjning eller bidragsförsörjning? Invandrarna, arbetsmarknaden och välfärdsstaten, rapport från integrationspolitiska maktutredningen*, Stockholm: SOU.

Vindelman, A. and Öresjö, E. (2001) *Jobb istället för bidrag, 100-jobben etapp 2000/2001*, Arbetsrapport, Blekinge: Blekinge Tekniska Högskola.

Zaretsky, A.M. and Coughlin, C.C. (1995) 'An introduction to the theory and estimation of a job-search model', *Review (Federal Reserve Bank of Saint Louis)*, vol 77, no 1, pp 53-65.

FOURTEEN

Feelings of insecurity and young people in housing estates

Manuel Aalbers, Agnieszka Bielewska, Franck Chignier-Riboulon and Anna Guszcza

Introduction

Many residents on large housing estates experience feelings of insecurity. Some of the estates have serious problems involving juvenile crime, while on other estates youngsters just hanging around cause *feelings* of insecurity. Residents and officials label such behaviour as deviant, and apply different types of measures to attempt to decrease the level of insecurity that it causes in a neighbourhood. The solutions to these problems can be divided into environmental (or physical), socialisation, and criminalisation strategies. In this chapter we discuss examples of criminalisation and socialisation strategies in France, the Netherlands, and Poland. The advantages and disadvantages of both strategies are described; by comparing examples from different countries, we assess which are the most successful in dealing with feelings of insecurity. We have taken our examples from three different countries: the Netherlands, where very explicit links are made between young immigrants and feelings of insecurity; France, where this link is also explicit, but where officials are reluctant to discuss it for ideological and political reasons; and Poland, where immigration is not a major issue, but where similar links are made between the presence of young people in public spaces and feelings of insecurity. The issue at stake is not just a problem in these three countries, however: it is also recognised elsewhere. In her widely cited study of housing estates in Europe, Power (1997) noted that issues of insecurity and violence among disaffected youth had become a common problem. In several of the RESTATE reports, similar points are raised. In Italy, for example:

> Minor delinquent behaviour such as painting graffiti or breaking windows is common. ... Young people do not

have many attractions here or places to meet, so they gather in the streets. Their behaviour concerns the rest of the inhabitants, who have no contact with young people and do not connect with their anxieties and needs, but feel that tension between the generations is growing (Mezzetti et al, 2003, p 47).

In Slovenia, 'the youngsters have taken over the space and the elderly residents complain about their boisterous activities' that discourage other residents 'from moving freely in the neighbourhood during the evening hours' (Černič Mali et al, 2003, pp 43 and 52), while in Germany 'often young people in the street, especially those from ethnic minorities, are seen as a danger in public space and to be avoided' (Droste and Knorr-Siedow, 2004, p 47).

We have not conducted a theoretical analysis of the criminalisation and socialisation strategies, but have used them as an analytical framework for our discussion. In our analysis, we concentrate on factors influencing feelings of insecurity. We have taken into consideration different types of disturbing incidents that, to a large extent, influence the residents' perception of danger on housing estates. In this respect, we follow the sociology of deviance, which takes a broader, more heterogeneous category of behaviour as its object of study than traditional criminology does. The sociology of deviance takes into account any behaviour that is socially defined as deviant. Fear of crime is often subjective and not always related to crime statistics (Grémy, 1996). We concentrate on those incidents which residents stress cause their fear.

In the next section we briefly discuss the two types of strategy that function as a framework for the presentation and discussion of the policies in the three countries. We then discuss some of the reasons behind youth crime, and also their link with immigration. In subsequent sections the three cases are discussed. For each country an account of a problematic estate is followed by descriptions of the criminalisation and socialisation policies adopted on it. The chapter concludes with a reflection on the two strategies and the different policies applied. We conclude that good policies are characterised not only by the right mix of strategies, but also by a collaborative approach that involves all the parties concerned.

Strategies

Police, local government authorities, and the residents in a neighbourhood respond to juvenile crime and feelings of insecurity in various ways. In this chapter we concentrate on two response strategies: criminalisation and socialisation. A third kind of strategy is referred to as 'environmental' or 'physical', and several strategies have been widely applied on housing estates; they often focus on reducing feelings of insecurity through redesigning public and semi-public spaces such as elevators, staircases, hallways, and porches. Although environmental strategies can often reduce *feelings* of insecurity, critics have suggested that they do little to improve *actual* security because most insecurity problems are social, not physical in nature. 'Insecure places' do not cause, but merely facilitate deviant behaviour. In other words, design cannot explain the social problems (Laé, 1991; van Kempen, 1994), and redesign cannot solve them, but only slightly reduce them.

Criminalisation strategies can be described as defensive; they focus on the punishment of juvenile crime. Socialisation strategies look at the roots of juvenile crime and aim to improve the situation of young people (often young men) by providing them with a future perspective through education or through increasing social, inter-generational, and sometimes also inter-ethnic integration. It is often argued that criminalisation is a short-term policy that leads to more social harm and injustice. Restorative models of crime prevention can be more effective at repairing relationships among victims, offenders, and communities than models based on retribution or vengeance (Braithwaite, 1989; Lauderdale and Oliverio, 2001).

As many authors argue (Lauderdale and Oliverio, 2001; Wacquant, 2001, for example), the late 20th and the early 21st century have witnessed an unprecedented worldwide expansion of criminalisation and incarceration. However, before 1970, when social control was interlinked with religion and social manners inspired by courteous behaviour, this expansion was still very low (Muchembled, 1998) and led to less poverty. The fact that the criminalisation trend is worldwide does not mean that policies have become identical or that criminalisation strategies have the same dominance all over the globe. European countries are not blindly copying US-style policies; the European scenarios suited to the different European political and cultural traditions are characterised by 'a conjoint, twofold accentuation of both the social regulation and the penal regulation of social insecurity' (Wacquant, 2001, p 407). In other words, they are characterised by the co-existence of socialisation and criminalisation strategies. As many studies show, incarceration often leads not to (re)socialisation in (mainstream) society but to socialisation within criminal networks. Thus, imprisonment typically aggravates and amplifies the problems it is supposed to resolve (Wacquant, 2001), partly as a result of the weakness of the state in relation to the social inclusion of ex-prisoners. As Mauer (1999) argues, existing data are not very supportive of a strong relationship between locking up offenders and reducing crime. However, imprisonment by the state is not done for the sake of the offender, but for political purposes, and should be viewed as the state's reaction to diverse social problems (Braithwaite, 1989; Mauer, 1999; Wacquant, 1999), and as a response to social demands.

Determinants of criminality in neighbourhoods

There is a common recognition that the social and economic difficulties of households have consequences for the level of security in the neighbourhood and for the residents' sense of security. Factors such as poverty, racial composition, family disorder, economic inequalities, unemployment, and residential mobility are implicated as direct or indirect causes of high rates of violence in some neighbourhoods (Hawkins et al, 1998). Unemployment and inequalities in the division of wealth are cited as the main economic reasons. Visible discrepancies between the standards of living of neighbouring households create feelings of frustration among low-income residents and may lead to attempts to achieve wealth through unlawful activities. One of the theories seeking to explain this mechanism was put forward by Merton (1938). According to Merton, pressure on acquiring material benefits without the opportunity to achieve enhanced standards of living in a legitimate way triggers different forms of anti-social behaviour. Attitudes promoting consumption and restricted financial resources might sometimes lead the poor to commit a criminal offence.

Moreover, the increasing social and economic polarisation involves a concentration of deprived households in the worst neighbourhoods. Deprived households from ethnic minorities are often concentrated on the estates with the worst reputation in the city. The residential segregation and clustering of immigrants in some neighbourhoods may cause them to harbour a concentration of criminality (W'gleDski, 2001). Additionally, the active neighbourhood life of young people, especially when it is centred on public and semi-public spaces, influences the development of criminality. Thus, there is a criminality of exclusion (Salas, 1997) that integrates the ethnic dimension. Young people with foreign roots feel they are not considered equal to other citizens. They often suffer from discriminatory attitudes on the labour and housing markets. Moreover, young estate residents have built up an image in which policemen have racist attitudes towards them and they feel that the police pay them excessive attention and exert unnecessary control. That this indeed is often the case is borne out by research (Body-Gendrot and Wihtol De Wenden, 2003). Police departments explain their focus by arguing that their presence is justified by the relatively high local crime rates. Finally, for some young people, neighbourhood attitudes may facilitate neighbourhood inclusion (although more deviant than other types of inclusion), but hinder their inclusion within the wider society (the city, the nation).

Young people may emerge as real local actors. According to this point of view, they play a dominant part in neighbourhood life – often in an informal rather than a formal way (Lepoutre, 1997; Bordet, 1998). We can observe that, for them, the estate is not just a neutral space; it is their territory, which they appropriate with certain patterns of 'exclusivism'. For these young people the estate is like a village (Lepoutre, 1997; Chignier-Riboulon, 2000); they build a real neighbourhood society, with its own norms and rules. This local society is founded on a dynamic local social hierarchy: everyone tries to improve their position and reputation inside their group of friends and within the estate. The power of the neighbourhood on inclusion processes is therefore important.

Major issues in France, the Netherlands and Poland

Usually, young people with foreign roots take an active role in the neighbourhood. Immigrants and immigration are major issues on the Dutch and French estates. However, because of their insignificant numbers, they are minor actors on the Polish estates. Strikingly, the problems in the three countries are similar. Thus, while the discourse in France and the Netherlands stresses immigration as a major issue, what is at stake is not just national inclusion, but primarily social/ economic exclusion. This is often connected to educational problems and social class. We do not argue that immigration is only a *discursive* problem: the 'migration factor' plays an additional role. In France and the Netherlands young (male) immigrants from low-income, poorly educated families make up a large share of the groups at risk of exclusion, while in Poland a large proportion of the groups at risk consists of indigenous Poles (who also come from low-income, poorly educated families).These groups are the most in danger of committing crime and manifesting anti-social behaviour.

There is, however, a clear 'immigration' or 'ethnic' factor in both France and the Netherlands in the public discourse that imputes a process of tougher attitudes in which minority ethnic groups are approached with increased suspicion and often seen a priori as a problem (Gastaut, 2000; Prins and Slijper, 2002; Uitermark et al, 2004), such as the Moroccans in the Netherlands and the Arabic groups in France. In connection with this is a media discourse in the Netherlands that stresses the over-representation of young Moroccan males in crime statistics and gives wide coverage to incidents such as gang rape, murder, and harassment of the elderly (Uitermark et al, 2004, for example). Currently, the question of a larger criminality of young people also officially exists in France (Schosteck, 2002), but police statistics are not broken down into racial categories out of respect for the French republican principle of equality.

The Netherlands

In this section, we discuss the criminalisation and socialisation strategies implemented in the Netherlands. The focus is on one large housing estate in Amsterdam: Nieuw West. Before describing and analysing the strategies, we first describe the Nieuw West estate and stress the growing political attention paid to safety issues (based on Aalbers et al, 2003; 2004). What makes this case special is that criminalisation and socialisation strategies take place side by side and are sometimes integrated within one programme. Several of the programmes involve a variety of parties, and can therefore be considered collaborative.

The Nieuw West estate in Amsterdam

Nieuw West used to be an area that accommodated predominantly indigenous Dutch, middle-class families. Nowadays, the number of first- and second-generation immigrants has increased to 61,000 of the area's 140,000 inhabitants – a proportion that rises to over 80% in some neighbourhoods. The changing ethnic composition of the neighbourhood is seen as a matter of great concern by both the indigenous Dutch and immigrants. Not only do the remaining white people regret the loss of other white people (and they often want to move out themselves); their departure is also seen as a loss by many immigrants.They are left wondering how their children are supposed to become full members of Dutch society when almost all the Dutch have left the neighbourhood.

The older inhabitants' appreciation of Nieuw West has declined markedly. The most important negative point they mention is the change in the composition of the population, especially the influx of minority ethnic groups. Many people make a direct link between immigrants and increasing criminality and pollution. The decline of the area is not seen to be the result of poor town planning, or the quality of the housing. Older inhabitants find that the area is no longer under their control; instead, specific parts are dominated by the young and by foreigners. So the quality of the domain in terms of accessibility, security, and respectability (authority constraint) is going down.

Almost all the shopkeepers have problems with crime and with youths giving them trouble: 'some enter the shop just to be thrown out'; others shoplift small things. Municipal police records show that the crime rate is highest in Nieuw West among the 12- to 17-year-olds. Furthermore, the police note a declining average age of juvenile offenders. The major problems are shoplifting and vandalism (Aalbers et al, 2003). There have been many small and some large-scale disturbances involving Nieuw West youths and the police. The most highly publicised example is that of the riots in early 1998 when several hundred young Moroccans rebelled against society and demolished shop windows, shop interiors, and public space artefacts.

Youth and safety policies

Since 1995, the Netherlands has had an integrative Big Cities Policy (BCP) (see Aalbers et al, 2004). The BCP was originally organised around three themes: physical, economic, and social development. A few years ago a fourth theme of safety was introduced. There are two main reasons for this addition. First, together with the upswing of right-wing politics in the Netherlands, calls for safe environments reached peak levels. Second, parties involved in areas that were already implementing renewal plans indicated that safety was a major issue that had not been adequately addressed in the previous renewal plans. The issue of safety has become increasingly important and has gained momentum in national and local policy discourses (Aalbers et al, 2004).

Criminalisation strategies

Criminalisation strategies are normally connected to both the Police and Justice departments. However, police intervention per se does not imply criminalisation. The Netherlands has a long tradition of socialisation by the police in cooperation with social workers. A policeman has often been portrayed as the social worker of last resort. Recently, however, the dominant discourse portrays the policeman less as a social worker and more as a menial from the justice department. So although recent 'inventions' such as 'Police Youth Target Teams' (which are also active in part of Nieuw West) apply a strong criminalisation discourse, they can – and do – also intervene in other ways. We focus on one specific programme, *Justitie in de Buurt* (JIB) [Justice in the Neighbourhood], and not on neighbourhood policing and justice intervention in general.

Since 1997, the JIB project has been opening offices in various Dutch cities. There are currently almost 30 of them, with six located in Amsterdam. The aim is for these offices to contribute to the overall safety and feelings of security in communities with serious problems in this field. The Ministry of Justice hopes that the JIB project will encourage organisations to work together and think of ways of tackling these community-related problems more swiftly than was the case in the past. A collaborative approach is therefore used to achieve better results.

In a JIB office, the Public Prosecution staff work together with staff from other (justice) organisations to deal with problems such as juvenile crime. The physical presence of these community officers makes them more readily accessible not only to other organisations in the community, but also to individual citizens. The short lines of communication enable them to acquire a better insight into the problems arising in the community, which helps them to respond swiftly and effectively. In order to avoid lengthy procedures, criminal cases are settled out of court wherever possible. It is important to stress that 'Justice in the Neighbourhood' is not necessarily a criminalisation strategy, since the Public Prosecutor has the discretionary power to refrain from prosecution on public interest grounds, even when a criminal offence has been brought to the Public Prosecutor's attention.

A first evaluation carried out by the 'Centre for Research and Documentation on the Ministry of Justice' in 1999, showed that one of the most significant results achieved by the JIBs is the speed with which cases are processed. In 2001/02 a second evaluation was carried out, which showed that particularly close partners (police, local government authorities, and so on) were pleased with the JIBs' achievements because the integrated approach not only ensures a more direct and rapid response, but also a response which is likely to be more in line with the requirements of the specific situation. The true strength of the JIBs lies in their implementation, because they give a special impetus to cooperative working in actual cases or problems, resulting in effective action on the part of government organisations. The centre's researchers criticise the project, however, for failing to be sufficiently embedded in the working methods and procedures of the organisations involved.

There is a similar policy in France known as the *Maisons de la justice et du droit* (MJD) (see the next section, which covers France).

Socialisation strategies

Reducing the number of educational drop-outs is an important objective in the local 'educational-arrears policy'. In Amsterdam there is also a policy concerning compulsory education that concentrates on reducing the level of non-attendance at school and the number of early drop-outs. There is also a system of taking note of non-attendance and pupil registration. Young people at risk of dropping out can therefore be identified. Youth networks approach these young people to get a complete picture of the situation and help solve problems together. Within those networks the Regional Educational Centres, Secondary School Boards of Governors, welfare organisations, youth organisations, and trade and industry cooperate (for more details see Aalbers et al, 2004, Chapters 6 and 7). In this subsection we concentrate on two specific programmes: 'New Perspectives' and 'Neighbourhood Fathers'.

New Perspectives

The *Nieuwe Perspectieven* (New Perspectives) project aims at a coherent approach towards the most difficult teenagers who find themselves in multiple problem situations typically involving family, school, and the police. The Amsterdam City Council set up this programme in cooperation with the police, the Public Prosecutor, and the Child Protection Council. The aim of the original project, which took place in Amsterdam-West between 1993 and 1996, was to help these young people go back to school or work. The project tries to build a bridge between the living environment, young people's networks and the formal network of social services that can be used to help these youngsters.

Feedback from the young people who completed the intervention programme indicated that they had greatly benefited from New Perspectives and felt more self-confident and able to manage their lives in a better way. The attention they were given, through daily conversations and the practical nature of the project aimed at solving problems at school and work, was particularly effective. The follow-up care provided in New Perspectives is particularly important for the success of the project. The cooperation between the authorities providing help, the police, schools, and New Perspectives was the key success factor in the project. Given the positive results of New Perspectives, this project might be a useful model for districts with a similar population make-up and similar problems concerning young people.

Through the success of New Perspectives in Amsterdam-West, the project has also been implemented in other parts of Amsterdam and in other cities. In Amsterdam, the project currently supports approximately 800 young people per year. Sometimes the project also takes on people who have been referred to the project's staff by a JIB office. This, however, is not to say that coordination between different projects and parties is so abundant that young people cease to create problems or to be labelled as deviant. Local key players as well as residents report that problems have only mounted since the riots of 1998 (Aalbers et al, 2003). Neither is it to say that the JIBs and New Perspectives have completely failed, since the problems might well have been worse without these projects.

Neighbourhood Fathers

In Nieuw West, the *Buurtvaders* (Neighbourhood Fathers) programme was developed in areas where male Moroccan youths were causing considerable nuisance and trouble. A group of Moroccan fathers took the initiative to walk through the neighbourhood, following a timetabled schedule to ensure that some of them were always present. They approach the boys in a personal way. Fourteen fathers started in the spring of 1999 by making daily rounds through the neighbourhood. Initially, many young people called them names, such as 'traitors'. Gradually, however, not only the young people, but also other parents came to accept the *Buurtvaders*. Not only does the *Buurtvaders* project make neighbourhoods safer; it also promotes social cohesion within and between groups, and between generations. While many indigenous

Dutch people were very sceptical at the beginning, they have also come to appreciate this initiative.

According to De Jong (2000) a striking feature of the project is that it makes positive use of 'Northern Moroccan village culture' in which authority over young people is less individualised than in Dutch (urban) culture, but shared with other adults. De Jong speaks of 'informal external social control'. It is not claimed that all the young people who hang around in the neighbourhood accept the *Buurtvaders*. As one 14-year-old Moroccan youngster says:

> "They talk too much. This way everyone knows all about everything. That's not right. No, I don't listen to them. I don't like them" (De Jong, 2000, p 482).

Nevertheless, the programme works so well that it has been copied not only within Amsterdam, but also in other Dutch cities. Organisations in other countries have also shown an interest.

France

In France, the insecurity issue is strongly combined with political and ideological issues. So, in 1977, Raymond Barre's liberal-right government passed the Security and Freedom Act. Trade unions and left-wing parties organised debates, demonstrations and so on to protest at the restrictions on human rights introduced by the Act. The left-wing politicians therefore decided to implement a different policy and there was broad discussion of feelings of insecurity.

Then, in 1981, Les Minguettes came to the fore as one of France's most symbolic large housing estates in terms of the rights of young foreigners, the alternative conception of insecurity policy, and François Mitterrand's presidential campaign. The Les Minguettes riots in the summer of 1981 had national consequences for urban, social, and security policies. But these types of policy failed and, in response to popular demand for security, the socialist vision of insecurity changed; the Socialist party acknowledged the importance of insecurity in 1997, when Lionel Jospin was Prime Minister (Le Roux, 1997). The Socialist party accepted this change because the districts most concerned about insecurity were working class. Before 1997, insecurity was acknowledged only as a social issue and the security demands of inhabitants as a middle-class concern. The extreme Right *Front National* party currently presents a huge problem in political debates and development. The leaders of this party are probably fascist, but the government's only response was, until 1997 at least, to say 'don't listen to them, they are fascist', without attempting to understand why people voted for them.

The Les Minguettes estate in Lyon

The Les Minguettes estate is located in the southern part of greater Lyon within the older industrial municipality of Vénissieux. Since the municipal elections of 1935, Vénissieux has had a Communist mayor. Today, more than 20,000 people live in the neighbourhood, a marked decline from 35,000 in 1975. It used to accommodate indigenous workers and French people returning to France following Algerian independence. During the late 1970s and 1980s the population changed and the proportion of first- and second-generation immigrant households increased markedly; in some districts young people with foreign roots accounted for 60-75% of the total youth population.

Increasing unemployment, poverty, spatial concentration, and riots contributed to the rising crime rates. For 2003, the crime rate was about 92 reported incidents per thousand people, a medium-to-high level for the city of Lyon. On the one hand, high crime rates in the commercial district of the Lyon city centre may be caused in part by young people from the estates (Chignier-Riboulon, 1999). On the other hand, crime rates in Les Minguettes are lower than might be expected in relation to the local atmosphere; however, people are reluctant to lodge complaints because they are afraid of reprisals from young people, or because they have lost faith in the justice system. Lastly, according to the Mayor of Vénissieux, official figures show a 'quantitative improvement in comparison with 2002, but hide a serious new evolution in qualitative aspects'.

Criminalisation strategies: the general French approach

The last two decades have seen two types of development. On the one hand several measures were implemented in order to increase socialisation in neighbourhoods in a state of decline. On the other hand, there has been a development of criminalisation strategies, mainly since the 1990s. In most cases, new laws to combat crime keep some patterns of socialisation; finally, young people (under the age of 18) benefit from *l'Ordonnance de 1945* (the 1945 Act) described below.

The aim of the 1945 Act was to protect minors. This Act has three principles. First, the focus is on education rather than on criminalisation. The second principle defines a specific justice system for minors:

specialist youth judges ('judges for children') with special courts, and a close relationship between the judge and the young people concerned. Third, for the same criminal action as an adult, a minor receives a less severe punishment (usually a 'half-punishment'). This Act was the basis of French judicial policy for young people, but it has gradually been changed since the 1980s: first, on large estates in decline, 'social insecurity' creates conditions for criminality and trouble; second, minors are often victims, too; and finally, since 1982 (Bonnemaison, 1982), it has been acknowledged that prevention is better than cure, or in this case punishment. So penal regulation and social regulation are mixed; the aims of alternative punishment such as 'work in the community' (*travail d'intérêt général* (TIG)) are: to replace short prison sentences (to avoid recidivism); to improve the self-knowledge of young criminals (by working in a hospital or in an urban environmental city service); and to facilitate social integration.

Penal regulation is, however, increasingly important. This development is linked with increased social difficulties on the estates in decline (Fitoussi et al, 2004) and the social demand for safety. Such demands are reflected in EU policy, especially with respect to urban criminality (Amsterdam Treaty). Usually, the political translation is a faster public response. The objective is to restore safety in neighbourhoods and, consequently, 'Republican Law'. The last Home Office Minister enforced police activity and penal legislation. The latest relevant piece of legislation, the 2003 Domestic Safety Act makes gathering in the entrance hall or stairwell of an apartment block a criminal offence if daily disturbances (abusive or violent behaviour to tenants, and so on) ensue.[1] Enforcement of the law is difficult, however. How can a nuisance that makes tenants afraid of young people be characterised? Moreover, social landlords and prosecutors prefer to negotiate to obtain long-term results. Finally, most of those involved do not want to penalise minor delinquent behaviour. Prison is no longer considered capable of providing an appropriate solution to attitudes in neighbourhoods in decline, not only for moral reasons, but also because of quantitative (too many juvenile delinquents for the number of judges) and qualitative (for instance, conditions for minors in Lyon's prison are comparable with those described by Dickens in the 19th century) concerns (Schosteck, 2002, p 155). Therefore, other measures are being developed, such as 'Justice in the Neighbourhood'.

Justice in the Neighbourhood

In a previous section the Dutch 'Justice in the Neighbourhood' policy was discussed. A similar policy has been developed in France under the name *Maisons de justice et du droit* (MJD). Currently, 98 MJDs have been set up in France. There is a partnership between the Ministry for Neighbourhoods in Decline, the Ministry of Justice, and the municipalities. One of the main aims of the partnership is to bring justice closer to the inhabitants of communities in decline. Thus, the objective is to achieve more equality in the justice system, because some residents have lost confidence in it, and to demonstrate with more transparency the action of the justice system: a justice system that is more direct and less solemn. Each MJD has two sides: information work about legislation, and actions to combat feelings of insecurity. Inhabitants and stakeholders are uneasy about miscreants who have not been brought before the courts because there are too many cases to try and the prosecutors can only select some of them. The time lag between the date of commitment of a crime and date of sentencing is on average 18 to 24 months. Under these conditions, a prison sentence serves no useful purpose because the young delinquents may have forgotten the particular offence, and have probably gone on to commit further offences, and so resocialising them only becomes harder. Some critics argue that there are no real effects in the long term and perhaps the MJD is merely 'Justice for the poor': a 'sub-justice system' for estates in decline.

Socialisation strategies

The French Ministry of Education has a specific policy to improve educational achievement in neighbourhoods in decline. This policy is the establishment of *zones d'éducation prioritaire* (ZEP) (zones of educational priority) since 1981, with additional funding. Unfortunately, as is usually the case in France, too many schools were incorporated and there has been no real evaluation. Improving school results for educational drop-outs involves further activities. One of these consists of 'temporary classes' inside or outside secondary schools for pupils who have fallen behind in the education system. In 2002, there were 3,650 pupils included in 233 classes. The programme works through contracts between the family and the school. Contracts are drawn up on a case-by-case basis. Even if reintegration within the secondary school is difficult, experts consider that this programme has *'very positive results'* (Dussaut and Isambert, 2003, p 120), with one third of the students displaying a better social attitude and more than 50% of them remaining in education and training (secondary school or other institutional structure).

In order to obtain better profitability, urban services employ fewer people. However, during the 1990s, the growth of reported crime and increased feelings of insecurity required the return of 'social intermediaries' in urban areas, especially at subway stations, on buses, and in neighbourhoods in decline (particularly during the night). Many new jobs were created (with public money) to maintain a human presence and to increase social mediation, with many new job titles such as '*agent local de médiation sociale*' (local agent for social mediation), or '*adulte-relais*' (adult person involved in the social life of the estate), or '*équipes emplois-insertion*' (teams for employment inclusion), and so on. All these initiatives aim to prevent crime and correct anti-social attitudes, on the one hand, and, on the other, to facilitate an inclusion process for the residents on the estates. Often, these new jobs are given in priority to residents of the neighbourhoods. In Rillieux and Vénissieux, for example, one of the current actions is the *présence tranquillité* (Quiet Presence) (Belmessous et al, 2004) implemented in partnership with the local authority, social landlords, and the police. The wardens walk around the estate during the day and also at night to observe any dysfunction or problems in the public and semi-public spaces. The wardens use mediation, or they can call police services when talking is insufficient. According to the stakeholders, feelings of insecurity seem to have declined, but the wardens' jobs often last only for a limited period. Some argue that this type of policy (social mediation) may be appropriate for the long-term management of neighbourhoods in decline (Schosteck, 2002, p 102), with probably more temporary jobs not requiring any qualifications. Others add that mediation is a new form of managing poor people because social translators are needed, and they fear further stigmatisation of large estates. According to Schosteck's report, this type of action should be proliferated. In relation to these perspectives, independent evaluations will have to be expanded.

Poland

The concentration of crime and different symptoms of pathology on the estates are caused by many complex factors. As illustrated above, the case study estates in France and the Netherlands are predominantly challenged by problems connected with the concentration of minority ethnic groups. In the case of the Polish estate of Wrzeciono, poverty and the lack of prospects for the younger generation are considered to be the main causes of anti-social behaviour. The Wrzeciono estate can be perceived as a typical case representing the situation on many Polish estates that in the past were inhabited by blue-collar workers who became unemployed after the socioeconomic transformation.

The Wrzeciono estate in Warsaw

The Wrzeciono estate in Warsaw is an example of an area that was affected particularly negatively by the changes after 1989. It is typical of the estates in Poland built in the 1960s and 1970s. At the beginning most of the residents were blue-collar workers in the steel industry working in the Luccini Steelworks located next to the estate. The changes of 1989 brought about a crisis in the heavy industry sector. As a result, many people working for the Luccini Steelworks lost their jobs. Now, Wrzeciono has become an area of high unemployment, which has influenced the social composition of the estate. Moreover, some families have lived on social welfare benefits over two generations. Thirty-eight per cent of the people in this region receive social welfare benefits. A socially excluded community characterised by common problems of unemployment and with few opportunities on the labour market generates various pathological patterns such as petty crime, domestic violence, and alcohol and drug abuse. The transformation has been followed by the steady inflow of the more prosperous newcomers who bought newly-built dwellings on the Wrzeciono estate. Unfortunately, in most cases their blocks of flats are well protected, and separated from the rest of the area by high walls (gated communities), a situation which does little to promote integration with the local community.

Socialisation strategies

In 2001, local authorities and institutions such as the Bielany Social Welfare Centre set up a Programme for improving the quality of life among Wrzeciono residents' on the Wrzeciono estate. The strategy was established to improve the quality of life in several social respects. Wide-ranging attention is paid to mobilising local community activity and to reducing poverty, as well as counteracting criminality and other risk factors such as alcoholism and drug addiction; the improvement of safety is set as one of the most important goals.

In order to diagnose area problems and key issues effectively, the emphasis was placed on gaining an understanding of the local context. The tasks for the years 2002-06 were worked out on the basis of the data obtained from special research, workshops with the residents, and consultations with local institutions. Having recognised that the insecurity issue on the Wrzeciono estate is of major concern to residents and that it is strongly interrelated with many other social problems, the agenda for improving residents' quality of life was drawn up in an holistic way: the agenda embraces a set of initiatives and projects and is to be realised in association with other projects run by various bodies functioning on the site. Considerable attention has been paid to particularly vulnerable social groups such as children and young people from deprived families.

Special attention is given to the organisation of after-school and vacation programmes for young children and teenagers. It is assumed that providing opportunities for young people to use their spare time in a socially acceptable way is the best remedy for youth delinquency. This assumption applies particularly to young people who have no positive social patterns in their family environment.

One of the parties on the Wrzeciono estate that plays a significant part in the realisation of the 'Programme for improving the quality of life among Wrzeciono residents' is the 'Centre for Out-of-school Activities'. It runs cultural and educational activities for young people. The provision has been extended; it also provides activities related to avoiding unemployment, in addition to artistic, dancing, or model-making workshops.

After-school programmes are offered within the framework of the 'Open Schools' project. Teachers lead hobby circles where students can develop their interests and skills. Schools also provide students with catch-up programmes. Teachers help students with particular learning difficulties in compensatory classes; some students may have problems with dyslexia, for example. Opening the school gyms and sports fields and making them available after school under the supervision of sports trainers has been very helpful in promoting sports activities. Some gyms and sports fields have been extended and renovated within the programme. Sports activities are particularly popular among young males, who often join school sports clubs and become members of teams that participate in interschool competitions and other sports events. The programme attempts to build an effective, interdisciplinary system of support for children and families at risk. On the agenda for enhancing the well-being of estate residents, street-based educators were employed to talk to the groups of young people just hanging around. Street-based educators' activities are intended to reduce the negative peer pressure that aggravates criminal intent.

Institutions frequently combine educational workshops and sociotherapeutic activities. Within the framework of Wrzeciono's strategy, special funds were set aside for preventive services led by non-governmental organisations operating on the estate. One of these – the Youth Assistance Society *Gniazdo* ('Nest') – manages the centre where children and young people can spend their spare time under the supervision of specially trained volunteers. They take care of children with a deprived background, and organise socio-therapeutic workshops that help children and youths to overcome their everyday life problems and cope with stressful situations. The volunteers also teach their young clients how best to react to aggression. Additionally, the programme takes on the organisation of self-support groups for withdrawal from alcohol and drug abuse, and enforcement of the prohibition of selling alcohol to children younger than 18 years of age.

Following the administrative reorganisation of Warsaw, some of the actions previously undertaken are being continued; however, the new authorities cancelled some of the plans that had initially been intended. Although the programme was planned for a period of four years, policy makers have raised doubts that the new administration will complete the adapted agenda. The new authorities are more willing to finance repressive actions than actions promoting community socialisation.

Criminalisation policies

In Warsaw, in 2002, newly elected centralised city authorities[2] announced the improvement of safety as the key feature of the city's strategy. The slogan 'zero tolerance for criminal offences' has become the principle for action to enhance peace and order in the city. The authorities started by reforming and increasing the number of City Guard Patrols. The scope of cooperation with the Warsaw Police Headquarters was expanded and a Customer Service Centre was established to receive complaints and accept proposals concerning safety in the city. The citywide project 'Warsaw's Safety Map' was prepared to combat criminal behaviour in all Warsaw's districts, including the Wrzeciono estate.

In the initial phase of the project, on the basis of meetings with residents and consultations with police officers, a list of unsafe areas was prepared and reinforced police patrols were allocated to areas regarded as particularly troublesome. Additionally, video cameras were installed in locations selected on the basis of the residents' statements. Police patrols on bicycles and motorcycles also patrol the Wrzeciono estate. The programme was largely devoted to the promotion and assurance of safety for students in school. Specialised groups of trained police officers and city patrol guards inspect school grounds. The patrol's task is to supervise the environment surrounding the school and intervene in risky and threatening situations. The underlying basis of the programme is to encourage headteachers to cooperate closely with school police patrols. Headteachers are required to keep up-to-date information about troublesome pupils (pupils who play truant, use drugs or alcohol, or are members of gangs or violent youth groups) (Węcławowicz et al, 2004).

The project 'Warsaw Safety Map' was established on the authorities' conviction that the effective reduction of violence and crime and the assurance of peace and quiet in the city can be achieved by 'fast and determined reaction by police, by the city patrol force, and by other auxiliary services to every disturbance of public order, without ignoring even the slightest signs of vandalism or troublemaking' (Kielak-Ciemniewska, 2003).

As a result of placing extra police patrols in selected areas, disruptive incidents were reduced. The improvement in feelings of safety is influenced to a great extent by the presence of uniformed police officers, which, according to the residents and headteachers, effectively deters potential perpetrators of crime. However, it should also be noted that, during the evaluation meetings, residents also made critical remarks. They complained that police officers frequently do not react to hooliganism firmly enough, avoid confrontation with young people and are reluctant to take effective initiatives.

The strategy of scaring criminals away undoubtedly meets the residents' basic expectations, but does not necessarily mean that safety in the neighbourhoods has been permanently secured. According to the residents' statements, once the police patrols were removed, acts of vandalism resurfaced. A successful criminalisation strategy requires permanent monitoring of the neighbourhood by police services. Additionally, using the 'safety map' to select and show the most dangerous places in the neighbourhood (especially when it is published in the local press) may lead to a situation in which residents feel more endangered and consequently try to avoid these areas, which in turn may worsen an area's bad reputation. A strong fear of crime can itself constitute a criminogenic (= crime-triggering) factor (Osiecka, 1998).

Conclusions

The so-called 'deviant' attitudes of local groups of (mainly male) young people in neighbourhood spaces may create feelings of insecurity. Other inhabitants and users of common spaces may disapprove of the behaviour of the groups of young people who gather and chat in the entrance halls of the apartment blocks, break letterboxes, urinate in the lifts, store bottles on the stairs, and so on. Their behaviour is a matter of concern for many of the other inhabitants, in particular the elderly, who complain about these young people but are often afraid to talk to them.

The risk factors of criminality and the causes of insecurity mentioned above are often linked together; undoubtedly, they must be treated as mutually dependent variables. Particular causes vary in intensity in different societies. Their presence and the extent of their influence and dynamics depend on the social context, type of society, and prevailing social trends in a community.

Social scientists have often favoured socialisation strategies over criminalisation strategies since, they argue, socialisation strategies combat problems at the root and thus combat a whole problem process, while criminalisation strategies only take care of the symptoms without addressing the causes of these interlinked problems. We argue that, while general socialisation strategies work better in the long term, criminalisation strategies are also needed to supplement socialisation strategies so as to combat crime and feelings of insecurity in the short term. Thus, although we agree with Wacquant (2001, p 410) that 'the best means of making the prison recede is, again and always, to strengthen and expand social and economic rights', we also believe that, on a practical level, nuisance sometimes has to be criminalised to be able to ensure safety. Moreover, punishment can also be a long-term action, but only if the social services for socialisation and integration processes are developed with proper state involvement. The policies implemented will therefore require large-scale public expenditure if they are to succeed.

The adequate handling of safety problems requires the implementation of a collaborative approach within which different actors can participate (see Chapter Three). Short-term, separate actions do not usually achieve the expected effects. The examples given show that, when preparing a strategy agenda, a comprehensive and integrating approach is fundamental in solving crime problems at neighbourhood level. Such an approach points to the involvement of different kinds of local players when undertaking actions and at the same time bringing these actions closer to the community. Proper communication and swifter information flow between all parties involved is also seen to be a key to success. While, on the Polish Wrzeciono estate, the engagement of residents is limited mainly to an informative role, residents on the Dutch and French estates are involved in more direct action such as 'neighbourhood watch' schemes. These kinds of action play a significant preventative role. However, one must be careful when implementing extensive control over an area. Sometimes this may turn out to have the reverse effect to that sought. As has been noted in the case of the 'Neighbourhood Fathers' project in Amsterdam Nieuw West, local young people may perceive the increased control negatively. Young people tend to rebel against extensive control over their behaviour and territory. They treat additional controlling patrols as intruders, which can also intensify their anger, leading to the inflammation of conflict between them and the rest of the community and police. Obviously the implementation of neighbourhood patrols is helpful in tackling youth crime, but examples show that they must be supplemented by strategies that first pull young people away from anti-social behaviour. In general these strategies involve showing young people other perspectives and giving them the opportunity to spend their time in a socially acceptable way.

The main challenge for policy makers and other local parties is how to approach young people in the place where they live. In the Polish case, different institutions provide various educational, cultural, and sports workshops designed for children and young people living in the surrounding blocks of flats. Giving young people the chance to develop their interests is very important, especially during vacations. The organised workshops often constitute the only source of positive activities for young people in their environment. In French and Dutch neighbourhoods, educational aspects are stressed first of all. Most attention is given to enhancing the levels of educational attainment of marginalised young people and, as a consequence, improving their position on the labour market and within society.

While in the Dutch example neighbourhood-based social programmes are addressed at distinct groups at risk, in France and in Poland the target groups of the programmes are not clearly specified. An insufficiently implemented collaborative approach leading to a lack of proper communication between institutional actors and the community can be a direct cause of the failure of even the best projects. When planning a socialisation strategy, the involvement of the recipients of the programmes should be one of the priorities for policy makers. And, finally, the effects of public policies should be publicised more widely, with, in the French case and, above all, in the Polish one, real evaluations.

Notes

[1] A previous piece of legislation enacted under the socialist government (the 2001 Everyday Safety Act (15 November 2001)) authorised police intervention in entrance halls of apartment blocks.

[2] Before October 2002, Warsaw was a municipal association of 11 Warsaw boroughs, which to a large extent functioned independently of the municipality. Since the end of 2002, when the new Act on the Structure of Warsaw came into force, the whole of Warsaw became one borough. The former boroughs have been abolished and transformed into districts/auxiliary units of the city of Warsaw. Districts have lost their independence to create their own policies. The role of a district has been reduced to administrating current affairs, while budgets were reduced by 50% from those of the previous boroughs.

References

Aalbers, M., Van Beckhoven, E., van Kempen, R., Musterd, S. and Ostendorf, W. (2003) *Large housing estates in the Netherlands: Overview of developments and problems in Amsterdam and Utrecht*, Utrecht: Urban and Regional research centre Utrecht, Faculty of Geosciences, Utrecht University.

Aalbers, M., Van Beckhoven, E., van Kempen, R., Musterd, S. and Ostendorf, W. (2004) *Large housing estates in the Netherlands: Policies and practices*, Utrecht: Urban and Regional research centre Utrecht, Faculty of Geosciences, Utrecht University.

Belmessous, F., Chemin, C., Chignier-Riboulon, F., Commerçon, N., Trigueiro, M. and Zepf, M. (2004) *Large housing estates in France: Policies and practices*, Utrecht: Urban and Regional research centre Utrecht, Faculty of Geosciences, University of Utrecht.

Body-Gendrot, S. and Wihtol De Wenden, C. (2003) *Police et discriminations raciales, le tabou français*, Paris: les éditions de l'Atelier.

Bonnemaison, J. (1982) *Face à la délinquance: Prévention, répression et solidarité*, Report for the Prime Minister, Paris: la Documentation française.

Bordet, J. (1998) *Les jeunes de la cité*, Paris: PUF.

Braithwaite, J. (1989) *Crime, shame and reintegration*, Cambridge: Cambridge University Press.

Černič Mali, B., Sendi, R., Boškič, R., Filipovič, M., Goršič, N. and Zaviršek Hudnik, D. (2003) *Large housing estates in Slovenia: Overview of developments and problems in Ljubljana and Koper*, Utrecht: Urban and Regional research centre Utrecht, Faculty of Geosciences, Utrecht University.

Chignier-Riboulon, F. (1999) *L'intégration des Franco-maghrébins*, Paris: l'Harmattan.

Chignier-Riboulon, F. (2000) 'La "banlieue", entre culture populaire de l'honneur et sentiment de marginalisation', *Géographie et cultures*, vol 33, March, pp 71-88.

De Jong, J.D. (2000) 'Marokkaans gezag in de publieke ruimte', *Rooilijn*, vol 33, no 10, pp 479-84.

Droste, C. and Knorr-Siedow, T. (2004) *Large housing estates in Germany: Policies and practices*, Utrecht: Urban and Regional research centre Utrecht, Faculty of Geosciences, University of Utrecht.

Dussaut, J. and Isambert, J.P. (2003) *Dispositifs relais et écoles ouvertes*, Report for the Ministry for Education, Inspections générales de l'éducation et de la recherché: 03-016, 03-033.

Fitoussi, J.P., Laurent, E. and Maurice, J. (eds) (2004) *Ségrégation urbaine et intégration sociale*, Report by the Conseil d'analyse économique, Paris: la Documentation française.

Gastaut, Y. (2000) *L'immigration et l'opinion en France sous la Ve République*, Paris: le Seuil.

Grémy, J.P. (1996) 'La délinquance permet-elle d'expliquer le sentiment d'insécurité?', *Les Cahiers de la sécurité intérieure*, vol 23, pp 54-67.

Hawkins, J.D., Herrenkokohl, T., Farrington, D.P., Catalano, R.F. and Garachi, T.W. (1998) 'A review of predictors of youth violence', in R. Loeber and D.P. Farrington (eds) *Serious and juvenile offenders: Risk factors and successful interventions*, Thousand Oaks, CA: Sage, pp 106-46.

Kielak-Ciemniewska, E. (2003) *Safe city. Safer streets*, Interview by Ewa Kielak-Ciemniewska with Deputy Mayor of Warsaw WBadysBaw Stasiak, The Warsaw Voice on line.

Laé, J.F. (1991) 'Crise des banlieues, le béton n'est pas en cause', *Regards sur l'actualité*, Juillet (July) pp 23-34.

Lauderdale, P. and Oliverio, A. (2001) 'Preventing or reinventing crime?' *International Journal of Comparative Criminology*, vol 1, no 1, pp 107-18.

Lepoutre, D. (1997) *Cœur de banlieue*, Paris: Odile Jacob.

Le Roux, B. (1997) *Une politique au plus près du citoyen*, Report for the Prime Minister, Paris: la Documentation française.

Mauer, M. (1999) 'Symposium: why are tough on crime policies so popular?' *Stanford Law and Policy Review*, vol 9, pp 11-41.

Merton, R.K. (1938) 'Social structure and anomie', *American Sociological Review*, vol 3, October, pp 672-82.

Mezzetti, P., Mugnano, S. and Zajczyk, F. (2003) *Large housing estates in Italy: Overview of developments and problems in Milan*, Utrecht: Urban and Regional research centre Utrecht, Faculty of Geosciences, University of Utrecht.

Muchembled, R. (1998) *La société policée*, Paris: Le Seuil.

Osiecka, J. (1998) *Poczucie zagrożenia przestępczościąoraz społeczne opinie o policji w świetle sondaży opinii publicznej*, Rapport no 151, Biuro Studiów i Ekspertyz Kancelarii Sejmu.

Power, A. (1997) *Estates on the edge: the social consequences of mass housing in Northern Europe*, London: Macmillan.

Prins, B. and Slijper, B. (2002) 'Inleiding', *Migrantenstudies*, vol 18, no 4, pp 194-210.

Salas, D. (1997) 'La délinquance d'exclusion', *Les Cahiers de la sécurité intérieure*, vol 29, pp 61-75.

Schosteck, J.P. (2002) *Commission d'enquête sur la délinquance des mineurs*, Rapport du Sénat: 340, Paris: la Documentation française.

Uitermark, J., Rossi, U. and Van Houtum, H. (2004) *Urban citizenship and the negotiation of ethnic diversity: An inquiry into actually existing multiculturalism in Amsterdam*, Research programme 'Governance and Places' working paper 2004/4, (www.kun.nl/), Nijmegen: University of Nijmegen.

van Kempen, E. (1994) 'High-rise living: the social limits to design', in B. Danermark and I. Elander (eds) *Social rented housing in Europe: Policy, tenure and design*, Delft: Delft University Press, pp 159-80.

Wacquant, L. (1999) *Les prisons de la misère*, Paris: Raisons d'agir Editions.

Wacquant, L. (2001) 'The penalisation of poverty and the rise of neo-liberalism', *European Journal on Criminal Policy and Research*, vol 9, no 4, pp 401-12.

Węcławowicz, G., Guszcza, A. and Kosłowski, S. (2004) *Large housing estates in Poland: Policies and practices*, Utrecht: Urban and Regional research centre Utrecht, Faculty of Geosciences, Utrecht University.

W'gleDski, J. (2001) *Miasta Ameryki u proguXXI wieku*, Warsaw: Scholar.

FIFTEEN

Restructuring large housing estates: does gender matter?

Christiane Droste, Irene Molina and Francesca Zajczyk

Introduction

All over Europe, large housing estates are currently undergoing fundamental structural change. In terms of direction and aiming at *good* urban governance (UNCHS, 1998), the complexity of the problems encountered seems to produce a contradiction between a demand for top-down urban development involving the devolution of governmental responsibilities to governance-oriented structures, and a new esteem for bottom-up initiatives.

Assuming that urban governance needs to be gender sensitive to be equitable, sustainable, and effective, the question that arises is whether gender mainstreaming is an important issue for the restructuring of large housing estates and current urban and estate development policies. Has the implementation of the top-down gender mainstreaming strategy had an impact on local governance? The problem is to identify which urban or estate development policies and steering concepts may be efficient in supporting the political commitment to gender mainstreaming. Following a brief explanation of the gender terminology and its adoption in urban planning and governance, we examine the compatibility of *gender mainstreaming* and Healey's concept of *collaborative planning*, mainly from a German perspective, but also including Swedish and Italian examples.

Although these approaches have some similarities, this chapter reveals the differences that are particularly related to the different welfare systems in which each of the gender perspectives on urban issues is rooted, representing the "three worlds of Europe" (Esping-Andersen, 1990). Sweden is a Nordic country with a highly developed welfare system, within the social policies of which gender is strongly mainstreamed. Germany, representing Central Europe, is undergoing a change from a 'supportive' welfare state system to an 'enabling' approach and a retreat of the state. A similar top-down approach to mainstream gender is being realised in this context and there is a slowly increasing demand on changing breadwinner models. Finally, in Italy, as a Southern European country, the gender mainstreaming approach has gradually been incorporated into the political and social culture of a country which is still strongly characterised by a familistic welfare system. We then discuss different structural frameworks for the implementation of gender mainstreaming in urban and large housing estate development and the gender sensitivity (or blindness) of these developments.

Gender mainstreaming in large housing estates

Gender refers to the culturally and socially determined differences between men and women, the relationships between them, the diversity of their roles in the community, and the power structures in which they are embedded. Gilligan's book *In a different voice* (1993) played a catalytic role in the feminist move from the *difference theory* to *gender theories*. Underlining that "the crucial issue becomes not difference, but the difference, difference makes", Rhodes (1990) indicated that recognising difference in the gender ratio demands more far-reaching societal, legal and political consequences. Butler (1990) and Lorbeer (1995) define gender as a societal construction and social institution, and one of the main principles of societal order. Awareness of this "doing gender" (West and Zimmermann, 1987) underlying any societal and individual action requires individual education as well as educational processes within institutions. *Mainstreaming* policies or strategies in urban governance can be explained as a process of "changing corporate policies, reallocating resources, reshaping services and improving accessibility" (Audit Commission, 2004).

Gender mainstreaming is the process of making gender-sensitive criteria a routine element in the development of organisations and policies. The EC defines *gender mainstreaming* as a "process of assessing the implications for women and men of any planned action, including legislation, policies and programmes, in any area and at all levels" (European Commission, 1998). The process is applied in both a top-down and a bottom-up manner promoting the gender perspective and the traditional empowerment of women. The main challenge is "to change the male-streaming and androcentricity of organisations rather than seeking to help women to fit into male institutions and cultures" (Rees, 1998). This paradigm shift necessitates the inclusion of men as the subject of identity change. After its political breakthrough at the 1995 Beijing World Conference on Women, the gender mainstreaming strategy was ratified as a statutory requirement for all member and accessing states of the EU in the 1999 Amsterdam Treaty.

'Women planning' has been on the agenda of European feminist research and theory from the late 1960s. Sandercock's book *Making the invisible visible* (1999) presented an overview of feminist knowledge about the different ways men and women use the city and contribute to it. The title also serves as a metaphor for the insufficient political recognition of this knowledge. Since "policy and planning with an understanding of gender does not come naturally to professionals, whether women or men" (Beall, 1996), gender mainstreaming has some essential prerequisites. Apart from political will, implementing gender mainstreaming in governance organisations and processes requires a resolution on gender policy guidelines; a top-level commitment to mainstream gender; a resolution to guarantee necessary preconditions (gender-training sessions, for example), and appropriate means of implementation, control, and evaluation.

In urban governance, gender mainstreaming entails the analysis of the tangible effects experienced by men and women through planning and governance. Important tools are the known objectives of gender planning (the spatial integration of work and reproduction, optimised trip-chains, for example). But matters of land use, such as zoning divisions and subordinating places for reproduction for gainful employment are also addressed (Matrix, 1985; UNCHS, 1998; Bundesamt für Bauwesen und Raumordnung (BBR), 2002a). In accordance with the UNCHS criteria for good governance, gender mainstreaming in urban governance strives to enhance the capacity building of women, particularly those in community-based organisations and local authorities. Since civic engagement is one of the basic elements of governance, the consideration of the future male role in this field also becomes relevant. A crucial element in 'gendering' urban governance is the implementation of gender budgeting, which implements cost-benefit analyses of public budgets with respect to men and women.

Large housing estates may be valued as focal points of gender mainstreaming for several reasons. The most obvious is their demographic structure: densely populated areas, with largely social housing, associated with large families, high densities of young people, immigrant populations, and ageing cohorts of mostly female residents. Single or divorced women, mothers, and widows are globally estimated to represent one third of all households; women-headed households are becoming increasingly pervasive in dense urban areas (Beall, 1996;

Becker, 2003). Women's independent access to housing is an important issue; however, it represents only one of the many spatial dimensions of social exclusion. This fact needs to be taken into account, particularly in situations, which arise in France, where the management of house relocation on a massive scale takes place on large housing estates following the demolition of social housing.

The construction of replacement housing is often postponed; and once replacement housing is provided it is different in quality and quantity, so that women are affected by a consequent gap in affordable housing. Despite massive feminist criticism of large housing estates, women experts who carried out one of the first advocacy planning processes in the Federal Republic of Germany, in a large housing estate in Hamburg-Kirchdorf South, concluded that this type of housing also provided advantages for women.

In the setting of the current integrated and governance-oriented urban renewal processes on many large housing estates, our interest is directed at the double role of women as both actors and the targeted group. Our interest in the latter role concerns the close proximity of space for work and reproduction increasingly required through changing gender contracts and the spatial demands of the knowledge-based society. On the other hand, the difference between spaces related to work and/or reproduction and those for revitalisation and self-fulfilment are likely to become more significant for women (Dörhöfer and Terlinden, 1998), not least if the Lisbon 2010 objective concerning the employment of women is to be fulfilled. This Lisbon strategy aims to narrow the gaps between women and men in employment, education and research and increase women's employment. Women continue to be more vulnerable to employment and economic inactivity than men, in particular women with low level education and older women (Commission of the European Communities, 2004) The sectors in which women are predominantly working (education, healthcare and social services, public services and retailing) contribute to local social cohesion, but at the same time, the urban environment often forms one of the barriers hindering women from equal participation in the labour market.

The modernist urban design of separated functions therefore needs to be reconsidered, but estates have the potential to adapt to a growing diversity of living arrangements through their technical preconditions.

Gender-sensitive governance by collaborative planning?

Healey's basic assumption underlying the concept of collaborative planning is that cities are complex diverse entities experienced in different ways by different people (see also Chapter Three); she also draws a distinction between male and female experience. Her conception develops a normative planning model, appropriate for building the institutional capacity for planning in the context of a diverse, fragmented, and uncertain society. The main aim is to set an agenda for inclusive city planning which acknowledges the right of all stakeholders, interest groups, and individuals to a voice in the decision-making process. This inclusiveness requires structures and strategies appropriate to diverse groups; it requires local knowledge and partnerships, networking structures, and institutional capacity building (Healey, 1997; 2003; Cars et al, 2002). A collective, consensus-building decision-making process is called for, referring in principle to Habermas's Discourse Ethic. This makes the case for the "equal participation of all who are affected" and a 'real' argumentation in which those who are affected participate cooperatively and are not excluded through 'expert discussions', assuming a 'place-holder function' for those in the given discourse structure who are not capable of representing themselves (Habermas, 1983; 1990). In political decision making, this role is usually attributed to (poor) women and ethnic minorities.

With regard to the compatibility of *gender mainstreaming* and *collaborative planning*, we can identify both gender-sensitive elements, explicitly included by Healey, and a structural framework. These, like gender mainstreaming, require inclusiveness with respect to gender and ethnicity, the reshaping of steering processes, the acceptance of difference and conflicting interests, and the claim for transparency and equality in decision-making processes. One of the core objectives of this concept is *place making*, which the author describes as the promotion of the social, economic, and environmental well-being of urban places and the building of institutional capacity (see also Chapter Three). From a structural perspective, place making perfectly suits the inclusion of the socio-spatial dimensions of gender.

Collaborative planning is intended to reframe how people think about winning and losing. It requires a discourse about power relationships and male and female roles in civil society. The remaking of gender identities, the rethinking of home and family, and diversifying lifestyles constitute important goals in the changing dynamics of urban regions, but also target renewed gender contracts. The recognition of the power relationships of everyday life experience is said to be of critical importance in developing practices for collaborative local planning. Healey draws attention to four key questions to be considered when changing the systemic design of government forms, which again correspond to gender mainstreaming criteria (Healey, 1997):

• the nature and distribution of rights and duties;
• the control and distribution of resources;
• the specification of criteria for redeeming challenges; and
• the distribution of competencies.

Assuming *collaborative planning* to be the instrument to shape governance, the central elements jointly shaping governance to be institutional capacity (merging intellectual capacity, social capacity, and political capacity (Fichter et al, 2004)) and the latter to be a crucial precondition to impose gender mainstreaming, this approach may be considered appropriate to the achievement of gender equality and democracy.

Mainstreaming gender in European urban policies

In comparison with employment policies, the role of EU and governmental gender policies in urban or estate development and governance is minor. Consequently, the frameworks of gender mainstreaming implementation and the gender sensitivity of urban development and participation in European countries vary widely. The particular points of interest in choosing Sweden, Germany and Italy as examples are the different ways of implementation: top-down and 'prescriptive' in Sweden and Germany; and 'permissive' in Italy. Despite the fact that none of the three countries has an explicit focus on urban development in this context, we were interested in the impact of the gender mainstreaming strategy and related policies in these different settings of policy implementation. In Sweden and Germany, gender policies have been implemented through a top-down legislative framework (considerably staggered) and followed through with specific strategies, pilot projects, and gender-training courses; however, their impact on the different fields of policy varied considerably. In Italy, gender policies have also been developed through legislative interventions, but they are rarely followed through with actual strategies or specific actions. Moreover, gender policies mainly refer to actions at regional and provincial level, while urban and estate-level initiatives are less widespread.

Gender and urban development: the case of Sweden

Sweden is well known for the advanced policies, with respect to gender equality, it has implemented during the last 30 to 40 years. One of the major successes for the gender equality movement is the mainstreaming policy, including all sectors of society, and the Equal Opportunities Act 1991. But there is an evident lack of gender perspective in urban policies, despite the various transformations towards a more gender-equal society. It is feared that the lack of gender-disaggregated data will challenge gender-sensitive housing policy. Among the important social transformations which occurred on the Swedish housing market during the 1980s was a growth in the representation of the elderly, low-income households, single mothers, and young people on the municipal rental-housing market (Lindén, 1989). The statistics reveal a hardening attitude in terms of an increased rate of expulsions of debtors owing rent from the dwellings. The expulsions seem to be gender selective, since single mothers are identified by NGOs concerned with homeless people as a dominant group among those recently expelled from municipal rental housing (Nordfeldt, 1999).

Gender and urban planning

A well-known local initiative to mainstream gender put into force in Uppsala during the 1990s is the *checkalistan* ('check list') (Referensgruppen för jämställdhet i kommunal plannering, 1990) for the gender evaluation of local government authorities and their handling of gender issues. The gender sensitivity of local urban planning and governance in Sweden is weak, although one of the main goals of the Metropolitan Programme (*Storstadssatsningen*) is explicitly gender sensitive, aiming "to stop social, ethnic, and discriminatory segregation in the metropolitan regions, and to work for equal and comparable living conditions and gender equality amongst the people living in the cities". The *lokala utvecklingsavtal* (LUVA) (local development agreements) addresses the integration of ethnic minorities into Swedish society and constitutes an important component of the programme. Among the projects the LUVA supports have been several projects aiming to increase civic participation in terms of deeper and broader citizenship and to promote local multi-ethnic inclusion. The main channel for political participation is through the political bodies.

The fundamental precondition for the allocation of support in the top-down programmes LUVA and 'Periphery Effort' (another locally generated Urban Development Programme) is for there to be a bottom-up initiative. *Livstycket* in the Tensta large housing estate (Stockholm), financed by the Periphery Effort, was created as a combined bottom-up and top-down initiative. The Women's Centre, supported by the LUVA programme, was started entirely from the bottom up, as a local initiative of women of different ethnic origin. Both projects can be classified as empowerment oriented, since they tend to improve life circumstances through enhanced skills, language learning, and other such collective activities. Public attention paid to the issue seems to be marginal; in contrast with the heavy criticism levelled at the programme's perspective targeting ethnicity and integration, the situation regarding gender has not as yet been an issue, even though only two of the 14 projects in progress on 2003 were specially oriented to women's development programmes.

Conclusion

The gender perspective in Swedish urban policy making is fairly weak, but the two examples mentioned earlier show an important link between top-down and bottom-up initiatives: the interstices left by the urban development programmes enhancing governance-oriented structures on the estates are used increasingly by grassroots women's movements. In the long term, the conjunction of rhetoric and spontaneous praxis might indeed change the status of gender issues in local urban policy making. For both the municipally organised measures and programmes to counteract growing exclusion and segregation on large housing estates, the systematic incorporation of a gender perspective would be necessary and perfectly viable.

However, to incorporate a gender perspective in all aspects of Swedish urban governance, there remains the necessity to explore gender relationships in the housing market, especially on the large suburban housing estates forming part of the 'Million Homes Programme'. Other decisive factors to be taken into account might be gender discrimination through financial market actors (taking the heterosexual nuclear family and its traditional income situation as the norm (Cox, 1992)), the impacts of gentrification on women's housing, and the question whether non-European immigrant women experience ethnically selective discrimination on the Swedish housing market.

Mainstreaming gender: German policies and the Berlin case

In Germany, women's empowerment and gender equality developed rather slowly, from an Article in a 1949 Act on Equal Rights to the 1999 Gender Equality Act concerning the implementation of gender mainstreaming and compulsory gender-training sessions for the top level of governmental and state administration. Gender mainstreaming was appended to the ministerial procedural rules and the reform of administration, but the federal system results in different modes of implementation at governmental, state, and municipal levels. At the municipal level, women's empowerment has mainly been implemented since the late 1980s by representatives of women's and equal rights movements, acting across sectors. In an increasing number of cities, gender mainstreaming is implemented through the modernisation of administration and service provision and reference to models for the city.

Urban and housing policies

The 1970s second wave of the feminist movement was considerably influenced by feminist urban research, but only in the context of careful urban renewal in the late 1980s were gender-sensitive criteria included in municipal urban development manuals and models. The feminist criticism of the mono-functionalism and the floor plans of the large housing estates constructed in the 1960s and 1970s led to several pilot housing projects being designed by women architects and planners since the late 1980s. They are providing today's models to mainstream gender in urban housing (Zibell and Schroeder, 2002), particularly because changing lifestyles and the increasing number of women-headed households are slowly producing an impact on housing cultures and markets.

Apart from the gender-sensitive models or projects established in the context of the *Lokale Agenda 21* (a programme of the UN Division for Sustainable Development), the outlines of the current national urban development programmes are gender blind. Despite objectives necessarily leading to gender sensitiveness, the visionary *Stadt 2030* programme neglected this issue; it was up to individual municipalities to take the initiative to include gender criteria in their projects. The *Socially Integrative City* (about one third of its target areas are on large housing estates) lacks a conceptually binding obligation to implement gender mainstreaming, although the model provides effective instruments to impose the strategy through its organisational structure.

Women do, however, play a crucial part as initiators of community-building initiatives, as persons supporting dissemination of information in an informal way and as professionals within the programme's local intermediary and steering process.

The *Urban Regeneration Programme*, targeting the shrinking housing stock that is the major structural change in German urban development, includes no gender-sensitive criteria. The ExWoSt project *Gender Mainstreaming in Urban Development* launched in 2003 by the Bundesamt für Bauwesen und Raumordnung [Federal Office for Building and Regional Development] (BBR, 2002b) is in this context a pragmatic and symbolic step. Its objective is to reveal, systemise, and generalise experiences in implementing gender mainstreaming and equal opportunities policies in urban development practice and to draw on two pilot projects, one of which includes the rebuilding process of a large housing estate in Dessau. The means by which gender sensitivity can still be implemented in the terms of the *Socially Integrative City, Urban II,* and the *Urban Regeneration Programme* will be defined.

Gender mainstreaming in Berlin: first steps of an ambitious project

The 2002 government statement on gender mainstreaming in Berlin led to the establishment of three steering channels playing a key role within the overall process: the *Gender Mainstreaming Office* (overall steering and interdisciplinary coordination), the *State Secretary and Expert Commission* (targeting *gender budgeting*, which will start with the 2006 budget and the conjunction between gender mainstreaming and the administrative reform) and the *Districts Steering Committee* (coordination and knowledge transfer). Forming part of the envisaged process is the establishment of pilot projects to be carried out in the Senate Departments of Legal Authorities, Inner City Urban Development, Health and Social Welfare organisations, and the Economy, Work and Women, and in eight districts all of which are managed by a female and a male executive officer and benefit from an external gender consultancy organisation. The overall project will be carried out in phases (a one-year pilot phase followed by a two-year main phase) and includes events to impart information and create awareness and compulsory gender-training sessions for responsible political and executive officers.

The Marzahn-Hellersdorf case: gender becomes an issue

The Marzahn-Hellersdorf district forms part of the largest agglomeration of industrially produced housing in Central Europe. Approximately 73% of its 250,000 inhabitants (with a slight female majority) live on the estate. As a result of the increasing number of apartment vacancies and social segregation, parts of the estate participate in the Urban Regeneration and Socially Integrated City programmes; these seek to introduce collaborative planning and governance structures. Despite a tendency in post-unification East Germany to consider women's empowerment unnecessary, today a considerable number of women's projects targeting qualifications, employment, health issues, language skills, and social inclusion are actively encouraging bottom-up initiatives, especially within the migrant community. The Women's Centre, the Girls' Refuge Flat, and the *Babybauch* (an initiative to support teenage mothers) are some of the cornerstones of their work, building social capital and capacity. Two projects for men (one for those found guilty of domestic violence, and a fathers' group to improve educational competence and parenting skills) constitute the first attempts to change some male patterns of behaviour. A girl's playground and a Centre for Women Starting New Businesses are projects resulting from administrative initiatives. Two professional networks, the *Frauen-Netz-Marzahn-Hellersdorf* and the Working Group against Domestic Violence support women's rights at a structural, bottom-up level, although within the administrative system.

Marzahn-Hellersdorf is one of the pilot districts for gender mainstreaming. In April 2003, the district established some pilot projects in the Departments of Economic and Social Affairs (annual social economic report; gender budgeting) and of Youth Work (the department itself and youth leisure facilities). The *Lokale Agenda 21* seeks to include the gender mainstreaming strategy in its model. Interaction between those involved in women's empowerment and those involved in the gender mainstreaming project or capacity building together with other actors involved in the project does not seem to be intended, although this approach would correspond with the double-track character of the strategy. The main intermediary between the various parties seems to be the women's representative, increasingly playing the part of moderator.

Conclusion

In Germany, most urban policies currently lack the theoretical foundations that could link different cross-sectoral policies strategically. State and municipal authorities recognise gender-sensitive urban planning and governance as an instrument to secure quality, but the form and intensity of the implementation of gender mainstreaming in urban governance still depend to a large extent on informal knowledge transfer, personal gender competence, and the power and fields of action of the respective responsible persons (Droste, 2002; Bock, 2004). Frequently, political or personal change still means a backward step for gender-sensitive instruments; the sustainability of top-down intensive courses in gender mainstreaming may be doubted. Most attempts remain sector-based, but phased models of implementation provide an important space for institutional learning (Weinmann, 2003). Careful monitoring is needed of the tendency to misuse the commitment to gender mainstreaming, cutting funding for women's empowerment, or failing to provide any funding at all, even for male trend setting. The general administrative resistance to cross-sectoral cooperation (Droste and Knorr-Siedow, 2002) and the subordination of gender issues to budgetary pressure need to be considered as components in the interaction space within which gender mainstreaming is to be implemented in urban governance. To verify the validity of this statement, it would be important to include the role of the various parties in ex-ante and ex-post evaluations.

Recent gender policies in Italy and Milan[1]

In Italy, the 1948 Italian Constitution first sanctioned the principle of parity between men and women through the recognition of an active and passive electorate, but only in 2003 was the Constitution revised in order to sanction actions designed to reduce the disparities in elective assemblies and in public office. Political power remains a male privilege; women account for 8.1% of the elected members of the Senate, 11.5% of the Chamber of Deputies, and only two out of 23 national ministers. Nevertheless, visible female presence in politics and administration is increasing: 13.2% of the councillors in regional administrations and 16.1% of the councillors in municipalities with fewer than 15,000 inhabitants are women (Arcidonna, 2003; Censis, 2003; Donne nelle istituzioni, 2003).

New initiatives from the 1980s onwards, aiming to strengthen female participation, were rarely followed by specific strategies or actions despite the opportunities provided by two lines of legislative intervention: 1) the promotion of positive action to overcome gender gaps in education and the professions; and 2) the provision of ad hoc institutions monitoring the implementation of equality principles. The legislation to impose these objectives promotes positive action for equal opportunities at work, female entrepreneurship, provision for maternity and paternity support, the right to care, the right to education, and the coordination of city time schedules. The institutions to promote gender equality set up at national level include the Ministry for Equal Opportunity and the National Committee for Equal Opportunities at Work. Gender policies are mainly referred to at regional and provincial level, whereas municipal and estate-level initiatives are less widespread (Zajczyk, 2003).

The main local institution is the 'Gender Councillor' (*Consigliere di Parità*), appointed at national, regional, and provincial levels. This person's role is the promotion and monitoring of the achievement of gender and non-discriminatory principles at work, testing the coherence of local development policies with the actual implementation of gender policies through public and private players operating in the labour market, and collaboration with the Gender Commissions at all administrative levels, with female association representatives, and 'Pink Centres'.

Considering the identity of the actors who implement policies and the endurance and coherence of the actions which have been implemented, public institutions are the most active actors in the different local contexts. Their main tools are EU-funded projects, generally also being promoted by other local actors. But a large variety of actions and policies are dependent on the initiative of single local actors who do not always network. They lack a strategic vision and precise action planning and risk arbitary closure, always endangered by the constant cuts in public budgets.

Time policies: an Italian peculiarity

The most striking example of gender sensitivity in Italian urban governance is the matter of city time schedules as an issue of public intervention and a variable affecting the quality of life. The first urban time-schedule policies were brought about in the early 1980s by the centre-left feminist debate on the complexity of the temporal experience of women and their double presence on the labour market. The policies go back to the 1989 PCI (Partito Communista Italiano) Act ('Le Donne Cambiano i Tempi', 'Women change times'), and the early 1990s, after the reform of public administration. Concentrating on how the system of city time schedules influenced the organisation of family life, women's access to the labour market, and the harmonisation of working and non-working life, women demanded the re-organisation of urban space, improved accessibility to public services, reduction of bureaucratic boundaries, the redistribution of care work in the social organisation and accessibility objectives. Two Acts designated mayors as responsible for the coordination of public service timetables according to the needs of users and the transformation of the time schedule organisation for social aims. This legislative measure was soon implemented in several Italian cities.

Relevant good practice examples are the 1990s 'Mobility Plan of Bolzano; the case of Cremona, where the administration has introduced experiments involving the timetables of commercial services, schools, and other services; the city of Bergamo, which is experimenting with the systematic planning of social services; and Milan, the first city to introduce a 'City Time Plan'. Milan also introduced a system of time schedule exchange in the 16 Banks of Time. Unfortunately none of these is located in a RESTATE research area. The Time Policies are characterised by fragmentation and depend on the initiative of the administrations. From a governance perspective, the complex actions undertaken on timetables enhance networking and the exchange of experiences among the different districts and increase the involvement of the different local players.

The case of Milan

Milan seems to be characterised by a lack of public planning in all domains, although the city has a variety of parties (unions, cooperatives and women's association, non-profit organisations) and programmes involved in gender policies. These parties and programmes are not always publicly coordinated, and they are of different impact and quality. Two examples of women-empowerment policies illustrate the main lines of municipal intervention in local policies (the support of female participation on the labour market/harmonisation), the roles of the different parties (EU, local authorities, firms), and the increasing public–private collaboration.

The 'Pink Counters' (*Sportelli Rosa*) are an ESF-funded initiative of the City Council of Milan. They were started on an experimental basis in December 2002. Now that they have become a permanent service of the local neighbourhood councils, they help women seeking jobs in all districts of the city. The city council will devote €200,000 per year to the promising Pink Counters that have been set up in all nine Milan districts. However, owing to the 1999 transformation of the administrative structure that made the districts very large, identifying a specific and direct impact on a single estate is very difficult.

In Milan, despite the falling birth rate, the supply of day nurseries has never met the demand: in 2001/02, the 110 public daily nurseries could only accept about two thirds of the applications for places. The lack of public resources has forced the local administration to try out two policies involving the private sector in the management of education services: Enterprise Nursery Schools and Estate Nurseries. Whereas Enterprise Nurseries cater for the families of a company's employees, the Estate Nurseries are opened and managed by cooperatives, associations, or private individuals, authorised and financially supported by the local authority. They receive grants through public competition. Criticism was levelled at the local authority's lack of control over these educational projects, certain management aspects, and the failure to integrate these nurseries into the public system.

Conclusion

Italy is a forward-looking country in relation to experimentation with specific actions and policies, for example to support female entrepreneurship and time schedule policies. In these fields, gender policies are innovative and the contents include integrated interventions. Tools for implementing gender mainstreaming are not yet well developed; policies remain fragmented and lack analysis of the complex circumstances involving gender differences. For regional and urban governance, the lack of horizontal policies resulting from a lack of cooperation amongst the various departments and levels is problematic (Barbera and Vettor, 2001). The current local interventions are criticised for their poor survival rate, fragmentation, and irregular character. The growing participation of women on the labour market is not reflected by a corresponding representation in legislative and executive institutions. The achievement of corresponding rights, guarantees, and interventions at the legislative level to address the newly-identified societal phenomena, such as increasing occupational flexibility and societal and economic transformation, is still awaited. Since awareness of gender issues in Italy is traditionally linked with the Left, the future progress of gender policies would seem to depend on women's capacity to develop a critical mass within institutions. In the context of the next EU elections, this lack of representation has revived the centre-left coalition debate on imposing quotas for women, resulting in the implementation of a 30% women quota system for European and administrative elections.

Conclusion

In this chapter, we come to the conclusion that the gender sensitivity of urban and large housing estate development and governance is of great importance, even though current urban policies hardly respond to it. We have set out the various constraints hindering the successful introduction of gender mainstreaming in urban governance and the combination of top-down strategy and bottom-up initiatives. Despite all the differences, there is one common feature: the EU political impulse and financial support provide the determinant incentives to gender mainstreaming in all European countries, particularly through the 'IV Action Programme' (1996-2000) and the structural funds programmes ('Equal', 'Interreg', and 'Urban II', for example), which also affect governance in the context of integrated urban policies. However, the need for gender-specific data and research related to housing quality, access to affordable housing, lifestyles, and urban development on large housing estates has become self-evident. One current attempt found at the German federal office of the Ministry for Building started in late 2004. It involves a research project targeting the implementation of gender mainstreaming in the housing economy and industry aiming at basic information and strategies to implement pilot projects in the restructuring process of the German housing market.

Reviewing policies and actions in the RESTATE research areas concerned with women's empowerment and gender mainstreaming, it is evident that these rarely appear as priorities or structural elements in urban governance. Despite important single initiatives to make urban development more gender sensitive, there is no systematic approach. Against the background of the different political and welfare systems in Europe, Behning and Pascual (2002) classify five different approaches to mainstreaming gender. Since the RESTATE research had no intentions regarding professional gender assessment, it is beyond the scope of this analysis to distinguish transnationally the biases of these different approaches within their national welfare systems or assess the efficiency of the more 'prescriptive' policies compared with the more 'permissive' policies. Since the implementation is still at an early stage, the impact of the top-down policy strand is difficult to assess. In general, gender-sensitive enactments only trickle down slowly from the governmental to an administrative and urban governance level. In the context of a whole city, even a comprehensive project like the Berlin case remains marginal behind other policies. In fact, for the countries concerned, an intertwining of both structures (and thus a collaborative approach) and linked action through women's empowerment and gender mainstreaming channels would probably produce the most effective results in term of gender sensitivity. Hitherto, the top-down strategy has been most effective when it meets bottom-up initiatives (as in structural funds projects), especially where the most deprived groups of the population are concerned.

At the municipal and estate level, we attribute an increasing competence to mainstream gender, especially through participatory and collaborative planning processes. Integrative urban renewal seems to be the core sphere where gender-sensitive attempts from different fields of action intertwine in governance-oriented structures, not least because this is where social exclusion and a lack of gender equality coincide most frequently. Traditionally, women are over-represented in community building. Healey stated that "in discussions about plans, strategies etc, and in community development work, it is very often women who articulate and bring forward daily life perspectives of people who live more at home, or with children and have responsibilities for elderly and disabled care" (2004). The growing proportion of women involved in participative planning processes, at the local political level and in steering positions in neighbourhood management, suggests a slow change. Integrated urban development, a necessity for most of the large housing estates, increasingly shows project-oriented planning as its organisational structure (Wotha, 2000). Through this structure, women officials are involved at executive level and the participation of equal rights representatives is becoming the rule (BBR, 2002b). This fact confirms research on participation showing that gender gains importance in the development of large housing estates. Studies of female political participation have revealed that, whereas female participation in highly institutionalised 'classical' fields of participation is low, the gender gap in more unconventional forms of participation is considerably less. Despite the fact that the latter is also closely related to disposable social and cultural capital and financial resources, participatory planning processes that address a diversity of everyday life experience and capacity provide opportunities for female participation (Bock, 2004).

Summarising these observations, the improvements essential to gender mainstreaming becoming a reality would seem to be:

- integrated, collaborative, local intervention in all fields and levels of action and consistent policies;
- a national legislative framework identifying an appropriate system of budgeting and the required typologies of action;
- an improved combination of top-down and bottom-up structures and space for locally based implementation;
- time to change awareness and renew professional patterns of thinking together with subsequent evaluation and control and sanctions in the case of the non-fulfilment of gender criteria;
- high-level PR work and educational programmes;
- a stronger European involvement in housing issues.

However, these recommendations involve some of the necessary preconditions to overcome institutional barriers: the relationship between planning and political theory, the underlying concept of urban governance, and the role of the actors in this space of interaction are other decisive factors to be taken into account. With respect to political theory, Fainstein and Fainstein (1996) classified traditional, democratic, incremental, and equity planning approaches. We focus here on equity planning because within this concept planning is understood as a political process, including aspects of democratic planning and reliance on the public as the ultimate authority in the formulation of planning ends and means. Above all, equity planning acknowledges the multitudinous nature of the conflicting social interests within a transforming society. Equity planning favours redistribution goals and the examination of the distribution of the costs and benefits of public decision making for all societal groups. Bauhardt (2003) revealed that, through its recognition of marginalised interests, 'equity planning' most appropriately links feminist planning criticism, the deconstruction of the dualist conception of gender in societal relations of power, and the gender mainstreaming strategy as an instrument to change the latter. Assuming this, we come back to Healey's concept of collaborative planning and urban governance (Healey, 1997; 2003), which we consider to be a concept of equity planning and also appropriate for adoption in the gender mainstreaming strategy.

Understanding networks as a basic structure of both urban governance and gender mainstreaming, the fourth perspective we recommend should be taken into account, when evaluating the constraints to gender mainstreaming, is the 'Actor Network Theory' (Callon, 1986; Latour, 1991; Law, 1992). This theory, developed from the 1980s in social science studies, defines social relationships, including organisational or power structures, as network effects. In this context, actors are not only human beings, but "any element which bends space around itself, makes other elements dependent on itself and translates their will into the language of its own" (Sarker and Sidorova, 2003).

Keim (2000) applied this theory to urban sociology and unequal situations in urban life. Analysing the 'translation' and 'alignment' of problems and shared (or conflicting) interests through examples of the socio-technical networks embedding single households and neighbourhood management, he revealed that the 'Actor Network Theory' also provides an effective approach to the analysis and counteraction of social exclusion and societal inequality, a major factor of which is gender inequality. To turn gender-sensitive urban policies and governance into a reality, we suggest paying attention to: (a) the inconsistency of policies and (b) time (long-term perspectives), space, resources, and knowledge having a considerable impact on the process of mainstreaming gender.

Note
[1] For this part of the text, Francesca Zajczyk collaborated with Barbara Borlini.

References

Arcidonna (2003) *Osservatorio sulla presenza femminile nei centri decisionali della politica e dell'economia*, Palermo: Luxograph.

Audit Commission (2004) (www.audit-commission.gov.uk/), last accessed 28 January 2004.

Barbera, M. and Vettor, P. (2001) 'The case of Italy', in U. Behning and A. Serrano (eds) *Gender Mainstreaming in the European employment strategy*, Brussels: ETUI-Press, pp 259-72.

Bauhardt, C. (2003) 'Equity Planning und Geschlechtergerechtigkeit', *PlanerIn*, vol 1, no 3, pp 39-41.

BBR (Bundesamt für Bauwesen und Raumordnung) (2002a) *Gender Mainstreaming und Städtebaupolitik*, Werkstatt: Praxis 4, Bonn: BBR.

BBR (ed) (2002b) *Gender Mainstreaming und Städtebaupolitik – Internet-Fassung der Expertise im Auftrag des BBR, Teil III, Verfahrensbezogene Kriterien für Gender Mainstreaming in der Stadtplanun,*. (www.bbr.bund.de/), last accessed 29 December 2003.

Beall, J. (1996) *Gender in urban development* (www.undp.org/), last accessed 12 January 2004)

Becker, R. (2003) 'What's wrong with a female head? The prevalence of women-headed households and its impact on urban development and planning', in U. Terlinden (ed) *From the local level to the global level and back again*, City and Gender: International Discourse on Gender, Urbanism and Architecture, Opladen: Leske und Budrich, pp 151-73.

Behning, U. and Serrano Pascual, A. (2002) *Rethinking the gender contract? Gender mainstreaming in the European employment strategy*, Brussels: ETUI-Press.

Bock, S. (2004) *Genderperspektiven im Forschungsverbund 'Stadt 2030'*, (www.newsletter.stadt2030.de), last accessed 3 March 2004.

Butler, J. (1990) *Gender trouble. Feminism and the subversion of identity*, London: Routledge.

Callon, M. (1986) 'Some elements of a sociology of translation: domestication of the scallops and the fishermen of St. Brieuc Bay', in J. Law (ed) *Power, action and belief. A new sociology of knowledge?*, London: Routledge & Kegan Paul, pp 196-233.

Cars, G., Healey, P., Madanipour, A. and De Magalhaes, C. (2002) *Urban governance, institutional capacity and social milieus*, Aldershot: Ashgate.

Censis (2003) *Donne e politica. Vecchie legislature e nuove chances*, Rome: Censis Foundation.

Commission of the European Communities (2004) 'Report on the equality between women and men, 2004', (COM(2004) 115 final), (http://europa.eu.int/eur-lex/en/com/cnc/2004/com2004_0115en.pdf), last accessed 28 April 2004.

Cox, J. (1992) 'Kvinna i den manliga staden', in J. Öhman (ed) *Urbana samhällen och processer*, Uppsala: Nordisk Samhällsgeografisk Tidskrift, pp 82-94.

Donne nelle istituzioni (2003), (www.cmparita.governo.it), last accessed 2 February 2004.

Dörhöfer, K. and Terlinden, U. (1998) *Verortungen. Geschlechterverhältnis und Raumstrukturen*, Basel: Birkhäuser.

Droste, C. (2002) 'Von Rostock bis München: Gender im Mainstream von Stadtentwicklung und Stadtplanung?' *Gender Mainstreaming in der Stadtplanung*, Werkstattberichte 50, Stadtentwicklung Wien, Magistratsabteilung 18, Wien: Magistrat der Stadt Wien, pp 59-66.

Droste, C. and Knorr-Siedow, T. (2002) *The Berlin case studies'*, online publication, (www.nhh.no/geo/nehom/), working material, NEHOM, Erkner,

Equal Opportunities Act (1991) (SFS 1991:433) Including amendments up to and including SFS 2000:773, (www.regeringen.se/), last accessed 2 January 2004.

Esping-Andersen, G. (1990) *The three worlds of welfare capitalism*, Cambridge: Polity Press.

European Commission (1998) *Incorporating equal opportunities for women and men into all community policies and activities*, Progress report from the Commission on the follow-up of the communication 'Incorporating equal opportunities for women and men in all community policies and activities' (COMg8.122fin,4.3.g8): Brussels: European Commission.

Fainstein, N. and Fainstein, S. (1996) 'City planning and political values: an updated view', in S. Campbell and S. Fainstein (eds) *Readings in planning theory*, Cambridge, MA: Blackwell, pp 265-87.

Fichter, H., Jähnke, P. and Knorr-Siedow, T. (2004) 'Governance capacity für eine wissensbasierte Stadtentwicklung', in U. Matthiesen (ed) *Stadtregion und Wissen. Analysen und Plädoyers für eine wissensbasierte Stadtentwicklung*, Wiesbaden: Leske und Budrich, pp 309-36.

Gilligan, C. (1993) *In a different voice*, Cambridge, MA: Harvard University Press (re-issued edition).

Habermas, J. (1983) *Moralbewusstsein und kommunikatives Handeln*, Frankfurt: Suhrkamp.

Habermas, J. (1990) *Discourse ethics: notes of a program of philosophical justification*, Cambridge: MIT Press.

Healey, P. (1997) *Collaborative planning: Shaping places in fragmented societies*, London: MacMillan.

Healey, P. (2003) 'Creativity and urban governance: an institutional perspective', in K. Kunzmann (ed) *Creativity, culture and urban development*, (forthcoming).

Healey, P. (2004) 'The treatment of space and place in the new strategic spatial planning in Europe', *International Journal of Urban and Regional Research*, vol 28, no 1, pp 45-67.

Karhoff, B., Ring, R. and Steinmaier, H. (1993) *Frauen verändern ihre Stadt: selbstorganisierte Projekte der sozialen und ökologischen Stadterneuerung: vom Frauenstadthaus bis zur Umplanung von Großwohnsiedlungen*, Dortmund: Edition Ebersbach.

Keim, K.-D. (2000) 'Aktor-Netwerke und die Konstruktion von Handlungsfähigkeit in ungleichen Städtischen Lebenslagen', in A. Harth, G. Scheller and W. Tessin (eds) *Stadt und Soziale Ungleichheit*, Opladen: Leske und Budrich.

Latour, B. (1991) *Wir sind nie modern gewesen. Versuch einer symmetrischen Anthropologie*, Frankfurt: Fischer.

Law, J. (1992) 'Notes on the theory of the actor–network: ordering, strategy and the heterogeneity', in *Systems Practice*, vol 5, no 4, pp 379-93.

Lindén, A.L. (1989) *Bostadsmarknadens ägarstruktur och hushållens boendemönster. Förändring och utveckling 1975-1985*, Rapport från forskargruppen boende och bebyggelse: Sociologiska institutionen, Lund: Lunds universitet.

Lorbeer, J. (1995) *Paradoxes of gender*, New Haven, CT:Yale University Press.

Matrix (1985) *Making space, women and the man-made environment*, London: Pluto Press.

Nordfeldt, M. (1999) *Hemlöshet i välfärdsstaden. En studie av relationerna mellan socialtjänst och frivilliga organisationer – i Stockholm och Göteborg*, Uppsala: Uppsala universitet.

Rees, T. (1998) *Mainstreaming equality in the European Union. Education, training and labour market policies*, London: Routledge.

Referensgruppen för jämställdhet i kommunal plannering (1990) *Checka listan*, Uppsala: Uppsala Kommun.

Rhodes, D.L. (ed) (1990) *Theoretical perspectives on sexual difference*, New Haven, CT:Yale University Press.

Sandercock, L. (1999) *Making the invisible visible*, London: University of California Press.

Sarker, A. and Sidorova, S. (2003) *What is actor-network theory (ANT)?*, (www.carbon.cudenver.edu/), last accessed 2 January 2004.

UNCHS (United Nations Centre for Human Settlements/Habitat) (1998) *Policy paper on women and governance*, (www.ucl.ac.uk/dpu-projects/), last accessed 19 January 2004.

Weinmann, U. (2003) *Erster Bericht über Gender Mainstreaming in der Berliner Politik und Verwaltung*, Berichtszeitraum 2002/2003, (www.berlin.de/SenWiArbFrau/frauen/), last accessed 18 December 2004.

West, C. and Zimmermann, D. (1987) 'Doing gender', in *Gender & Society*, vol 1, no 2, pp 125-51.

Wotha, B. (2000) *Gender Planning und Verwaltungshandeln*, Kieler Arbeitspapiere zur Landeskunde und Raumordnung 42, Kiel: Geographisches Institut.

Zajczyk, F. (2003) (ed) *Chi comanda non è donna. Il ruolo della donna nell'odierno sistema istituzionale lombardo*, Milano: Guerini e Associati.

Zibell, B. and Schroeder, A. (2002) *Auf den zweiten Blick, Städtebauliche Frauenprojekte im Vergleich*, (edok01.tib.unihannover.de/edoks/), last accessed 9 October 2003.

SIXTEEN

Knowledge management and enhanced policy application

Thomas Knorr-Siedow and Iván Tosics

Large post-war housing estates provide some of the most striking examples of the mismanagement of knowledge in recent European urban development. The symptoms are manifold. Some apparently mediocre large estates have fared well on the housing markets or have achieved a turnaround after a problematic past, while other, previously highly acclaimed, model housing estates of the second half of the 20th century were demolished after only a few decades as they had become unsustainable, ungovernable or were just no longer in demand. A third group of estates remain in constant need of refurbishment; neither the original plans nor repeated attempts at urban repair have proved able to curb physical and social decay. The question is: what constitutes the differences between these groups?

The central argument of this chapter is that it was not only the quality of the estates, their social structure and status, or a lack of means or political and professional goodwill, that led to the failure of the efforts made to improve the large estates. A partial neglect of available knowledge and, in particular, an inappropriate management of knowledge as a basis for policies of change are seen as important reasons for many obviously problematic decisions and practices.

In this chapter, knowledge management in housing is contrasted with the development practice reflected in some of the RESTATE cases. Some of the difficulties in adapting the different paradigms of knowledge management to the development of the large estates are debated and a communicative model is presented of knowledge management as a reflexive methodology to support the sustainable development and change of the estates.

Knowledge and the large housing estates

Over the years, different examples of mismanaging knowledge have emerged. Technological and engineering knowledge may clearly have been neglected during planning and building of the large housing estates (Gibbins, 1988, p 46). The evidence for this can be found in the serious deficiencies which have often only emerged a decade or so after the residents moved in (Gibbins, 1988, p 22). Second, existing knowledge about the social and economic use of built-up space seems very often to have been given scant attention in the planning phase, in the day-to-day management of the estates, and during the repeated attempts at rehabilitation that some estates have experienced. Third, the tacit (that is, unwritten) knowledge of residents and other local society members, whose experience and understanding of the estates' affairs is often decisive, has only reluctantly been used in the running and sustainable improvement of the estates.

The evidence from current evaluations of many of the integrated policies for neglected urban areas in Europe is that the mismanagement of knowledge is still a key factor in the failure of the implementation of these policies (Difu, 2002; Neighbourhood Renewal Unit (NRU), 2003; Droste and Knorr-Siedow, 2004). Despite the common jargon of integration and collaboration to 'ensure that policies and decisions build on existing knowledge and are evidence based' (NRU, 2003), the barriers between the different holders of professional planning, administrative, and political knowledge on the one hand and the everyday knowledge of residents, shopkeepers, wardens and so forth on the other often remain high. As a result, the potential benefit of shared knowledge for the planning process (Healey, 1997, p 160) and for running the estates cannot be harvested. Finally, an international transfer of knowledge about success and failure factors has only taken place to a limited degree, and mistakes are constantly repeated. A rare historic opportunity was missed after the fall of the Iron Curtain, when the transfer of knowledge to the emerging new market economies was only very limited and strongly dominated by political considerations on both sides.

Certainly, the reasons for the observed neglect of knowledge that could have been a permanent asset in the steering of development are not to be found exclusively in deficient forms of knowledge management. Economic and political power overruled the use of knowledge in many cases. Sometimes knowledge was suppressed as irrelevant – over decades in the West as well as the East – since what had been done could not be questioned. The neglect of knowledge was particularly striking in the countries of Eastern Europe. Despite Eastern European countries' experience with technological faults and social problems as early as the 1970s, which led Western countries to stop this type of construction, all former Eastern block countries continued building large estates right up to the implosion of their economic system at the end of the century. Had Western knowledge of the 1970s and 1980s not been deliberately blocked, the staunchly held assumption of a sustainable special relationship between the socialist personality and the panel–construction apartment block could easily have been stripped down to its rational core (Kipta, 1989).

Knowledge types and their place in the rehabilitation of large housing estates

It is important to provide a broad definition of knowledge here in order to describe its management. The emphasis is on the difference between data, information, knowledge, and learning.

Whereas *data* are representative of conditions and differences without any specific value being attributed to them, *information* combines data with criteria of relevance. In consequence, without a system of references there is no information, and different parties with different systems of reference can easily conclude quite different information from the same data.

Knowledge, however, relates information to context; the process seeks to externalise irrelevant information and is combined with a process of sense-making and reflection. Knowledge 'implies comparisons, consequences, linking and dialogic practice, has to do with experience, judgement, intuition and values' (Matthiesen, 2004). Knowledge describes the process and the result of learning and is 'a thing' and 'a flow' (Snowden, 2002). Snowden describes three important features of knowledge:

- 'We only know what we know when we need it.'
- 'We always know more than we can tell.'
- 'Knowledge can only be volunteered, not conscripted.'

Of course, as soon as more than one party is involved there can never be only one version of knowledge, since it is the result of individual cognitive processes. Thus, finding a common understanding is a spiralling process of enhancing knowledge, which involves learning as well a readiness to see the views of others before new knowledge can emerge in a following round of reflection.

Only respect for the differences between data, information, knowledge and learning as a process leads to the development of new or enhanced knowledge. Especially in those parts of the RESTATE national reports that deal with the recent history of policies and actions for the estates' improvement, a lack of contextualisation of data and differences in the systems of reference regarding information between the various players is stated.

Account needs to be taken of the differentiation between the different forms of knowledge and the links between them in order to reach a concept for the utilisation of knowledge in socio-spatial development (Willke, 1998). Matthiesen (2004) states that the commonplace dual schemes of explicit/implicit knowledge, codified/uncodified knowledge, and institutionalised/personalised knowledge 'are helpful, but not sufficient'. To obtain a working understanding of knowledge in spatial research, he suggests structuring the knowledge landscape according to the following interrelated and partly overlapping fields.

Before its value in estate management became apparent, *everyday knowledge* of common-sense relevance for action in an everyday environment was often considered irrelevant and dismissed. Everyday knowledge, however, is by no means a simple form of knowledge. Local housewives with children have a different form of understanding of how their estate ticks than a plumber or a manager who may only work there. Age, gender, and ethnicity are factors shaping individual everyday knowledge, as well as specific inflows from other types of knowledge.

Expert and professional knowledge describes the scientific and codified knowledge about technology, the social situation, the institutional (and legal) structures, and what lies behind them. Expert and professional knowledge is often directed towards the refinement of professional practices and the generation of new expert knowledge. This realm of professionals, planners, administrators, and politicians – the place-makers in a narrow sense – is often characterised by hermetic separation from other types of knowledge. Technicians tend to live in a world that is decisively different from that of social workers or housing managers, and often the separation of expert knowledge is cultivated to secure professional identities. Competition often prevents the building of bridges between these enclosed fields of expertise, since it is feared that sharing may endanger autonomy for action.

Milieu knowledge describes the social conception of 'how things are' within social networks and milieus. Large housing estates accommodate different milieus, ranging from the different resident groups (with regard to ethnicity, gender, age, social status, institutional embedding, or a mix of these factors) to the estate management, economic, political and administration realms. Milieu knowledge reaches out beyond the estates, although the extent of the reach differs for different individuals and social groups. There is a wide difference between the ranges of *locked-in* milieus (and their exclusive knowledge of an often ethnic character) and *open* milieus (that readily allow a more distanced and reflexive look at life on the estates).

Institutional knowledge is knowledge about the processes within organisations and institutional arrangements. In relation to the large housing estates, institutional knowledge is unevenly distributed between the different milieus. Whereas professional milieus often have considerable capacity to use their institutional knowledge, culturally marginalised milieus, such as the elderly or children, are often the bearers of important bits of local knowledge, but they usually have little institutional knowledge to make that local knowledge heard or transform it into the improvements they need. Thus groups with a low level of institutional knowledge are highly dependent on socially inclusive forms of knowledge management if they are to make useful contributions to sustainable change.

Local knowledge, combining different forms of knowledge, is based on and enhances the perception of local potentials and deficiencies. On the estates, the concept of local knowledge (Knorr-Siedow and Gandelsonas, 2004) combines the different forms of knowledge that are available within the specific circumstances of a specific locality. Sectoral knowledge of the different milieus needs to be communicated into a joint space (Snowden, 2002, p 6). Thus, the local knowledge of socio-spatial entities, including the large estates, differs for different milieus and actors, but can be enhanced and activated by appropriate forms of management.

Reflexive knowledge, finally, links types of knowledge and context, and includes the capacity for the critical understanding of relationships (see Figure 16.1). Reflexive knowledge at the estate level is produced over time, for example in forums.

The utilisation of different forms of knowledge was explicitly addressed within the RESTATE research project. Local knowledge was considered in the Dutch and German cases, where residents were seen as providers of specific knowledge for improved development/ action planning, and in Hungary and Poland for the understanding of regional processes with an influence on the locality. Training the unemployed and especially migrants (Sweden, Spain) falls within the same realm as improving inclusion into the neighbourhood through the introduction of specific knowledge for the non-specific goal of allowing for greater individual and neighbourhood identity (the UK).

The lack of specialist knowledge was reported as a decisive factor in enhancing sustainable estate development (the UK, the Netherlands,

Figure 16.1: Landscape of knowledge

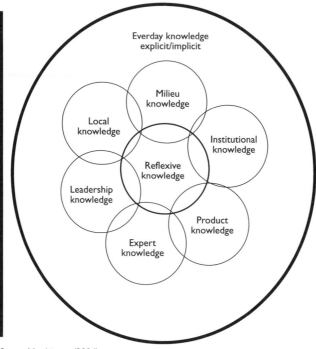

Source: Matthiesen (2004)

Germany). Building new knowledge about condominium management (Hungary) was seen as a major factor for a resident-oriented development of the estates. And a lack of knowledge about the allocation of residents and institutions (Italy) was found to lead to counter-productive consequences from well-intentioned policies.

In planning and policy making, the management of specialist knowledge was seen to be a prerequisite; introducing elements of the knowledge society into peripheral estates (Sweden) and enabling local populations to take part in policy-related action (Spain) was considered essential for more socially inclusive developments leading to better opportunities for individuals and groups.

Despite an underlying notion that a lack of knowledge may be problematic and that the means of carrying and combining different forms of knowledge to better secure the success of rehabilitation processes are usually insufficient, there is hardly any explicit mention of a need to enhance the area of reflexive knowledge, placed centrally on the map of knowledge (see Figure 16.2).

In general terms, the reports show that knowledge in its differentiated form has not usually been understood as a resource for the housing

Figure 16.2: Knowledge flow and relational ties in a rehabilitation process

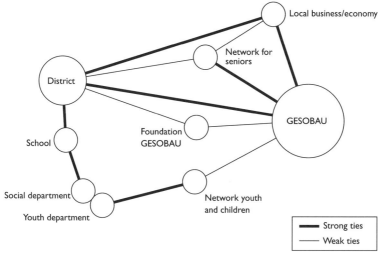

Source: Droste and Knorr-Siedow (2004)

Figure 16.3: Iterative workshop in Marzahn/Hellersdorf estate management

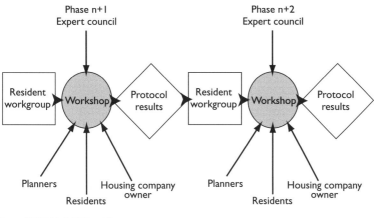

Source: STERN Ltd (2003, p 14)

estates, and that appropriate knowledge management could lead to ways out of the dangers of not knowing or understanding why policies or actions fail or succeed.

The theory and practice of knowledge management

Knowledge management has been infiltrating the economic world since the late 1980s (Grünberg and Hermann, 2003). It became obvious that a casual and random combination of existing knowledge could not lead to sufficiently robust and realistic estimations of given situations nor to the production of satisfactory, sustainable innovation. It was hoped that organised forms of a strategic management of knowledge would lead to a targeted exploitation and recombination of existing knowledge in order to further the emergence of new usable knowledge that has social and economic relevance (Katenkamp and Peter, 2003). Knowledge management frequently featured in attempts to enhance the competitiveness of individual organisations as it became clear that, in the context of the acceleration of knowledge production and the decreasing time span between knowledge production and knowledge utilisation, new efforts had to be made. The associations' intentions ranged from wanting to improve their position in the contest for innovation to their desire to raise self-awareness processes, often in crisis situations.

The *theories of knowledge management* are mostly rooted in the social sciences, ranging from psychology to the sociology of knowledge, and are often influenced by the managerial sciences (Peter, 2003). In contrast, the *practice of knowledge management* has branched into two strands, only one of which is related to the social theories of knowledge and interaction. On the one hand, a large number of information-technology based methods and tools is labelled knowledge management. Even simple databases or intranet solutions are proclaimed to be knowledge management. On the other hand, there are complex communicative methodologies that are based on the social sciences. For the housing sector and collaborative urban development strategies that were found to form the background to the sustainable change of large housing estates in the RESTATE project, the technology tools are of some interest. The availability of information as a basis for the development of reflexive knowledge is vital as this is the most rational possible form of strategic action.

Different models of knowledge management have been debated recently in the literature. Roughly, four types of strategy have emerged (Katenkamp and Peter, 2003, p 24):

(1)   technology-oriented knowledge management;
(2)   knowledge networks;
(3)   process-oriented knowledge-flow concepts;
(4)   hybrid models of a mixed nature.

While technology applications are usually targeted at making information available in a readily accessible and well-organised form, the other three strands are related to institutions (rules of actions) and forms of social organisation.

In urban and estate planning and management, the *technology-based* forms of knowledge management are probably of minor importance for securing context awareness and reflexivity. They have, however, changed the everyday work in housing and estate management markedly by making existing specialist and codified knowledge widely available, thereby helping to convert many housing associations and local government authorities from knowledge hierarchies to more open institutions, and allowing more flexibility. The internet and intranets have opened up previously hermetically sealed forms of expert disciplinary knowledge such as legal case databanks and other information to all staff within the housing associations; residents putting complex problems to desk-workers linked to an intranet or the internet can be given answers that were formerly only available to the legal professions. Even across the boundaries of organisations, tenants and tenant organisations also have increasingly easy access to these kinds of information.

But even though deliberately opening up access to different forms of IT-based expert knowledge (as in a German case) can change the internal culture of housing associations, knowledge flow and network-oriented forms of knowledge management were found to be of greater influence in generating the new action-oriented knowledge-based capacity (Fichter et al, 2004) that was vital for the turnaround of problematic estates. These forms are targeted at interdisciplinary and collaborative work, which was found frequently as an action paradigm within the RESTATE projects. These forms are about sharing personalised knowledge and enhancing the depth of knowledge across the interests of the individual parties involved.

- *Knowledge networks* are targeted at securing a rationale linking available knowledge and sustainable action. As a sub-form, *storytelling* amongst knowledge workers became a prime source of securing the success of complex action, linking knowledge and experience. Knowledge networks are dependent on a certain level of infrastructure (specific meetings, access to databanks, and so forth); teamwork should bridge hierarchic and disciplinary boundaries. Communicating about work rather than just collaborating in work should also be understood to be a prerequisite for the development of reflexive networks. Usually, knowledge networks have a thematic core and are limited to specific tasks to prevent them from becoming too time-consuming and then petering out (Brödner et al, 1999a; 1999b).

- *Communities of knowledge* are usually oriented towards resolving limited focal questions through the development of new knowledge. Originating in multinational organisations, communities of knowledge bring the various parties together, either in person or virtually, through e-communication, or in mixed forms. Once set up, communities of knowledge continue in principle (although often to a limited extent) outside their everyday working structures and develop their own codes of conduct. In managing large housing associations, strategic planning groups are often organised as communities of knowledge.
- *The culture of knowledge* and *hybrid approaches* often use elements of the forms of knowledge management mentioned above and spread them throughout the various parties' institutional framework. The aim of these approaches is to abstract from single-targeted actions in order to change attitudes and to question structural and institutional limitations to the use of knowledge. Approaches oriented towards the culture of knowledge are often implicit in policies for urban problem areas when public participation and cross-departmental and collaborative strategies and practice are required to secure the use of local knowledge (Mega, 1999).

Although knowledge management was introduced largely to serve the demand for innovation within single organisations, cases of project-oriented knowledge management across organisational boundaries are also numerous, especially in advanced industries that are highly dependent on their relationships with their suppliers (Howaldt et al, 2003). These approaches will be of most interest in an urban context of managing knowledge within complex networks of participants, since city and estate are paradigmatic fields of interrelated actions performed by actors with different agendas and often conflicting interests.

Knowledge managers and moderators of networks and communities have been found to be instrumental in contributing to the avoidance of self-referential processes and improving problem-solving capacity. Pardon (2003, p 144) states that communicative performance is the key to success and that any deficiencies frequently lie in institutional structures that discourage communication. In particular, a lack of institutional competence, something which is often missing in traditional administrations and bureaucratic environments, is a barrier to the successful utilisation of knowledge.

Knowledge, housing, and estate development

In one respect, introducing knowledge management into the development of large housing estates differs from most other industrial and administrative practices. The sustainable development of large housing estates incorporates (at least) three often contrasting fields of action, which are in themselves characterised by a multitude of actors and contrasting interests: *urban and neighbourhood development* in a broader socio-spatial sense, *housing*, and *social policy*.

At the neighbourhood and estate level, urban and neighbourhood development, although greatly influenced by economic factors, is generally a highly politicised field. The sharing of knowledge, as well as the inclusion of the residents in the planning process, has been an important aim since the 1970s. In contrast, housing has not been a traditional focus of knowledge-driven innovation from outside the professional and expert realm, although the scope differs widely throughout Europe. Whereas in Central and Eastern Europe actors have only recently become more market-oriented, French and German housing associations, for example, usually have long traditions of moving between the poles of public interest and the market (Donner, 2000; Hall et al, 2003).

For a long time, many actions of the housing industry and local government authorities were routine-driven. In the German rehabilitation programme for the large housing estates, for example, even government evaluators stated that public funds allocated to integrative socio-spatial projects were used mostly by the housing actors within traditional routines, rarely referring to anything other than specialist knowledge. As late as the 1990s, the inclusion of the everyday and local knowledge of residents and other interested parties from business and civil society was judged to be beyond the imagination of most German housing managers (Bundesanstalt für Bauwesen und Raumordnung (BBR), 2004). Modern management methods have only recently infiltrated this sector, since the publicly owned sector responsible for social housing lost its unfettered package of subsidies and at the same time there was a constant undersupply of quality homes at an affordable price.

Above the level of direct customer relationships (contracts, repairs), the managers of large housing estates opted to incorporate residents' everyday knowledge by adopting *resident councils* and other forms of participation in all the RESTATE cases, often as a direct consequence of public debates about disturbing urban problems. Different forms of knowledge other than the associations' expert knowledge were exploited, from *theme-centred public debates* on what the public thought about projects for rehabilitation to asking residents and other specialists in general terms to share their knowledge in *permanent tenant councils*, forums, steering group models, community planning, and other processes.

The graph describing the decision-making process of a successful rehabilitation of one of the case-study areas shows the different demands for shared knowledge and cooperation (Figure 16.3). The quasi-non-governmental housing association established a network of links and shared knowledge, which brought about a mix of expert and everyday knowledge from different agencies, associations, policy makers, and – not to be forgotten – the residents. The development of the economy, of employment and of cultural diversity often becomes more important for the sustainability of the estates than the internal processes within the association. As a result, the external knowledge relationships of the association have become just as important as the expert knowledge within the association for the estates' rehabilitation process.

Each of the circles in Figure 16.1 stands for a complex network in itself. Ways need to be found to include different parties' knowledge across organisational and competition boundaries, while at the same time respecting their position as competitors and their different vested interests in the running of an estate. The aim must be to find a common space of overlapping interests and match it pro-actively with methods that respect conflicting interests.

A knowledge-milieu and capacity-oriented approach to knowledge management

Starting from the notion that knowledge is best developed, processed, and reflexively adapted in a milieu context (Matthiesen, 2004), a milieu-oriented approach to knowledge management for the sustainability of large housing estates is proposed. By *knowledge milieu* we mean the parties' special socio-spatial relationships, which allow communication above the single discipline and single agency level that is rooted in a common culture and the acceptance of a certain set of joint topics (Matthiesen, 2004). As in Markusen's concept of 'sticky places' (Markusen, 1996) that attract innovatory economic actors, the 'stickiness' of the environment for communication is a main element, making a knowledge milieu productive as an open and interesting environment for life and work. On the one hand, the joint understanding within a milieu encourages parties to become and remain involved, while on the other, the institutional scope is opened up for the inclusion of the different types of knowledge especially in its more tacit forms.

Thus, a knowledge milieu can become a space for the development of a new capacity to act in a socially embedded manner, based on reflexive knowledge. However, a milieu, which at its best can drive development, can also produce inflexible forms of communication.

Since knowledge management as such has yet to become an explicit type of action in the housing environment, forms of action found within the RESTATE project's case studies have been analysed for their openness towards an implicit use of knowledge.

Between planning and project

In the 1980s and 1990s, the trend towards rigid planning concepts for estate development turned to more targeted projects that were achievable in a given time and with set means. A project orientation makes it easier to include the knowledge needed for a project's short-term 'technical' success, but can also lead to the neglect of the context knowledge that is necessary for long-term sustainability in a given context. East Germany's experience of rehabilitating its large housing estates is an appropriate example; although excellence was achieved on a project level through the inclusion of expert technical knowledge, the demographic and economic context was ignored, since the everyday knowledge of the residents and their wishes were neglected. In consequence, tens of thousands of the 1.3 million empty flats in East Germany are on freshly rehabilitated panel construction estates. Keeping the balance, through appropriate management, between avoiding information overload and neglecting knowledge could have saved billions of euros.

Targeted planning and action groups

The establishment of thematically oriented groups has become almost everyday practice in the development of large housing estates. These groups usually include representatives from different areas, uniting specialist technical, economic, and housing knowledge. Since the problems have been generally understood to be of a dynamic and non-linear type, collaboration and contributions of different forms of knowledge by different parties over a longer time period are called for. Thus, the context of a project usually becomes clearer as different professional views enrich each other and knowledge gaps between interested parties are acknowledged. A collaborative work form that does not externalise context questions (*'we have extra specialists for that'*) and still manages the process according to targets, has proved essential for a successful rehabilitation process. Building trust and allowing open communication seem to have unleashed new opportunities. However, the exclusion of residents from work- and action-teams with an outwardly technical theme still frequently leaves out the perspective of the end-user, who will finally determine the sustainability of the estate. Iterative workshops are often used as an element stabilising the development of knowledge across actor boundaries. This apparent need for the professional management of groups – knowledge networks, communities of knowledge or other forms – shows that, even in this field, expert knowledge is in demand.

Action planning

Community action planning, planning cells (Dienel, 2002) and *planning for real* (Neighbourhood Initiatives Foundation, 1995) exercises have been successfully introduced as a means of opening up professional planning to include the everyday knowledge of residents. As part of the conceptual planning processes for longer-term physical and social development, the exercises provide an infrastructure and space for a social process of joint cognition professionally translated into concepts and plans. Often an initial stage for more prolonged forms of sharing knowledge between experts and lay people, the major problem with these short-term time capsules of knowledge production is keeping the momentum going after the show is over.

Forums

Inviting the public to a civic discourse allows the holders of expert and professional knowledge to be confronted with knowledge existing outside their own milieu, namely forms of everyday and local knowledge. If these forums become specific communities of knowledge planning (as in the case of the Forum Marzahn, see Droste and Knorr-Siedow (2005)) and open spaces for debate, they provide easy access to the trends and constant feedback from the everyday life of the estates. The meetings can be very informal, although theme-based, and held regularly in a public place, or they can be highly structured with regular plenary sessions and workgroups linked to the planning and running of the estate's affairs. The advantage of such forums is that they activate different forms of knowledge, since newly appearing problems can be introduced into the debates at an appropriate time. In contrast with the methods mentioned above, which have a background in professional planning practice, forums need a higher degree of content- and process-management, including knowledge management; special roles need to be defined in order to identify relevant topics that arouse the interest of non-professionals and lead to their knowledge being brought into the open.

An outstanding example of a comprehensive form of a knowledge-oriented forum is the Platform Marzahn in Berlin (see Figure 16.3). It has proved to be a focal point for professional debate and at the same time a link to the residents' more tacit knowledge for more than a decade. The regular exchange of knowledge in an inner professional circle and a wider debate with residents has enabled a new culture of communication to develop. The experts were provided with unexpected information from a previously unknown realm, and the residents were enabled to follow and even criticise actions on the basis of a new proximity to expert knowledge, which would have been closed to them without this forum.

Integrated policies, programmes, and projects

Integrated policies, programmes, and projects are a response to the difficulty of matching action within individual disciplines with the complexity of the urban problems faced by the estates. In all EU countries, elements of integrated measures were found that allowed action to be targeted to problems by combining social, economic, and cultural action with spatial change. However, a high degree of process and knowledge management seems to be essential for producing optimal links between the different actors and their actions. Codified professional knowledge as well as tacit knowledge must be activated to override sector-based routines, hermetically sealed professional cultures, and often the simple fear of losing authority as others take a look over the professional fence. Besides managing different forms of knowledge – that is, the logics of engineering and social work – the interdependencies of different actors and actions need to be understood in order to avoid obstructions.

Single rehabilitation budget or neighbourhood budgeting

Current discussions in many European countries seek to formulate an answer to the withdrawal of the state from direct policy intervention and enable local participation by turning round the old logic of top-down budgeting to bottom-up steering of local affairs based on the utilisation of local knowledge. Examples both from developing countries (Brazilian Porto Allegre, for example) and Europe (the Berlin district of Lichtenberg, for example), community-centred British neighbourhood development, French urban policy, and the German social city programme seem to demonstrate that single-budget strategies provide accountable solutions to problems, motivate citizens to take responsibility for their affairs, and save money, since less extra work for action is needed. However, neighbourhood budgeting is highly dependent on knowledge exchanges between all the relevant parties, a strong local civil society and local democracy.

Capacity building as an outcome and prerequisite for utilising knowledge

Central to the establishment of a knowledge-driven development is a joint institutional capacity (Fichter et al, 2004) among the parties concerned with the sustainable improvement of large estates. Lack of awareness of the importance of joint knowledge was as frequently reported as institutional inhibitions, also implying the need for institutional change and the introduction of specific individuals as agents for change.

An independent party or contractor can work at some distance from the process, which probably allows an easier inclusion of participants other than those routinely involved, since the process involvement is on a professional basis rather than based on loyalty to one party, be it the housing association or the local government authority. The personal and institutional elements of knowledge management – balancing the openness required and targeting the action – can be facilitated through these informing and enabling people, who often come from local civil society. These people can also establish links to the technology-driven parts of the exercise and provide access to databanks and other forms of codified knowledge. Such tasks within planning processes, at present often undertaken by professional planners, are likely to change the planning professions as much as association management and social intervention in spatial issues has changed urban management in the last few decades.

Conclusions

The question raised in this chapter was whether knowledge management could be fashioned into a tool for the development of large housing estates. It has been found that balancing the collecting, processing, and evaluation of information in order to make it usable cannot be achieved by applying a single tool. Knowledge management should be understood as a process leading towards a culture of openness to information that constantly needs to be reconsidered with respect to its aims and means. Information can only be transformed into the generation of new knowledge if it is integrated into the actor–network structures of the development and management of an estate as a reflexive structural element of running the estate. A process of constantly gathering information, developing it into knowledge-based action, and checking the outcome of actions in order to fine-tune the next steps is required. In order to make use of the relevant information, knowledge management should be context related and should therefore stretch across the boundaries of the estates; knowledge management needs to be inclusive in order to avoid overlooking important items. This leads us to the conclusion that utilising knowledge in an estate context has, as a prerequisite, democratisation at the local level and the enabling of players to participate in the sustainability of large housing estates.

Knowledge management is a relatively new phenomenon, one not yet regularly discussed in the planning and housing literature. The practical application of the results achieved within this approach so far is especially important in the cities of Central and Eastern Europe, where the phenomenon is not only less well known (because of language barriers), but also the conditions for its application are not so well developed. Important actors within the knowledge management process are lacking power (the civil organisations) or not yet interested (politicians and housing managers). Knowledge management in these countries could be important not only in regard to the substantive issues, such as the improvement of large housing estates, but also because of the partial replacement of the public authorities which have been pro-active in the urban development field, and which is largely missing at the moment.

For all these reasons, helping to improve knowledge management skills in these societies is of prime importance, not only for enabling sorely needed knowledge transfer, but also for the improvement of the institutional structures and policy making. In addition to bilateral technical assistance programmes, the EU could also play an important part here with the introduction of the 'Open Method of Coordination' for social policy with specific attention to urban development.

Finally, if knowledge management can become an important asset to the sustainable rehabilitation of large housing estates, it will ease the way into collaborative forms of development action and open up the scope for more democratic forms of action by putting the parties involved on a more equal level with regard to information and enhancing capacity. Also, especially in urban and estate development, a conscious form of introducing knowledge management can be interpreted as a sign that this sector is finally entering the knowledge society. But, since knowledge cannot be conscripted, the power balance and the cultural framework encouraging or discouraging the utilisation of knowledge finally remains decisive for the opportunities it opens up.

References

BBR (2004) (Bundesanstalt für Bauwesen und Raumordnung) *Nachbesserung von Großsiedlungen der 50er bis 70er Jahre*, (www.bbr.bund.de/), last accessed 15 June 2004.

Brödner, P., Hamburg, I. and Schmidke, T. (1999a) *Strategische Wissensnetze: Wie Unternehmen die Ressource Wissen Nutzen*, Gelsenkirchen: Informationsdienst Wissenschaft, (idw-online.de).

Brödner, P., Helmstädter, E. and Widmaier, B. (1999b) *Wissensteilung. Zur Dynamik von Innovation und Kollektivem lernen*, München: Mering.

Dienel, P. (2002) *Die Planungszelle. Der Bürger als Chance*, Wiesbaden: Verlag für Sozialwissenschaften.

Difu (ed) (2002) *Die Soziale Stadt, Eine erste Bilanz*, Berlin: Difu.

Donner, C. (2000) *Wohnungspolitiken in der Europäischen Union, Theorie und Praxis*, Wien: Donner.

Droste, C. and Knorr-Siedow, T. (2004) *Large housing estates in Germany: policies and practices*, Utrecht: Urban and Regional research centre Utrecht, Faculty of Geosciences, Utrecht University.

Droste, C. and Knorr-Siedow, T. (2005) *Large housing estates in Germany, Berlin: opinions of residents on recent developments*, Utrecht: Urban and Regional research centre Utrecht, Faculty of Geosciences, Utrecht University.

Fichter, H., Jähnke, P. and Knorr-Siedow, T. (2004) 'Governance capacity für eine wissensbasierte Stadtentwicklung', in U. Matthiesen (ed) *Stadtregion und Wissen. Analysen und Plädoyers für eine wissensbasierte Stadtentwicklung*, Wiesbaden: Leske und Budrich, pp 309-36.

Gibbins, O. (1988) *Grosssiedlungen*, München: Callwey.

Grünberg, U. and Hermann, T. (2003) 'Wissensmanagment in der Praxis', in O. Katenkamp and G. Peter (2003) *Die Praxis des Wissensmanagments. Aktuelle Konzepte und Befunde in Wirtschaft und Wissenschaft*, Münster: LitVerlag, pp 72-82.

Hall, S., Lee, P., Murie, A., Rowlands, R. and Sankey, S. (2003) *Large housing estates in United Kingdom: overview of developments and problems in London and Birmingham*, Utrecht: Urban and Regional research centre Utrecht, Faculty of Geosciences, Utrecht University.

Healey, P. (1997) *Collaborative planning: shaping places in fragmented societies*, London: Macmillan.

Howaldt, J., Klatt, J. and Kopp, R. (2003) 'Interorganisatorisches Wissensmanagement im Kontext wissensorienter Dienstleistungen', in O. Katenkamp and G. Peter (2003) *Die Praxis des Wissensmanagments. Aktuelle Konzepte und Befunde in Wirtschaft und Wissenschaft*, Münster: LitVerlag, pp 169-95.

Katenkamp, O. and Peter, G. (2003) *Die Praxis des Wissensmanagments. Aktuelle Konzepte und Befunde in Wirtschaft und Wissenschaft*, Münster: LitVerlag.

Kipta, E. (1989) *Manuscript transforming housing in post-socialist Poland*, Karlskrona: The Swedish Urban Environment Council.

Knorr-Siedow, T. and Gandelsonas, C. (2004) 'Lokales Wissen in Stadt- und Quartiersentwicklung', in U. Matthiesen (ed) (2004) *Stadtregion und Wissen. Analysen und Plädoyers für eine wissensbasierte Stadtentwicklung*, Wiesbaden: Leske und Budrich, pp 309-36.

Markusen, A. (1996) 'Sticky places in slippery spaces: a typology of industrial districts', *Economic Geography*, vol 72, no 3, pp 293-314.

Matthiesen, U. (2004) *Stadtregion und Wissen. Analysen und Plädoyers für eine wissensbasierte Stadtentwicklung*, Wiesbaden: Leske und Budrich.

Mega, V. (1999) *The participatory city – innovations in the European Union*, Management of Social Transformations (MOST) Programme, discussion paper no 32, Paris: UNESCO House.

Neighbourhood Initiatives Foundation (1995) *A practical handbook for 'Planning for Real' consultation exercise*, London: Neighbourhood Initiatives Foundation.

Neighbourhood Renewal Unit (NRU) (2003) *New deal for communities*, Research report 7, London: NRU.

Pardon, B. (2003) 'Kommunikationsorientiertes Wissens-management: Konsequenzen für die Gestaltung von Wissens-prozessen' in O. Katenkamp and G. Peter (eds) (2003) *Die Praxis des Wissensmanagments. Aktuelle Konzepte und Befunde in Wirtschaft und Wissenschaft*, Münster: LitVerlag, pp 143-68.

Peter, G. (2003) 'Wissen managen, Von der Wahrheitsfindung zur Ressourcenorientierung?', in O. Katenkamp and G. Peter (2003) *Die Praxis des Wissensmanagments. Aktuelle Konzepte und Befunde in Wirtschaft und Wissenschaft*, Münster: LitVerlag, pp 5-15.

Snowden, D. (2002) 'Complex acts of knowing: paradox and descriptive self-awareness', *Journal of Knowledge Management*, vol 6, no 2, pp 1-14.

STERN Ltd. (2003) *Grosssiedlung Hellersdorf - Kaulsdorf Nord, ein Quartier entwickelt sich*, Berlin: STERN GmbH.

Willke, H. (1998) *Systemisches Wissensmanagement*, Stuttgart: UTB/Lucius & Lucius.

SEVENTEEN

Conclusions

Stephen Hall, Ronald van Kempen, Iván Tosics and Karien Dekker

The aim of this book

Large post-Second World War housing estates are a significant physical and social phenomenon in most European cities. Many of these estates are unproblematic, functioning efficiently within the urban housing market, and considered to be agreeable places in which to live by actual as well as potential residents. However, many other estates are suffering from a multitude of problems. Because so many people live in these kinds of areas and because in a number of cases they are increasingly seen as dysfunctional areas in their cities and beyond, action is needed. In contrast with other, 'developed' parts of the cities, housing estates are artificial areas in that they are self-contained, planned developments rather than neighbourhoods that have developed organically over several generations. Moreover, as we have previously argued, their development was informed by economic and social assumptions that no longer apply in the contemporary world. They therefore need concerted, more complex actions when they deteriorate.

The need for action is enhanced by a growing dissatisfaction among the different kinds of people living on the estates, especially among those who do not have the financial means to move elsewhere. The population that is forced to stay suffers increasingly from a multitude of problems, which were defined in Chapter One of this book. These include: the physical decay of the housing stock and public spaces; the increasing concentration of workless and low-income households; social and racial tension between residents; high turnover leading to the erosion of social cohesion; and the deterioration of local private and public services. The call for action comes from parties of all kinds: central government, local government authorities, housing associations, private builders, and, not to be forgotten, the inhabitants of the large housing estates.

On the basis of an EU Fifth Framework research programme carried out in 29 large post-war housing estates in 16 cities in ten European countries, this book addresses a number of issues considered important in the present situation and in the future developments of these estates. In Chapter One, we stated that three questions were to be regarded as central in this book. They are:

- Which factors and developments are crucial for the future progress and present state and position of large housing estates in European cities?
- What ideas inform potential policy interventions in European large housing estates? What are the advantages and disadvantages of these approaches?
- Which policy interventions are important in large housing estates in European cities? How are they organised? How effective are they?

We use these questions as guidelines in this final chapter. First, we place the questions in a broader societal and theoretical framework. We then focus on the present social and economic position of large housing estates and the factors and developments that can be considered crucial in this respect (question 1). Next, we summarise the discussion on the advantages and drawbacks of some concepts that can be seen as generic images and visions applying at the societal level, and some more specific images that seem more directly related to the large housing estates in this book (question 2). We go on to draw some general conclusions on policy interventions, their organisation, and their effectiveness (question 3). Finally, we put forward some general observations concerning the future of large housing estates in European cities.

The context: a diverse, fragmented and uncertain urban society

We argued earlier in the book (Chapter Four) that the basic assumptions that informed the genesis of the large housing estates were not relevant to the contemporary world. The past 20 years have witnessed a transition from one social, economic, political and cultural paradigm to a new one.

The certainties that characterised the second half of the 20th century – sustained economic growth and full employment underwritten by a Keynesian welfare state in the West, and Socialist central planning in the East – have diminished. As a result of the epoch-making changes that have occurred (globalisation, deindustrialisation, tertiarisation, for example), new forms of economic and social polarisation have emerged. Perhaps the most important of these has been the fragmentation of the labour market into a core group of well-paid, highly skilled beneficiaries of the 'knowledge economy' on the one hand, and a peripheral pool of unskilled workers occupying a more vulnerable position in the labour market on the other. These economic changes have a spatial dimension since regions, cities, and neighbourhoods are increasingly differentiated according to their position within the new economic hierarchy. In addition to these economic trends, there has been a transition within social and political discourse from a preoccupation with narrow class-based questions to a greater awareness of a diversity of issues such as gender, ethnicity, disability, sexuality, and so on.

These are all broad societal changes. What are their specific implications for large estates?

First, the Modernist design paradigm that informed the building of the estates that emphasised, for example, large-scale development and the separation of land uses has been superseded by new urban forms that emphasise vernacular building scales and social and land-use mix. These principles, surprisingly, do not necessarily imply that large estates represent redundant urban forms. A challenge for policy makers in the context of regeneration is to acknowledge the part that housing estates play in the sustainability of the broader urban structure. Despite all the criticisms, the large housing estates built in the decades following the Second World War constitute a relatively compact form of urban living, sometimes well connected to public transport networks and equipped with environmentally friendly heating systems and green open spaces. If all the residents on the estates were to move into suburban single-family houses, the sustainability of the conurbation could well be undermined. In addition, the related rational, technocratic approach to planning has also given way to an understanding of the need to develop more collaborative forms of planning, typical of a transition from government to governance. This shift is considered in more detail in the following section.

Second, the function played by large estates within the urban housing market has changed and the population base has become more fluid as a result. The estates were, typically, conceived as desirable, long-term mass housing for families and households of differing incomes. In many countries, the role of housing the most marginal sectors of society has fallen to the large estates. They have increasingly become the depository for those people who have not benefited from new forms of economic activity or are new entrants to the labour market. These residents might live there for the rest of their lives. But the estates also attract young starters on the housing market. Many of these people will only stay on the estates on a temporary basis. When the starters are in the majority, the large estates will be characterised by a higher level of population turnover than in the past. The housing estates in the post-socialist cities are yet to experience these changes, although mass privatisation and the rapid growth of alternative housing forms point in the same direction, especially in those cities where there are no longer any housing shortages.

Third, if one of the defining characteristics of the residential base of the large estates is that the people who live there do so through compulsion rather than choice, the diversity of the population on the large estates should also be acknowledged. The population, typically, includes elderly long-term residents, younger, often temporary, residents, and, in many countries, minority ethnic communities. These people have a diversity of needs and aspirations that may, in some cases, be irreconcilable.

The differentiated, dynamic nature of the population base of large estates presents a formidable challenge to policy makers. Estate regeneration raises a number of important questions. For example, what are the aims and objectives of regeneration? Is regeneration intended to improve the quality of life and life chances of the existing residents? Is regeneration intended to maintain demand for housing from potential residents and, thus, protect the fixed investments of the state in the estates? Or does regeneration combine these objectives? How is it possible to reconcile the diverse interests of the different stakeholders, not least the residents? Most fundamentally, what type of planning is appropriate in the context of a society characterised by diversity, fragmentation, and uncertainty, and how can the institutional capacity for this type of planning be developed?

Place making, communicative planning, power, and governance

In Chapter Three we set out an analytical and theoretical framework for this book. Following Healey (1997; 1998a; 1998b), place making was defined as the promotion of the social, economic, and environmental well-being of diverse places and the development of the institutional capacity to achieve this well-being. What does this definition mean in the context of the large estates? In many European countries, the state plays an important part in meeting and/or supporting the basic social and economic needs of the residents of many urban neighbourhoods, not least those living on large housing estates. This role of the state also applies in the Central East European countries, where housing has been extensively privatised, but the state or the local government authority owns the public spaces and has general responsibility for social services. However, the state's role in the housing estate areas has only too often become passive, routine-driven, and bureaucratised. The notion of place making implies a more proactive mobilisation of stakeholders in support of a long-term, holistic vision to improve the quality of life and the life chances of urban dwellers. Ideally, an integrated and collaborative (multi-agency) approach to policy making is called for, involving all the relevant stakeholders, the exploitation of local knowledge (professional and resident), and the building up of relational resources to facilitate the above. Several of these aspects have been dwelt upon in various chapters in this book.

Collaborative planning theory (Healey, 1996; 1997; 1998a; 1998b; 2002) is based on the idea that a collective and 'objective' understanding of the world – and, by implication, places – can be achieved through free and open discussion. In all European countries, planning policy is informed by a dialogue between stakeholders on the nature and potential of places: regions, cities, and large estates. Of course, the extent to which this process is exclusive or inclusive depends in each case on the specific political context. Important influences include: the degree to which the state and municipal authorities have tended, historically, to pursue didactic, top-down intervention on the one hand, or the promotion of local initiatives on the other; the different constitutional traditions and the relative importance these afford to representative or participative democracy; and the capacity of citizens and associations to mobilise so as to pursue their collective interests locally. These factors differ significantly in the various European countries and have different consequences at the level of the large estates.

Collaborative planning can be seen as an *aspirational* model for promoting place making in the context of a fragmented, diverse, and uncertain society. Cities and their neighbourhoods, including the large housing estates, are experienced and interpreted in different ways by different parties and different people. Thus, a multiplicity of interpretations or images of any given place emerges. The idea of place making, based on the principles of collaborative planning, becomes, therefore, both a challenge and an imperative. On the one hand, the sheer number of potentially competing images of a place may be difficult, if not impossible, to reconcile. On the other hand, according to Healey at least, the promotion of place making through the development of an inclusive dialogue that entertains as many ideas on, and images of, the nature and potential of a place as possible, is the only viable form of creating the institutional capacity for planning in the contemporary world. We return to these problematic issues later.

The process of place making through dialogue described above is not evenly balanced. Certain ideas and images of an estate will doubtless prevail over others. Power is never distributed equally between actors. Power is, in part, generated by individuals' economic, social, cultural, and symbolic capital. The differential distribution of power between stakeholders is a defining feature of the restructuring processes in large housing estates and may give rise to conflicts and unwanted outcomes. This logic can be applied at a sectoral level. For example, public agencies may play the dominant part in estate regeneration at the expense of the business or associational sector. Power may be unevenly distributed between geographical levels so that, for example, central government might dominate the processes of urban restructuring (or, at the other extreme, central government might play almost no role at all in urban policy making, as is the case in many East Central European countries). The logic can also be applied at an individual level. For example, certain assertive local residents may emerge as natural, but not necessarily representative, community leaders, while others may be perceived as troublemakers by public officials who may exclude them from decision-making processes.

It is within the process of governance that a dialogue on competing ideas and images related to an estate emerges and policy responses are formulated. We have argued above that a proactive approach to place making is imperative in addressing the social and economic problems of large estates. Furthermore, this process may be informed by a dialogue between stakeholders who have different images of the estates, interpretations of their problems, and ideas for tackling them. This process is uneven by its very nature. The key challenge for the governance of planning is, therefore, to construct an institutional apparatus to promote positive relations between government, citizens, and business where information, knowledge, and understanding can circulate and be fully exploited in the pursuit of positive economic and social outcomes.

Place making, collaborative planning, and local governance can all be considered as an essential foundation for improving the future of large housing estates. These tools and procedures aim to maximise the involvement of all the local partners with their knowledge and readiness for action. All these ambitions might fail, however, if the problems of a given estate are determined to an overriding extent outside the area (as is the case with problems of high unemployment, social segregation, and so forth) and the local governance efforts are unable to achieve significant control over these external factors.

Large housing estates in this book: developments and backgrounds

In Chapter One, we argued that local developments had to be interpreted in their proper context. It is therefore difficult to generalise about the different experiences of the estates. Nevertheless, some generalisations can be made about the large housing estates that are central to this book. The physical layout is in most cases the same: medium-rise or high-rise apartment blocks with large green public spaces seem to predominate. In general, the architecture is simple, but at least at the time the estates were built the layout of the estates was quite revolutionary. Large apartment blocks, large open parks between the blocks, and a separation of functions were characteristic features. At the time of construction the dwellings were considered in most cases to be spacious and affordable. Many of the estates were socially cohesive communities in which a considerable number of residents were involved in neighbourhood activities.

At present, many dwellings on most estates show clear signs of physical decay and sometimes long lists of physical housing problems can be enumerated: unsafe balconies, poorly functioning lighting systems, defects in the heating systems, leaking roofs, defects in water and sewage systems, crumbling plasterwork, problems with heat insulation, and so forth. Furthermore, housing on most estates is relatively cheap, which attracts those households who cannot afford to live elsewhere. Many estates serve an important function for those at the bottom of the housing market.

Nearly all city estates have relatively high unemployment rates. Educational levels are generally below the city average. Increasingly, the estates are inhabited by elderly people as a consequence of a process of ageing *in situ*. Most Western estates also increasingly accommodate households from minority ethnic groups.

The estates also experience problems with liveability and safety: the separation of functions that is so typical of most of these estates leads to unsafe places and conflicts about the maintenance of public space. Safety problems on the estates are related to vacant apartments, drug abuse, the lack of meeting places for youngsters, and the anti-social behaviour of some groups of people.

Despite some similarities in the physical, economic, and social development of large housing estates in the last few decades, there are also some significant differences in their positions. The present situation on these estates is to some extent the consequence of broader processes in the city and the country as a whole (immigration, employment, spatial mobility). At the same time, national and city-level policies can significantly alter the consequences of the more general trends and their spatial concentration. Finally, there might be causal factors operating at an estate level. As a combined result of all these features, the housing estates all occupy specific positions within the local hierarchy of housing classes: some estates might be well accepted and placed around the middle of the hierarchy, while others are unpopular and ranked close to the bottom. An estate's position is expressed in the relative value of its housing units compared with values elsewhere in the local housing market (the city and agglomeration), and also in the differences in vacancy rates. (In the cases where public sector rentals are dominant, the expression might be in terms of the length of the waiting lists for flats.)

It is probably this relative measure, the position of the estate in the local housing market (and its interaction with the local labour market), which explains most of the differences between housing estates. Two physically similar estates could easily occupy very different positions and therefore exhibit differences with regard to economic and social processes and problems (see also Chapter Eight).

Emerging images, visions and concepts

Is it possible to develop generally applicable visions and ideals for large housing estates when the local reality and interpretation of problems is so diverse? Indeed, as we have previously argued, even apparently similar estates in the same city can exhibit very different economic and social characteristics. Perhaps even more important is the fact that, in some cases, the purported advantages of fashionable policy concepts are accepted uncritically. In this section we pay attention to some of these concepts: social mix, social cohesion, and spillover effects.

We argue above that there is a strong correlation between the nature and extent of the physical, economic, and social problems experienced on large estates and their position within the local housing market. It is logical, therefore, to suggest that the potential to regenerate estates is equally dependent on this position within the local housing hierarchy. It determines, for example, the potential of the estates to attract new residents (from higher income groups if the objective of policy is to encourage greater social mix) or new investment (if the objective of policy is to encourage greater diversity of land use), and the impact that the regeneration of an estate may have on the housing market in the surrounding neighbourhoods. The local housing market context is, therefore, a decisive factor in influencing what type of policy response is feasible and desirable in the case of a specific estate.

Social mix

Socially mixed neighbourhoods are seen in many countries as desirable objectives of policy intervention. Such neighbourhoods are often presented as an ideal type in contrast with homogeneous neighbourhoods. The latter are often stereotyped in terms of spatial concentrations of low-income households, minority ethnic groups, or a combination of these. Homogeneous areas characterised by a concentration of affluent residents are seldom considered to be problematic.

Large housing estates can sometimes be seen as places where low-income households have been concentrated. This happens because these estates often represent the most inexpensive options within the urban housing stock. As such, they do, of course, have an important function. On the estates in Western European cities in particular, the low-income concentrations currently have a strong and increasing ethnic component. Some of the estates (in France, the Netherlands, Sweden, for example) have evolved from areas with a concentration of white, middle- and working-class indigenous households into areas with concentrations of various low-income minority ethnic households, sometimes mixed with indigenous households unable to move elsewhere. This kind of transition may prompt unrest, social and 'racial' problems, misunderstandings, and a variety of inter-ethnic conflicts. We do not want to say that multicultural areas are by definition problematic, but finding post-war large housing estates where this change has passed unnoticed among the long-term inhabitants is a difficult task.

In considering 'homogeneous' large housing estates, it seems somewhat illogical to refer to these as 'multi-cultural' areas since this term implies a certain heterogeneity. Large estates are often, in fact, more diverse than many other areas. The factor that can be considered as more or less homogeneous is the low income position of the households. It is this income homogeneity that is seen as problematic by local authorities and other landlords of the housing stock, such as housing associations. From Chapter Seven, however, it has become clear that, at least for Sweden, the large housing estates are often highly mixed with respect to income. It may therefore be concluded that, at least in some cases, income homogeneity on large housing estates only exists in the minds of policy makers. It should be noted, however, that in North West Europe the socioeconomic heterogeneous population structure is related to the housing allocation, rent, and social welfare systems. In most other countries in the South and East of Europe income homogeneity is a major problem.

In certain cases, there is a clear reference to the possible problems with respect to ethnic homogeneity. In practical situations, trying to disperse spatial concentrations of low-income households often means dispersal of a spatial concentration of minority households.

What is wrong with spatial concentrations of low-income households? In the urban geographical and sociological literature concentrations of low-income households have been claimed to lead to deviant values and norms; deviant behaviour; low staying-on rates in post-school education; criminal behaviour; and teenage pregnancies. On the one hand, individuals living together in the same area may influence each other negatively, while on the other hand stigmatisation by external institutions and individuals may increase the social isolation of such areas. Large housing estates, with their particular housing and urban structure, may even reinforce the undesirable effects more than would be the case in more flexible inner city areas or single-family neighbourhoods.

In cases where people use an area for a variety of activities, such as shopping, going out to bars and restaurants, social activities, sports, and so forth rather than merely as a place of residence, the neighbourhood can influence residents' behaviour in a number of ways. Neighbourhood effects may occur.

It seems, then, logical to disperse spatial concentrations of social and economic problems. Large housing estates with large concentrations of low-income households or minority ethnic groups should become more mixed, for example by demolishing a part of the inexpensive stock and increasing the number of more expensive dwellings (and introducing a greater functional mix, for example, by establishing workplaces on the estates). However, some considerations are necessary here:

- Most of the literature on negative neighbourhood effects is based on research in US cities. We should not automatically draw on this literature in European situations, although that is not to say that neighbourhood effects do not exist in European cities. The basic contexts, for example the role of the welfare state and the importance of 'race', differ markedly between the US and Europe, and also between countries in Europe. Mixing does not guarantee either the elimination or the stimulation of neighbourhood effects: local contexts are probably very influential.

- In many cases, the people who live on large housing estates spend most of their social lives elsewhere, so the neighbourhood cannot be so very influential on the lives of the residents. In some cases, taking part in activities somewhere else is the consequence of an individual's clear choice, but in other cases people are more or less forced to live part of their lives outside the estates, for example when the estate itself does not offer the opportunities for, say, sports or employment. Working towards a greater functional mix is probably a better strategy in these cases than working towards a greater social mix.

- Mixed neighbourhoods usually consist of a number of different groups (indigenous/immigrant, old/young, old/new, low-income/high-income households) who do not live together with each other, but have their own separate activities, their own social contacts, and so forth (see Chapter Seven). Spatial mixing does not automatically lead to all kinds of beneficial social contacts between groups. Creating a social mix often seems more like creating separate living worlds than creating a cohesive neighbourhood. Of course, the aim may very well not be to create social cohesion (see below), but just to eliminate an acute concentration of problems in order to make the area a better place to live.

The conclusion should be that mixing neighbourhoods is not always, and definitely not automatically, a panacea. A social mix within an estate can be an advantage, but this is definitely not universally and automatically the case. In the housing estates of the post-socialist countries, the problem of income and/or ethnic homogeneity is not yet visible to the same extent as in Western Europe. The reasons for that include the smaller proportion of immigrants and the relatively high position of the housing estates on the local housing markets. Income differentiation is, however, growing within these societies; with the emergence of alternative housing forms, income homogeneity can be predicted to develop very soon in these countries, too. Thus the experiments of the Western countries are of particular relevance for the post-socialist countries, even offering the opportunity of intervening before the worst consequences of income and ethnic segregation become visible.

Social cohesion

In the past few years the concept of social cohesion has gained immense popularity. This is, at least in part, the result of EU-programmes in which this concept figures prominently. Social cohesion is a concept that can be used on many spatial scales and comprises a number of features, such as common values and norms, social solidarity, social control, social networks, a feeling of belonging to each other and to to the local community and to one's place of residence. In many policies and communications, social cohesion is seen as something very positive, something that should be striven for. However, in Chapter Six, Dekker and Rowlands point out clearly that social cohesion should not always be looked at exclusively in a positive way. Social cohesion can very well lead to situations in which people still only have contacts with people of their own kind. Granovetter (1973) talks about bonding capital: ties and contacts between people who do not give new beneficial information. Unemployed people, for example, might have many contacts with other unemployed people, but, in drawing on these contacts, they are unlikely to increase the possibility of finding ways to get a job (Morris, 1993). Exchange of information and goods may lead to a situation in which the bonds with other people, and the rest of urban society, may be weakened (Healey, 1997). Another potential danger of strong cohesion between people with similar characteristics can be the exclusionary approach to people belonging to different social strata.

That is not to say that we are against social cohesion. The existence of social cohesion may lead to all kinds of positive aspects for the people involved, and also to all kinds of important associations and neighbourhood activities. Living on a socially cohesive estate may be more agreeable than living on an estate where people do not see each other, have no contacts, and are not interested in each other. However, we do see the possible negative implications of creating the wrong kinds of social cohesion. A form of social cohesion where some groups of people belong, while many others do not is probably not desirable. A form of social cohesion in which bonding capital creates situations that might even resemble cultures of poverty is equally inadvisable. The rhetorical, uncritical advocacy of social cohesion on an estate is, thus, little more than an empty gesture.

In the chapter on social cohesion, Dekker and Rowlands argue that the ideals of collaborative planning can be very useful when aiming to improve social cohesion in ethnically diverse housing estates. It is important to consider whose cohesion is being pursued; identifying the groups which are involved in designing the policies that shape the estate and how powers are divided within and between groups is essential. The future of social cohesion in ethnically mixed large housing estates rests on the acceptance of the fact that they are increasingly multi-ethnic and will not form one big cohesive community. Rather, the estate community consists of several separate communities that overlap to some extent.

Spillover effects

Policy interventions in one part of a city invariably affect policies elsewhere. This statement seems very logical, although policy makers rarely acknowledge this reality, deliberately or otherwise. Addressing a problem in one area might give the impression that the problem has been resolved, but in many cases it has probably only been displaced. The most obvious example is a policy that is aimed at the de-concentration of a certain kind of group: low-income households or minority ethnic groups, for example. De-concentration may be achieved by demolishing inexpensive dwellings and replacing them with more expensive ones that the original inhabitants cannot afford. In the end, the area will accommodate fewer of these original inhabitants. There is a significant chance, however, that concentrations of the same kind of people might emerge in another area where inexpensive housing is still available. Musterd and Ostendorf demonstrate the existence of such a spillover effect in Chapter Eight of this book.

Do all policies have unintended consequences? They probably do. Knowledge about how things work out, what the side-effects are, and what the experiences from similar situations and policies have been, seems to be crucial for effective action. Too often policies and policy makers are focused on just one area and seem to forget what might happen in other areas when a policy is implemented. Any intervention in a large housing estate will always affect neighbouring areas, or areas that are similar with respect to the housing stock, for example.

We have given some critical remarks on some concepts that seem to be relevant in the present discussion on the restructuring of large housing estates. We have also indicated that we should be aware of spillover effects. But we definitely do not conclude that we should stop carrying out policies on large housing estates because there are always so many disadvantages and dysfunctions in the concepts involved. There are numerous opportunities for positive action, and we elaborate some of them, again critically where necessary, in the next section.

How to improve the estates?

The various countries have all made numerous attempts to improve the situation of their large housing estates. Chapter Four gives a short overview of these attempts, pointing out the change in approaches over time from smaller physical towards more complex interventions, some including economic and social features and the increased involvement of local stakeholders.

It is important to ask whether it is possible to develop universally applicable policy tools and processes. The local housing and labour market context will, of course, enable or constrain particular policy options on any given estate. In terms of the potential to develop the inclusive governance processes associated with place making and collaborative planning, this is likely to be determined, in the first instance, by national political traditions (the primacy of state *dirigisme* [top-down edict] versus 'grass roots' activism, representative versus participative democracy, etc.). However, it is equally important not to discount the influence of local contingent variables (for example, the vitality, or otherwise, of civil society).

Demolition

In recent years, more radical interventions involving substantial demolition have gained ground in some countries. Although demolition is clear evidence that certain previous interventions have failed, demolition does not prove the general failure of complex interventions. Rather, the conclusion to be drawn is that, in extreme situations where the relative position of the housing estate becomes very weak within the hierarchy of housing stock in the local housing market (the estate reaches rock bottom, either through the rapid development of other, better housing stock, or as a result of the increasing spatial concentration of physical and social problems on the estate), no local solution other than the elimination of this part of the stock can be considered appropriate.

In some cases, demolition may seem to be the only solution to improve an estate. Demolition is a radical and drastic measure. By definition, it destroys an urban structure, and, even more importantly, it forces the resident population to move to other dwellings and often other places, thereby also destroying a social structure. If there are no satisfactory housing alternatives elsewhere, a new housing shortage may emerge. Belmessous et al (Chapter Ten) see this lack of alternatives as the most important problem with respect to demolition. It should also be said that, in many cases in European cities, the households to be replaced are taken care of and offered a dwelling somewhere else (or even in new housing on the same estate).

We strongly believe that in some cases demolition is necessary: for example, in housing markets with an extremely low demand for the types of dwelling to be found on the large housing estates. Flats in the large housing estates are sometimes considered outdated, because of construction problems, physical decline, and rooms that are too small. A high number of vacancies will undermine the financial viability of the landlords (such as housing associations) and may also lead to spirals of decline: the high vacancy rate might lead those who are still living in the blocks to feel less responsible for the area, which in turn might lead to anti-social behaviour, which then causes more people to move, and so on.

There are even examples where demolition of otherwise physically sound buildings has been unavoidable as the consequence of unsuccessful handling of social and/or criminal problems. If the very delicate borderline between low-income neighbourhoods and areas dominated by households with deviant behaviour is not correctly determined and the problem of the latter families is not dealt with in time, whole buildings may become so undesirable that demolition is the only solution.

In the previous section we indicated that in some cases demolition and rebuilding have been used to make an estate more diverse with respect to the housing stock and, as a consequence, differentiated with respect to the population. It is an open question whether such a radical physical measure does indeed create solutions for problems that do not find their origin in physical circumstances. In other words, social problems might be better dealt with by other measures for as long as and as far as is possible. In Chapter Eight, Musterd and Ostendorf have presented a critical view on the relationship between social problems and physical interventions. Their conclusion is clear: the assumptions that physical structures have a substantial impact on people's well-being and mental condition, and that these aspects are crucial variables behind social problems, can often not be supported. Restructuring the housing stock of a large estate may lead to the displacement of such problems as unemployment and criminal behaviour, but in most cases will not lead to their solution.

Tackling the problem of unemployment

In Chapter Two it was made clear that, on a considerable number of the large post-war housing estates, the number of unemployed is relatively high. To a significant extent, this is the result of the position of the large housing estates on the urban housing markets. The estates generally consist of a large number of relatively inexpensive dwellings that are therefore affordable for low-income households. The large housing estates, therefore, have an important function for these low-income households, including the unemployed. In many cases they will be unable to find a comparable affordable alternative elsewhere in the same urban area.

In Central East European housing estates unemployment figures are relatively low when compared to those of North Western Europe, or when compared to the national averages. This relatively low figure is related to the history of the estates, and their relative position on the housing market. Fighting unemployment is not specifically targeted at national level, but is a national concern.

Policy makers generally deem spatial concentrations of unemployed people to be undesirable. This can be the case for several reasons:

- Unemployed people living in spatial concentrations can affect each other negatively ('neighbourhood effect', as mentioned earlier).
- Concentrations of unemployed people can create spirals of decline in the neighbourhood: the unemployed may end up in criminal circles, making the neighbourhood an unsafe place to live.
- Concentrations of unemployed people may come together with concentrations of minority ethnic groups. In that case labour market problems may coincide with integration problems.

The causes of unemployment are mostly external to the estates. Therefore combating unemployment on the estate level does not seem very logical. However, some initiatives to create jobs in a local area and/or for people living in the area have been successful. A good example has been described for Sweden by Petterson and Öresjö in Chapter Thirteen. The main idea is that unemployed people are guided personally (and not as a group) on their way to a job. This individualised approach does not result in large numbers of people moving from unemployment into work, but at least a few people are helped. The personalised nature of the assistance seems to be crucial here.

Giving assistance to the unemployed is a radically different way of dealing with their plight than trying to disperse them from the large housing estates to other places, which, of course, results in displacement. There is a fair chance that unemployed people will not get a job through re-housing, at least not automatically. Attempts to generate a functional mix on the estate (encouraging incentives for job creation there) could be regarded as a better approach.

Dealing with the problem of criminality

Increasingly, criminality is becoming one of the main problems in European cities in general and on large housing estates in particular. In several RESTATE reports it has been indicated that large housing estates suffer from all kinds of criminal behaviour. This goes hand in hand with increased feelings of insecurity among the inhabitants of the estates. In Chapter Fourteen, Aalbers, Bielewska, Chignier-Riboulon and Guszcza have indicated that two general strategies to combat criminal behaviour can be identified. Punitive strategies may be described as defensive and focusing on punishment, while socialisation strategies focus on the causes of criminal behaviour. Socialisation strategies aim to improve the situation of criminals by giving them better future prospects through remedial schooling, for example.

We agree with the authors of Chapter Fourteen that socialisation strategies probably work better in the long run, but that punitive strategies are needed to deal with problems in the short term. Punitive strategies might not directly improve the behaviour of (petty) criminals, but may well lead to positive feelings among the inhabitants of the estates: they might get the impression that the problems on their estates are being addressed. Thus, special attention has to be paid to deviant behaviour, which can lead to serious effects on the desirability of living on an – otherwise physically sound – estate. On the other hand, to apply exclusively punitive strategies and/or controlling measures (such as CCTV) may not solve the problems, but lead to spillover effects, pushing them out to other areas.

The integration of different policies: governance as a useful concept

Governance is a catchword that gained momentum in the 1990s. In almost every European country the concept of governance has found its way into political discourse on different spatial levels. The problem with catchwords is that they are often used in an uncritical way. In the case of governance this is definitely not the case in theoretical terms (there are innumerable articles and books about governance), but it sometimes seems to be the case when talking about the practical use of the term. In general, we might say that the transition from single-agency intervention to the partnership working implied by the term 'governance' is seen as a solution to many problems. In practice, however, this ideal form of governance is often difficult to attain. In some of the chapters this difficulty has been indicated. Some examples are cited below.

In Chapter Eleven, Mugnano, Pareja-Eastaway, and Tapada-Berteli argue that contingent circumstances might stimulate or obstruct the promotion and functioning of partnerships. A lack of social cohesion in an area may obstruct the emergence and smooth working of partnerships (see also Chapter Thirteen). The same negative effect may emerge when the authorities do not stimulate, or may even frustrate, initiatives that come from the local population.

Partnerships fare best when there is some degree of parity between participants in respect of knowledge and the extent to which different forms of knowledge (professional expertise, local knowledge held by residents, for example), held by different participants, are equally valued (see also Chapter Sixteen). This is not always the case, however. Some parties are better equipped with knowledge than others. Consequently, a situation might arise in which those who have more knowledge (about legal aspects or financial arrangements, for example) also have more power in the partnerships. Those who do not have that power may in turn feel frustration, and may use an exit option (that is, leave the partnership) as the next logical step. The partnership may fall into a situation in which it is seen as an undemocratic body. Of course, this undemocratic nature may have been present from the beginning, when the partnership was created. At that point some people and organisations might have been left out, purposefully or otherwise (see Chapter Eleven).

Not everybody is interested in partnerships (see also Chapter Twelve, by van Beckhoven, van Boxmeer and Garcia Ferrando). Some inhabitants already know that they will live only temporarily on the estate and, as a result, display little interest in it and see no need to participate in activities that aim to improve the environment or the dwellings. In this respect housing estates dominated by owner occupation might be better able to attract participation than public-tenancy dominated estates, while the domination of private rental housing might create the least incentive for residents to participate.

The time factor also seems to play a part. At a certain point in time, the inhabitants participating in partnerships on an estate will want to see some results from their efforts. If results are not forthcoming, residents may feel disappointed and turn their backs on the partnership. They may eventually even turn against the estate.

We agree with van Beckhoven et al (Chapter Twelve) that local circumstances, such as the population composition of an area or the existing community and associational structure, will generally better determine the success of a partnership in which inhabitants take part than national exhortations to involve local people. Inclusive governance can be important in generating better results, but governance is also a process that has to be guided, coached, and monitored. Governance does not come about automatically and partnerships (an important aspect of governance) do not routinely last forever. Hard work is always necessary for them to work well, to endure, and to arrive at good results.

Inclusive, partnership-based governance is one of the most important prerequisites for the successful handling of problematic housing estates. In some cases, however, even this might not be enough: even the most actively participating residents might leave the estate if problems with deviant households remain unsolved, and/or if more desirable subsidised housing forms become available somewhere else.

The future of large housing estates

One of the main lessons to be learnt from the case studies is that extreme situations, notably the fall of the housing estate to the bottom of the local housing market hierarchy, should be avoided. To this end, influencing both the external causal processes and the complex interventions on the housing estate itself are necessary. The first requires an overall urban development policy at the national level, with a clear view of the consequences of economic, social, and spatial development on the potential future of the different parts of the urban housing stock. In addition, and related to this urban policy, complex local approaches are needed, with all the innovations of governance, to maintain and, if possible, to improve the relative position of the large housing estates.

The problem of large housing estates is not the same in different parts of Europe. In many of the Western European countries, both external and local factors lead to the large estates occupying a disadvantageous social and economic position. In these cases major public attention and substantial financial interventions have been deployed to find solutions. In the Central East European countries the share of large housing estates form a much greater proportion of the housing stock, and in most cases their relative position is not yet as bad as in the Western countries. However, the tendencies point to a similar decline. Even so, these countries are not able and sometimes not willing to expend similar public attention and financial resources on handling the mounting problems. Under such circumstances, qualified knowledge transfer, that is, adaptation of the Western experiences to the quite different Central East European circumstances, would be of prime importance.

This comment leads us to a final remark. By no means is the problem of large housing estates only a housing problem: the deterioration of the estates leads to serious economic, employment, social, ethnic, and environmental problems. To find the correct balance between seeking to influence external factors and the pursuit of complex, local governance approaches is difficult. Structured advice and knowledge transfer is needed, especially with regard to the new member states of the EU, where the largest housing estates are to be found.

All things considered, the exclusionary approach of the EU towards the large housing estates (with reference to the fact that housing is not part of the common policies) should be re-examined (Tosics, 2004, p 87). The EU should take on at least a limited role with regard to this problem, obliging national governments to set up the required national urban policy frameworks. With the introduction of pilot programmes for complex housing estate improvements, and the application of the Open Method of Coordination (resulting in the compulsory setting up and comparative analysis of National Action Plans similar to the existing practice in the social policy field) to the case of policies for urban housing development, the EU could help take a first, very important step towards sorting out the problems of the large housing estates on the national and local level.

References

Granovetter, M.S. (1973) 'The strength of weak ties', *American Journal of Sociology*, vol 78, no 6, pp 1360-80.

Healey, P. (1996) 'The communicative turn in planning theory and its implications for spatial strategy formation', *Environment and Planning B*, vol 23, no 2, pp 217-34.

Healey, P. (1997) *Collaborative planning: shaping places in fragmented societies*, London: MacMillan.

Healey, P. (1998a) 'Building institutional capacity through collaborative approaches to urban planning', *Environment and Planning A*, vol 30, no 11, pp 1531-46.

Healey, P. (1998b) 'Collaborative planning in a stakeholder society', *Town Planning Review*, vol 69, no 1, pp 1-21.

Healey, P. (2002) 'On creating the city as a collective resource', *Urban Studies*, vol 39, no 10, pp 1777-92.

Morris, L. (1993) *Dangerous classes: The underclass and social citizenship*, New York, NY: Routledge.

Tosics, I. (2004) 'European urban development: sustainability and the role of housing', *Journal of Housing and the Built Environment*, vol 19, spring 2004, pp 67-90.

The context of this edited volume

This edited volume was written as a result of the first half of the work undertaken for RESTATE, a research project funded by the EU. RESTATE is the acronym for Restructuring Large Housing Estates in European Cities: Good Practices and New Visions for Sustainable Neighbourhoods and Cities. The project running time was from November 2002 to October 2005. Ten European countries are involved and data have been gathered from 29 estates. This appendix provides some basic information on the RESTATE project. The primary objective of RESTATE is to deliver evidence-based knowledge drawing on experiences in cities in all parts of Europe. It is hoped that the results will be useful for researchers and policy makers seeking to discover the contexts in which measures taken to improve large urban housing estates have been, or can be expected to be, successful.

Research questions

Seven research questions have been formulated for the RESTATE project. They are as follows:

(1) What are the structural and other factors that explain the difference between success and failure of large post-war estates? What types and combinations of problems have been identified in different cities and what factors are associated with these problems?
(2) What is the philosophy underlying the various existing policies with regard to large housing estates in different European cities? What are the main policy aims? What are the main activities included in these policies, and what is the balance between these activities?
(3) How are these policies organised? Who participates in the policy and who has decided about this participation? Can the policy be seen as a top-down or as a bottom-up process? What are the advantages and the disadvantages of these approaches? Has the policy, the way in which it has been organised, and the way it is perceived by residents and others changed over the time period that it has been in place?

(4) Who profits from the developments and the policies? Who experiences clear disadvantages?

(5) Which aspects of policies are seen to have been successful and which are seen to have failed in different situations, and what explanations for this difference can be given?

(6) How far and in what ways can we generalise from the results of the different projects?

(7) On the basis of the evidence obtained about what has been achieved, what scenarios and visions for the future can be proposed for large post-war estates and the cities in which they are located? What policies and processes will be most effective in achieving successful developments in these areas?

Case studies

The case studies are the heart of the project. Each study aims to:

• identify why certain post-war estates are successful and others are not;

• establish general information about the estate: its history, its characteristics, its demographic, social, economic, and physical development and problems;

• identify the philosophy and aims of the policies that are being promoted on the estates, how policies have matured over time, what the effects of the policies have been, and how this process can be evaluated;

• analyse how the policies are organised, who participates, who decides, who profits, and who experiences disadvantages.

Research areas

The cities involved in the RESTATE project are shown on the map (see Figure A1). The specific features associated with the different estates in the selected cities and countries are set out more fully in Chapter Two of this book. The estates are briefly outlined here within their national contexts. Table A1 gives some information about the basic physical characteristics of the estates that are featured in the project.

Figure AI: The countries and cities in the RESTATE project

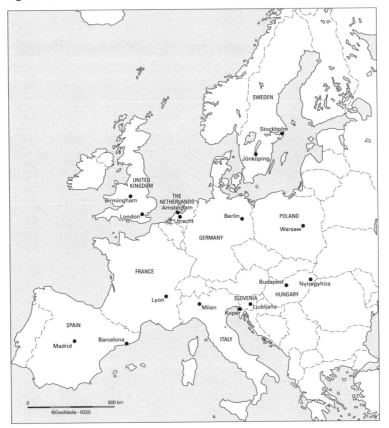

Source: Own research

Research methods

The same research questions are posed and the same methodologies used in all the research countries, cities, and estates. Comparability is fundamental in this project. The chapters in this book have been written on the basis of two essential phases in the RESTATE project. These phases are briefly outlined below.

Table A1: Basic physical characteristics of the estates

Country	City	Estate	Size (ha)	Main building period	Number of dwellings	% of rented dwellings
UK	London	Bow HAT	23	'68-'77	2,285	77
	London	Poplar HARCA	62	'30s-'70s	6,304	93
	Birmingham	Central Estates	94	'30s-'70s	3,305	46
	Birmingham	Hodge Hill	137	'30s-'50s	3,937	4
Sweden	Stockholm	Tensta	196	'68-'72	5,931	54
	Stockholm	Husby	183	'70-'75	4,725	53
	Jönköping	Öxnehaga	320	'69-'78	2,041	68
	Jönköping	Råslätt	120	'66-'72	2,657	99
Netherlands	Amsterdam	Bijlmer-East	408	'68-'77	12,296	85
	Amsterdam	Kolenkit	69	'46-'55	2,634	83
	Utrecht	Kanaleneiland-Noord	66	'56-'61	2,674	78
	Utrecht	Nieuw-Hoograven	–	'54-'65	2,595	85
France	Greater Lyon	Les Minguettes	220	'67-'74	8,190	92
	Greater Lyon	La Ville Nouvelle	160	'60-'76	7,422	81
Italy	Milan	Comasina	32	'54-'63	2,218	25
	Milan	Sant'Ambrogio	33	'65-'72	2,338	93
	Milan	San Siro	60	'31-'73	8,137	59
Spain	Madrid	Orcasitas	127	'74-'76	7,382	0.4
	Madrid	Simancas	229	'57-'59	9,923	10
	Barcelona	Trinitat Nova	55	'53-'63	3,215	20
	Barcelona	Sant Roc	46	'62-'65	3,395	–
Germany	Berlin	Marzahn/Hellersdorf	280	'77-'89	13,800	86
	Berlin	Märkisches Viertel	370	'60-'75	16,000	–
Slovenia	Ljubljana	Nove Fužine	68	'77-'88	4,332	8
	Koper	Žusterna-Semedela	32	'73-'89	2,040	6
Hungary	Budapest	Havanna	54	'77-'83	6,200	20
	Nyíregyháza	Jósaváros	36	'70-'79	3,600	–
Poland	Warsaw	Wrzeciono	944	'60-'70	13,122	26
	Warsaw	Ursynów Pn.	234	'76-'81	13,143	0.4

Source: Musterd and van Kempen (2005)

Identification and clarification

The first step in data gathering was a literature search and the analysis of secondary sources and interviews, with the aim of identifying the main problems on the large housing estates and clarifying these on the basis of existing knowledge. This preliminary overview led to a review of the literature that addresses the question of which structural factors constitute the difference between the success and failure of large housing estates – both in theory and, from examples, in practice.

The main problems were then identified in the research areas themselves. The fieldwork concentrated on the following variables:

- physical structure (quality of the buildings and the environment, tenure, price and type of dwellings);
- demographic developments (age structure, income distribution, household and ethnic composition, migration patterns);
- economic developments (employment and unemployment, number, type, and size of firms on the estate);
- sociocultural developments (changing values and norms within the estate, changing cultural identity).

This phase resulted in quantitative data as well as qualitative information (meaning, evaluation, and so forth) for the estates and the cities in which they are located. In this way, specific developments of the estates can be traced. The interviews in this phase dealt with problems relating to social inclusion, social cohesion, sustainability, demographic change, multicultural developments, well-being, housing, and access to services (with respect to the residents), and policies, measures, governance and management (with respect to local government authorities and estate management). The interviews were conducted according to detailed guidelines.

During the spring of 2003 at least 15 interviews per estate were held with, for example:

- (former) directors/relevant persons involved in housing associations;
- (former) real-estate developers;
- (former) members of the local government;
- (former) schoolteachers;
- (former) members of active organisations in the area, such as associations of shopkeepers, churches, or residents' organisations.

Policy analysis

When the situation on the estates had been identified and clarified, the focus was shifted to policy analysis. The analysis of reports and memoranda, interviews, and discussions with stakeholders and end-users has resulted in papers that address the question of which philosophies and aims are central in the policies being promoted in the estates under review. Of course, an important question to be addressed was how these policies are organised, what activities are included, how these policies have matured and changed over time, and how these philosophies, aims, and organisational aspects can be evaluated.

During a second interview round held in the autumn of 2004, the following topics were addressed: the role of the stakeholders; urban governance arrangements; the main areas of policy intervention (housing, employment and the economy, safety, education, health and well being, social aspects); community involvement; the role of networks; and best practices and evaluation. At least 15 interviews were held per estate with people of similar characteristics, as in the first interview round.

For further information

For further general information, please contact the coordinator of the RESTATE programme, Professor Ronald van Kempen r.vankempen@geo.uu.nl. The results (reports, papers, evaluations) of the RESTATE project can be downloaded from our website (www.restate.geo.uu.nl).

Reference
Musterd, S. and van Kempen, R. (2005) *Large-scale housing estates in European cities: opinions of residents on recent developments*, Utrecht: Urban and Regional research centre Utrecht, Faculty of Geosciences, Utrecht University.

Index

NOTE: Page numbers followed by *f* and *t* indicate information in a figure or a table respectively.